THE ACTION GUIDE TO GOVERNMENT AUCTIONS AND REAL ESTATE

by George C. Chelekis

A Complete Investigation of the Government Agency Auctions in the United States and How To Succeed at Those Auctions

This publication is designed to provide accurate information on the subject matter covered. Procedures and addresses may vary in local areas. All information is effective as of September, 1989.

The publisher is not engaged in rendering legal or accounting advice. Use of a competent and recognized attorney is advised in certain areas.

REX PUBLISHING COMPANY
P. O. BOX 390
CLEARWATER, FLORIDA 34617-0390

FIRST EDITION -- JANUARY, 1989

SECOND EDITION
 First Printing - February, 1989
 Second Printing - March, 1989
 Third Printing - April, 1989
 Fourth Printing - May, 1989
 Fifth Printing - July, 1989
 Sixth Printing - August, 1989

THIRD EDITION -- OCTOBER, 1989

Library of Congress Catalog Card Number: 89-62835
ISBN: 1-878214-01-2

PRINTED IN THE UNITED STATES OF AMERICA

ACKNOWLEDGEMENTS

The author wishes to thank Elizabeth Gay, Vice President of Research; Jeanne Yarbrough, Director of Research; Dianne Blasciuc, Director of Editing; Lynnette DeMontmollin and Edward Schwartz, Assistant Directors of Research; Peter Stern, Computerization; Samantha Bailey, Technical Editor; and the staff of researchers who have spent countless hours on the telephone extracting auction information from sometimes reluctant public servants.

Their work is what makes this publication unique, for they have eliminated the tough research work you would have had to face to actually arrive at a government auction.

Use their labors and the information in this book to your advantage.

FOREWORD

Applause! Finally a book on government auctions that presents an opportunity to take the "rip-off's" out of the market place. I find this book to be thoroughly researched and highly understandable, and it brings to the auction arena a vast amount of integrity, information and help to the prospective auction-goer.

I especially liked the section on "Rules for Auction-Goers." Auctions can be fun and profitable if you follow the rules and do your homework.

The auction method of marketing is as old as the hills or as modern as today's computers. Recorded history describes auctions as early as 500 B.C., and later the Roman Empire was sold using the auction method of marketing. The Oxford English Dictionary dated 1595 contains the earliest English reference to auctions. Auctions can be found all over the world with all kinds of people claiming to be auctioneers. This method has certainly survived the test of time. It is a modern way of selling most any item. Almost every type of merchandise you can find in the retail market can be found at auction. Real estate sales people are becoming more aware of the auction method of marketing real estate through local and national seminars and are getting richer. Even our United States Treasury Bonds are sold at auction. Obviously, the U.S. government thinks this is a viable method to dispose of properties and merchandise.

The U.S. Government many times uses private auctioneers to market the merchandise they have on hand. Most of these auctioneers are the same people who have to look you right in the eye on Sunday morning or during the week in the workplace. Also, they need to protect the reputation of their company. Because of this, it will be rare for the auctioneer to take advantage of the consumer. If this does happen, however, you do have recourse. If the auctioneer is a member of your State Auctioneer Association or the National Auctioneer Association, please notify them. We adhere to a strict code of ethics, and proper action will be taken. The address for notifying the National Auctioneers Association is: 8880 Ballentine, Overland Park, Kansas 66214.

Again, this book is full of information on government auctions. Read it and follow the instructions given. You will enjoy attending these auctions once you get started.

Ronald W. Faison

Ronald W. Faison, President
National Auctioneers Association

AUCTION SUCCESS STORIES

When we first published the <u>Action Guide to Government Auctions</u>, our intention was to provide the "definitive auction guide". One of the points we have made in presenting this book to you is that there *are* bargains to be had. In an effort to ensure that government auctions truly are a viable way to purchase merchandise at significantly less than retail cost, our Research Department called around the country to find out what is actually being sold at these auctions. The following are just a few of the many bargains we found:

Riverside County Garage - Riverside, CA

A Porsche with a book value $60,000, with only 500 miles on the odometer, sold for $39,000.

U.S. Postal Service - San Francisco, CA

The Postal Service auctioned off a batch of over 150 guns and rifles, including one rifle worth $2,500. A San Francisco resident bought the entire lot with a bid of $1,500. Had he known at the time that his was the *only* bid, he could have purchased the lot for only one dollar!

An antique doll with an appraised value of $3,000 was sold for $200.

Wayne County Sheriff's Department - Detroit, MI

A $5,000 mink coat with the price tag still on it sold for $600. A full length white mink coat, valued at $18,000 was sold for $1,400.

Fulton County Sheriff's Department - Atlanta, GA

A home with an appraised value near $150,000 sold for *$15.00!* This does not happen often but there are instances when a buyer will place an extremely low bid and then find that his was the only bid.

U. S. Postal Service - St. Paul, MN

An abandoned Persian rug valued at $1,200 was auctioned for $250.

U.S. Marshal's Service Providence, RI

About 15 people attended the auction of a $55,000 fishing boat. A resident of Maine started things rolling with a bid of $10. No one else spoke up, and the boat was sold to the man from Maine.

Harris County Sheriff - Houston, TX

Brand new G.E. washer and dryer: $50 each.

U.S. Postal Service - Philadelphia, PA

A brand new Pioneer stereo system - including dual cassette deck, digital tuner, equalizer, 150 watt amplifier - sold for $90.

U.S. Marshal's Service - Sioux Falls, SD

A horse sired by Secretariat was auctioned for $4,500. The horse has won $20,000 in purses.

We would love to hear about YOUR auction success stories. Also tell us of any questions or comments you may have regarding the contents of this publication. You may write to the author at:

REX PUBLISHING
P.O. BOX 390
CLEARWATER, FL 34617-0390

TABLE OF CONTENTS

CHAPTER 2..39

Real Estate Auctions and Sales

SECTION FOUR 357

CITY DIRECTORIES

INTRODUCTION

You are now holding in your hands the result of nearly one year's work and the expenditure of nearly $200,000 in research costs. No one has ever assembled this much information about the government auction and related real estate sales in a single volume or home-study course. The entire book has been laid out in a home-study course format so that you can find out about all the government agencies which have auctions, contact them directly for auction information and get all the practical insider information needed for your auction success.

During the course of our research we have discovered that the most outrageous things have been auctioned and we have found bargains of a lifetime bought by many very lucky individuals. One man bought a $50,000 boat for only $10. Another woman bought a $279,000 home for less that $50,000. Another man bought a $250,000 apartment on New York City's wealthy Upper East Side for less than $100,000. Others have reported amazing bargains on cars, some bought for as little as $25. Desks have sold for 53 cents apiece. Mink coats have sold for pennies on the dollar. One person has even been reported to have bought a $150,000 home for only $15. Some have bought homes for $1.

Can you get bargains like these? Time and auctions under your belt will tell. Even if you don't hit the auction lottery, you can certainly find bargains you could only dream about and at savings which you might not even believe years after you've gotten them.

For the first time ever you'll find out where used car dealers often shop to buy cars for their car lots and sell to you at more than double the price they, themselves, paid for that car. You will read about real estate that you can buy at large discounts; perhaps you can even buy your own first home that way. Others will find investment property that they might otherwise never be able to purchase.

Some people have said that information such as this is "free and available to anyone" but that statement is nonsense. To gather this much information has taken thousands of hours, enormous phone bills and subscription costs that have run into many thousands of dollars. I sincerely doubt that anyone, on their own, can find out this information without spending many days, weeks and months and then only if they were to use this guide as a working manual to direct them. The amount of information that a full-time research team had to sift through to bring this single volume to you was enormous.

No one has ever written such a complete book nor fully researched it as thoroughly as has been done here. A few people have written cheap government surplus manuals, but upon reviewing those, I found their information was incomplete, inaccurate and misleading.

A lot of those manuals were simply copies of someone else's that had been written years ago. Information was outdated, their phone numbers usually incorrect and the addresses no longer usable.

Why should I have written a book on government auctions? Because no one had ever bothered to research as thoroughly as I had wanted it researched. You won't find anything in this book which hasn't been checked, re-checked and re-checked again. No stone has been left unturned. The hard part of the research has been done. This is not just a telephone directory, but a complete manual that will prepare you for auctions. It's a step-by-step instruction manual which will take you from not knowing about government auctions or agencies, to fully informing you about the key elements of the government agencies and their participation in the auction process. We will provide you with not-well-known information and re-emphasize the important points so that you will become successful at auctions.

Did you know that there are billions of dollars of merchandise sold each year at government auctions? Did you know that various government agencies and private companies, congressionally chartered, now hold potentially $400 billion worth of real estate? Did you know that many are eager for your calls and wish you would find out about their auctions and go to them? Did you know that you can buy a house, a car, a boat and practically anything you ever dreamed of at a government auction for a fraction of the price you would normally pay elsewhere? Did you know that many professionals regularly attend such auctions and routinely pick up merchandise for which you probably pay full price? Did you know that many professionals wouldn't ever think of paying a wholesale price on something let alone the retail price you've been paying all these years? Well, now you can change all that. You can read the next few hundred pages and change your lifestyle, improve your bank account, start a new career or simply pick up a few bargains which might have been out of your grasp yesterday or last week. Now, you have a tool which can give you an advantage over your co-workers, neighbors and friends.

You are going to be required to do some work. You are going to have to practice and prepare yourself well. You will have to make phone calls and follow auction information. The enormous, nearly impossible, task of data-gathering has been done for you. You'll have to read this book and perhaps re-read it. You'll have to refer to it from time to time in order to polish off what you have already learned.

I do know that if you follow the easy instructions laid out for you in this book that you will have success at auctions. I know many people who have gone to auctions and succeeded. It does not require superior intelligence, nor does it require an overwhelming drive for success. Many people have simply not succeeded at auctions because they did not go to the ones where there were bargains or because they did not have the practical experience described later in this book. Some simply gave up because past books on the subject provided them with false information or even incorrect phone numbers.

New agencies are continually being formed, changed or deleted. If you follow this guide properly and stay on top of the auctions and the agencies mentioned in this book, you'll have the capability of always being informed about such changes. And you'll be able to use this book for the rest of your life. If used properly, you'll be able to pass this on to your children and other relatives so they can take advantage of these bargains as well.

And when you succeed at these government auctions, please drop us a line and let us know how you did at them. We're always happy to hear from you. Our customer service department is open during business hours to answer your questions and help you succeed at these auctions. Please contact them when you can, if you need help.

Remember that we're here to help you succeed at the auctions. I wish you the very best of good fortune. Now you finally have the tools so get started!

How To Use this Book

This book was designed as a course to help educate you in the auction procedure. Many people will want to flip through the pages and simply find one or two government agencies to call. I strongly advise you to use this book as it was written. It was written after researching how one can be best prepared to attend and succeed at a government auction.

In **Section One** you'll find out about all the government agencies which have auctions or real estate sales and how they go about obtaining such inventory for resale to you. You may read of familiar names or of unfamiliar ones. You'll learn about their procedures and advice on how to deal with them properly so they may be effective for you.

In **Section Two** you'll find out exactly what goes on at an auction and the different types of auctions there are, how they work and how you can obtain financing to purchase your bargain. Virtually every insider tip which exists has been assembled for your use. Many people have been consulted to provide you with useful and practical information.

3

In **Section Three** you'll get the hard-won research of thousands of hours and a king's ransom in money. There you'll find the names, addresses, phone numbers and other information for every agency involved in the auction process. It was not an easy task nor was it obtained for free. No one, up until now, took the time to provide you with all of this information in an easy-to-follow format.

In **Section Four** you'll find the city pack directories which contain pertinent information for many of the major United States cities. For those who travel and for those who want to find out what's going on in their city, as well as in cities they might wish to visit, we've isolated the data for quick use and fast reference.

At the end of the book you'll find a complete glossary for your properly defining words which have a specialized or legal use. Many of these words may be new to you. When you run across such a word, please turn to the glossary so that you may properly define that word. If you pass such a word and fail to get the proper definition, you may find yourself unable to fully understand that part of the book which you are reading. It is important that you use this glossary.

SECTION ONE

INTRODUCTION

This entire section exists to give you a quick rundown on all of the government agencies which are in any way related to the government auction process. You will find out which government agencies have auctions, which ones do not, where the merchandise comes from and what you should expect to find at each auction.

For your convenience, I have split this section into two main chapters: personal property auctions and real estate auctions. This allows you the choice of reading both or concentrating on the section you prefer. If you want to purchase cars, boats or furniture, the Personal Property Chapter will be the one you will need to read. Conversely, if you want to purchase property, then the Real Estate Chapter will help you. I hope the way the agencies are presented fills your needs and facilitates your ability to make purchases at an auction faster and easier.

There are very important terms found in the glossary for specialized words. Please use the glossary to prevent any confusion you may have in understanding the auction process.

A Word About Government Agencies

Please remember that you are dealing with human beings. Each has a job to do and some do it well. Most government agents are bureaucrats and they are expected to follow "party lines". Some are cranky and difficult, but overall, our research team found most of them very willing to help. As you call these agencies, you may hear that this information is readily available in libraries or "all you need is one simple address to obtain all of this information". Unfortunately that is not true. We have scoured libraries and spent thousands of hours interviewing government agents to find the truth about these auctions and the correct data so that your job will be easier.

The government has said there are no bargains at these auctions. That statement is just a reflection of the frustration the government has regarding the disposal of all of this material. The government is defeating its own purpose. While they do not want to be bothered with phone calls and inquiries from the novice auction-goer, they are failing to realize the "sales potential" the novice brings. In the June 1989 issue of Reader's Digest there are documented facts that disprove this government line. The article found that HUD homes are generally discounted 10% to 40% below market value. One man bought a boat valued at $50,000 for only $10. I would be committing fraud if I said this and these facts were not true. Our Research Department works overtime, carefully checking and re-checking these facts to ensure that you are receiving the most accurate and complete data. The point here is there are bargains at government auctions.

Many people complain that the government is difficult and uncooperative. Apparently they sometimes forget that your tax dollars pay their salary. I hope that you receive the help you need but if you don't, please be patient. If the people you contact after reading this book tell you "there are very few auctions", try asking them these questions: "Why do I see the advertisements all over the United States? Why do so many professionals go to these auctions?"

Some agencies feel that if they actively publicize these auctions they will get into trouble for "giving this property away". Don't worry about the government agencies as they will take care of themselves. Be persistent and follow through until you talk to a person who can help you. Get the auction notices, go to the auctions and see for yourself what is available.

You'll find that the information given to you has been carefully researched and has been determined as factual and complete. No matter what the official line is, make your own observations. I believe that you will make the same determination I have. You will find success. Good luck at the auctions.

CHAPTER 1

Personal Property Auctions and Sales

Seized and Confiscated Merchandise
Government Surplus Merchandise
Abandoned and Unclaimed Merchandise
Repossessed Merchandise

General Services Administration

Corres. Symbol 4FBS

75 Spring St., SW
Atlanta, GA 30303

Official Business
Penalty For Private Use $300

Sale No: 04FBS89107

Sealed Bid

FIRST CLASS MAIL

Postage and Fees Paid
U S General Services
Administration
GSA-361

**Sale of
Government Personal Property**

Sale No: 04FBS89107

Bid Opening – Date/Time: JULY 26, 1989
12:30 PM, LOCAL TIME

Bid Opening – Location: SEE ITEM BID PAGE

Inspection: JULY 17 THROUGH 21, 1989

ELIZABETH GAY
519 CLEVELAND, #113 FL 346150000
CLEARWATER

10

Personal Property Auctions and Sales

In this chapter you'll read about cars, boats, tractors, trucks, golf bags, coins, books, motorcycles, jewelry and other assorted personal property. You'll learn the sources of the merchandise, who auctions it and a basic rundown on that agency. You will find the phone numbers and other means you may use to find out about these auctions in **Section Three**. This section gives you the important briefing on the agencies and where you are likely to find the best bargains.

Seized and Confiscated Merchandise

For some reason, many, many people are more interested in this section than in any other. Perhaps there is a certain glamor in buying property or merchandise from someone who has broken the law. Many people are convinced that, because the government seized this personal property, they will give it away. Many others will not buy this merchandise because they think the drug dealer will come back and take it away from him. None of that is true. Yes, there are many bargains one can find at these auctions. Because of increased publicity, various government agencies are hesitant to practically give things away, although in some cases you'll still find this going on. Drug dealers are given many opportunities to retrieve their possessions by posting bonds through the Drug Enforcement Administration's Asset Forfeiture Unit with the Office of the Chief Counsel. You'll find notices printed almost every Wednesday in the newspaper, USA TODAY. It is in the classified section and takes up nearly two full pages in the newspapers. You should look through it sometime to see just how much is being confiscated.

There are five basic ways that personal property can be seized or confiscated:

- Through the National Asset Seizure and Forfeiture Program.
- By U.S. Customs for a variety of reasons.
- By the local sheriff when local laws are violated.
- Through the IRS asset seizure program.
- By the local police when local laws are violated.

Of the above, U.S. Customs, sheriff and police agencies also have merchandise at their auctions which come from a different source. And that will be discussed later in this chapter. Let's run through the various government agencies and see who does what.

The National Asset Seizure and Forfeiture Program

This is conducted by the U.S. Marshal's Office. None of the U.S. Marshal's Offices maintain a mailing list. Contacting the U.S. Marshal's Office won't get you very far, as they are busy disposing of this property and running their offices. They have a specific procedure, although confusing, in disposing of this property.

The personal property that we are talking about here is the drug-related merchandise: cars, boats, jewelry and other luxuries of those who deal drugs and suck out the life from our youth in order to have a more comfortable life. They live quite spectacularly but many are losing their accumulations and those accumulations are being sold at public auctions. You'll find Rolls

Royces, Mercedes, Jaguars, BMW's, Porsches and a lot more at auctions held under this program. But you'll also find late models or junk, American cars and foreign cars of lesser value as well. You'll find boats, trucks, pick-up trucks and other accoutrements of the drug criminal at these auctions. You'll find furs, computers, jewelry and other fancy merchandise.

The government claims to keep half of it for use by other agencies. This may or may not be true. I am constantly surprised by how much is seized and how little actually does come up for auction. This year's estimates include over $1 billion by just the Drug Enforcement Administration alone. If you know or have found out about anything unethical going on in this area, I will pay you $1,000 reward money if the information helps lead to the indictment and conviction of the government official involved in the unethical behavior with regard to the disposal of this personal property.

Their procedure for disposing of the merchandise goes as follows: The Marshal's Office can either auction the merchandise themselves or they can turn the merchandise over to the GSA. If the auction is through the GSA, it is not going to be a great place to find bargains. The GSA usually tries to get fair market value for all merchandise. If the merchandise is not relinquished to the GSA, it will be auctioned through a private auctioneer. All real estate is handled by local real estate agents.

With the in-house auctions, some Marshal's Offices will have hot-line phone numbers so that you can listen to dates of auctions in your area. It depends on the Marshal in your area. You can call and suggest that a hot-line number be set up. If enough people call, I'm sure he'll accommodate eventually.

At various times, Marshals will advertise in the classifieds of the newspapers, usually very small ads that are hard to find. We've done our best to provide you with in-roads into their auctions. Check **Section Three** under U.S. Marshals for the most up-to-date advice.

Some people will expect the Drug Enforcement Administration or the FBI to handle their own auctions. They do not. They turn it over through the National Asset and Forfeiture Program to the U.S. Marshals who, in turn, distribute it in the manner prescribed above. Do not call the FBI or the DEA about auctions. They don't have them, they don't maintain mailing lists and are pretty upset about being called about their auctions since they don't have any. Save yourself some time and aggravation by following the above procedure and referring to **Section Three**.

United States Customs

Many years ago U.S. Customs had their own auctions. They obtained their merchandise through drug seizures or from companies which had tried to smuggle merchandise into this country without paying duty or import tax or from those people who simply failed to declare their merchandise properly when returning from a vacation or business abroad. They would have regional Customs auctions around the United States.

As the drug seizures increased and as a result of budgetary problems in disposing of this merchandise, U.S. Customs hired a private contractor to dispose of the personal property seized or confiscated by the agency. That private contractor is a subsidiary of Northrop World-Wide Aircraft. I had heard for many months that customs auctions were atrociously bad for bargains. Yet there were still some bargains to be found from time to time.

Occasionally, someone would brag about some fantastic bargains they had found at one of them. Currently, a Federal Grand Jury in Texas is investigating Northrop for overcharging the government on this auction merchandise. Customs will seize aircraft, boats, cars and other lesser items from suspected drug dealers. Apparently, the government is making allegations that Northrop is performing poorly in running their auctions and is charging the government exorbitant fees for storing property or towing cars (example: $750 to tow a car less than 50 miles!).

Northrop still handles the auctions for U.S. Customs. I expect that this will change within the next few years and will either get scattered among private auction houses, be handled by another government agency or be run similarly to the U.S. Marshal's National Asset and Forfeiture Program. In the meantime, you can find out about these auctions as discussed in **Section Three**.

You'll also hear about this in greater detail in the media as news breaks on this subject. Congress is also investigating this contract so fireworks should occur shortly.

Local Sheriff's Sales

Sheriff's Deputies are usually used at auctions to sell off foreclosed property such as homes and farms. However, there have been various research findings showing that some sheriffs are also selling drug-related personal property and other crime-related property in various counties around the United States. That is one area where we have found pronouncements of great bargains. For example, at one sheriff's sale, a $5,000 mink coat with the price tag still on it sold for only $600. I guess the bidders didn't believe the price tag or was that fair market value?

One way to find out about these auctions is simply to call and ask when and where the next auction is to be held. Another way is to send a small packet of self-addressed stamped envelopes to the local sheriff and ask him to mail you any notices or fliers of upcoming auctions. Some will be reluctant or unwilling to do so. Each county sheriff's office has their own peculiarities. Remember, they are elected officials and you can always vote against that person if he is unfriendly or unhelpful to you.

IRS Sales

These are not well-publicized but can provide you with the most incredible deals. When someone fails to pay his taxes, a lien can be brought against his property or a levy against his salary. In the past eight years IRS liens on property owners have skyrocketed from $371,000 to $837,000 annually. That's a lot of properties but with salaries it's even greater: from $465,000 to $2.1 million annually!

As a result, there could be a great amount of property (see Chapter Two of this section) and merchandise up for auction by the IRS. They will generally conduct their auctions themselves. The IRS only wants its back taxes from the auction sale. One man reported to me that several years ago an expensive house in Sacramento was sold for under $1,000 at an IRS tax auction.

The IRS will notify you if there are any known encumbrances on the property or merchandise, stating the fact clearly on their public auction notices. This can affect your bidding on that item. Who would want to pay $2,000 on a $5,000 car and then discover there's a $3,000 loan also due on the car?

The IRS has a national 800 number which will connect you with the IRS Office in your area or state from which you can ask to receive mailings, forms for sealed bids and more. You can also write to them. Addresses are provided in **Section Three**.

You'll find cars, boats, land, homes, jewelry and other merchandise at these auctions. The value of them depends on the amount the IRS wants back in past-due taxes, penalties and interest. Bargains have ranged from spectacular to fair, depending on the condition of the merchandise. Many people will not go to IRS auctions out of sympathy for the former owner of the property for fear that something like this could happen to them or even their distaste for the IRS. Others will go to them because they can find fantastic bargains and don't mind the above.

Police Auctions

These operate under similar conditions to the sheriff sales. A local criminal is arrested and his property seized in the course of breaking the law. The police may also confiscate stolen merchandise which is not reclaimed by the rightful owner. After a time it is put up for auction. At big city police departments, many people do not recover their personal property because it is not clearly identified. Since so much can be "hauled in" on a day's work from big city crime, some of it won't be recovered. It ends up at a police auction.

The police also deal with abandoned vehicles which are covered later in this chapter under Abandoned Merchandise. **Section Three** covers all the police auctions in the major cities.

This covers the seizures and confiscations part of this book. For more specific information and contact points for you, please turn to **Section Three** so you can begin contacting the various government agencies that have this type of merchandise.

Government Surplus Merchandise

You've probably heard about classified ads stating "Jeeps for $49" or some such nonsense. This stuff is simply not true. That is probably someone's outright fraud or copying of an old marketing campaign from the late 1960's or early 1970's. I remember seeing such things advertised in magazines or comic books but someone still persists in advertising this now in tabloids. Those jeeps were surplus and were declared unfit for driving by the Department of Transportation in the early 1970's.

There is an enormous amount of merchandise up for auction in the government surplus area. There are five distinct categories where you might look: The General Services Administration, the Defense Department, the U.S. Postal Service, State Surplus Sales and City Surplus Sales. There may be others but those are the primary ones for surplus merchandise.

NOTICE OF
PUBLIC AUCTION
CARS & TRUCKS
SATURDAY, JULY 8, 1989 - 10:00 A.M.
6100 S.W. 87TH AVENUE, next to ORR Water Plant

1.	*Dodge Aries 4dr.,'85	8746	31.	Dodge Pick-up,'81	13-0916
2.	*Ford LTD 4dr.,'83	7270	32.	GMC Pick-up,'79	7890
3.	*Dodge Aries 4dr.,'85	8726	33.	*Ply. Reliant 4dr.,'84	7553
4.	Int'l Step Van,'69	13-0205	34.	AMC Concord 4dr.,'79	5009
5.	Chevy Van,'81	6039	35.	GMC Pick-up,'79	7921
6.	*Plymouth Reliant 4dr.,'84	7565	36.	Dodge Pick-up, '81	13-0923
7.	*Ford LTD 4dr.,'83	7333	37.	Ford Pick-up,'80	9-0056
8.	*Ford LTD 4dr.,'83	7265	38.	Dodge Pick-up,'81	7798
9.	*Dodge Diplomat 4dr.,'85	8458	39.	Chevy Pick-up,'80	8214
10.	GMC Pick-up,'80	7835	40.	GMC Step Van,'79	13-0543
11.	*Ply. Volare 4dr.,'80	5239	41.	*Dodge Diplomat 4dr.,'87	9016
12.	Dodge Pick-up,'82	13-0952	42.	*Dodge Diplomat 4dr.,'87	9009
13.	*Ply. Volare, 4dr.,'77	4042	43.	*Dodge Diplomat 4dr.,'87	9017
14.	*Dodge Diplomat 4dr.,'85	8241	44.	*Dodge Diplomat 4dr.,'85	8259
15.	Ford Van,'85	8494	45.	*Dodge Diplomat 4dr.,'87	9004
16.	GMC Van,'76	3767	46.	*Dodge Diplomat 4dr.,'85	8446
17.	GMC Pick-up,'84	13-1094	47.	*Dodge Diplomat 4dr.,'85	8277
18.	*Ford LTD 4dr.,'83	7228	48.	Old Regency 98 4dr.,'83	6627
19.	Chevy Chevette 4dr.,'84	8069	49.	Ply. Horizon 4dr.,'81	7689
20.	GMC Pick-up,'75	13-0885	50.	Dodge Pick-up,'83	13-0722
21.	*Ford LTD 4dr.,'83	7256	51.	Chev. Pick-up,'79	7821
22.	*Ford LTD 4dr.,'83	7313	52.	Chev. Pick-up,'83	7135
23.	*Ford LTD 4dr.,'83	7262	53.	Ford Van,'78	13-0689
24.	Chevy Chevette 4dr.,'83	7053	54.	Couri Pick-up,'76	4103
25.	*Ford LTD 4dr.,'83	7290	55.	Chev. Pick-up,'67	1793
26.	*Ford LTD 4dr.,'83	7229	56.	Dodge Pick-up,'82	7852
27.	*Ford LTD 4dr.,'83	7312	57.	Olds Regency 98 4dr.,'83	6994
28.	*Ford Pick-up,'80	8245	58.	*Honda ATC 3whl,'82	31-0404
29.	AMC Concord 4dr.,'77	6630	59.	*Honda ATC 3whl,'82	31-0405
30.	Olds Regency 98 4dr.,'83	6995	60.	Thunderbird 30'Boat,'80	23-2126

NOTE: Vehicles denoted with an asterisk (*) have been used as police vehicles.

Pursuant to Chapter 274, Florida Statutes, the above listed equipment is being sold at auction in an "AS IS, WHERE IS" condition with no guarantee, written, expressed or otherwise. Inspection allowed from 8:00 A.M. to 10:00 A.M. on day of sale. Terms are CASH or Cashier's Check (made out to the Board of County Commissioners), full payment or, a deposit of $200 per vehicle at time of sale. Vehicles must be removed immediately after full payment. General Services Administration employees, members of their immediate family are not eligible to bid on or purchase County vehicles.

The sale will be subject to the complete terms and conditions specified in the "Rules of Dade County Auction Sales" which will be read aloud at the auction and the Bid receipt signed by each purchaser. Dade County makes no warranty, expressed or implied as to description of any of the property, or it's fitness for any use or purpose. All sales are final, no refunds or exchanges, and are subject to State sales tax collection at time of sale. The General Services Administration Director reserves the right to waive any informalities in, or to reject any or all bids.

BOARD OF COUNTY COMMISSIONERS
DADE COUNTY, FLORIDA

CI-89-13

By: Victor J. Monzon-Aguirre, Director
General Services Administration

AUTO AUCTION

STATE OF CALIFORNIA - DEPARTMENT OF GENERAL SERVICES
OFFICE OF FLEET ADMINISTRATION

WHERE

LOS ANGELES STATE GARAGE
122 SOUTH HILL STREET
LOS ANGELES

WHEN
JULY 15,
1989

10:00 A.M.

INSPECTION
JULY 15,
1989

8:00 A.M. TO
10:00 A.M.

SURPLUS STATE
VEHICLES & MISCELLANEOUS
ITEMS WILL BE SOLD TO
THE HIGHEST BIDDERS

OPEN BIDDING · PUBLIC INVITED

IF YOU ARE NOT IN THE MARKET FOR A CAR THIS MONTH - PASS THIS FLYER ON TO A FRIEND

General Services Administration

This government agency plays a large role in the auction business. As with seized and confiscated merchandise, they'll handle their auctions in-house, using GSA auctioneers who are government employees. GSA employees and their families, other government employees and military personnel, unless there is a specification to the contrary in the conditions of sale, are not permitted to bid at these and other GSA auctions. They're not permitted to have an agent at those auctions trying to buy merchandise for them either.

The GSA will auction surplus merchandise from all the non-military government agencies around the United States. That's a tall order. It is considered to be the world's largest auction house by many in terms of sheer amounts of merchandise offered to the public at their auctions.

At these auctions you'll find all the used merchandise from the GSA and other government agencies: typewriters, desks, surplus vehicles (some of which have warranties), medical and dental equipment, photographic equipment and many other items too numerous to mention. They'll send catalogs of merchandise out on a regular basis. This is most frequently done on a sealed bid basis (see **Section Two** for more information on sealed bids). You'll either be asked to make a bid over a certain minimum amount ($25, $50, $100 or more) without submitting any deposit with your bid or you'll have to submit a deposit with your bid, usually 20% of the bid amount, which is refundable if you fail in buying the merchandise. Items will go to the highest bidder.

Most of the merchandise they offer is in fair to poor condition. Some of it will require repairs. There is a major disadvantage: it is scattered at government warehouses or offices around the United States. That will make it difficult for you to correctly appraise the merchandise. Often, a custodian's name and phone number is listed along with the item to be auctioned. That will give you a window of opportunity to judge if the item is worth making a long-distance trip to see for yourself. Such merchandise does get sold so there may be bargains there for you. You can find out what the merchandise is being sold for by using the techniques described in **Section Two.**

Department of Defense

Within the vast caverns of the Department of Defense is the Washington-based Defense Logistics Agency. Subordinate to them are the various field level offices called Defense Reutilization Marketing Offices, also known as DRMOs. Supervising the DRMOs within each part of the country are regional offices, which are not worth contacting for auction information.

Many people equate these auctions, incorrectly, with the National Bidder's List which comes out of Battle Creek, Michigan. This is a large wholesale operation for sealed bids. If you want to purchase one typewriter, go to the DRMO auction; however, if you are in the market for 150 typewriters, then try the National Bidder's List.

All the DRMOs in the country are listed in **Section Three**. The way to get on the National Bidder's List is also described in the appropriate chapter of that section.

These local auctions are probably the best place to go on the retail level. Of course, if you are a large wholesaler and want to start a retail specialty store or you already own an Army-Navy Surplus store, the National Bidder's List is the way you would go. Many do already. I've heard from the professionals about phenomenal bargains at these national sealed bid auctions.

The local auctions will be conducted in one of three ways. The first and most common, being a "public oral auction". This method is used where there is a wide variety of small quantities of property. You must be present at these auctions to make your bids.

If there is a variety of property with substantial interest and demand in the local market, they'll use a method called the "spot bid" (more on this in **Section Two**). You'll submit your bids on forms provided by the selling activity so you must be there to make this form of bid.

The last method used to dispose of surplus merchandise is through "retail sales". Small quantities of individual items of property will be offered from time to time at the DRMOs with fixed prices. Contact the local office for retail sale information. On the national level, the Defense Reutilization and Marketing Service has a single contact point for buying merchandise wholesale and in large quantities. You'll be sent an application on which you can note your particular buying interest, both geographically and with respect to the class of property in which you are interested. Don't mark *all* the items, as your application will get lost in the shuffle. You'll then be identified as a crank and probably won't get any mailings.

On the national level you must make sealed bids regularly or your name will be removed from their list if you haven't bid after receipt of five catalogs.

DEPARTMENT OF DEFENSE

DEFENSE REUTILIZATION AND MARKETING SERVICE

CONDUCTED BY

LOCAL AUCTION

SALE NO. 27-9502

DATE AND TIME	SALE SITE
26 JULY 1989	BUILDING T-64 FOR REGISTRATION/INSPECTION 21 JULY THRU 25 JULY 1989
9:00 AM	SALE CONDUCTED IN BUILDING T-6297 - 26 JULY 1989

CONTACT

MRS. SHARON MCMILLION - AC (301) 677-6367

REGISTRATION T-64(21 thru 25 July 1989)
T-6297(26 July 1989)

OFFERING

OFFICE FURNITURE	TRAILERS
OFFICE MACHINES	BOATS
HOUSEHOLD FURNITURE	VEHICLES
TYPEWRITERS	REFRIGERATORS
COMMUNICATION EQUIPMENT	PALLET JACKS
ELECTRICAL/ELECTRONIC EQUIPMENT	
BICYCLES	

INSPECTION BEGINNING   REGISTRATION REQUIRED PRIOR TO INSPECTING - PHOTO ID REQUIRED!
21 JULY 1989 THRU 25 JULY 1989   8:00 AM to 12:00 PM and 12:30 PM to 3:00 PM

(Excluding week-ends and Holidays)

BIDDER ELIGIBILITY NOTICE: The following DoD and U.S. COAST GUARD MEMBERS and EMPLOYEES are NOT ELIGIBLE to bid on this sale: (a) A civilian employee of the Department of Defense or the United States Coast Guard whose duties include any functional or supervisory responsibility for or within the Defense Reutilization and Marketing Program.   (b) A member of the Armed Forces of the United States, including the United States Coast Guard, whose duties include any functional or supervisory responsibility for or within the Defense Reutilization and Marketing Program.   (c) An agent, employee, or immediate member of the household of personnel in (a) and (b) above.

AUCTION 27-9502

1. COMBO FILE CABINET	1 EA	25. OPTICAL MICROSCOPE	1 EA	50. MEDICAL/LAB EQUIP ARTICLE(S): C07	1 LT
2. COMBO FILE CABINET	1 EA	26. IBM SEL II TYPEWRITER	1 EA	51. HOUSEHOLD FURNITURE ARTICLE(S): C15	1 LT
3. CANON COPIERS	1 LT	27. PROGRAMMABLE CALCULATOR	1 EA		
4. ELECTROSURGICAL APPARATUS	1 LT	28. BENCH DRILL	1 EA	52. ELECT/ELECTR EQUIP ARTICLE(S): C31,C32	1 LT
5. LAB EQUIPMENT	1 LT	29. PHOTO EQUIPMENT	1 LT	53. ADP EQUIPMENT	1 LT
6. OSCILLOSCOPE WITH CART ARTICLE(S): C31,C32	1 EA	30. AIR SMOKE-EATER	1 EA	54. OSCILLOSCOPES ARTICLE(S): C31,C32	1 LT
7. ELECT/ELECTR EQUIP ARTICLE(S): C31,C32	1 LT	31. OFFICE MACHINES/SUPPLIES	1 LT		
		32. REFERENCE/MISC BOOKS	1 LT	55. AO SPENCER MICROSCOPE	1 EA
8. MEDICAL/LAB EQUIP	1 LT	33. ELECT/ELECTR EQUIP	1 LT	56. END TABLES	1 LT
9. OSCILLOSCOPE WITH CART ARTICLE(S): C31,C32	1 EA	34. TELEVISIONS ARTICLE(S): C31,C32	1 LT	57. END TABLES	1 LT
10. ADP EQUIPMENT ARTICLE(S): C31,C32	1 LT	35. TELEVISIONS ARTICLE(S): C31,C32	1 LT	58. END TABLES	1 LT
11. OSCILLOSCOPE WITH CART ARTICLE(S): C31,C32	1 EA	36. ADP EQUIPMENT ARTICLE(S): C31,C32	1 LT	59. ELECT/ELECTR EQUIP ARTICLE(S): C31,C32	1 LT
12. OFFICE MACHINES	1 LT	37. ELECT/ELECTR EQUIP	1 LT	60. COMMUNICATION EQUIP ARTICLE(S): C08	1 LT
13. HARDWARE/HAND TOOLS	1 LT	38. REFRIGERATOR	1 EA		
14. ELECT/ELECTR /LAB EQUIP	1 LT	39. ULTRA-MICROTOME	1 EA	61. ADP EQUIPMENT ARTICLE(S): C31,C32	1 LT
15. VIDEOCASSETTE RECORDERS	1 LT	40. ELECT/ELECTR EQUIP ARTICLE(S): C31,C32	1 LT	62. DESK ATTACHMENTS	1 LT
16. ELECT/ELECTR EQUIP ARTICLE(S): C31,C32	1 LT	41. ELECT/ELECTR EQUIP ARTICLE(S): C31,C32	1 LT	63. ELECT/ELECTR EQUIP	1 LT
17. MEDICAL/LAB EQUIP	1 LT			64. TEAM RALEIGH BICYCLE	1 EA
18. LAUNDRY SEALERS	1 LT	42. COMBO FILE CABINET	1 EA	65. CHEMICAL CARTRIDGES	1 LT
19. ELECT/ELECTR/COMM EQUIP ARTICLE(S): C08	1 LT	43. COMBO FILE CABINET	1 EA	66. BOOKS	1 LT
		44. SAFE	1 EA	67. TELEVISIONS ARTICLE(S): C31,C32	1 LT
20. ELECT/ELECTR EQUIP ARTICLE(S): C31,C32	1 LT	45. ELECT/ELECTR EQUIP	1 LT		
21. END TABLES	1 LT	46. HARDWARE/PLUMBING EQUIP	1 LT	68. RANDOR GALAXY BICYCLE	1 EA
22. END TABLES	1 LT	47. PHOTO EQUIPMENT ARTICLE(S): C01	1 LT	69. EXHIBIT BOARD	1 EA
				70. EXHIBIT BOARD	1 EA
23. END TABLES	1 LT	48. ELECT/ELECTR EQUIP/COMPS	1 LT	71. HENNES JUNKERMANN BICYCLE	1 EA
24. END TABLES	1 LT	49. HUFFY ECHELON BICYCLE	1 EA	72. DESK ATTACHMENTS	1 LT
				73. LOTUS BICYCLE	1 EA

PAGE 1

FRIDAY, July 14, 1989   United Feature Syndicate
JACK ANDERSON and DALE VAN ATTA

WASHINGTON MERRY-GO-ROUND

Government auctions virtually a giveaway

By Jack Anderson

and Dale Van Atta

WASHINGTON — Dick Textor catches what the government spills.

His driveway is coated with green Army tennis court paint. His Brandywine, Maryland home shines with a layer of Coast Guard white and Navy gray. He drives an $18,500 electric truck that Uncle Sam sold him for $120. He can serve dinner on hand-painted White House china and sign letters with Ronald Reagan's automatic autograph machine — all picked up at government surplus auctions.

Textor drives the government crazy. A self-confessed "loud-mouth," he hangs out at government auctions barking about how our bureaucrats run the worst business in the nation. In a booming voice, he asks his fellow bidders how the government can afford to pay thousands of dollars for something, and then sell it for pennies. He marvels aloud about the Secret Service safe he bought. It had a blueprint of the White House grounds stuffed in the bottom drawer. Then Textor takes home a perfectly good fax machine for $10.

What Textor has seen is the flipside of the Pentagon's $640 toilet seat. At supply depots across the country, the government runs auctions to flush the products it claims it no longer needs.

Here are some things the taxpayers bought at a premium and then dumped for a pittance: copy machines, televisions, computers, forklifts, video cameras, night-vision scopes, scales, safes, emergency flares and more.

Hydraulic scales go for $5, eight televisions for a total of $110, 62 cases of Xerox copier toner valued at about $6,000 for $2. Monte Hall never dished out better deals.

In February, Textor figured it was time to alert George Bush to the giveaway. He wrote a letter to the president saying that the laws governing the sales are routinely broken, that the government could get much more for its surplus goods, that he has bought radioactive materials without warning labels and military equipment that wasn't supposed to be sold.

Textor bought one auto-signature pen for $25 and sold it for $500. He picked up a scale for $5 and resold it for $500. Why can't the government get a better return too, he asked Bush.

Four months after Textor wrote the letter, the Defense Reutilization and Marketing Service (the Santa Claus at the Pentagon) solved the problem in its own way — it banned Textor from auctions of military goods. Now Uncle Sam can go about its foolish business without being bothered by the facts.

(MORE)

MERRY-GO-ROUND   7-14-89   ADD 1

The Pentagon justified its move saying Textor had tried to rig the bidding simply because he bantered with other bidders.

The Pentagon told our associate Jim Lynch that Textor's letter to the president had nothing to do with the attempt to ban him from auctions.

We asked a spokeswoman for the Defense Reutilization and Marketing Service why the government doesn't listen to Textor's marketing ideas. "It's not that kind of marketing," she said, likening the program to a garage sale. "If you have ever had a garage sale, you know things don't go for top dollar."

In other words, the Pentagon doesn't do the smart thing because it's not in the business of doing the smart thing.

Postal Vehicles

From time to time the local post office has to replace their vehicles. They'll sell their vehicles, either by auction or at a fixed low price, to those who wish to purchase them. Generally, though, they'll have those little cube vans or trucks up for sale or even the Jeeps. There is no set pattern in most cities nor a regular schedule. Some cities haven't had auctions in years; others have auctions every few months. In New York City, they have ongoing sales of Jeeps, one-ton vans and 4-wheel drive trucks at their postal garage throughout the year. See **Section Three** for their phone number.

Some bargains have been found with vehicles in this category. Keep in mind that you are not getting new vehicles here. Some are very old and very used.

State Surplus Sales

In many states this is probably your best place to look for a vehicle. They're often overlooked because most people have the idea they only sell used state police cruisers. Some do but many don't. At these auctions you'll likely find phone trucks, Department of Transportation vehicles, boats, general purpose vehicles, pick-up trucks and a wide assortment of surplus merchandise. Some will have office equipment and other fine items for sale.

Each area is different. Some states turn their vehicles over to dealers who will then re-sell them to you. That's bad if you're in one of those states. I have seen many used car dealers attend and buy cars at these auctions. You'll be surprised to find the auction selling price and the car dealer's asking price to be wide apart on the car dealership's lot - yet another reason why you should go to these auctions.

City Surplus Sales

These are usually held once a year. At the last one in my area I heard about the most incredible bargains. Cars going for a silly fraction of their Blue Book value. Call your local city hall and ask when or if they'll be having one of these auctions in your area soon.

SAN FRANCISCO POLICE AND SHERIFF DEPARTMENTS
AUCTION SALE OF UNCLAIMED PERSONAL PROPERTY
With Additions From "STING" Operations
SATURDAY AUGUST 5th At 9 A.M.
Gold & Costume Jewelry, Tools, Radios, Tape Decks, V.C.R.s, Cameras, Clothing, Bikes, Scales, T.V.s, etc.
EXHIBITION: 8 AM to 9 AM on Morning of Sale
Sale Held in Garage of Hall of Justice, Seventh St. Entrance 850 Bryant St., San Francisco, Ca.
NOTE: Cash or Certified checks only Accepted
Oscar D. Kaufman, Auctioneer Ca. License #165 P.O. Box 2071 San Francisco, Ca. 94127

POLICE AUCTION JULY 22, 1989
ASSORTED POLICE VEHICLES, MANY WITH HEAVY DUTY COMPONENTS, COMPOSED OF 1980-85 YEARS OF VARIOUS MANUFACTURERS MAKES AND BODY STYLES.
These vehicles will be sold at Public Auction by the Sheriff of Cook County on July 22, 1989, at 10:00 A.M., at the Sheriff's Police Auto Pound, 3146 South Archer Avenue, Chicago, Illinois. The vehicles may be inspected one hour prior to the start of the auction. Transfer of titles will be effected upon payment of vehicles purchased. VEHICLES MUST BE PAID FOR IN CASH AT TIME OF PURCHASE. NO DEPOSITS ACCEPTED. County employees, their relatives or their agents are not permitted to bid. VEHICLES ARE TO BE SOLD AS IS, NO GUARANTEE. For information, contact Officer Robert Neubauer at 890-3355.
JAMES E. O'GRADY
SHERIFF OF COOK COUNTY

Abandoned and Unclaimed Merchandise

This has been one of the better kept secrets around the United States. True, you won't find merchandise going for a few dollars but you will find a steady stream of great bargains at many of these auctions. Merchandise like this comes about because it was "lost". Things get lost through the mail, cars get towed away, coins and jewelry in safe deposit boxes are abandoned and even passbooks that have money in them are forgotten about. Imported merchandise is sometimes not claimed or given up for one reason or another. All the above falls under the category of abandoned and unclaimed merchandise.

The agencies which oversee the disposal of this personal property are as follows: U.S. Postal Service (in five locations throughout the United States), Local Police Departments, State Unclaimed Property Divisions and U.S. Customs. Each has its own categories of merchandise.

United States Postal Auctions

Here is one of the better ways to find bargains. No, they won't give this merchandise away but some of the offices contacted seem very eager to attract bidders. You should find the region nearest you and get to their next auction. Not only do they provide great experience but some of them have inexperienced auctioneers who could care less about appraising the merchandise.

Anything that has been lost through the mails or material which has been damaged (the loss paid for by the Postal Service) will be sold at one of these auctions. If your city doesn't have these auctions, it's because the personal property has been sent on to that city's main region. Postal Auctions are held at these locations only: New York City, Philadelphia, St. Paul, Atlanta and San Francisco.

At these auctions you'll get to preview the merchandise the day of the auction only. You'll have to pay that day. Bidding generally has a $25 minimum bid and increments go up in $2 or $5 amounts. You must remove merchandise the day you buy it. Bidding is done in "lots" so that you may have to bid on a "tub of books", as opposed to the few you'd like.

Here are some examples of the different types of merchandise you'll find at these auctions: books, compact discs, video cassettes, audio cassettes, baby strollers, welding and cutting outfits, electrical appliances, baby's car seat, cutlery, typewriters, cowboy boots, men's shirts, model airplanes, ladies' shirts, coats, computer software, leather jackets, clocks, birthday candles, cameras, toys, baseball gloves, cassette players and more. The list really does go on and is very long. You can find everything from luggage to Christmas decorations at these auctions.

Generally, they are held monthly in each of the regions. Since so much can and does get lost through the mail or goes unclaimed, you should take advantage of these bargains. You'll get further details in **Section Three**.

State Unclaimed Property Divisions

In some states this is under a different name. **Section Three** provides the correct name for each state. Not every state has these types of auctions. They are held irregularly in most states, if at all. Among other items, you can expect to find the contents of safe deposit boxes at these auctions, generally coins or jewelry.

Simply contact your state, as indicated in **Section Three**, for details. Some put out a nice catalog, others don't do anything except place a classified ad in the local paper.

While we're on this section, here's another tip: If you've ever had money in a bank and forgotten about it, this may be one way to recover it. Some entrepreneurial spirits sell this information for about $30-$40. In some states, not only can you recover your own money which you've forgotten but you can also hire yourself out as a finder of lost money. You either buy or rent lists of people who have forgotten about their money, then contact them and, for a finder's fee, recover it for them. Some states charge for this list, others don't and still others forbid the practice or demand that you be licensed for it. You can order these lists by mail for a fee or view them for free by appointment only, with some restrictions per your state. It could be an extra way for you to make some spare cash if you need to do so.

Local Police Departments

Now, this is one place where many don't bother to look for bargains. And there are good reasons to do so and not to do so. The police departments have auctions in major cities (and in many smaller cities) on a regular or annual basis for cars which have been abandoned. Sometimes towing companies have these auctions for them.

Cars can either be seized or taken away by police departments when someone doesn't want to pay their traffic tickets. The situation in New York City has gotten very unrealistic with some people running up thousands of dollars in unpaid parking tickets. In those cases, the person is better off allowing his car to be sold at public auction and remain out of the picture.

For every great car at these auctions there are probably 10-50 clunkers or cars not worth bothering about. The wonderful thing about police auctions is that some have about 10 times as many cars as participants in the auction. Another is that at some of these auctions, auctioneers can get overwhelmed by sheer numbers and not properly auction off the cars for the "fair market value". At one auction some cars were auctioned off for $15-$25 per car at the end of the auction, simply because there were so many and the auctioneer was frantically trying to get rid of them.

What's the down side to police auctions? Quite a bit. For one, you can't start the cars up to see if they even work. Who knows what you're getting? That's one of the reasons prices are so low. A locksmith will come at the end of the auction to open the car and make you a set of keys (for which you'll have to pay an additional $30-$50).

If you can overcome the above and find a good-looking car and keep your bid low, you can probably do all right at these auctions. There are various problem-spots to look for while inspecting these vehicles (as covered in **Section Two**). Please try to inspect the car as much as you can within these limitations. Some people have done very well at these auctions and have found "unreal" bargains. Others are turned off by the clunkers. Just don't bid on the clunkers.

U.S. Customs Auctions

Once again, U.S. Customs does not have auctions. They turn over their merchandise to Northrop World-Wide Aircraft for auction. As stated earlier, Northrop is under Federal Grand Jury and Congressional investigation and is likely to lose its contract with U.S. Customs. As this will make news, as it has already, you'll find out in the media who will then do their auctions for them.

There is one unmentioned note to U.S. Customs. They also have unclaimed merchandise up for auction. An import company may have merchandise brought in from a foreign country and then go out of business or be unable to pay the duty or import tax. If that happens, U.S. Customs will turn it over to Northrop for auction. See **Section Three** for address and phone information.

This covers the unclaimed merchandise section of this chapter. If you wish to immediately pursue this area to get onto various government mailing lists, then please contact the applicable agencies in **Section Three.**

Remember to read the **Auction Information** in **Section Two** before attending your auctions, though. I want you to be well prepared for auction success.

Repossessed Merchandise

Most of us are familiar with bank repossessions or home foreclosures but there are more areas than that available at auction. Some in this area are not auctioned but turned over to be sold by various agencies or auctioneers. This is one unpleasant area of the auction process because it contains the element of loss, similar to an IRS auction. I have spoken to a few people who hesitate to go to these auctions because they are taking advantage of someone's personal loss.

PUBLIC AUCTION

On the Premises:

BY ORDER OF THE UNITED STATES BANKRUPTCY COURT

ARROW GLASS COMPANY
3740 El Camino Real
San Mateo, CA

FRIDAY, JULY 7TH – 11:00 AM

STOCK IN TRADE – VEHICLES – FIXTURES
MACHINERY – TOOLS – HOUSEBOAT
OFFICE FURNITURE AND EQUIPMENT

FRAMED MIRRORS – HARDWARE – GLASS STOCK – WINDOWS
WIRE – SILICONE – GLUES – MUCH MORE!

INCLUDES: MILWAUKEE ELECTRIC HAMMERS – GLASS
DRILLS – ROUTERS – MAKITA SAWS – TABLE SAW – RADIAL
ARM SAW – BENCH GRINDER – CHOP SAW – SOMNICK GRINDERS
DRILLS – PARTS – CABINETS – WALL RACKS – CLAMPS –
LADDERS – HARDWARE – DESKS – CHAIRS – FILE CABINETS –
OLYMPIA ELECTRIC TYPEWRITER – SUPPLIES, ETC.

VEHICLES: GMC Sierra 35 Pick-up
1 Ton DODGE Ram, Custom 200 w/ glass rack
MAZDA B 2000 Pick-up w/glass rack

INSPECTION: Morning of the Sale 9:00 – 11:00 AM

DIRECTIONS: 101 Take Hillsdale Blvd Exit, West to
El Camino Real, Left on El Camino to
Auction Site, Signs will be posted.

AUCTION OF HOUSE BOAT

FRIDAY, JULY 7TH – 2:00 PM

DOWNTOWN MARINA
1548 Maple Street
Redwood City, CA

26 Foot Fiber Form HOUSEBOAT, Berth available for
berthing at $4.25 a foot, or living on the boat for
$125.00 extra.

INSPECTION: ONE HOUR BEFORE THE SALE

DIRECTIONS: 101 Take Woodside Road Exit, West to
Veterans, Right on Maple to Downtown
Marina.

AUCTIONEER'S NOTE: THE AUCTIONEERS WILL NOT BE RESPONSIBLE FOR ANY PENALTIES ON
PAST-DUE REGISTRATIONS CONCERNING ANY VEHICLES SOLD BY THE
AUCTIONEERS. IT IS THE BUYER'S RESPONSIBILITY TO CHECK PLATES
AND/OR TAGS. CERTAIN VEHICLES MAY NOT HAVE REQUIRED SMOG DE-
VICES. SMOG COMPLIANCE CERTIFICATES WILL NOT BE PROVIDED.
INSPECTION OF VEHICLES FOR SMOG, MAJOR COLLISION REPAIR,
FRAME DAMAGE, ETC, IS THE BIDDER'S SOLE RESPONSIBILITY.

TERMS OF SALE: CASH OR CASHIERS'S CHECK. A BANK LETTER MUST ACCOMPANY ALL PERSONAL
OR COMPANY CHECKS. FULL SETTLEMENT TO BE MADE DAY OF SALE.

ASHMAN COMPANY

California State Lic. #370
LLOYD ASHMAN, AUCTIONEER

21 Massolo Drive • Pleasant Hill, California 94523-2405 • (415) 682-8100

However, keep in mind that no matter how bad it gets, it cannot possibly get as bad as it has gotten in some countries in the past few centuries. People who couldn't pay their debts in England a few centuries ago didn't get another chance to have their property sold and start over. They were imprisoned within debtor's prisons. There are no debtor's prisons in the United States. Some of our earlier immigrants had come from English debtor's prisons, quite a few as the result of the efforts of William Penn, the man who helped settle Pennsylvania.

You are giving the person a chance to settle his debts and start over when you buy at these auctions. And you are giving yourself a business or personal advantage by buying merchandise at discounts. One auctioneer told me that the very best auctions to attend are the bankruptcy auctions, since that is where he's gotten his lowest prices for merchandise. And if an auctioneer tells you that, then you know that's one of the better places to go.

For this type of auction there are five primary places to look: Bankruptcy auctions, which are held through the U.S. Trustee's Office; City and County Marshal's sales in those cities and states where such sales occur; local Sheriff's auctions where merchandise is sold after a court order; bank repossessions using a private auctioneer; and Small Business Administration repossessed equipment which is sold through the bank or a private auctioneer.

Let's look at each of these individually.

Bankruptcy Auctions

Eventually, these are held by a private auctioneer in nearly all cases when the person has declared straight bankruptcy, also known as Chapter 7 bankruptcy. Such a bankruptcy happens so that the debtor can pay off his debts to creditors and creditors can receive part of the debt owed them.

The process for bringing about bankruptcy is not widely known. The person normally uses an attorney to petition the bankruptcy court in his district for the right to declare bankruptcy. Corporations are the main source of bargains at bankruptcy courts, since they most frequently have greater assets to sell off. They'll also have to petition the same bankruptcy courts in their area for that right to declare bankruptcy. Personal property or real estate is then turned over to the Bankruptcy Trustee to manage for them and to liquidate, subject to court confirmation. Now, depending on the area of the country, the economic conditions at that time and the availability of the merchandise on the general market, prices can vary. You'll find some Bankruptcy Trustees giving an unequivocal official statement stating that merchandise is sold at fair market value (boy, what an overused phrase!!!). Other Trustees will remain silent.

Attempts will be made to keep prices in a fair range. Anxiety on the part of the Trustee, restlessness within the court itself to dispose of such property in order to satisfy the creditors and other factors can bring about great bargains.

The Bankruptcy Trustees will hire a private auctioneer to sell the merchandise at an "equitable price", another one of those phrases which really mean nothing more than "best price we can get". While a list of the various U.S. Trustees Offices, which you can contact directly, are provided, your fastest method is simply to begin calling auctioneers from your local yellow pages (under "Auctioneers") and ask them when their next bankruptcy auction is being held for the merchandise you want. Ask to be put on their mailing lists and you'll see a flurry of fliers in your mailbox from which you can pick and choose to your heart's content!

City/County Marshal's Sales

These government employees act in the same way as county sheriffs act in various parts of the country. For instance, if someone loses a court judgment and now won't pay, their property will be seized by the County or City Marshal and sold at auction. In most cities they are called City Marshals, while in California they're known as County Marshals. The result is the same. They are operating under the same or similar procedure as the local sheriff.

In **Section Three** you'll find out how to contact them, how often their auctions are held (some very infrequently) and whether or not they hold the auctions themselves or have a private auctioneer to do it for them.

At these auctions you'll find both real estate and personal property being sold. Some have great bargains: In Atlanta, Georgia, the private auctioneer who holds their auctions says that buyers keep coming back for more and that autos usually go for $500 to $1,100, all in good condition. You'll find jewelry, cars, VCR's and other small things which can be seized and easily transported for auction. Some will maintain mailings for their auction-goers. Others, such as in NYC, will advertise in the major newspaper in that city.

U.S. Marshal's Sales

Because of the Comprehensive Crime Control Act of 1984, merchandise is supposed to be auctioned through commercially feasible means. The U.S. Marshal's Offices utilize the services of auctioneers, brokers and other commercial sellers to dispose of property.

If you desire a particular type of asset, such as a Ferrari, Mercedes, Cigarette racing boat or fancy home, one method you may employ is as follows: get the Wednesday edition of USA TODAY and turn to the classifieds. The section you are looking for usually takes up two full pages and contains legal notices of assets seized from drug dealers. It comes under the heading of "Legal Notice" (an example of such a notice is reproduced below). Contact the U.S. Marshal's Service, from the addresses listed in **Section Three**, in the district where the merchandise or property is located. Write a note with your name, address and telephone number on it. Provide the asset type, case number and any other descriptive information you can from this listing. Contact only by mail. Do not call! Mail this in to the U.S. Marshal's Office at the address given in **Section Three** nearest the location of that asset. The Marshal's office does not *guarantee* that you will be notified but they will make every effort to notify you when it is time for the merchandise to be sold or auctioned.

Here is an example taken directly from USA TODAY's listings:

> *55763, 1988 Porsche 928 Turbo, Miami Beach, Florida, (name omitted), 04/07/89, $5,000*

For legal reasons we've omitted the name from the above example; in the actual listing in USA TODAY you would see the person's name listed.

The "55763" at the beginning of the listing is the "case number," which identifies the particular legal proceeding or court case, involved. The date after the name is the date the item was seized. The $5,000 is the "bond amount" which will give you an idea of the item's appraised value - in this case, $50,000 - since the bond amount will be for 10% of the appraised value.

Again, remember to keep your communications with them in writing. Only send a letter. Do not call. Repeat, if necessary, in writing but do not call. They have been bombarded by callers in the past and do not appreciate verbal communications about the auction programs for which they are responsible.

Listed in **Section Three** will be a list of hotline numbers you may call for a "recorded message" regarding their auction updates. If a hotline number for your area is not listed, it is because there is none as yet.

Local Sheriff's Sales

There are various ways that personal property can end up in the sheriff's hands for auction. One common and very little-known method is through storage or warehouse liens. A person can drop off something to get repaired and not want to pay for repair costs or can store something and forget about it. Such merchandise can end up on the sheriff's desk or parking lot and be auctioned.

Another more common method is through judgments which have been rendered by the court. This can be for car repossessions, although many banks will do it themselves to save money or for other personal property. Many sheriff sales are quite popular and there can be numerous bargains at them.

Bank Repossessions

This is probably the auction most frequently attended by used car dealers. They generally can find bargains to resell on their used car lots. Rather than going through the sheriff, banks will have the cars auctioned by a private auctioneer. I don't think enough people know about these.

One of the fastest ways to find out about them is to simply call your local banks and ask them if they have any repossessed cars up for auction. Ask them who to call if they don't. Many banks will even keep their cars in storage companies and take three sealed bids, awarding the car to the highest bidder. Some will even finance the purchase or refer you to someone who does this financing (another bank for instance). A quick trip through your yellow pages will help here. Some banks will even advertise their cars in the classifieds.

If they don't sell them in the sealed bid as described above, then rest assured that they will sell them at private auctions. One friend who attended such an auction found the used car dealers stood out quite vividly: they all had cellular phones and Blue Books! In a steady stream of activity, they'd be calling their dealership and asking various questions about the cars. The smart auction-goer waited until the dealers dropped out of the bidding and then bid a few dollars more ($25, $50 or even $100 more). If those cars had been bought by the used car dealers, they would have been offered on their lots to others at thousands of dollars more.

As it would be inconvenient and unnecessary to list all the banks in the United States having bank repossessed autos for auction, simply call various banks from your yellow pages directory. Look there first in buying a car.

The Small Business Administration

They do not have auctions but they do have equipment and merchandise which does get auctioned. One SBA office told our Research Department that all they're looking for is the loan amount. Since many of these loans are only 70% (or up to 90%) insured, that alone can save you some money if you buy from them. Also, don't forget the person has probably made some payments on the loan amount. I have heard of various bargains at SBA auctions, so make a point of calling them as well.

When you call you'll probably be referred to a private auctioneer or even a bank for the auction notice. The SBA is primarily in the business of insuring loans and is not very well staffed. Please do not take up a lot of their time. Just ask about the SBA auctions in your area and how you can find out about them. They'll either take your name and refer it to the private auctioneer or they'll tell you who to contact and refer you to the bank or auctioneer for disposal time, place and date. A full listing of the SBA offices is located in **Section Three.** The SBA is responsible for the auction of real estate, developed and undeveloped, as well as various personal property.

Estate Sales and Probate

There is one other way to get bargain merchandise which some people have popularized under the category of "estate sales". A variation on that is what is called "probate sales". After someone dies there is an estate to be settled. There may be real estate and general merchandise which the heirs or executors of the estate wish to sell.

Sometimes that will go up for public auction at an estate sale. Bargains depend upon the skill of the auctioneer employed and the turnout of the crowd. These are generally advertised in the classified section of newspapers if there is valuable or adequate inventory of things to be auctioned.

However, one method you may employ to get to the merchandise faster and perhaps successfully is this: contact your local courthouse about probates and the various stages they are in before the will is settled. This may require a personal visit. In some cases you may be referred to the estate's attorney.

Contact him and find out what is available for auction. Ask if you can see the merchandise. Sometimes there are cars, furniture, jewelry and more which the heirs do not want. Frequently, there are arguments over settlement of the estate. In any case, you can contact them through their attorney and offer them a resolution by buying the merchandise. Getting to them before it goes to an estate sale gives you an edge over others. This has worked very well in the past with real estate, although I also know of individuals who have picked up cars at discounts and have gotten bargains on other merchandise.

Just follow the above procedure to avoid the public auction.

CONCLUSION

Now that you've finished reading Chapter One of this section, you should be aware of the various merchandise up for auction by different government agencies on the federal, state and local levels.

You may proceed to **Section Three** if you wish to contact the agencies which interest you most. Some have great bargains, others don't. It all depends on what you are looking for and what you're willing to pay for the merchandise. Be selective and avoid those which don't have the best bargains (like the GSA for vehicle auctions).

I would strongly advise you not go to an auction without having carefully read **Section Two,** which follows the next long chapter. In **Section Two** you'll learn about the important things to watch out for at an auction, what you must do to be successful and how to prepare yourself for the auction. Many people have told us that this information was important to them, so please do go over it thoroughly.

In the next chapter we'll cover the important real estate sales and auctions and how you can take advantage of them. If your interest is real estate investment or you would simply like a new house to live in, then please turn to Chapter Two.

PUBLIC AUCTION
Sale of Used Postal Vehicles

SUMMARY OF VEHICLES TO BE SOLD

Light, medium or heavy trucks, suitable for delivery vans for contractors, carpenters, electricians, plumbers, painters and farmers.
Note: Our ¼-ton delivery vehicles were not designed as passenger vehicles.

SALE DATE SATURDAY, JUNE 24, 1989 **TIME** 10:00 A.M.

SALE SITE WESTERN AVENUE AUXILIARY GARAGE
2301 WEST 51st PLACE - CHICAGO, IL 60609-9603

INSPECTION DATES THURSDAY, JUNE 22, 1989 - FRIDAY, JUNE 23, 1989

DURING THE HOURS FROM 9:00 A.M. **TO** 2:00 P.M.

TERMS

- Vehicles will be sold to highest bidder. Payment must be made by cash, certified check or money order made payable to Disbursing Officer, U.S. Postal Service. Full payment must be received by JUNE 30, 1989

- Vehicles must be removed from Postal premises by JUNE 30, 1989

- Vehicles are sold "as is, where is" without warranty or guarantee.

- All bidders are urged to inspect the vehicles prior to bidding. Bidders must register to be eligible to bid. All bids are final - no refunds.

- THE POSTAL SERVICE IS NOT OBLIGATED TO SELL VEHICLES AT UNACCEPTABLE PRICES AND RESERVES THE RIGHT TO REJECT ALL BIDS THAT ARE CONSIDERED UNREASONABLY LOW

RELEASE OF VEHICLES

- Upon receipt of payment for the vehicle, the Postal Service will issue to the buyer a certificate of release of a Motor Vehicle, Standard Form 97. The buyer can then title and license the vehicle.

For additional information, call THE OFFICE OF THE Fleet Manager
Phone Area Code (312) 765-4122 or visit sale site

NOTICE 139
January 1982

NO LIMIT   NO RESERVE

BY ORDER OF
U.S. BANKRUPTCY COURT
PUBLIC
AUCTION
AGUNDEZ CONCRETE & M&C
PAINTING CONTRACTOR
302 W. 19TH ST., NATIONAL CITY, CA.
(W 18TH TO HARDINGE ST, SOUTH 1 BLOCK,
EAST ON W. 19TH, NEXT TO PARK)
TUESDAY JULY 18TH - 10 A.M.

CONCRETE TOOLS & EQUIPMENT
(5) WHITEMAN & WISCONSIN GAS CEMENT FINISHERS - BOSCH JACK HAMMER - MAKITA JACK HAMMER - MIKASA GAS WACKER - MIKASA TAMPER - CONCRETE VIBRATOR COMPACTOR - CONCRETE STAMPS - SKILSAW - (2) REBAR CUTTERS - SPECTRA PHYSICS EL-1 ELEC LEVEL - DAVID WHITE ALT 6-900 TRANSIT - MISC CEMENT FINISHING TOOLS

PAINT EQUIPMENT & SUPPLIES
HYDRA PRO IV AIRLESS SPRAYER - (5) BRIGGS & STRATTON 8 HP AIRLESS SPRAYERS - WAGNER 8500 & GLIDDEN 500 AIRLESS SPRAYERS - (10) ALUM EXT. LADDERS - (14) ASST STEP LADDERS - 100'S OF GALLONS OF MISC PAINT

ROLLING STOCK
MASSEY FERGUSON MF 4D SKIP LOADER W/ SCRAPER - (2) 80 - 85 CHEVY EL CAMINOS - 80 FORD F250 P/U - 79 FORD F350 FLATBED - 69 FORD F600 FLATBED - 63 FORD F350 DUMP TRUCK - 67 FORD F100 SERVICEBODY P/U - 67 INT FLATBED - 71 DODGE 300 FLATBED - 78 FORD GRANADA - DAVEY TRAILER AIR COMP - 12' EQUIP TRAILER

MATERIAL & MISC.
MISC BRICK, BLOCK, STONE - FORM LUMBER - P/U TOOL BOX - TRUCK RACK - MISC SUPPLIES ETC.

INSPECT MONDAY JULY 17TH, 10AM - 4PM
TERMS:DEPOSIT AND PAYMENT CASH OR CASHIER'S CHECK ONLY

FISCHER AUCTION CO.   (619) 233-1851
STATE LIC #C1460

CHAPTER 2

Real Estate Auctions and Sales

Federal Agencies
Other Federal Real Estate Disposal Agencies
Local Methods of Obtaining Real Estate

U.S. CUSTOMS SERVICE
Real Estate Auction
Sale No. 89-52-383

Friday • June 30, 1989 • 10:00 a.m.

Home Located in Florida Keys
158 Iroquois Drive • Islamorada, FL

Open House	Viewing/Inspection	Open House

Sunday • June 11, 1989 • 12:00 Noon-4:00 p.m.
Sunday • June 25, 1989 • 12:00 Noon-4:00 p.m.
Final Inspection/Registration: Day of Sale • 8:00 a.m.-10:00 a.m.

Atlantic Ocean accessible by boat from property. 2-story house on steel stilts. 3-bedroom, 2-baths, fireplace, ceiling fans. Screened porch, patio, storm shutters and paddle fans. Concrete seawall, boat dock with boat access to open water. *Furniture and Miscellaneous Items Included!* Bedroom furniture, living room furniture, kitchen furniture, and accessories. Lots of odds and ends. Approximate price range $120,000 - $150,000.

Directions: Take Mile Marker 74 off of U.S. 1 South.

Legal Description: Lot 7, Block 1, Lower Matecumbe Beach, according to the plat thereof, recording in Plat Book 3, at page 34, of the Public Records of Monroe County, Florida.

Real Property Taxes: 1987 taxes are delinquent in the amount of $1,339.22 plus penalties and interest. 1988 taxes are due in the amount of $1,241.97 plus penalties and interest. Alt. Key No. 1477052

Real Property Terms: Property will be sold for cash to the highest bidder subject to confirmation and compliance to terms of sale including: All bidders are required to present a $15,000 Cashier's Check made out to themselves at registration to obtain a bidder number. The successful bidder may endorse his Cashier's Check to Northrop as payment deposit against purchase at the time of sale, balance due on or before July 14, 1989.

For additional details and information on viewing and sale, call (405) 357-3797, ext. 407 between the hours of 8:00 a.m.-5:00 p.m. (CT). For information on how to become a subscriber, call (405) 357-9194 between the hours of 7:00 a.m.-7:00 p.m. (CT).

NORTHROP
Northrop Worldwide
Aircraft Services, Inc.

U.S. Customs Service
Support Division

This sale is conducted by
Northrop Worldwide Aircraft Services, Inc.,
on behalf of the U.S. Customs Service
with all proceeds directed to the U.S. Treasury.

F91350S

Real Estate Auctions and Sales

There are probably no better buys in the United States in real estate than in the ways I am going to show you throughout this chapter. The amount of real estate which the United States Government holds in foreclosure through its various government and related agencies and through the foreclosed savings and loans institutions has recently been estimated at over $400,000,000,000! That's $400 billion worth of real estate.

While an astounding number of would-be first-time home buyers are waiting on the sidelines for their home, the Federal Government is fretting about what all this real estate dumped on the market will do to depress real estate prices. My goodness, doesn't that seem ironic? On one hand we have people unable to buy property and, on the other hand, we have our vast government worrying about what to do with the property they are now holding!

Eventually, enough people will find out about this real estate and it will get sold. As mentioned earlier, a recent magazine article pointed out that one government agency's inspector general had found that this agency's homes were being sold at 10% to 40% below market value! That's quite a discount.

If you've been following the newspapers during 1989, you'll have concluded that there is a whole lot of real estate and the government doesn't know what to do with it. What they're not telling you is that if you made a few dozen phone calls you could find out about all the real estate you'd ever want to hear about. While Americans fret about foreigners buying up American real estate, many don't realize that our real estate is up for sale. You just have to know how to get to it. And that's what we're going to talk about in this chapter.

Federal Agencies

The Veterans Administration

The VA was formed to provide our ex-military personnel with certain benefits. These benefits included assistance for education, hospitalization and funding for housing. Many bought homes with these benefits and some had their homes foreclosed. Such property was then put through the VA system for reselling. At any given time, you are likely to find between 10,000 and 30,000 homes to be resold by the VA. That's a lot of homes!

As of April, 1989, there were over 18,000 properties available. Some people think, incorrectly, that you must be a veteran to buy a VA repossessed home. You do not have to be a Veteran to buy a VA repossessed home. In fact, you do not even have to live in such a home to buy one.

These homes come in all sizes and conditions, ranging from very good to major repairs required and you must go through a real estate broker to purchase one. There are three primary listings which you should be aware of in buying these homes:

- **Regular Listing:** Offers must be made at the listed price. Offers below the listed price will not be considered except on homes you wish to purchase with your own financing or for all cash.

- **Special Listing:** These properties are available at listed prices and terms. Reasonable offers below the listed prices will be considered. Remember that a reasonable price could be 10-20% below their listing if the property has been on this special listing for a while.

- **New Listing:** Offers on these must be at list price. If you provide your own financing you can save 10% except on those properties which state all cash. Bids must be received in five days.

The VA has recently been reluctant to provide financing. Budget difficulties and the high amount of real estate they are currently holding has contributed to this. When you see "all cash," that means you provide your own bank or mortgage company financing or you pay all cash for the house.

Down payments, where the VA will finance for you, range from no money down (rare) to a small down payment percentage (under 5%).

VETERANS ADMINISTRATION
SALES LISTING (MULTIPLE) MAY 5, 1989

SECTION "A" REGULAR LISTING
****
Offers must be at listed price and terms only. Offers below list price
cannot be considered.
****

Location	Price	Description		Management Broker	Spec. Code	VA File No.
ANGIER						
RT 1 BOX 399-B	34,900	6/3/2	MANUF	HILL	c	PMLH 361557
	31,410	CASH		REPAIRED		
BLACK CREEK						
211 WILLIAMS ST	47,800	6/3/1.5	BV	BISSETTE	a	PMLH 436530
WITHOUT EXCEPTION	43,020	CASH				
CHARLOTTE						
5421 DOLPHIN LN	42,550	5/3/1.5	BV/FR	BERRYHILL	a	PMLH 354392
WITHOUT EXCEPTION	38,295	CASH		TITLE PENDING		
2117 EMERYWOOD DR	72,250	8/4/2.5	BV/SD	BERRYHILL	a	PMLH 421546
WITHOUT EXCEPTION	65,025	CASH				
4533-H SHARON CHASE	48,500	4/2/2	FR	COUSAR	a	PMLH 343596
WITHOUT EXCEPTION	43,650	CASH				
8123-D TREMAINE CT	49,550	4/2/2	FR	COUSAR	a	PMLH 430363
WITHOUT EXCEPTION	44,595	CASH				
CLEMMONS						
105 BRIARWOOD CT	99,000	9/4/3.5	BV	VANBUREN	a	PMLH 415006
WITHOUT EXCEPTION	89,100	CASH				
DALLAS						
2410 DEVON DR	41,500	6/3/1	BV/FR	BARIERI	a	PMLH 382341
WITHOUT EXCEPTION	37,350	CASH				
RT 3	33,650	5/3/1.5	FR/SD	BARBIERI	a	PMLH 322155
WITHOUT EXCEPTION	30,285	CASH		TITLE PENDING ROOF TO BE REPAIRED		
DELCO						
RT 1, BOX 131	34,200	5/2/1	FR	FROST	a	PMLH 422492
WITHOUT EXCEPTION	30,780	CASH				
		WELL PUMP AND TANK TO BE REPLACED AT CLOSING				
DUDLEY						
113 LAKEHURST DR	74,100	6/3/2.5	FR	PERKINS	a	PMLH 365138
WITHOUT EXCEPTION	66,690	CASH				
DUNN						
RT 6 BOX 470	48,900	8/3/2	BV	HILL	a	PMLH 410897
WITHOUT EXCEPTION	44,010	CASH		TITLE PENDING		

6

VA FORM 26-6719A (DEC 1984)
EQUAL HOUSING OPPORTUNITY

VETERANS ADMINISTRATION
SALES LISTING (MULTIPLE) MAY 5, 1989

SECTION "B" SPECIAL LISTING
5-DAY PERIOD ENDS MAY 15, 1989

These properties are available at listed prices and terms. However, a
reasonable offer below the listed prices will be considered for acceptance.
This is not an offer/counter offer procedure. It will be to the purchaser's
advantage to continue to submit offers at or above the stated sales price.
Brokers are advised that if a purchaser chooses to submit more than one offer
for the same property, but at different prices, VA will consider only the
higher price.
****

Location	Price	Description	Management Broker	Spec. Code	VA File No.
FAYETTEVILLE					
6512 ADDINGHAM CT	54,950	6/3/2 BV/FR	POOLE	b	PMLH 389136
	49,455	CASH	STOVE TO BE REPLACED		
2609 ADEN PL	34,000	5/3/1.5 FR	WALTERS	a	PMLH 424613
WITHOUT EXCEPTION	30,600	CASH	TITLE PENDING		
1966 ASPEN CR	45,100	6/3/1.5 BV	MATTHEWS	b	PMLH 393586
	40,590	CASH	TITLE PENDING		
413 BAYBERRY CT	65,200	5/3/2 FR	MATTHEWS	b	PMLH 355647
	58,680	CASH			
1264 BROMLEY DR	64,600	6/3/2 SD	MATTHEWS	b	PMLH 390517
	58,140	CASH	TITLE PENDING		
7062 CALAMAR DR	62,850	5/3/2 BV/FR	HILL	c	PMLH 393931
REPAIRED	56,565	CASH	TITLE PENDING	REDUCED-RELISTED	
7060 CANDLEWOOD DR	42,100	5/3/2 FR	WALTERS	a	PMLH 373810
WITHOUT EXCEPTION	37,890	CASH		REDUCED-RELISTED	
2533 CARRIAGE RD	47,500	5/3/2 MOD	COUNCIL	b	PMLH 433041
	42,750	CASH		REDUCED-RELISTED	
319 DURANT DR	33,200	5/3/1 BV	POOLE	a	PMLH 439150
	29,880	CASH			
7226 GODFREY DR	64,550	7/3/1.5 BV	WALTERS	b	PMLH 399088
	58,095	CASH			
548 HICKORYWOOD DR	52,850	5/3/2 SD	MATTHEWS	b	PMLH 392636
	47,565	CASH	TITLE PENDING		
314 JEFFERSON DR	29,850	5/3/1 BV	HILL	a	18-4-7694
WITHOUT EXCEPTION	26,865	CASH			
5901 JUSTIN CT	48,950	7/3/2 BV	HILL	a	PMLH 403352
	44,055	CASH			
1023 KERROW RD	72,000	7/3/2.5 BV/FR	HILL	b	PMLH 389523
	64,800	CASH			
415 LOBLOLLY CT	62,000	6/3/2.5 SD	COUNCIL	a	18-4-9271
WITHOUT EXCEPTION	55,800	CASH			
3900 NASHVILLE DR	44,200	5/3/2 FR	WALTERS	b	PMLH 402164
	39,780	CASH		REDUCED-RELISTED	
5240 REMINGTON RD	64,600	7/3/2 SD	COUNCIL	a	PMLH 399937
WITHOUT EXCEPTION	58,140	CASH	TITLE PENDING		
7105 SAN JUAN DR	56,900	5/3/2 SD	COUNCIL	b	PMLH 387496
	51,210	CASH		REDUCED-RELISTED	
510 TOXAWAY CT	54,700	4/2/2 FR	COUNCIL	b	PMLH 446654
	49,230	CASH		REDUCED-RELISTED	

9

VA FORM 26-6719A (DEC 1984)
EQUAL HOUSING OPPORTUNITY

Speculators who wish to buy the property and rent it out to others, will be asked to put 5% down payments. But even this can be relaxed under many circumstances.

Your broker will show you the VA homes you wish to view and assist you in many ways. You will have to fill out VA FORM 26-6705 in making your bid offer. The broker must have four copies made with one going to you. You will have to put up $100 earnest money into the broker's escrow account for the VA. Please answer your questions truthfully, as falsification of any kind will cause you to lose out on this opportunity and your earnest money may be forfeited to the VA.

With your offer, you'll be required to submit a $5.00 application fee by certified check or cashier's check. Your broker will notify you if your offer has been accepted. On the new listings you should make your offers in $50 increments above the listing price if you expect competition on the bidding to go beyond the VA's listing price. Example: If the house is $21,250 and you wish to increase the amount above the listing price by 3%, you should bid $650 more, not $637.50 more.

Here is the priority of selecting the winning bid that the VA uses:

- All cash offers (when not below 10% of the listing price).
- Amount of the purchase. Highest bid wins.

- The amount of the down payments. For example, if the bids are the same and one person offers a larger down payment, when it exceeds the required down payment by 3% or more of the list price.

- The degree of acceptability of your credit compared to others. Those with poor credit will lose out to those with better credit.

- Purchase for your own occupancy or use.

- Veterans over non-veterans will get higher priority if the above still hasn't broken the tie.

- If everything else is equal the first offer will get the house as opposed to later offers.

In order to qualify for VA-repossessed homes and financing by the VA, you will need to meet three simple criteria: "Have you been on your present job for at least six months?" "Do you have satisfactory credit rating?" "Are you financially able to assume the obligation of home ownership?" Those are very simple qualifications that a large percentage of Americans should be able to fulfill.

The VA will pay closing costs up to a certain extent if you use their financing but you will have to pay a 1% funding fee. Additionally, you'll have to obtain the necessary insurance, prepay interest for the rest of the month, prepay a tax deposit on upcoming property and other applicable taxes and the normal recording fees for the Deed and Deed of Trust. These are all the usual fees you would have to pay in buying any house.

I do recommend that you obtain your own financing, as the VA doesn't want to get burned twice and their financing and type of mortgage may require more time than normal in obtaining bank or mortgage company financing. You'll save on the price of the house purchase by as much as 10%.

However, if you don't have the down payment, this is one excellent way to buy real estate with a very low down payment, using the government's financing. There aren't many banks where you can obtain 5% financing, even as a speculator, in buying a home you can then rent out. VA financing is limited to $144,000.

A full listing of VA Offices can be found in **Section Three**. Or you can simply call real estate brokers in your area where you wish to purchase the home. Even non-Americans can buy VA-repossessed homes. Many have. They're excellent investment vehicles and people do rent them, even if they can't buy. And if you do this right and look hard enough, you won't have to rent the same house you could be buying.

The Department of Housing and Urban Development

This agency, an outgrowth of the Federal Housing Administration (FHA), guarantees home mortgage loans. There is quite a bit of controversy brewing on the topic of housing and on the subject of HUD in Washington during 1989. The current limit for FHA financing is $101,250, which makes it very difficult for a young couple to find a home in some parts of the country: Orange County, California, San Francisco Bay Area, New York City and the adjacent counties, Northern New Jersey, Boston or Connecticut. There is talk in D.C. about raising this limit for some parts of the country.

Other controversy over HUD focuses on how HUD has not been doing its job properly and how some speculators easily deceived HUD officials on some of their properties and made a fast buck. Lost in the headlines is the ongoing fact that there are normally about 45,000 HUD homes on the market most of the time. Some of these homes are available to both investors and owner/occupants for 10-40% below market value (according to Reader's Digest: June 1989 issue, page 136, column 2, paragraph 1). Depending on the region of the United States, it is possible for you to buy your home for $100 down payment. That shoots down those complaints about unaffordable down payments.

Some of these 45,000 homes are not in the best condition. It may require work to make them liveable or rentable to others. However, there are many, many homes available which are in move-in condition. If the house requires hard work on your part to make it liveable, remember that this is still better than renting. With home ownership you are blessed with many advantages, among them: possible real estate appreciation (along with profit when you sell and the potential of trading up to a better home), tax deductions on your mortgage interest (which means part of your house payment is recouped in tax deductions as opposed to rent which is not deductible), having the status of home ownership (which still counts in many circles) and the capability of borrowing against equity you build up in your home as you pay off your mortgage monthly and as your home appreciates. No wonder so many people want to buy a home!

There are over 12,000 HUD-approved real estate brokers in the United States. The best way to find out about these homes is to watch the classifieds in major newspapers on Fridays, Saturdays and/or Sundays. That's the fastest way to find out about the listing. The broker, himself, calls for the key to the house after he sees the ad in the paper so that the property can be shown.

HUD has a few different ways they list properties about which you should know.

- **CODE I** listings: FHA-insured properties, which you can get with a $100 down payment or $500 down payment on the house.

- **CODE III** listings: not FHA-insured and you have to provide your own financing.

As with the VA homes there are certain explanations necessary on these properties. A HUD home is put on the market for a short period of time, usually with an expiration date right on the ad for the date of the sealed bid.

You must have your sealed bid placed by the time of the due date, such as "March 15, 4:00 p.m.", via your real estate broker or your bid will not be accepted. If no bids or only unacceptable bids (those below HUD's asking price) are received, then you can expect to see the same property again placed under Extended Listings.

If the buyer's financing fell through or a winning bid was tossed out because the FHA did not approve financing through their agency, then the

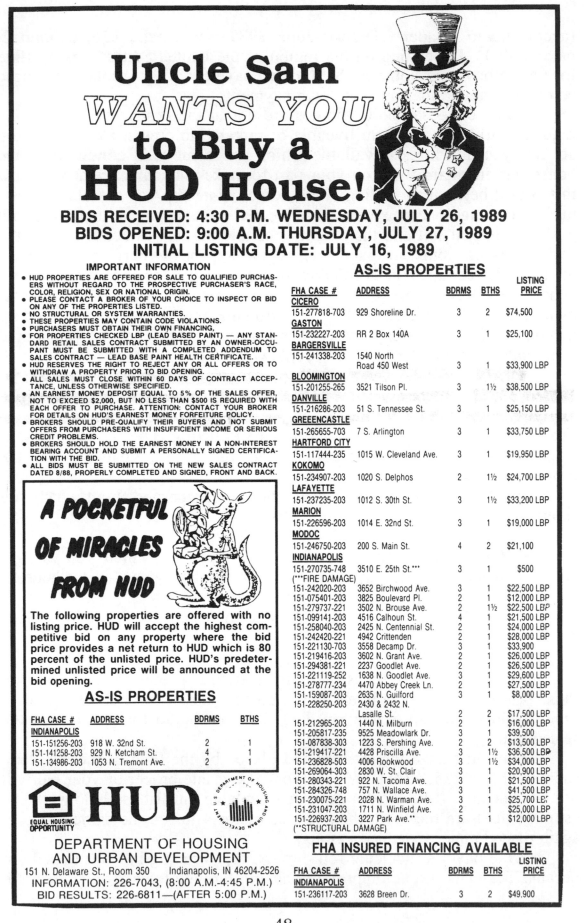
48

home is returned to the market. The listing will state: returned to the market. Occasionally, homes that were on the Extended Listings and did not sell (or receive bids) are withdrawn and returned at a later date. Those homes may even be fixed up so they may attract buyers.

Back to the Extended Listings. These probably afford you the best deals. A house's price is lowered the longer it stays on the market. If HUD continues to advertise homes through Extended Listings, that means they are not receiving the bids they wish to have. For instance, in one Denver newspaper, there was a 20 page supplement of listings, many of which were Extended Listings. If you see homes on the Extended Listings and you like them, you probably have an excellent opportunity to buy one. Bids are received on a daily basis for these.

There are certain precautions or restrictions with which you should be prepared to deal. If you buy the house for your own occupancy, there may be lead-based paint. If so, you may choose to have HUD remove this paint prior to your occupancy. If you are an investor, you *must* agree, as a condition of sale, to have this done. Investors are often required to post escrows (sometimes $1,500 or less) so that they have an incentive to remove the lead-based paint. Escrows are returned after the lead-based paint has been removed.

All properties will be offered in "as-is" condition and may contain code violations for which HUD will assume no liability. Offers can be made only through real estate brokers. That doesn't mean you can't call HUD directly for assistance or to get your questions answered. It just means that you can't make a bid directly to HUD. In Denver, for instance, HUD has set up a Consumer Hotline to answer your questions: 1-800-443-4483. HUD offices are set up to really help you and there is adequate staff to answer your questions about buying their homes, the loan process or anything else.

If you are going to use a bank or mortgage company for your property, you'll have to close within 60 days. If closing will take longer than 60 days, you'll have to pay a non-refundable extension fee for that right. A house for which you'll have to obtain financing is designated as all cash. That doesn't mean that you have to pay all cash for the house; you just have to provide your own financing.

One important thing to keep in mind is that just because you submit your bid and others don't, particularly on Extended Listings for which you are making a low bid, HUD does reserve the right to reject any and all offers. HUD will accept the offer giving the highest net return to HUD, so keep that in mind. HUD will consider all offers.

Your real estate broker will explain the various details on making your offer and will help you fill out the paperwork. Your offer must be submitted on FORM-9548 (HUD's Sales Contract) with an earnest money deposit of $500. You may be required, with some properties, to make a larger deposit, $1,500 for example.

Are there any HUD deals? Of course there are. Not only are many HUD homes offered and sold below market value, there is shocking news for you, the U.S. taxpayer: HUD, during fiscal year 1988, lost about $20,000 per home. In 1987 HUD sold 59,194 single family homes for an aggregate loss of $1.2 billion! And if you're going to have to pay higher taxes to offset Uncle Sam's real estate losses, then you should at least buy one of them, so you have something to show for these higher taxes.

Lastly, certain HUD homes are listed under the "Mortgage with Repair Escrow Program". Eligible homes requiring up to $3,000 in repairs may be FHA insured with a cash escrow that would allow you to complete the needed repairs. The one catch is that this program is only available to owner/occupants. If you're buying the house for you own occupancy, you may get such funding if that home qualifies.

Federal National Mortgage Association

You have probably never heard about this company, nor realized how vast their influence is in the housing finance market. Let me give you some details. The Federal National Mortgage Association, better known as Fannie Mae, is a stockholder owned, Congressionally chartered corporation. It was originally created by the Federal Government in 1938 and signed into law by Franklin D. Roosevelt as part of the National Housing Act. Fannie Mae was, at first, a subsidiary of the Reconstruction Finance Corporation. It became owned by private stockholders in 1954. A major change occurred in 1968 when Congress split up this corporation into two separate corporations: Fannie Mae (as we know it today) and the Government National Mortgage Association (GNMA). GNMA helps finance government housing programs within the Department of Housing and Urban Development (HUD).

Newly chartered by Congress, Fannie Mae's job is to raise money and provide a constant stream of money into the secondary market of America's mortgage lenders. Fannie Mae has been a private corporation since 1970 when it was bought by its shareholders for a mere $216 million. Fannie Mae is very large - the nation's third largest in terms of assets and the largest source of conventional mortgage funds in the United States.

What does Fannie Mae really do? They purchase mortgage loans from many local lenders, including commercial banks, mortgage finance companies and savings & loan associations. Where do they get this money? Well, they raise it in the "capital markets", such as Wall Street. Michael Miliken, formerly of Drexel, Burnham, Lambert, was one of the "junk bond specialists" who helped provide hundreds of millions of dollars to the housing industry via Fannie Mae.

Stop for a moment and realize that what happens is this:

- You go to a bank for a mortgage.

- The bank or mortgage company lends you the money.

- The bank then borrows its money from Fannie Mae to replenish the reserves from which they lent you the money.

In some cases the above takes several hours or days, depending on the availability of funds.

Think for another moment about what would happen if Fannie Mae went out of business or got into serious financial troubles, as some of our other major U.S. corporations have. Well, it's time to get a little concerned. By the end of 1988 Fannie Mae had only $2.3 billion of equity to support over $278 billion of mortgage lending. That means for every $1 in equity they have more than $100 in debt! Of that $278 billion in mortgage lending, only $178 billion of it is backed by securities. Just think how devastated our real estate market would become if those shares crashed as a result of a stock market collapse. They are traded on the Stock Exchange as a corporation. Investors are lulled into a false security that there are "implied federal guarantees", Because of this misunderstood relationship with the government, Fannie Mae's prices have risen about 1250% in the past year (The Economist Magazine, June 17, 1989 Issue, Page 92).

Now that you've heard the bad news, why should you want to deal with Fannie Mae? They have properties on the market which they wish to sell you. These properties have come to them from the sources for which they have guaranteed the mortgages and provided liquidity for banks and mortgage companies. They now possess a large number of homes in great condition.

Fannie Mae takes great care of their homes when re-marketed for sale. They have a tremendous advantage in that they can sell for whatever price they wish and are not restricted by Federal regulations. Our Research Department has concluded in conversations with bankers and others that Fannie Mae is an aggressive home marketer. For example, if the home needs a new roof to make it move faster, they'll pay for a new roof. We have gotten inside information that Fannie Mae often will sell their homes below market value to stay competitive, sometimes as much as 25% below market value.

Fannie Mae is pleasant to deal with; they'll send you the listings of properties they have available in the area about which you want to know. You'll get the address, city, the type of property available, how many bathrooms and bedrooms it has, the list price, the name of the real estate broker, the agent handling that property and the phone number to contact. Turn to **Section Three** to find out how you can acquire their properties. I recommend them highly.

The Federal Home Loan Mortgage Association

Freddie Mac, as it is affectionately known, is a government chartered corporation which was created in 1970. Congress chartered Freddie Mac for the same purposes as Fannie Mae. They are not, as Fannie Mae is, owned by stockholders and traded on the stock market. Freddie Mac is owned by America's savings institutions through common stock held for them by the Federal Home Loan Banks.

Freddie Mac purchases mortgage loans from individual mortgage lenders, groups the mortgages into pools (which range from $1 million to $100 million of these loans) and resells them as Mortgage Participation Certificates. These PCs, as they are called, are sold to investors in order to provide liquidity to Freddie Mac. Basically, this "government sponsored enterprise" is nothing more than a conduit for capital from Wall Street (or foreign investors) to mortgage lenders to the homeowner.

How safe is Freddie? By the end of 1988 this corporation had equity of $1.6 billion with which to support a credit risk of $243.2 billion. No normal business could get away with this. In fact, the Annual Budget, which describes Freddie Mac, notes that the timely payment of interest and the full return of the principal is solely backed by "Freddie Mac" reserves. It is not guaranteed by the Federal Home Loan Bank Systems nor by the full faith and credit of the U.S. Government. Ouch!

Fannie Mae and Freddie Mac hold about 12,000 homes. If you wish to look for a house in your area, I would recommend you contact Fannie Mae. Freddie Mac is for those who wish to buy pools of such properties, starting at $1 million and upward. If you are a large investor or hope to become one, then Freddie Mac is where you would look. Both are covered in **Section Three**. With over $300 billion loaned annually in mortgages, Freddie Mac may have a lot of property up for auction, particularly because of the S & L crisis.

Federal Deposit Insurance Corporation

FDIC are initials you have probably seen before. They are on the signs near a bank's name. If you've ever looked carefully inside your bank or in its literature, you're bound to have seen FDIC.

What is the FDIC? It's an independent agency within the executive branch of the government. It's run by a Board of Directors, a three man team consisting of the Comptroller of the Currency and two Presidential appointees. The FDIC insures deposits in national banks and in state banks which are members of the Federal Reserve System. Other state banks which meet their requirements and apply for Federal Deposit Insurance will also have their deposits insured as well. All deposits are presently insured up to $100,000.

There is tremendous turmoil at this time because of the savings and loan crisis. If you've been following the newspaper stories on this crisis, you've probably heard about the massive new corporation being proposed by President Bush's administration to take over the real estate portfolios which helped bring this crisis about. It is called the Resolution Trust Corporation. Many of the troubled or failed S&L's will fall under its jurisdiction to unload on us. Some feel that the FDIC will take over these S&L's real estate for resale to buyers.

The FDIC is being considered because it has done an aggressive job managing properties and reselling them. At this time they hold only about $400 million worth of properties and are actively promoting them. They fall under the category of REOs, an acronym for Real Estate Owned properties.

The FDIC has eight regional offices around the United States which try to market properties to buyers. This is another excellent way for you to buy real estate cheaply. Many are sold at market value; however, with properties that have been held for a while, there have been offers accepted for 10-15% below market value. The acting director for the FDIC's Liquidation Division stated in a news magazine article recently: "It's rare that we will end up with more than the original loan was made for."

There you have it. The FDIC Liquidation Division's acting director believes that there are properties you can buy for *less* than the loan value. When the person bought the property, the total price he was paying consisted of the loan amount *plus* a down payment - anywhere from 5% (one of the lowest down payments one can usually make on a property) to 20% .So if you are able to pick up the property for an amount *equal* to the loan amount, right off the bat you are saving between 5 and 20 percent. What about properties that were purchased several years ago and have seen a rise in value? When those default and you purchase the property at approximate loan value, you may have made a swift killing in the real estate market.

Turn to **Section Three** for the applicable phone numbers and addresses in contacting the FDIC. Depending on your region of the country, you'll get a listing of the properties the FDIC is administering for banks, including: the bank number, asset number, address and description of the property, the local broker, his phone number and the asking price of the property.

FEDERAL DEPOSIT INSURANCE CORPORATION
DIVISION OF LIQUIDATION
DALLAS REGIONAL OFFICE
DALLAS, TEXAS

CONSOLIDATED
LISTING OF REAL ESTATE PROPERTIES OWNED BY
THE FEDERAL DEPOSIT INSURANCE CORPORATION
IN ITS LIQUIDATION CAPACITY

AS OF 6/30/89
(Quarterly Report)

STATES

OKLAHOMA
TEXAS
ARKANSAS

DALLAS REGION
OWNED REAL ESTATE
AS OF JUNE 30, 1989

OFFICE: Addison Consolidated Office

ADDRESS: Federal Deposit Insurance Corporation
          P.O. Box 802090
          Dallas, Texas 75380

TELEPHONE: (214) 239-3317

BANK NO.	ASSET NO.	DESCRIPTION	ADDRESS/LOCATION	STATE	PRICE
2928	351000001	5 BLDGS ON 10.872 ACRES	ARLINGTON	TX	$1,425,000.00
2932	351000070	5.3902 ACRES +/-; L-T LEASE W. ESCALATION	TYLER	TX	$1,085,000.00
5914	3510P0016	144 LOTS, SHIREWOOD ADDITION	BRYAN	TX	$1,000,000.00
2781	353000001	OFFICE BLDG 42,563 SF +/-	FARMERS BRANCH	TX	$ 915,000.00
2691	353000011	MINI WHSE-104 UNITS; 43,344 SF	AUSTIN	TX	$ 875,000.00
2724	353000030	2/1; 852 SF EA; 52 UNITS APARTMENT	WAXAHACHIE	TX	$ 850,000.00
5824	353000099	ACREAGE; 365.13; PHASE 6, TOWN CREEK	KERRVILLE	TX	$ 666,350.00
2828	354000008	1.5 ACRES +/-	FT. WORTH	TX	$ 546,000.00
5923	353000014	4.796 ACRES +/-	N. RICHLAND HILLS	TX	$ 440,000.00
2898	3510P0001	SHOPPING CENTER; 23,600 SF	WATAUGA	TX	$ 420,000.00
2936	351000001	4 CONDOS, 2/3/2 1,270 SF EACH	DALLAS	TX	$ 405,000.00
5923	3530P0008	HORSE FARM 75.36 ACRES	HOT SPRINGS	AR	$ 387,500.00
2691	351000006	1 MSNRY BLDG, 2MTL BLDGS	AUSTIN	TX	$ 325,600.00
5923	353000015	AUTO SERVICE - 5,000 SF	FT. WORTH	TX	$ 320,000.00
2979	351000010	2.6448 ACRES +/-	MESQUITE	TX	$ 305,000.00
2465	353000034	336.41 ACRES +/-; 214 ACRES +/-	CRESSON	TX	$ 300,000.00
2465	353000035	320 ACRES +/-; 62 LTS	CRESSON	TX	$ 300,000.00
2979	351000005	4.796 TTL ACRES +/-	ROCKWALL	TX	$ 275,000.00
5824	353000080	89 LOTS-GUAJIA BAY, BOX CYN ESTATES	DEL RIO	TX	$ 272,800.00
2764	351000005	4.1908 ACRES +/-; TR 3,4, 5 UNIMPROVED	MARBLE FALLS	TX	$ 242,000.00
2936	351000007	76.761 ACRES +/-	LANCASTER	TX	$ 241,000.00
2764	353000014	MTL OFFICE/WHSE - 7,500 SF +/-	AUSTIN	TX	$ 236,500.00
2663	351020020	565.29 ACRES +/-	CLARKSVILLE	TX	$ 225,000.00
5923	353000009	MTL BLDG, 5,400 SF +/- + .76 ACRE	DALLAS	TX	$ 220,000.00
2952	351000006	STRIP MALL 3,690 SF +/-	AUSTIN	TX	$ 215,000.00
2952	3510P0005	14 UNIMPROVED LTS SIGNAL HILL SUBD. PH 2	AUSTIN	TX	$ 214,958.00
4006	351000018	ONE STORY OFFICE/WHSE; 9,584 SF	PFLUGERVILLE	TX	$ 199,000.00
4006	351000020	OFFICE BLDG - 5,767 SF	AUSTIN	TX	$ 189,000.00
5920	353000003	35.412 ACRES	AUBREY/PILOT P	TX	$ 181,500.00
2803	3530P0009	4-UNIT APT BLDG, 2/2 EACH	DALLAS	TX	$ 176,000.00
5920	353000004	18 UNIT APT COMPLEX	DALLAS	TX	$ 172,000.00
2693	353000007	RETAIL/WAREHOUSE 12,777 SF	FRISCO	TX	$ 168,300.00
2979	351000003	WAREHOUSE BLDG - 9,990 SF +/-	ROWLETT	TX	$ 155,000.00
5781	353000020	10 UNIT APTS, 8,034 SF +/-	LAGO VISTA	TX	$ 155,000.00
2936	351000006	62.161 ACRES +/-	LANCASTER	TX	$ 149,000.00
5629	3510P0002	44 UNIT APTS COMPLEX	MEXIA	TX	$ 145,500.00
2583	353000004	4/3/2; 2947 SF	SAN ANGELO	TX	$ 142,000.00
4002	3510P0019	34 RESIDENTIAL LOTS	DUNCAN	OK	$ 130,000.00
2803	351000002	BLDG 6559 SF +/-	DALLAS	TX	$ 126,500.00
2830	353000024	0.423 ACRES +/-; UNIMPROVED	AUSTIN	TX	$ 121,000.00
2830	353000025	0.423 ACRES +/-; UNIMPROVED	AUSTIN	TX	$ 121,000.00

1201R/5

55

DALLAS REGION
OWNED REAL ESTATE
AS OF JUNE 30, 1989

OFFICE: Houston Consolidated Office

ADDRESS: Federal Deposit Insurance Corporation
           7324 Southwest Freeway, #1600
           Houston, Texas 77074

TELEPHONE: (713) 270-6565

BANK NO.	ASSET NO.	DESCRIPTION	ADDRESS/LOCATION	STATE	PRICE
6854	353000090	31,275 SF LAND ZONED COMMERCIAL	1401 LOUISIANA, HOUSTON	TX	$2,252,000.00
6854	351000025	SHOPPING CENTER WITH APPROX 73,233 SF	701 UNIVERSITY, COLLEGE STATION	TX	$1,440,000.00
2964	351000005	72,000 NET RENTAL AREA OFFICE/WAREHOUSE	9777 HARWIN, HOUSTON	TX	$1,125,000.00
5924	353000010	MINI WAREHOUSE WITH APPROX 51,850 SF	2510 FM 1960 W, HOUSTON	TX	$ 985,000.00
5908	353000048	15.8 ACRES VACANT LAND	HIGHLAND MEADOWS SUBDIVISION, HARRIS COUNTY	TX	$ 875,000.00
5908	351000026	67,944 SF LOCATED ON 3.952 ACRES	1673 BRIARCREST DR., BRYAN	TX	$ 850,000.00
2819	351000004	11 ACRES N OF DEERBROOK MALL	GEOFFREY COURT, HUMBLE	TX	$ 850,000.00
5908	353000049	27,900 SF MISSION VERDE	14880 BELLAIRE BLVD., HOUSTON	TX	$ 810,000.00
2561	353000025	UNIVERSITY INN (100 UNIT MOTEL)	1400 UNIVERSITY, EDINBURG	TX	$ 775,000.00
5908	351000021	35,000 SF RETAIL SPACE WITH 180 PARKING	1712 FIRST ST., HUMBLE	TX	$ 710,000.00
5908	353000040	149.7087 ACRES VACANT LAND	N SIDE US 90, KATY	TX	$ 579,000.00
5908	353000054	3.3 ACRES OF LAND	PARK & LANGHAM, HOUSTON	TX	$ 550,000.00
2968	351000004	30,000 SF 3.3882 ACRES	10818 POINT LOOKOUT, NASSAU BAY	TX	$ 515,000.00
5867	353000008	244.5 ACRES VACANT COMM LAND	BRENHAM	TX	$ 500,000.00
6954	353000094	13.1088 ACRES 1 BLK N OF FM 1960 E	13.108 A W SUGAR PIN, HOUSTON	TX	$ 497,000.00
6854	353000095	11.141 ACRES 1 BLK N OF FM 1960 E	11.141 A E SUGAR PIN, HOUSTON	TX	$ 425,000.00
5908	353000052	9.7 ACRES COMM LAND	9512 FM 2222, AUSTIN	TX	$ 425,000.00
6854	353000107	BUILDING A 17,135 SF/BUILDING B 10,500 SF	NWC of SH 146 & LOOP 201, BAYTOWN	TX	$ 405,000.00
2818	351000001	INDUSTRIAL SITE $60,000/YR INCOME	SH 146, DAYTON	TX	$ 400,000.00
5908	353000053	10,100 SF RESTAURANT ON 1.2 ACRES	8611 MO-PAC, AUSTIN	TX	$ 375,000.00
5908	351000003	21,250 SF	1515 SYLVESTOR RD., HOUSTON	TX	$ 345,000.00
4018	351000012	1300 SF FARM HOUSE, BARN FENCE	FM 102 2 MILES W OF WHARTON, WHARTON	TX	$ 324,000.00
2728	353000083	8,640 SF RETAIL BLDG ON 1/2 ACRE TRACT	14501 NW FRWY/E OF WINDFERN RD., HOUSTON	TX	$ 315,000.00
2513	353000083	16.26 ACRES UNDEVELOPED LAND UTIL AVAIL	E DRIVE, BTWN WOODFORD RD & BROOKVIEW DR, HOUSTON	TX	$ 298,000.00
2968	351000012	3 ADJACENT TRACTS TOTALING 5.63 ACRES	NASA ROAD & REPSDORPH RD., SEABROOK	TX	$ 290,000.00
2937	351000003	3.252 ACRES	FM 1960 E/PINE ECHO, HOUSTON	TX	$ 286,000.00
6854	353000106	10,000 SF COMMERCIAL BLDG. 28.0606 ACRES	3708 GREENHOUSE ROAD, HOUSTON	TX	$ 275,000.00
5959	351000015	2.558 ACRES	SH-3 S OF PENNSYLVANIA, WEBSTER	TX	$ 270,000.00
2655	351000001	VACANT LAND	EGRET BAY & NASA I, WEBSTER	TX	$ 250,000.00
4018	351000011	14.8457 ACRES W/5 METAL QUANSET HUTS	HWY 60 S OF WHARTON, WHARTON	TX	$ 250,000.00
5959	351000016	281.5756 ACRES	NEAR SH-35 SOUTH OF PEARLAND, PEARLAND	TX	$ 235,000.00
5908	351000007	2.79 ACRES VACANT LAND	W. AIRPORT BLVD., HOUSTON	TX	$ 234,500.00
2779	353000012-B	11.8 ACRES COMMERCIAL LAND	LOOP 224, NACOGDOCHES	TX	$ 234,000.00
5957	351000010	70 ACRES OF LAND ZONED COMM	HARRIS COUNTY	TX	$ 220,500.00
5924	351000001	14.5 ACRES OF VACANT LAND	E SIDE CALDER RD, LEAGUE CITY	TX	$ 220,000.00
4012	351000009	31.11 ACRES 510' FRONTAGE ON MORTON	N SIDE OF MORTON RD. 1/2 MILE W OF PITTS RD, KATY	TX	$ 202,000.00
5955	351000010	12.5 ACRES UNIMPROVED UTILITIES AVAIL	SH 146N OFF NASA ROAD, SEABROOK	TX	$ 199,000.00
5959	351000020	2.8005 ACRES	FM 3005, GALVESTON	TX	$ 180,000.00
4012	351000015	280.04 ACRES OF FARM LAND	WEATHER COUNT ROAD 335, MILAN & BURLESON COUNTIES	TX	$ 180,000.00
5936	353000012	3.2003 ACRES	CORNER FM @(@) & PRESSMMON DRIVE, TOMBALL	TX	$ 175,000.00
4004	351000001	145,490 SF OF RAW LAND	206 TIDWELL (NE CORNER YALE & W OF TIDWELL)HOU	TX	$ 175,000.00

1201R/7

56

Federal Savings and Loan Insurance Corporation

Just as the FDIC insures national and state banks, the FSLIC insures our savings and loans. And right now it's having a rough time of it. Many do not expect the FSLIC to survive its current crisis and some suspect a major change is under way in how its successor will be doing business in the future. The FDIC has taken control of over 220 savings and loans for the year just halfway into 1989!

The FDIC steps in, locates the problem, determines the gravity of the situation and then turns it back over to the management with an FDIC managing agent left behind to oversee matters.

One Wall Street Journal article in March, 1989, described in gory detail how the FSLIC mismanaged a home builder as part of its loan disposition and could rack up an enormous bill for the taxpayers to settle over the next few years. The FSLIC is simply not equipped nor capable of properly disposing of the vast amount of property it now holds.

Additionally, they are restrained by the FDIC from just giving away the property to get it off their books. Right now the official line is that they can't go "much below market value." However, our research team has also pried a few details out of them. The banks are quite willing to work out down payment deals, interest deals, offer special terms, discount the property and so forth. What would you do if you were holding onto billions of dollars of real estate and didn't have immediate buyers?

FSLIC will mail you a quarterly catalog of their available properties, which include real estate from these categories:

- Improved and Unimproved Land
- Retail, Office and Industrial Properties
- Hotels, Motels and Resorts
- Condominiums
- Multi-Family Housing
- Single Family Housing
- Mobile Homes and Miscellaneous Property

There's something there for everyone. The book will contain the property's address and a description of the property, the asking price for the property and the contact's name and phone number. It's yours free of charge when you call the FSLIC regional office nearest you which is listed in **Section Three**.

At a Houston, Texas Savings and Loan auction held in July, a
1957 Bentley sold for $10,000.[1]

---

[1]Photo reprinted with permission, Time Magazine - July 21, 1989

<u>Federal Asset Disposition Association</u>

This agency, more commonly known as FADA, has been selling off savings and loans thrift assets (mainly property) for the past four years. According to a Wall Street Journal article mentioning FADA, they "have been skewered in Congress for mismanagement, cushy salaries and slow sales."

FADA will send you a catalog if you call one of their four regional offices which will list properties in many states. Primarily, you're going to find very large properties, often listed in the $500,000 to $10 million price range, although occasionally you'll find property well below that. $27,500 for acreage is one example found in their May/June, 1989 catalog.

Your first issue is complimentary. After that you'll have to purchase a subscription for 3 or 6 issues, published bimonthly, for $30 or $50 respectively. Their catalog contains listings for undeveloped land, condo units, motels and various other categories listed below.

In their May/June, 1989 catalog here's the breakdown of what's available:

TYPE of PROPERTY	NBR. of PROPERTIES
Apartment Bldgs.	58
Condos/Townhomes	40
Hotel/Motel/Resorts	20
Industrial	25
Land-Commercial	48
Land-other	19
Land-Residential	71
Office Bldgs.	38
Other	9
Residential	16
Retail	55

TOTAL PROPERTIES: 399

Here are the states where the properties are
located:

STATE	NBR. of PROPERTIES
Arizona	14
Arkansas	4
California	32
Colorado	38
Florida	47
Georgia	2
Illinois	1
Louisiana	4
Maryland	1
Mississippi	1
Missouri	1
Nevada	4
New Mexico	1
North Carolina	1
Oklahoma	15
Oregon	9
South Carolina	5
Tennessee	1
Texas	217
Wyoming	1

As you can see, Texas has the lion's share of these properties, more than 54% of those available. But there are still many interesting bargains available in their listings. For example, in their May/June catalog one 20 unit condominium project in Florida had brand-new 2 and 3 bedroom condos on beach front property at below market value. Texas, once we see higher oil prices (an inevitable outcome before the end of this century), will be an attractive real estate dream for those who bought now at fire sale prices.

FADA does not own these properties. They are just the FSLIC's marketing associate. In many of these listings, properties have already been turned over to private realtors for disposal. Many are still handled by FADA's regional offices or their national marketing office in Washington,

PROPERTY TYPE	CITY	REFERENCE NO. NAME & ADDRESS	SIZE DESCRIPTION	PRICE
Industrial	Woodward	8 – V – 1430HS **Wen-Clay Industrial Buildings** NWC Oklahoma Ave & N 48th Street	**16.5 acres** Property consists of a 31,080 sq. ft. office building and a drilling rig fabrication facility comprised of seven industrial buildings which contain approximately 54,000 sq. ft. FADA National Marketing (800) 225-3968 US / (800) 621-1219 Texas.	$775,000
Land - Other	Moore	17 – V – 7701UN **Sports Time** NEC of I-35 and South 19th	**22.45 acres** Vacant land zoned C-4, Planned Shopping Center. FADA National Marketing (800) 225-3968 US / (800) 621-1219 Texas.	$700,000
Land - Residential	Edmond	18 – V – 7802/7773AF **Chisholm Lake Subdivision** East of Santa Fe and South of Edmond Rd.	**140 lots** Residential building sites within the 364 lot Chisholm Lake Subdivision. Approx. 1/2 of the subdivision has been improved with single family residences averaging $65,000. FADA National Marketing (800) 225-3968 US / (800) 621-1219 Texas.	$891,000
Office	Norman	18 – V – 1537HS **Sooner Federal Building** 401 West Main Street	**1.1 acres** Property consists of an existing 4-story office bldg. and a 1-story annex bldg. on an irregularly shaped tract of land totalling 73,500 sq. ft. The site is comprised of a leasehold estate from a ground lease encompassing 28,000 sq. ft. and the fee simple estate totalling 45,500 sq. ft. FADA National Marketing (800) 225-3968 US / (800) 621-1219 Texas.	$1,150,000
Office	Tulsa	18 – V – 9050KY **Skyline Tower** 5810 East Skelly Drive	**104,541 gross sq. ft.** A 20-story office building with an underground parking garage built in 1983. The net rentable area is 81,354 sq. ft. and is presently 80% leased. FADA National Marketing (800) 225-3968 US / (800) 621-1219 Texas.	$3,800,000
Other	Midwest City	18 – V – 7751SH **Grissom Mobile Home Park** 900 North Oakview	**7.15 + 2.25 acres** A partially improved, but never occupied 62 space mobile home park on 7.15 acres and four lots zoned for commercial use containing 2.25 acres. FADA National Marketing (800) 225-3968 US / (800) 621-1219 Texas.	$328,900

PROPERTY TYPE	CITY	REFERENCE NO. NAME & ADDRESS	SIZE DESCRIPTION	PRICE
Land - Residential	Aurora	18 – V – 9442SL **Concord** Near Hampton & Tower Rd.	**20 lots** Finished single family lots located in the Seven Lakes Subdivision ranging from 6,000 to 7,000 sq. ft. each. FADA National Marketing (800) 225-3968 US / (800) 621-1219 Texas.	To Be Determined
Land - Residential	Castle Pines	18 – V – 9074KY **Glen Oaks**	**25 lots** Single family home sites in Glen Oaks Subdivision at Castle Pines North. FADA National Marketing (800) 225-3968 US / (800) 621-1219 Texas.	$1,125,000
Land - Residential	Colorado Springs	12 – V – 3141F **Bear Creek Land** Skyview Lane & Pecan Street	**17.31 acres** Consists of 67 developed and 90 undeveloped lots situated in the Community at Bear Creek. FADA National Marketing (800) 225-3968 US / (800) 621-1219 Texas.	$520,000
Land - Residential	Colorado Springs	9 – D – 2358FF **Cedar Heights** Residential Subdivision	**329 lots** Single family lots in a partially completed master planned community. Stuart Scott, Ltd. (719) 578-8800/Rocky Scott.	$7,500,000
Land - Residential	Colorado Springs	11 – V – 3122F **La Posada Land** Fontmore & Mesa Rds	**30 lots + 6 acres** Property consists of 31 fully developed single family lots and approx. 6 adjacent acres of unplotted development land (roughly triangular in shape, at the east side of the project). Zoning is PUD. Paragon Properties (719) 634-5564/Jean Miles.	$750,000
Land - Residential	Littleton	18 – V – 9421SL **Bowles & Sheridan** Junction of Bowles Ave. & Sheridan St.	**18.38 acres** Vacant land (including a single family residence) zoned agricultural but suitable for single family residential. FADA National Marketing (800) 225-3968 US / (800) 621-1219 Texas.	To Be Determined

D.C. The catalog you'll be getting contains the property type, city, description of the property, reference number and listing price.

They do not want to just give these properties away but FADA is always prepared to accept offers much lower than their listing prices.

The listing prices are generally for the original loan amount, sometimes a little more. Keep that in mind when making your offer. Now that Resolution Trust Corporation has become a concrete reality, FADA will likely be the first one to lose its properties. Properties do get sold every month as many of the listings change, so these properties are moving. Someone is buying them. If you can raise the amounts of money necessary to get involved in these (see **Section Two**, Financing Chapter), then you should call. See **Section Three** for FADA's addresses and phone numbers.

✓ Resolution Trust Corporation

The Resolution Trust Corporation was approved by Congress on August 9, 1989 and is responsible for the disposal of assets of failed savings and loan associations.

RTC offices have been, or are in the process of being, set up in major cities across the United States. Their purpose is to dispose of $100 billion dollars worth of real estate as quickly and economically as possible.

The savings and loans which are in conservatorship will be closed and banks or solvent S&L's will receive the good assets, cash, bonds or a combination of the above for their assumption of the failed S&L's deposits.

The lower dollar value per unit, low dollar value single-family homes and apartment buildings, will be offered first to low-income families, non-profit organizations and government agencies. Most properties will be available immediately to investors through the methods chosen by individual institutions responsible for liquidation.

Thirty billion dollars in bonds will be issued to pay for the clean-up of the insolvent thrifts. A five person overseeing board, composed of the Secretary of Treasury, the Chairman of the Federal Reserve Board, the Secretary of the Department of Housing and Urban Development and two Presidential appointees, will administer the operations of this agency.

For more information on the RTC, please consult the addresses in **Section Three**.

REOs Direct

Real Estate Owned property (REOs) can be bought before the bank gets into trouble and has had its assets seized by the FDIC or FSLIC. Various lending institutions have a frequent rate of foreclosures which they need to resell just to get them off their books. This can include property such as single family homes, condos, apartment buildings or other forms of residential or commercial real estate.

Don't limit yourself to just banks or savings & loan companies. There are mortgage and finance companies which have REOs as well. Many are eager to get these assets off their books and to sell them quickly. Keep in mind that a bank is a business. They have to report their profits and losses to Board of Directors every quarter. Lenders' jobs are at stake. And if a property has been foreclosed and not resold, the lender looks especially bad to his Board of Directors.

Because reports are made quarterly, you have to find out when a bank's quarter ends. Many banks have quarters which end on the last day of March, June, September and December. Just before those time periods are the best times of the year to call the bank. You should leave yourself enough time to work out financing. Although near the end of the quarter, depending on the condition of the bank or company, the lender or manager may be quite frantic to unload the property and give you a terrific bargain.

In contacting various savings & loan institutions around the country (those that weren't problem banks or seized already), our Research Department found a good deal of available property sitting on their books. Those properties have already been turned over to real estate brokers to be resold but various banks we contacted would send us complete packages of computer printouts showing their listings. The broker's name and phone number would be included but the listings were still sent to us.

You'll find out, if you follow this through, that banks are quite eager to dispose of this property. Many will send extensive listings for your perusal. Real estate brokers may be obstinate and demand close to market prices. You can always make offers and hope they'll accept them OR just move on to another property. It's not painstaking work and can be done in a few days spare time, just by calling the banks listed in your telephone book's yellow pages.

Banks, you should know, often have about 70-80% of the home's value tied up in their loan amount. Keep this in the front of your mind when making your offer. They may want fair market value or some such price but they only need to recoup their loan investment. If they can't get the property sold and it remains on the books for another quarter, they could be putting their jobs in jeopardy.

MIAMI SAVINGS BANK
REAL ESTATE OWNED PROPERTIES

PAGE 1 of 2

PROPERTY LOCATION	DESCRIPTION	ASKING PRICE
CONDOMINIUMS & TOWNHOMES -		
Horizons West Condo 8600 S.W. 133rd Avenue Unit #106 Miami, Florida 33183	2 Bedrooms/2 Bathrooms Den 1,028 Square Feet Monthly Maint.: $105.00 Monthly Taxes: $ 80.00	$ 49,900.00
Lakeshore Townhomes 6092 S.W. 41st Street Davie, Florida 33314	2 Bedrooms/1 1/2 Bathrooms 1,012 Square Feet Monthly Maint.: $78.00 Monthly Taxes: $53.00	$ 29,000.00
LAND -		
227 Avenue SW 232 Street Miami, Florida (Contract)	13.77 Acres Agricultural	$125,000.00
COMMERCIAL -		
Minorca Plaza Condo 951 SW 122 Avenue Miami, Florida	3 Offices Secretarial area, Reception Area, Storeroom 800 Sq. Feet. Monthly Maint. : $101.00 Monthly Taxes : 89.00	$ 61,900.00
New World II Shopping Center 1460-1470 N.W. 107th Avenue Units #7, 8, 14, 15, 28 #43 & 44 Miami, Florida	1,100+/- Square feet per unit Monthly Maint.: $ 65.00/unit Monthly Taxes: $178.00/unit	$ TBD

65

So, a bank can easily be a source of buying real estate below market value. They can afford to do so if you contact them near the end of their quarter. This bank could, and some often originate this themselves, provide you with excellent financing. After all, they have the luxury to do so. It is removed from their books as a foreclosed property and back on their books as a new mortgage. You can win both ways: cheaper house and great financing. The bank wins as well.

One young associate of mine applied this method quite successfully a few summers ago and purchased 10 homes in an economically depressed area for only $15,000 down payment. All were fully rented and all had a positive cash flow - a profit after expenses. The bank was happy to get them off its books and provide him with the financing to repurchase the bank's homes. If he was able to do it, it can be done by anyone.

At this writing I have found such a deal in a prospering area where I can buy a commercial office building, valued at $650,000, for about $400,000 directly from the bank. The bank will appraise the property at $640,000, sell it to me at the above price and then lend me 70% of the appraised value for the purchase of this building. In other words, they are going to lend me around $55,000 above and beyond the selling price of the building to take it off their books.

Look in your local phone book's yellow pages and call some banks.

Bureau of Land Management

At one time or another our Federal Government has owned 80% of our country's 2.3 billion acres. Now it owns about 1/3 of this property. Land was sold, as our country was getting started, to provide funds for the U.S. Treasury. In the mid 1800's Congress passed homesteading legislation which gave land to settlers who would farm it. This brought on a westward drive and expansion of our country. There have been battles, back and forth, over giving away Federal land, as well as selling it off. Conservationists have quarreled with developers since the turn of this century. Slowly, developers are gaining more and more real estate. During the Reagan administration the Bureau of Land Management gave away 20 million acres of public land for only $5.6 Billion. That comes to $280 per acre!

The BLM is now involved in two different sales: undeveloped land and oil/gas leases. Most of these land sales occur in the 11 Western states and Alaska, although there are parcels of land scattered around the Eastern United States. In order to qualify for purchase of these lands, you must be a U.S. citizen or have a corporation subject to Federal or State laws (non-

U.S. citizens can have corporations established within the United States and buy land this way).

Their sales are conducted by public auction or sealed bid. You do not have to be present at their auctions and can have an agent represent you. You'll have to make a deposit or pay a minimum down payment with your bid. Then you can obtain financing through private lenders. Sometimes direct sales are made to adjoining landowners and the auction process is avoided.

Keep in mind that this is undeveloped land, not surplus real estate and it does not include national forest land. If Congress authorizes such sales it may likely be done by the Forest Service. You can contact the Forest Service directly for details:

Forest Service
P.O. Box 2417
Washington, DC 20013

Aside from undeveloped land, one can participate in the BLM's oil and gas lease auctions. This has been called, by at least one government official, a big program. From their information sheet, they expect to have 13 of these sales throughout the United States from August 11 until November 17 in these states:

Nevada	Indiana	Florida
Wyoming	Ohio	Idaho
New Mexico	Illinois	Utah
Colorado	Michigan	Alaska
Arizona	Oregon	California

Such auctions will probably continue into the future. Call them for details. Those bidding on oil/gas leases should get expert information from auction participants and contact an attorney about various complications that may arise. This is not like those "cons or scam oil/gas lease lotteries" where you buy the right to have your bidding card drawn. Many of those companies were selling rights to bid for enormous amounts. You can do that yourself now without their "expensive assistance".

One private auction company which has just started auctioning off privately held oil and gas leases is Ebco Auctioneers, Inc. They can be reached at (405) 947-7400 or (405) 720-0313. They auction off wells to competitive bidders. With these auctions you can come in and pick up wells for as little as $100, getting a fractional interest of the well. Also, at these auctions you can get experienced information and practical knowledge about them before proceeding on to the BLM's oil/gas lease auctions.

See **Section Three** for the correct phone numbers and addresses of BLM offices you can contact for auction schedules and further information.

An additional function of the Bureau of Land Management and Forest Service is to provide information to any U.S. citizen who wishes to stake a claim on federally owned land in order to extract minerals.

In 1972 an act of Congress gave every U.S. citizen the right to stake a claim to 20 acres of land for the purpose of mining gold or other minerals. There are certain restrictions which apply but they are reasonable and easy to follow. The offices listed in **Section Three** will be helpful in answering any questions you may have.

You can state your claim in any state where government owned land is under the jurisdiction of the Bureau of Land Management or Forest Service. It is estimated that 90% of gold and other minerals remain untapped, waiting for the small prospector or large mining company to go in and find it.

This can be a hobby or full-time endeavor, depending on how you plan to approach it; a supplement to your present income or an opportunity to make a fortune. In either event, it can be a new experience that can provide a recreational outlet or a full-time project.

If this type of activity is of interest to you, we suggest you contact a company in California which publishes a booklet giving instructions on how to stake your own claim. Write or call:

> Public Lands Title
> P.O. Box 2082
> Grass Valley, CA 95949
> Tel.: (916) 273-1990

Farmers Home Association

The FmHA is a loan granting government agency, giving loans to people who wish to buy or build homes, to farmers who need money for equipment, seed, additional land and to rural cities who need hospitals, sewer systems and fire houses. They'll also make business loans in rural areas.

Although FmHA is in the business of giving out money, they are also in the credit counseling business, assisting borrowers who can't pay on time. For instance, if someone misses a payment, they can pay an extra $10 per month until their back payment is remedied. A person can also extend their loan payment period for up to two years if they cannot make their mortgage payments.

As a result, the Department of Agriculture, under which FmHA is based, lost $256 million in farm properties and $238 million on single family homes during fiscal year 1988. Despite the help given under the FmHA, properties are still being foreclosed, as well as prime farmland. Listings can include single family homes, apartment buildings, businesses, hospitals and all kinds of real estate.

You can contact the various state agencies for information on how you can find out about their properties in **Section Three**. They have 46 state offices with Property Management Divisions at those offices.

Other Federal Real Estate Disposal Agencies

Three previously mentioned Federal Agencies are also in the property disposal business: The General Services Administration, the IRS and the Small Business Administration.

The General Services Administration

The GSA auctions surplus Federal real estate and some undeveloped land. Their subordinate agency is the Federal Property Resources Service which publishes a quarterly pamphlet of real estate listings offered by the GSA. The first thing you should do is write for a booklet entitled, "U.S. Real Property Sales List". It may be obtained free from:

> Consumer Information Center
> Box 100
> Pueblo, CO 81002.

"U.S. Real Property Sales List" is published quarterly by GSA to list properties it currently has for sale across the country. The "Sales List" provides the name and location of properties currently for sale; their descriptions; types of sales (auction or sealed bid) and dates, times and places of sales. Also included are the addresses and phone numbers of the GSA regional offices responsible for the sales.

Within the "Sales List" are two coupons, one which you can mail in to receive the next issue and the other to get your name placed on the mailing list for real estate being sold in the price range and geographic areas of your interest.

IMPORTANT - PLEASE READ BEFORE BIDDING

SPECIAL TERMS AND CONDITIONS OF SALE

BIDDERS INDEBTED TO THE GOVERNMENT: Purchasers of surplus personal property must make arrangements to pay promptly all amounts administratively found to be due the United States Government arising out of their prior purchase of surplus personal property. Failure to pay any such amount upon demand may be cause for rejection of all future bids until such time as the debt is paid.

SALE TO GOVERNMENT EMPLOYEES: To the extent not prohibited by the regulations of any executive agency, an employee of such agency (either as a civilian or as a member of the Armed Forces of the United States including the U. S. Coast Guard, on active duty) may be allowed to purchase Government surplus personal property. The term "EMPLOYEE" as used in this statement includes any agency or immediate member of the household of the employee. GSA EMPLOYEES ARE INELIGIBLE TO BID. Other Federal employees should check their own agencies as to their eligibility to bid.

FORMS OF PAYMENT: ACCEPTABLE FORMS OF PAYMENT INCLUDE CASH, CASHIER'S CHECKS, OFFICIAL CREDIT UNION CHECKS (Federal/state chartered), MONEY ORDERS, TRAVELER'S CHECKS AND GOVERNMENT CHECKS (Federal, State or Local Government). PERSONAL OR COMPANY CHECKS WILL BE ACCEPTED **ONLY** IF ACCOMPANIED BY AN INFORMAL BANK LETTER GUARANTEEING PAYMENT. BANK LETTERS NEED NOT BE IN ANY SPECIFIC FORMAT BUT STATE IN ESSENCE THAT THE DEPOSITOR IS IN GOOD STANDING AND THE BANK WILL GUARANTEE CHECKS UP TO A SPECIFIC AMOUNT THROUGH A SPECIFIC DATE AND SHOULD STATE THAT THEY COVER THE PURCHASE OF U. S. GOVERNMENT PROPERTY ONLY.

REMOVAL RESPONSIBILITIES: PROPERTY CUSTODIANS ARE NOT RESPONSIBLE FOR AND WILL NOT MAKE ANY REMOVAL ARRANGEMENTS. THE SUCCESSFUL BIDDER MUST MAKE THESE ARRANGEMENTS, INCLUDING LABOR FOR PACKING, CRATING, REMOVAL, AND TRANSPORTATION. **TO RELEASE PROPERTY TO ANYONE OTHER THAN THE SUCCESSFUL BIDDER, WRITTEN NOTIFICATION MUST BE FURNISHED TO THE PROPERTY CUSTODIAN.**

CONSIDERATION OF BIDS: Qualified bids, bids specifying order of choice or **UNSIGNED BIDS** may not be considered. The Government reserves the right to reject any and all bids. **TELEPHONIC AND TELEGRAPHIC BIDS ARE NOT ACCEPTABLE AND WILL NOT BE CONSIDERED.**

The bidder warrants that he is **not under 18 years of age.** For breach of this warrant the Government shall have the right to annual any contract without liability. Identification may be required.

DISPUTES: Any contract resulting from this offering is subject to the Contract Disputes Act of 1978, Public Law 95-563 and is hereby incorporated by reference. A copy of the clause is available upon request from the GSA Sales Office conducting this sale.

RESULTS OF SALE: Bid results are not furnished by telephone. A bidder may request sale results by enclosing a stamped, legal size or larger, self-addressed envelope along with his/her bid. This action is necessary due to current budgetary limitations.

Condition of property is not warranted.

DESCRIPTION WARRANTY

THE GOVERNMENT WARRANTS TO THE ORIGINAL PURCHASER THAT THE PROPERTY LISTED IN THE INVITATION FOR BIDS WILL CONFORM TO ITS DESCRIPTION. IF A MISDESCRIPTION IS DETERMINED BEFORE REMOVAL OF THE PROPERTY, THE GOVERNMENT WILL KEEP THE PROPERTY AND REFUND ANY MONEY PAID. IF A MISDESCRIPTION IS DETERMINED AFTER REMOVAL, THE GOVERNMENT WILL REFUND ANY MONEY PAID IF THE PURCHASER TAKES THE PROPERTY AT HIS OR HER EXPENSE TO A LOCATION SPECIFIED BY THE CONTRACTING OFFICER. NO REFUND WILL BE MADE UNLESS THE PURCHASER SUBMITS A WRITTEN NOTICE TO THE CONTRACTING OFFICER WITHIN 15 CALENDAR DAYS OF THE DATE OF REMOVAL THAT THE PROPERTY IS MISDESCRIBED AND MAINTAINS THE PROPERTY IN THE SAME CONDITION AS WHEN REMOVED. AFTER PROPERTY HAS BEEN REMOVED, NO REFUND WILL BE MADE FOR SHORTAGES OF PROPERTY SOLD BY THE "LOT."

THIS WARRANTY IS IN PLACE OF ALL OTHER GUARANTEES AND WARRANTIES, EXPRESS OR IMPLIED. THE GOVERNMENT DOES NOT WARRANT THE MERCHANTABILITY OF THE PROPERTY OR ITS FITNESS FOR ANY USE OR PURPOSE. THE AMOUNT OF RECOVERY UNDER THIS PROVISION IS LIMITED TO THE PURCHASE PRICE OF THE MISDESCRIBED PROPERTY. THE PURCHASER IS NOT ENTITLED TO ANY PAYMENT FOR LOSS OF PROFIT OR ANY OTHER MONEY DAMAGES, SPECIAL, DIRECT, INDIRECT, OR CONSEQUENTIAL. CLAUSE NO. 2 OF STANDARD FORM 114C IS DELETED.

DEFICIENCIES, WHEN KNOWN, HAVE BEEN INDICATED IN THE ITEM DESCRIPTION. HOWEVER, ABSENCE OF ANY INDICATED DEFICIENCY DOES NOT MEAN THE ITEM MAY NOT HAVE DEFICIENCIES. **BIDDERS ARE CAUTIONED TO INSPECT BEFORE BIDDING. CONDITION OF PROPERTY IS NOT GUARANTEED.**

Once you have the "Sales List" in hand and determine that you have a definite interest in a particular property, you may contact a realty specialist in any of the GSA Regional Real Estate Sales Offices for further information and to obtain an Invitation for Bid. Or you may phone 1-800-GSA-1313 and request an Invitation for Bid. When using the 800 number, you must be able to cite the location of the particular property in which you are interested. Your call will be answered electronically and you will be asked to leave your name and address.

The Invitation for Bid contains a legal description of the property and information concerning bidding procedures and the obligations of bidders and the Government. Each bidder is required to display a substantial bid deposit in the form of a cashier's check made out to the General Services Administration. The check is applied toward the purchase price of the winning bidder.

The Small Business Administration

The SBA, as a result of business failures, possesses quite a bit of real estate in its foreclosed portfolios. In most cases they'll have a private auctioneer or local bank dispose of the property. As is usually the case, auctioneers will try to get as high a price as possible or demand a fixed price in their mailings, handling sealed bids they receive in whatever procedure they have to in order to dispose of the property. There can be good deals found here.

Obviously, banks will try to get their loan amount back from the property disposition. Depending on the bank, the region of the country and other economic factors about the property or the area, one should be able to negotiate with the bank for a bargain. You can find out who is holding property by contacting the SBA field offices located in **Section Three**.

The Internal Revenue Service

The IRS seizes property. As mentioned in Chapter One of this Section, the number of IRS liens on property owners has skyrocketed from 371,000 to 837,000 during the past eight years. That's potentially a lot of real estate on the market. Much of it is settled with the IRS. Since the establishment of the Taxpayers' Bill of Rights, the amount of seizures should drop because the length of time the IRS needs to seize the property from the delinquency notice has been extended from 10 days to 30 days.

There are still a number of properties that frequently go up for auction by the IRS. Because of the IRS formula in calculating a minimum bid and with few people attending their property auctions, one could find a bargain there. Minimum bids should be figured at 80% of the forced sale value of the property, minus any loans or other encumbrances outstanding.

You'll find a few disadvantages. The major stumbling block is that you have no more than a few hours to come up with the entire purchase price of the property as soon as you get the winning bid. You'll have to also assume responsibility for any mortgage, other liens (such as Ad Valorem Tax Liens covered later in this chapter) and any other encumbrances on that property.

The IRS has a sealed bid form they use (FORM 2222) which you can get for upcoming sealed bids by calling or writing the contact points in **Section Three**. When you make such a bid, you'll be required to include a deposit of $200 or 20% of your bid, whichever is more.

In other cases the IRS will send a flier announcing the auction, although they may not. By law the IRS must place notices of seized property sales in the newspaper where the property is located. They may, if there is not a sufficiently-sized newspaper, post notices in the nearest U.S. Post Office and in at least two other places. You can get on their mailing lists by calling the national 800 number or writing the addresses found in **Section Three**. They are not obligated to continue sending you mailings, although they may. One friend of mine gets all his notices of public auction sent directly to his home address. Just call them and ask to be put on their mailing list for "Tax Seizure Auctions". They may ask you whether you're interested in real estate or personal property auctions.

Because the IRS number is the same for all 50 states, you may wish to specify which counties you are interested in within your state or you may write to different states and ask to be put on the mailing lists for auctions in those states.

Although the ideal scenario is to sell property or merchandise at market values, keep in mind that, in practice, this has not always been the case. One man in Sacramento purchased a moderately-expensive home for under $1,000 a few years ago. Another businessman I know purchased numerous factory machinery items for 10¢ on the dollar. You may find incredible bargains at these auctions. It often depends on how hard the IRS promotes the auctions, how quickly they wish to dispose of the property, how many bidders show up and how aggressively they bid. Don't rule out the IRS auctions as one way of finding inexpensive property.

IRS AUCTION OF TSALICKIS BUSINESS DRAWS CROWD

A Tribune Staff Report

TARPON SPRINGS
Nearly 200 people turned out Thursday to bid on everything from comic books to bric-a-brac during an Internal Revenue Service auction at a business complex here where more than three tons of cocaine were seized last year.

The IRS sold the contents of Bogie's Upper Deck Cafe and Lounge and the Ultimate Health and Racquet Club to try to recover nearly

$100,000 in back taxes owed by two defunct businesses.

The businesses are in the Tarpon Financial Center, 855 U.S. Highway 19 S., where federal agents seized almost $60 million worth of cocaine at a warehouse in the complex.

The center's owner, prominent Tarpon Springs businessman Michael Tsalickis, was convicted last year on drug-smuggling charges and was sentenced to 27 years in prison. The IRS said the auction had nothing to do with the drug case.

The auctioned items consisted mostly of standard restaurant and health club equipment: stoves, ovens, treadmills and rowing machines.

But there also were items such as paintings from such Humphrey Bogart movies as "Casablanca" and "The Maltese Falcon." One such painting went for $175. Also, a slightly damaged satellite dish outside the complex went for $200.

IRS officials late Thursday had not calculated how much of the unpaid taxes they had recovered by the auction.[2]

---

[2]Reprinted with permission of the Tampa Tribune, 9/89

Local Methods of Obtaining Real Estate

Tax Sales

County governments assess property taxes on homeowners and other real estate investors. These are called "ad valorem" taxes. Such a tax is based on the value of the item being taxed. Example: A home may have just been sold for $125,000. However, the ad valorem tax may only be for the assessment, which could be as low as $49,000 in this example. The ad valorem tax may be for 1% of the assessed value ($1 for each $100 assessed value). So, while the house may be worth $125,000 on the market, the assessment would only be on the $49,500. If the ad valorem tax was 1%, the tax would come to only $495 on an annual basis.

Now, if someone does not pay that ad valorem tax, it becomes delinquent. Should this delinquency continue past a set time limit, the county will then put a lien on the property. Tax liens can be placed on one's property for failure to pay these taxes:

- City taxes
- Payroll taxes
- County taxes
- Sales taxes
- Estate taxes
- School taxes
- Income taxes

If you don't pay your income or payroll taxes, the IRS will seize and auction your real property or personal property, as the case may be. Your property may be seized and sold at auction for failure to pay other taxes such as the ad valorem taxes, county, city and school taxes. Here's how that happens: Frequently, a person cannot pay his taxes on the property or sometimes the owner has disappeared and abandoned his property. None of the tax authorities can reach that person. At that point, if the person has failed to pay the taxes, often for a time period such as two years, the taxing authority files a lien against the property.

In some cases the tax deed or certificate is sold at public auction. This may be redeemed by the property owner at a certain later date and the the winning bidder is reimbursed when he sells the property owner back his property, usually at a high interest rate. Some investors have even made this a profitable sideline, since you can pick up a tax sale certificate for around $5,000-$10,000 and then collect a high rate of return on this investment. The worst thing that could happen is that you would own the house outright, rent it out profitably or even re-sell it for an enormous profit.

There are a few caveats here of which you should be aware. To begin with, never, ever buy such a tax sale certificate unless you have first contacted a real estate attorney in the area where you want to buy the real estate. There may be local redemption laws to worry about or there may be other troublesome matters.

One of the biggest worries you can have in buying such a tax sale property is that there are likely going to be other encumbrances on that property. If the person hasn't paid his property taxes, he may also not have paid his income taxes or even other people may have then put liens on that property. Tax liens are superior to other liens; they may, sometimes, erase all other liens, excluding IRS liens, but that varies from state to state. If they don't, you will then have to pay those liens to fully own the property or you may then be responsible for those liens and have liens placed on property you already own.

The auction is held simply to raise the money to pay the back taxes. The minimum bid on that property or certificate is for the amount of back taxes plus interest, penalties and costs in disposition of the property. Payment is required, often on the day of the auction, although, in some cases, you may make just a deposit and pay the balance at some date in the near future. Their purpose is to get the back taxes paid so that the local government has money with which to pay its bills.

Some people sell courses on pre-foreclosures which show you how to contact the county recorder's office and to look for something called a "Lis Pendens". This is the legal term showing potential buyers that there are liens on the property. Before buying properties, you should do this or have someone do this for you and find out if there are liens on the property you wish to buy.

Tax sales are advertised in the local newspapers where the real estate is going to be auctioned. In some cases you might try calling your county recorder's office and find out if you can obtain a listing of the properties coming up for auction. Some will provide you with such a list. In **Section Three** you'll get a list of various counties which have tax sales and how you may contact them about such sales.

Not all tax sales and foreclosures are handled by the local courthouse. In some cases, city hall is involved or the local sheriff has them done. It can even be a combination of the above.

Be careful about redemption periods in various states. A person may redeem his property within that time period if he comes up with the money.

The following will list each state with the corresponding redemption period.

STATE	REDEMPTION PERIOD	STATE	REDEMPTION PERIOD
Alabama	12 months	Montana	12 months
Alaska	none	Nebraska	none
Arizona	none	Nevada	none
Arkansas	12 months	New Hampshire	none
California	none	New Jersey	10 days
Colorado	75 days	New Mexico	1 month
Connecticut	none	New York	none
Delaware	none	N. Carolina	none
Washington, D.C.	none	N. Dakota	12 months
Florida	10 days	Ohio	none
Georgia	none	Oklahoma	none
Hawaii	none	Oregon	none
Idaho	none	Pennsylvania	none
Illinois	12 months	Rhode Island	none
Indiana	3 months	S. Carolina	none
Iowa	6 months	S. Dakota	12 months
Kansas	12 months	Tennessee	none
Kentucky	none	Texas	none
Louisiana	none	Utah	6 months
Maine	12 months	Vermont	6 months
Massachusetts	none	Virginia	none
Michigan	6 months	Washington	12 months
Minnesota	6 months	West Virginia	none
Mississippi	none	Wisconsin	none
Missouri	12 months	Wyoming	6 months

State Departments of Transportation

From time to time, various Departments of Transportation have surplus land which they auction. Either there is no use for the land or the state treasury wishes to raise money for their coffers. Much of this land is unimproved or undeveloped land and minimum bids, in some states, are quite low. It may be zoned for commercial use only, so you may not be able to use it for residential building.

Occasionally, states may have buildings which they auction as well. These would come under the heading of State Surplus sales and still fall under the Department of Transportation for that area. Your best bet is to call the Department of Transportation in your state capital and ask about such property.

They may not have great real estate auctions but they do have wonderful bargains at many of their state surplus vehicle auctions.

Urban Homesteading Programs

Originally, such homesteading programs fell under the jurisdiction of Housing and Urban Development. Now, they are managed by each city. Not every city has them. Not every city that has them has property available year around. These are generally for low-income individuals who would like to buy a run-down home for as low as $1, obtain financing to rebuild the home and wish to live in it for at least 5 years.

There are minimum income requirements in order to have your application accepted and you must have good credit. These are foreclosed homes that are in such poor condition that they cannot be resold easily and which will require that you borrow money to fix them up. In some cases the local city will help you obtain financing to fix up the property.

Many of the agencies contacted sell their homes or practically give them away for very little money. Because of this, many people fill out applications in hope of being the "lucky one". As a result, cities are forced to have lotteries and draw the winning applications out of a box.

Sometimes there are restrictions, such as you cannot have owned property in that city for at least the past 12 months, you must be a resident of the city or this must be your first home, etc.

There are many cities which have these Urban Homesteading Programs. For those which we've contacted that have had such programs, please see **Section Three**.

You may not find your city listed. If so, please contact your local Department of Community Development and Housing and determine if they have plans to sell such homes in the future. As more buildings or homes are abandoned and turned over to city agencies to sell, we are likely to see more of these auctions going on in the future.

Those people who advertise $1 homes in the classifieds, trying to sell you a government auction book, are talking about such homes. As I said, these are not the best types of homes to look for and you have to have your application drawn from a box or barrel. There are far better properties available in the real estate market across the United States. If you have a hard time getting started in real estate and cannot afford or wish to look for other homes, this is your last resort. It is not your best resort but, if all else fails, there may be such property there for you.

Probate Real Estate Sales

When someone dies they often leave real estate behind which heirs will argue about with regard to the disposal of such property. If a will is left behind, for example, willing the house to "the children" or something like that, there can be endless arguments over what to do about this house or property.

One real estate guru from Los Angeles has sold home study courses for up to $350 which basically tell you to look at the classified ads in newspapers and follow up people's deaths by calling the attorneys handling the estate or the local courthouse. You then get details on that person's property and approach the heirs about buying the house or property, offering a price, usually about 40% below market value, just to get it off their hands.

The above can work and for those aggressive, ruthless individuals who easily overcome confronting a widow's grief or children's loss of parents (in hope of a quick profit), this can be one way to make a fast buck. Right after a person's death, there is the question of state probate taxes to be paid. Some inheritors may lack the cash and real estate sales are a quick solution. On the one hand, it does seem like a rotten thing to do, buy up someone's property, who has just lost a loved one. On the other hand, the person or persons may need to pay inheritance taxes and they don't have the cash with which to do so. If you have the stomach for this sort of negotiation and really want to buy property at far below market value, then be my guest.

Another, more civilized, though less profitable method is to call auctioneers right out of the phone book. Many auctioneers regularly hire themselves out for estate auctions, some for real estate property. This method is not the best place to find bargains unless the area is economically depressed.

One way to buy these properties through your local government is to call the Public Administrator in your city and get the listings of local estate property. These don't happen on a regular basis, except in larger cities that have them. Some are by sealed bid, others by open bidding. There have been cases where one can make a sealed bid on such a house and then bidders can make open bids to top the sealed bids once opened. Procedures vary from state to state. My parents, for example, bought their first home this way many years ago, with my father making an open bid after the sealed bids were opened. The property appreciated considerably even in a depressed real estate market and is now worth about four times what he originally paid.

The poorest way to find out about these auctions is through the classifieds for estate sales. There may be bargains but they are few and far between and the merchandise is going to have more sentimental value than resale value. This is not usually done with real estate.

If a property has been on the market for a while after a person has died, one could approach the heirs, rather than immediately after the wake and make an offer. By then, there may have been squabbles and quarrels and the right offer could quickly be accepted. Such activity does mean you'll have to be familiar with the neighborhood and keep notes, mental or written, about various properties. I have spoken to people who have bought property in this way and all seem to have done well, so this can pay off for you.

Pre-Foreclosed Real Estate

These are also known as pre-foreclosures, which means that the property has accumulated liens and/or the owners have fallen behind on their mortgage payments and the property is soon to be foreclosed upon. Not too many people know about this and investors who use this method certainly aren't going to share this well-kept secret.

You can now bypass the misery and problems in raising a down payment on your house by a simple visit to your local courthouse. How would you like to buy a house or property before it gets repossessed by the bank? Here's how you do it:

- Go to your local courthouse and ask to see the foreclosure filings. (This is where you get to ask about Lis Pendens that have been filed.)

- Find the properties where mortgage payments have lapsed between three and six months, not those that haven't made payments for longer than that (or you won't be able to do this successfully).

• Do this simple calculation: multiply the monthly loan payment due by the number of months lapsed since the last mortgage payment was made. Add that total figure to this: $1,500-$2,000. That is approximately how much you might be able to pay for that house.

• Approach the homeowner, either by phone call, in person or by letter and let him know that you are interested in assuming his property's mortgage. Some investors even use the phrase: "I'll take it off your hands."

What has happened to permit you simply to follow the above steps so easily in buying a house? The person may have lost his job, undergone a long illness, had a divorce or even had the death of a spouse. His American dream has gone sour. The biggest problem on that person's mind right now is to keep his good credit rating, not his home. Without good credit in this country at this time, a person's life is a maelstrom of misery!

That couple or that person has just stopped making payments and the bank has tried to get them to make payments. The bank will start with phone calls and then, after a short while, follow with a demand letter. Such a letter will state that the person must bring his payments up to date by a certain time. If not, then the bank will start foreclosure proceedings.

If you contact someone who's recently gotten a demand letter, you're likely to find one very distraught individual. At that point the person will either try to handle the situation, as it is a very dangerous one, get out of the trouble or is just going to give up.

In some cases the person will already have made plans to move; in others, the move will already have been made. Please keep in mind that the person's frame of mind is going to be that of a very "crushed individual". He knows he's going to lose his house. He's beaten down. Please be polite and use good manners in working out such a deal. Some of these people have even been known to throw the keys at you and say: "Here. It's yours."

When making such a deal with the person, you can either be firm and take it off their hands for their past due amounts and other fees, which we'll discuss or you can be kind-hearted and generous and give them whatever they ask. With the more expensive homes and, believe me, there are very expensive homes that can go through this process, you'll probably have to pay the owner some of his equity in the house.

Many investors just use a standard real estate contract, found in many stationery stores, in order to sign the deal. Others wish to use attorneys to make sure everything is properly done. You'll either have to do a title search yourself or have an attorney do it for you, for a fee.

This procedure does require that you be prepared to cover many of the homeowner's legal expenses. You'll have to pay the principal and interest on the past due mortgage payments, late fees, additional interest on a per diem basis on the loan that is due, court costs and other related fees which the bank will require.

Also, you will have to pay an "assumption fee", usually 1% of the mortgage amount, sometimes as little as $250. On VA or FHA homes that have assumable mortgages, the assumption fee is about $45. You may have to re-apply with the bank for the mortgage and have a credit check done and be approved to purchase this home. Obviously, some banks don't want to go through the foreclosure process all over again, although they shouldn't mind since they are getting all their fees paid by you anyway.

If you're doing this for the very first time, you should contact a real estate attorney at some point before you sign the real estate contract.There may be various state and local laws about which you might not know. For instance, if you don't get this home in the "pre-foreclosure" stage, you may have to wait until it is formally foreclosed to buy it. At this point you'll have to pay more money and you may still lose it, as some states have redemption periods of 10 days or more for the owner to re-purchase the home from the bank.

In nearly all states you may have to do this work yourself. Here are the three documents you should look for in your research:

> • **CIVIL COVER SHEET:** This is the form required by the courts stating who is filing this case against whom. On it you'll see the bank's name and the homeowner's name.

> • **LIS PENDENS:** This means actions pending and tells you the name of the bank and the homeowner against whom the action is filed and for what reason this action is being filed. This will also give a legal description of the property.

> • **COMPLAINT:** This will give you the necessary information about the case, such as who owns this property, how much is past due (the balance due) at the time of the foreclosure filing, when the last payment was made and other information about the mortgage holders, including other liens and mortgages. Such complaints can be very short or run into hundreds of pages.

Some of the costs you are going to have to pay once you get the person to agree to practically give his home away to you are:

- Title searches
- Attorney fees
- Court costs
- Filing fees
- Interest owed
- Late charges
- Process servers
- Principal amount of loan due now

Estimates given to me have ranged between $1,500 and $3,000 additional monies due above the past due mortgage amount. Still a tremendous bargain over the normal 20% down payment cost.

If one doesn't want to search for this information, there are people who do this for you, for a hefty fee. If you are going to subscribe to such a service, you should be guaranteed that you'll receive this information on their listings:

- Case number
- Plaintiff
- Interest rate
- Original loan amount
- Property address
- Plaintiff's attorney
- Legal description
- Monthly payment
- When the last payment was made
- Defendant
- Attorney phone number
- Assessed value
- Original loan date
- Other liens and mortgages

One such service which our research team found is located in the Florida area is:

The Foreclosure Bureau
Sandi or Jerry Wilkinson
(305) 720-0526

They are friendly, helpful people who will answer your questions on the pre-foreclosure process and give you helpful tips about how to buy such real estate in the Florida area. They handle only Florida at this time but then Florida is a great place to buy real estate right now. With their listings you'll get a 120 day notice before property will be auctioned on the courthouse steps.

Can you find bargains or even great homes through the pre-foreclosure process? One man I know has bought about 80 homes in the New Jersey market, resold them for enormous profits or rented them profitably. Recently I heard about one person who picked up a $500,000 home in the booming Orlando housing market for only $225,000. Quite a bargain!

There are many states which don't have mortgages; they have trusts instead, which means the foreclosure process can start within 21 days. That causes a lot of panic and helps you get a deal faster, although you won't have the convenience you'll have with other states.

STATES WHICH HAVE MORTGAGES:

Alabama	Louisiana	Ohio
Arkansas	Maine	Oklahoma
Connecticut	Massachusetts	Pennsylvania
Delaware	Michigan	Rhode Island
Florida	Minnesota	South Carolina
Illinois	New Hampshire	South Dakota
Indiana	New Jersey	Vermont
Iowa	New Mexico	Washington
Kansas	New York	Wisconsin
Kentucky	North Dakota	Wyoming

STATES WHICH HAVE DEEDS OF TRUST OR SECURITY DEEDS:

Alaska	Idaho	Oregon
Arizona	Maryland	Tennessee
California	Mississippi	Texas
Colorado	Montana	Utah
Washington D.C.	Nebraska	Virginia
Georgia	Nevada	West Virginia
Hawaii	North Carolina	

Judicial Sales

A judicial sale is one where property is sold by the sheriff or, in some cases, the City or County Marshal, under the authority of a court's judgment and writ of execution in order to satisfy an unpaid judgment, mortgage, lien or other debt of the owner.

When a person has failed to pay their mortgage on time and it goes past the due date set by the bank and the foreclosure proceedings have gone through their course, the property, by order of the court, is put up for auction.

The office where this is done is usually the sheriff's, unless he has it auctioned through a private auctioneer. You can either contact your courthouse to look for judgments against the types of properties you are looking for or you can contact your sheriff and send him self-addressed, stamped envelopes to be returned to you with fliers. Sometimes they'll advertise in newspapers or just post notices.

As mentioned in the tax sale sub-section earlier, some states do have redemption periods for those who wish to buy back their properties. Many sheriffs interviewed claim that once it's sold, the person rarely buys the property back.

THOSE STATES WITH JUDICIAL SALES ON FORECLOSED PROPERTY:

Delaware	Louisiana	Ohio
Florida	Montana	Oklahoma
Illinois	Nebraska	Pennsylvania
Indiana	New Jersey	South Carolina
Iowa	New Mexico	Utah
Kansas	New York	Washington
Kentucky	North Dakota	

In **Section Three** you'll find a listing of many local sheriffs which you can contact about these sales. You can also locate them by contacting the particular county where you want property and calling the local sheriff.

Power of Sale

This is a variation on the judicial sale. Its one primary difference is that the lender need not go through the court system. Most of the states which use the Trust Deed, as opposed to the Mortgage, will use Power of Sale and also not have a redemption period. This, of course, varies from state to state.

A Power of Sale is a clause inserted into the mortgage or trust deed which gives the lender or trustee the right and power, on default in the payment of the secured debt, to advertise and sell the mortgaged property at public auction without resorting to the court's authority. When this is done, the lender or trustee will pay the creditor from the sale of the house, convey the deed to the purchaser and return the surplus, if any at the sale, to the mortgagor. In most cases the mortgagor will lose all rights of redemption, with the exception of a few states: Alabama, Arkansas, Colorado, Michigan, Minnesota, Missouri, South Dakota and Wyoming.

These sales are often done by private auctioneers. You can contact local auctioneers from your phone book and find out from them when there will be auctions. In many cases the banks will be holding on to these properties as REOs (discussed earlier), or they can be done by sheriffs.

STATES WITH "POWER OF SALE:"

Alabama	Massachusetts	Rhode Island
Alaska	Michigan	South Dakota
Arkansas	Minnesota	Tennessee
California	Mississippi	Texas
Colorado	Missouri	Virginia
Washington D.C.	Nevada	West Virginia
Georgia	New Hampshire	Wisconsin
Hawaii	North Carolina	Wyoming
Maryland	Oregon	

Conclusion

I hope I've apprised you of the existing real estate market condition in this country. There is a surplus of homes on the market in many areas which can be obtained by using non-traditional methods. Many people who can't afford down payments or the high cost of housing in some regions can still use these methods.

Your goal should be first to buy a home for yourself using one of these methods, either as a first-time home, as a second home or a vacation home. After you've found something you're happy with, then you can move into the investment stage and begin accumulating property for your personal real estate portfolio. Many of our multi-millionaires and billionaires have made their fortunes in real estate. Many very well-to-do people have done so as well. These leads you are being provided with do require a lot of work. Much of the research and ground-breaking has been done for you. You must still read **Section Two** so that you can be forewarned of many of the pitfalls which can harm you.

If you wish to turn now to **Section Three** to begin accumulating literature, fliers and catalogs, please feel free to do so. But don't forget also to read **Section Two** so that you get more knowledge under your belt before going to an auction.

SECTION TWO

INTRODUCTION

Now that you understand the various government agencies which have auctions and what you might expect from them, I want you to carefully study this section before proceeding. It's very important that you understand the auction procedure and what may be expected from you. In this section you'll learn all about auctions; you'll get tips on how to succeed at auctions and you'll learn about financing methods for your purchases, both traditional and non-traditional sources.

The research team has made every effort to get tips on auctions and financing from auctioneers and from various government agencies. Nothing that we will provide for you is guesswork but is, in fact, actual experience. For your own protection, I recommend you use an attorney when purchasing real estate. There are various local laws, state laws and other idiosyncrasies for each area of the country. Preparation is nearly always the key to success.

In many, many cases you will be required to pay cash for an auction purchase or use certified checks, money orders or some other similar instrument requiring immediate payment. While this seems like a disadvantage - and it might even seem far simpler than merely buying something at the retail price and obtaining bank financing - keep in mind that all the other auction-goers and participants are under this very same disadvantage. The Financing Section is especially valuable to many who do not have immediate cash, as well as those who do have cash or access to it.

Please study the rules for auction-goers detailed in this section. You must read and understand these rules to prevent a disappointment or a tragedy at an auction. It summarizes the important points of your participation at an auction: what to prevent, what to do and what to avoid doing.

How Do the Auctions Work?

"The buyer needs a hundred eyes, the seller, not one."
--George Herbert

Auction History

AUCTION SALE: A public sale to the highest bidder; the sale of real property or goods by public outcry and competition bidding. With the fall of the auctioneer's hammer, or some other customary manner of ending the bidding, the sale by auction is complete. (Barron's Law Dictionary, Second Edition)

Few auction-goers know that it was the Roman conquests which expanded the Roman Empire almost two thousand years ago that brought about the auction process. After legions of Roman soldiers conquered a new region to add to their empire, they looted the "spoils of war" from their victims. The ordinary Roman soldier would assemble the booty with his fellow soldiers into a bid pile. These soldiers were eager to convert their profits into gold and silver. So, they had auctions. It was during this time period where we got the word "auctions." Since Latin, not English, was the common language at the time, the process was called: "auctio sub hasta", which translates into "to increase under the spear". At one of these auctions they would have a spear thrust into the ground with parcels of goods and merchandise divided into lots and various citizens of Rome would bid on them.

At these first auctions, bids would increase until the highest bidder was found and thus was the first method for property disposal developed. The spear continued in use for a while and dwindled down until just a spear painted on a banner was left. At about that time, the Romans began using a block of stone called an "auction block". That's where we get today's term: "to put it on the block for auction".

Even the important command: "Don't lose your head at an auction" came about from these Roman auctions. Two bidders once made bids on the entire Roman Empire. This caused widespread panic and civil war. The new Emperor, the gentleman who paid the highest price, was actually decapitated shortly after that auction and his head put on a pike for all to see.

One of the biggest fears people have about attending auctions also dates back to the Romans. At one particular auction, Caligula (a wild and crazy Roman Emperor) had put property up for auction. The bidding was crowded and the auction had a party-like atmosphere about it, with a great deal of eating and drinking. One of the bidders drank far too much and was in a stupor, half awake and half gone. During this auction he had nodded his head while snoring at a fairly regular pace. The auctioneer had taken his head-nodding as acknowledgment of bids made. And when the man recovered he had bought Caligula's merchandise. Today, people have a morbid fear that if they wink or sneeze, they'll suddenly have bought and be responsible for paying for an expensive, unwanted item. In many of the art gallery auctions, participants will use hand and eye signals and other body motions to offer bids to the auctioneer - but those are generally pre-arranged and mainly fluff or intended to discourage others from discovering the identity of those one is bidding against. At most auctions this is just not the case, so don't worry.

Rules For Auction-Goers

These are brief reminders, based on actual experience, on what you should and should not do at an auction. Please follow them or risk the problems you might face by not following them.

- **NEVER** get "stuck" on an item that is up for auction or get carried away by your desire for that item and permit yourself to actually bid more than it is worth.

- **ALWAYS** inspect the merchandise, real estate, property, vehicle or equipment on which you are going to make your bid or offer of a price. If you do not feel competent to evaluate its condition, then find someone who can. Otherwise, do not make a bid.

- **NEVER** go beyond a set limit for a bid. Set your limit based on data or information. You may get an evaluation of what the item is worth from a list (such as a Blue Book) or from one of the auction-goers who is a professional.

- **REMEMBER** that the auctioneer is a salesman. He is getting his commission on what he sells you. It is his job to get the price as high as he can.

- **NEVER, NEVER, NEVER** make a bid at your first auction unless it is so ridiculously low that you would walk off with the "bargain of a lifetime". Do not bid at your first auction after others have started bidding or come into that first auction to bid after a lull in the auction bidding and make a bid.

• **ALWAYS** go to several different auctions before buying an item. There are so many, many auctions going on in America and the one you are currently attending will not be your last.

• **ALWAYS** bring cash, money orders or certified checks to an auction on which you are going to make a purchase. Call ahead and find out what requirements there are for financing and removal of merchandise. Be prepared for each of those activities when you are ready to make your auction purchase.

• **ALWAYS** remember that there is nearly always going to be a professional auction-goer (used car salesman, computer dealer, etc.) at these auctions and that you should use those people in any way you can to have them help you in your judgment of the merchandise.

• **ALWAYS** read the conditions of sale before making your bid. Before attending the auction find out as much about the merchandise as you can, even if it requires time and effort. If the auction is going to be a waste of time, don't go to it.

• **WHEN** in doubt, contact a professional who will help you determine the value of something or warn you about legal obstacles you may encounter.

• **ALWAYS** contact an attorney in purchasing real estate, if only for advice and protection.

CHAPTER 1

Types of Auctions

Types of Auctions

Oral Auction

This is public sale where the auction is done openly and sometimes loudly, by calling out or waving your hand or showing your bidder's card. This is competitive bidding by public outcry. It just means to cry out your bid. And you don't always have to yell, either.

The auctioneer will call out a bidding price, either through a microphone (with a P. A. system) or just use his own voice, depending on how large the crowd is. Items will be tagged or marked with numbers and generally be listed in a booklet.

While the auction is underway you might wish to scout out the various merchandise listed in the booklet or sheet of paper and determine which goods you wish to bid on. You might wish to discuss with other auction-goers the value of the merchandise up for auction or you might wish to follow the auction proceedings. Oral auctions can take anywhere from a few minutes (for real estate auctions which have only one property up for sale) up to several hours or all day at many of the larger auctions where numerous items are up for bid.

The auction bidding goes like this: "$75, 75, 75. Do I hear $80? 80? 80? This fine desk for only $80. 80? Thank-you. Do I hear 90? 90? 90? 90? Do I hear $90? This beautiful, hand-made desk is worth more than $90. Who wants it? Do I hear $90? No one is going to bid $90? OK, Sold for $80 to Number 29!" The patter of the auctioneer is usually sped-up faster than you can read the above and may sound incomprehensible. But it isn't. If you spend a bit of time just concentrating on the auctioneer's voice and words, you'll come to understand the important words or numbers he's voicing.

Now, at these auctions you'll generally have a bidder's card assigned to you when you register. You may, however, at postal auctions and a few others, be given a bidding paddle to use with a number on it. The bidder's card is used solely for identification purposes. When the auctioneer sells you the tagged merchandise, his assistant will then note your number down on a list opposite the item's ID number. That will identify you as the purchaser when you go to pay for your item. Do not lose your bidder's card or casually toss it out after you've left the auction (if the auction is still under way) because someone could use that bidder's number to bid on other merchandise. It may not be valid but it could cause you an unnecessary headache.

Spot Bid Auctions

Spot bid auctions are very similar to public, oral auctions. A spot bid is also a public auction but it is not oral. The competitive bidding is done in secret and in writing. You do not call out your bid to the auctioneer and you do not know what your competitors are going to bid. There is no upward bidding.

At these auctions you will be given forms or order forms to fill out. You'll get one opportunity to write down your bid on the form, sign the form and turn it in. The auctioneer will gather up the forms and open them in public. The highest written bid accepted by the auctioneer will be the winning bid. Be certain you've given your written bid to the auctioneer or his assistant after making the bid. Those not received by the auctioneer may not be accepted.

Remember, you get only one opportunity to bid on each "lot" of merchandise. You cannot make multiple bids, you cannot increase the bid once the auctioneer has closed the bidding process nor can you offer a higher bid after the auctioneer has announced the winning bid.

When you register you will be given your forms and the brochure or booklet containing the listing of the items to be bid upon. At the registration you'll have to give them your name, address and telephone number. Some form of ID may be required to confirm your name and address, such as your driver's license. Once again, keep your bidder's card in your possession at all times while at the auction.

Be certain you sign your bid. If it turns out to be the winning bid and you haven't signed it, it will probably not be accepted by the auctioneer. Check your spot bidding card or form to review your bid and to ensure that you've signed it and filled out the required spaces.

Sealed Bid Auctions

These are trickiest of all auctions. Yet for many people who cannot attend an auction because of a lack of time or a distance being too great, it allows them to participate in auctions without attending. They are similar to the spot bid method in that you write down your bid. They are not voice bids. You get only one chance to make a bid. There are deadlines on these bids which are explained in the brochure you'll receive.

The most frequent type of sealed bid sales are those held by General Services Administration and the Defense Reutilization and Marketing Service. The IRS also has sealed bid auctions for seized property and

Department of the Treasury / Internal Revenue Service

Notice of

Public Auction Sale

Under the authority in Internal Revenue Code section 6331, the property described below has been seized for nonpayment of internal revenue taxes due from

_____ .

The property will be sold at public auction as provided by Internal Revenue Code section 6335 and related regulations.

Date of Sale: _____ 19_____

Time of Sale: _____ am

Place of Sale: Anthony J. Celebrezze Federal Building, 1240 East Ninth St., Cleveland, OH 44199
Room B-1

Title Offered: Only the right, title, and interest of _____ _____
in and to the property will be offered for sale. If requested, the Internal Revenue Service will furnish information about possible encumbrances, which may be useful in determining the value of the interest being sold (See the back of this form for further details.)

**Description
of Property:** Premises situated in the City of Parma, County of Cuyahoga and State of Ohio: And known as being Sublot No. 4733 in the H. A. Stahl Properties Co.'s Ridgewood Subdivision No. 6 of part of Original Parma Township Lot Nos. 13 and 20, Blake Tract as shown by the recorded plat in Volume 89 of Maps, Page 30 of Cuyahoga County Records and being 65 feet front on the Northerly side of Hollywood Drive and extending back of equal width 150 feet, as appears by said plat, be the same more or less, but subject to all legal highways. Permanent Parcel No.: 448-20-004

A single family, one story brick with three bedrooms. Has an unattached garage and basement. Lot size is 65 ft. wide by 150 ft. deep.

**Property may be
Inspected at:** _____

**Payment
Terms:**
☐ Full payment required on acceptance of highest bid
☒ Deferred payment as follows: 20% of the highest bid at the time of acceptance, with the balance by Noon on Monday, November 6, 1989.

**Form of
Payment:** All payments must be by cash, certified check, cashier's or treasurer's check or by a United States postal, bank, express, or telegraph money order. Make check or money order payable to the Internal Revenue Service.

Signature *S. Vuicich*	Name and Title *(Typed)* S. Vuicich, Revenue Officer	Date 09-18-89
Address for information About the Sale Internal Revenue Service, 2490 Lee Blvd., Rm. 246, Cleveland Hts., OH 44118		Phone 216-321-5549

Form **2434** (Rev. 3-84)

merchandise. Most of what is offered at these auctions is surplus merchandise.

Another use of the sealed bid method is done by the Department of Housing and Urban Development and the Veterans Administration on their real estate. HUD generally advertises their homes in the classified sections of the larger newspapers in most major cities. You would then be required to contact a real estate broker who handles these homes and has been approved by HUD and has the proper forms. Then, you'll have to make your bid through him. The Veterans Administration has a similar set-up but they generally advertise their listings in smaller ads.

As I mentioned earlier, the primary use you'll have for the sealed bid auction method is with government surplus. Such surplus auction information from the GSA will be sent to you on a regular basis in catalog form. You'll get a complete package of a pamphlet showing you the items up for auction, the location of the merchandise, from what agency this merchandise comes and a phone number and local contact (a custodian) so that you may inquire about the merchandise. You'll also get a "conditions of sale" and an order form, usually the last two pages in the booklet/pamphlet.

The pamphlet will also state on the front page (where your name and address appear) and on the order form, the deadline for the receipt of your sealed bid. You are usually given a few weeks to study the pamphlet, make your choice(s) on which item(s) you'd like to bid upon and mail it to the address given on the order form so that your bid will be accepted.

A great deal of the merchandise in these catalogs will be of no use to you. Some of the merchandise may state "repairs required" on it. Some of it may be just what you're looking for. Don't forget the United States government has millions of employees. Those employees utilize a vast wealth of equipment from our tax dollars and the quantity may include typewriters, computers, dental equipment or photo-developing equipment. The GSA's job is to dispose of it to the highest sealed bidder. The GSA has the right to withdraw the item or items if they feel the price is too low or not enough people bid on it.

If you wish to bid at a GSA auction using the sealed bid method, you'll ask for GSA FORM #3195 (Rev. 11-88). When you call, you may be told you have to apply first; they'll send you an application form. You may also ask to be put on the mailing list. If you do get on the mailing list, you'll be expected to bid at least once after having received five mailings or your name will be purged from their mailing list. I have gotten on several mailing lists from the GSA and not bid on those mailings without having had my name purged, so this warning may or may not be true.

What do you bid on an item? It's hard to say but here's one way you can find out what winning bids look like. When you get your first pamphlet, you could just bid the very least amount of money on the most expensive-looking item in the catalog and send in your bid. When you submit your bid, please include a letter requesting the "knock-down" prices of the items in the catalog or pamphlet and a self-addressed stamped envelope.

The "knock-down" prices are the prices actually paid by the winning bidders. This term, also known as the "hammer price", comes about from the tradition of the auctioneer hitting his hammer down to signify that bidding on that item is over and the last bid was the winning bid.

When you receive the "knock-down" prices from the GSA, you'll then be more able to determine exactly how great the bargains are (or aren't) with them or with any other auctioneer using this method. You may have to make a minimum bid. The IRS, in accepting sealed bids, demands that you include 20% or $200, when making such a bid. Others have varying practices or conditions which determine whether you include money or not and whether there is a minimum you must bid on an item. Read the order forms carefully and the conditions of sale as well.

Negotiated Sale

This may not always be available to you or the quantity of merchandise or property under these circumstances may make it prohibitive. At such a "non-auction", you simply make an offer to the seller (it may be a Bankruptcy Trustee, sheriff or some other official) to buy the merchandise or property at the price you wish to pay. In some cases, if the amount of merchandise happens to be clogging up the official's time and energy and even his capacity to unload the property, he or she may take you up on that offer. Giving a "low-ball" figure is not generally advised, unless you happen to be aware of the conditions under which this merchandise is going to be auctioned and it may not always work. For more information on this type of "auction", please continue in Chapter Three of this section.

CHAPTER 2

The Auction

The Auctioneer
Conditions of Sale
Shills

The Auction

Going to an auction can not only be a great bargain-hunting adventure but it can also be a wonderful way to meet people, trade stories, network, learn new ideas and generally just have fun. During the preview periods and even during the auctions, you'll be surprised to find how many people are willing to talk to you. Many auction-goers seem to go to see what the various items sell for. Others go as a way to spend a Saturday or Sunday afternoon. Still others hang out at auctions just to tell you how bad the bargains are or to complain about how much various items are being sold for. Many go completely uninformed of the value of the merchandise they are interested in and, as a result, pay far too much, more often than they should.

Most auctions you will be going to are generally friendly affairs, conducted by boisterous and amiable auctioneers. You'll probably see a few fellows fighting to "the death" over a particular piece of merchandise, trying to prove a point or simply desperate for that item. Be sure to stay out of debates like these as they usually result in higher than normal prices.

At several of the GSA auctions don't be surprised if you find participants booing and jeering the auctioneers. At some of those auctions the government auctioneer will start the minimum bid at far too high a price. Not everyone will take the advice of the crowd and usually the items are sold regardless of the higher price. Despite those auctions, most of the auctions you will attend will have very reasonable minimum bids and the crowd will be pleasant and have a high spirit of play.

The rule of thumb I've come up with as to friendly surroundings and participants is this: If the auction is being run by a professional auctioneer, it is more likely to be fun and organized than if a government employee is in charge. For example, Postal auctions are a great source of bargains and most auction-goers prefer them because of this. However, they are not well organized and are sometimes confusing.

Other auctions, like sheriff's sales, may not be at all pleasant even if a professional auctioneer runs it. At these auctions you are dealing with some one who has lost his house or other property and who may show up at the auction and display grief, bitterness or disappointment. While legally they have every right to match your bid or top it, the many sheriffs our research department spoke to said that nine out of ten times the home is sold to a new owner.

Car repossessions are handled in a more civilized manner. The bank either turns them over to a professional auctioneer who sells them or the banks maintain a storage area and accept sealed bids.

There are several different components of auctions which I advise you to study carefully before you go to your first auction. If you are familiar with the following information, you may save yourself a lot of heartache and money.

The Auctioneer

His entire role in the job is to get you involved, to get the last bid even higher and he'll use every trick he can to get the crowd under his control. Don't take it personally. He's just doing his job. Just as you would not believe every word coming out of the mouth of a real estate broker or used car salesman, why should you simply take his word that this 1987 Yugo is worth more than twice its resale value?

From the auctioneers I've seen, I trust them more than I would many other professionals. They're hard working, most are honest and nearly all require one form of certification or another to auction merchandise. And if the government contracts with them, either on the federal, state or local level, then they usually have earned a degree of trust in their profession.

The Auctioneer's Assistants

At nearly every auction you're going to attend you'll see people helping the auctioneer. When you register, you'll meet the assistants who log you in. They'll want to see proof of identity; usually a driver's license will suffice. They'll ask you for an address, either local or your home address, a phone number and, most importantly, how you plan to pay for the merchandise. They'll assign you a bidder's number and issue you a bidding card or a bidding paddle. They'll also fill out an index card for you so that you can be notified of future auctions and you will probably be sent numerous fliers and brochures concerning these later auctions.

When you register you should ask questions about payment and pick-up for the merchandise, whether or not there is a time limit of that day for pick-up or an extension of a few days.

There are two other types of assistants which you'll notice at auctions: Ringmen (spotters) and the record-keeper. Ringmen help the auctioneer by bringing out the bids. These are usually would-be auctioneers, who are getting their life experience by encouraging you to make bids. They are also in the crowd or in front of the crowd to spot bids for the auctioneer. These guys will shout out the bids for you, if you're shy or just wish to nod your head for them or raise a hand. They can stir up the crowd as well, which is part of their purpose. Don't let them get to you. That's easier said than done: the auctioneer may be several yards away but the spotter or ringman may be right next to you, asking you directly if you'd like to make a bid. If you don't want to bid, turn your back on him or simply look away. He'll move on to someone else.

The auctioneer's clerk or record-keeper logs the winning bids and the winning bidder's number along with the item sold. You may not even notice this person but he is there watching and listening, making sure the correct amount is recorded and getting the right bidder's number from the bidder's card or paddle.

After you've made the winning bid and your number has been logged, a runner will run that information back to the cashier. At many auctions the registrar will double as the cashier. You'll show your bidder's card and he will match up the bidder's number with the record-keeper's log. Often you can wait a short while before paying for your merchandise, as it takes time to get the information to the cashier.

Please determine, before you pay the cashier, how long a time you will be given to remove your merchandise. At some auctions you may be given a few days or up to two weeks to remove your purchase. However, at other auctions, if you don't remove your merchandise by a certain date or time, it may be reclaimed by the auctioneer or government agency. Leniency varies from auctioneer to auctioneer. The GSA, for instance, on various sealed bids specifies that the bidder must pay for the item within ten days of the award and must remove the merchandise within 20 days of the award.

Conditions of Sales

This is an often overlooked component of the auction by many novices. Veterans quickly scan through these conditions of sale immediately after registering to note any peculiarities or restrictions. It is usually a typed notice given to you with your pamphlet of merchandise-to-be-auctioned. Or it will be included with the sealed bid catalog. It is imperative you read this short notice.

The Conditions of Sale will tell you how you are expected to pay for your merchandise, warranties on the merchandise, if any, the auctioneer's "right to reserve" (to withdraw) property up for sale and the date for the removal of the merchandise. There are other types of information given on these sheets, which vary from auction to auction.

Even on the sealed bid forms, you'll notice conditions of sale that vary from region to region around the United States. On one recent notice a GSA sealed bid form gave two unusual restrictions:

- That cash would not be accepted nor personal or business checks. Instead they would accept Mastercard or Visa, certified checks, traveler's checks or money orders.
- That unless you arranged the appointment to pay before arriving, your payment would not be accepted.

Those are certainly different conditions from the usual ones in purchasing items at an auction. So please be careful to study these conditions prior to bidding. It can save you embarrassment or a financial loss.

Shills

You are not likely to find these people at most auctions but in the event such people are there, let's discuss them briefly. A shill is someone hired by the auctioneer to lace the auction process with false bids. Such a person is there to stir things up, to get prices higher; he never really buys anything. Most auctioneers do not hire such people. Others do and their presence brings an uneasy feeling to the bidding.

If you find yourself bidding on something against someone who just keeps raising the price, quickly look around you and see if that person is receiving signals from someone, signals such as a nod, a wave or some other sudden movement. He may or may not be a legitimate bidder. It might be difficult to tell. Such bidders can be very good actors. If you feel you're bidding against someone like that, just stop.

One way to catch shills, and I'm sure you can think of others, is simply "change your mind". Let's say you made the winning bid and you feel you've been taken. Just announce to the auctioneer and the crowd: "I'm sorry. I made a mistake. I don't want this." See what happens. If the "shill" also backs out, you've got your man. If he buys the merchandise and is quite excited, he probably is not a shill. If he merely accepts his merchandise or reluctantly does so, he may quickly be covering up for his "error", in which case the auctioneer will sell this stuff at another time. In any event, this tactic can work for you, especially if you feel the merchandise you wanted went for far more than you wished to pay for it. Don't, on the other hand, overuse this tactic or you may find yourself unwelcome at various auctions.

CHAPTER 3

Types of Bids and Bidding Strategies

Types of Bids and Bidding Strategies

There are many specialized terms regarding bidding and types of auctions. Basically, they boil down to these two separate categories: auctions with minimum bids and auctions without minimum bids.

Because people will try to find loopholes or auctioneers wish to embellish their auctions, other terms have evolved. Although the greater part of this chapter will concentrate on definitions, you should study this chapter very carefully to avoid any confusion or upset at your first few auctions.

Minimum Bid

At these auctions, particularly GSA (General Services Administration) auctions, a minimum bid will be announced. This amount given is the least amount the auctioneer will accept as an offer. That is the floor. They don't wish to permit any offer less than that amount.

Bidding Strategy:

Sometimes, the bid may be very high, such as $3,000 minimum bid for a vehicle worth about $3,500. Other times, the minimum bid will be a very low amount to get the bidding started, such as $25 or $10 or even $1. If the minimum or opening bid is too high by your standards, just don't bid. However, you might try an alternative tactic: offer a low amount; if the auctioneer asks for $3,000, offer $1,000 or even $2,000. It might not always work but the auctioneer may accept it to get the bidding started. I once offered $100 on a Jaguar XJE, which eventually sold for $4,700 and the auctioneer accepted it. Someone raised my bid to $200 and the bidding got heavy from there.

Auction With Reserve

This means the auctioneer may withdraw the merchandise if the bidding does not reach the level he wishes. Such auctions must be labelled "auction with reserve" or "reserve auctions". Read your conditions of sale to be on the safe side. You may think you've gotten the highest bid, only to discover the auctioneer just won't accept it.

Bidding Strategy:

Try to find out what the "floor limit" is on the merchandise on which you plan to bid. Attempt to start the bidding at so low a price that when you reach the "reserve price", you won't have many bidders left to bid against. As you approach the lowest acceptable price, set the highest limit to which you will go and then drop out if you pass that limit. This is a very tricky maneuver - be certain to stick to your set limit or face the consequences.

Auction Without Reserve

This means that there may or may not be a minimum bid but that the auctioneer must accept the highest offer made to him. He may not withdraw the merchandise once the bidding has started, once it has gone above the minimum bid. "The Uniform Commercial Code retains the common law rule for sales 'without reserve' in that once the auctioneer calls for a bid, the article for sale cannot be withdrawn unless there is no bid within a reasonable time."

Bidding Strategy:

You may wish to retract your bid if you feel it has gone too high. Otherwise, it's a free-for-all. Determine your "set limit" and stick to it. If you've gone beyond it and your bid wins, then retract your bid or simply walk away (cover-up your bidding card as well). I've attended auctions where the winning bidder just left. It is not the most polite thing to do and you're not going to be welcome there again if they remember who you are but it does beat getting stuck with something you didn't really want at too high a price, doesn't it?

Upset Price

This is a variation on the "auction with reserve". This is the lowest accepted price at that particular auction, generally a sheriff sale, bankruptcy sale or real estate auction. You must go beyond that price to purchase the merchandise or property. Here's a legal definition: "The price at which any subject, as lands or goods, is exposed to sale by auction, below which it is not to be sold. In a final decree in foreclosure, the decree should name an upset price large enough to cover costs and all allowances made by the court, receiver's certificates and interest, liens prior to the bonds, amounts diverted from the earnings and all undetermined claims which will be settled before the confirmation and sale." (Black's Law Dictionary, Fifth Edition).

The auctioneer will announce the upset price or you'll find it in your brochure. Auctions with upset prices as noted in the above definition, particularly having to do with real estate, do require the use of an attorney. I would rather you be absolutely protected in these matters and an attorney's fee is inexpensive compared to the headaches you may later get from not having had one. Prevention is the best medicine at these auctions.

Absolute Auction

There is no minimum bid. There is no reserve or upset price. The highest bidder gets the property or merchandise. At some auctions, advertised in the newspapers as "absolute auctions", you may find one to ten properties auctioned at the absolute price. Those auctioneers use those properties as a come-on to get a crowd there for the other properties which will have minimum bids. Sheriff sales may really be absolute auctions on real estate with minimum bids of $1 or $25 on a house but there may be liens against that property which have not been disclosed, so beware of that problem.

If you are ever fortunate enough to attend a truly absolute auction and there are very few bidders there, then count yourself very lucky indeed. At those auctions, unless someone corners the market (and it can happen) you may find yourself with that bargain of a lifetime.

Bidding Strategy:

Look for "absolute auctions". Call the number listed for more information and find out how much of it is really absolute, how well it has been promoted and then determine if you wish to go. Don't buy merchandise you don't really want or need just because you can get it at an incredible or fantastically low price. And if you do, then you're not that bad off, as you can probably unload it at a profit to someone who does need it.

Forced Sale

Also known as a judicial sale. This comes about when a court of law forces the sale through a judicial decree. This means that the party involved must make an immediate sale by finding, without time or opportunity, a buyer who will pay a price representing a sum approaching the reasonable value of the property. The key word here is "reasonable". That could mean 70% off as in many bankruptcy sales or sheriff sales. It could mean $3 for all the live pets in a pet store which one auctioneer told me about. It could mean $15 for a home worth over $150,000 at a sheriff's sale in an Atlanta suburb several years back. "Reasonable" is another one of those wonderful words which can mean anything. Another similar phrase which the GSA uses to protect its backside is "fair market value". This word is defined by The Dictionary of Business Terms (Second Edition) as "a value arrived at by bargaining between informed buyers and sellers". It could be any conceivable sum under the sun. And it has been. Let's put the shoe on the other foot: At some GSA auctions, buyers have been known to pay well above market value - say $12,000 or more on a $10,000 vehicle. Is that fair market value?

Bidding Strategy:

At a forced sale, consult your attorney for any advice as there may be state and local laws covering these sales, particularly with regard to liens or other holds against the property. If you get the go ahead, pray that there are few bidders or even auction-goers at this type of auction. It can be a bonanza to you under these conditions.

No Minimum Bid

This means there is no floor limit. You can bid anything your heart desires. One person bought chairs at an auction in Seattle several months ago for as little as 53¢. I've picked up a $250 desk for $45 at these types of auctions. Many auctions are held with no minimum bids and it's the auctioneer's job to get those prices up to a realistic final price. Sometimes, the auctioneer doesn't get lucky.

Negotiated Sale

As stated in Chapter Two, these types of auctions really aren't auctions, in that there is no competitive bidding. You simply contact the person in charge of the merchandise and offer to buy the items or real estate at a fixed price. The trustee or sheriff, because of an overload, may simply accept your offer or ask around for a better offer. There are points in your favor: the seller, creditor or the person-in-charge may not want to go to the expense of an auction. Auctions can cost money in promotion, commissions and so forth. And people who are over-burdened would like a quick end to something they don't really want. If you offer between 10% and 25% below market value or lower if the circumstances warrant it, your bid may stand a good chance of being accepted.

Bidding Strategy:

Locate sheriff's offices, bankruptcy trustees (especially in areas where there is a high amount of business failures) and ask for the person in charge of the auction. Inquire as to what merchandise is available. Research it where possible. Compare that merchandise with similar merchandise or property. Make an offer. If it is refused, you may wish to follow it with a written offer sent by certified mail. If that fails, try again.

Auctions Subject to Court Confirmation

Some auctions, such as bankruptcy auctions (or even judicial sales) may require court confirmation before your offer is accepted. Once again, be sure to read your conditions of sale in order to determine your set price and your participation on that particular auction.

Subject to Seller's Approval

This may be implicit or explicit. At various Marshal's Sales (whereas the Marshal orders the merchandise sold at an auction by a private auctioneer), the Marshal may have a "Subject to Seller's Approval" clause inserted in the conditions of sale. That prevents some auctioneers dumping the merchandise at low-ball prices in order to move onto the more glamorous inventory. Keep in mind that at many private auctions, there may be government-seized merchandise available. Usually auctioneers will offer those items first and, if the auction is slow to get underway, those items may be "sold" at lower prices to get the auction moving. Or the auctioneer will entice the crowd by quickly dumping those items, knowing they might not get seller's approval at those prices, to get his audience excited and involved.

Bidding Strategy:

Go ahead and bid low. If you win the merchandise at a very low price and it doesn't get seller's approval, you won't lose anything except the thrill of victory. And the seller may have other headaches going on at that time - such as storage costs on that vehicle or merchandise - and really just accepts the bid to rid himself of it or a clerk will slip it by his boss. One man DID buy a $50,000 fishing boat in February, 1989, by offering a "joke bid" of $10. It was accepted. To protect yourself from the trauma of winning a low bid and getting struck by the disappointment of a seller's rejection of your low bid, read the conditions of sale. Sometimes, there is no seller's approval clause at those auctions.

Important Bidding Strategies

There are a few different methods you can use to protect yourself at an auction. Because many auctions are attended by professionals (or bid on by professionals through sealed bids), you can use their expertise to your advantage.

Professionals

At an oral, public auction, look for the professionals. They may be used-car dealers at car auctions, computer dealers at computer auctions and so forth. At these auctions you may find they have NADA Used Car books (also known as Blue Books) which give the retail, resale and loan value of the vehicle. It seems that each profession has its own guide for appraising merchandise. At this public auction, pay attention to how the professional bids. Often he will drop out of the bidding when the price has gone too high in his estimation. At that point, you should offer a small amount more: for instance, if the auctioneer asks for a $100 increasing bid, offer $25 instead; the auctioneer asks for $1,100, you counter with $1,025. If nothing else this will at least slow down the bidding process. The professional has his own set limit. It may have been determined because his mechanic told him it would cost "X" amount to repair and he figured that into his final figure *or* he decided on that limit because he wanted to make a certain amount of profit on that particular vehicle. In many, many cases the pro will drop out if he believes you will definitely pay $25 more on whatever he's going to bid.

With this method you have the positive angle of using the car dealer's expertise, experience or his assistant's appraisal. The slight drawback is that the car dealer, if enough people use this technique, will take the bids higher just to get even. And, of course, you can cancel your bid and let him pay the higher amount you brought him up to. Another drawback is that many people using this same method against each other can force the price of the vehicle to an unrealistic level.

Sealed Bids

With sealed bids, if there are regular sealed bid auctions on which you will bid again and again, you might try the method described in Chapter One of the Section. That's where you obtain the knockdown sheet on that sealed bid auction by making a very small minimum bid and including a self-addressed, stamped envelope. Once you determine how much merchandise sells for at those particular auctions, you can then evaluate how much you plan to bid in the future.

If there is a tie in the bids you may want to write your bid in this way: $500 (your bid) +$1. Yours wins since you will pay $1 more than the bid. If the person bidding against you goes higher, you've obviously lost, so this doesn't always work.

Hand Signals

Hand signals are important at auctions and from them you can evolve a minor but important, tactic. Generally, the most frequent hand signal used is raising one's hand or bidder's card to acknowledge the auctioneer's asking price for the item. Most people automatically just raise their hands and take the auctioneer's offering price. However, by simply running your hand horizontally in front of you in a sideways, chopping motion, you can make a bid of one half the increase the auctioneer wishes to get. Example: If the bidding is jumping by a $100 each time, making that motion is an offer of $50 more instead of a $100 increase. In some cases the auctioneer will ignore this motion, particularly when the bidding is fast and furious. You may only be able to use this hand motion in the latter part of the auction when it has slowed down. If the auctioneer ignores your bid, then just shout out the amount: If he asks for $1,500 and the last accepted bid was $1,400, you can shout out $1,450 (or even $1,425).

Using the hand signals shows the auctioneer that you've been to an auction before and that you're a likely buyer, so you stand a good chance of being taken seriously. Additionally, if you can use this hand signal method throughout the greater part of the auction, it will slow the auction bidding to a less hectic pace - something the auctioneer dislikes having, as a rapidly moving auction usually gets higher prices. Try this out. It might save you money.

Auction Fever and Setting Your Limit

Once the auction gets underway and the bidding is fast and furious, many people throw caution to the wind. It's like acting on the stage your first time or facing a baseball pitcher - you can get butterflies. Being in the spotlight with a crowd watching you puts you at a disadvantage. Don't think the auctioneer doesn't know that and don't think the auctioneer won't use that advantage against you.

There are basically two things you can do wrong at an auction. You can pay too much or you can "choke" and never get started. If you get auction fever and get carried away, you can pay too much. If you never overcome your fear of overpaying on an item, you'll never get started.

By carefully sticking to your "set limit" (the amount you set and decide to never go past no matter what happens), you can avoid getting caught up in auction fever. By being absolutely certain you won't get caught up in auction fever and by preparing yourself with the information and advice you have read thus far (and what follows in Chapter Four), you can overcome your fear of "choking".

Keep in mind that whenever you do something new you may either make a number of mistakes or be self-conscious that you are going to make mistakes. To avoid getting trapped into an unwanted situation, please, please do not attempt to buy anything at your very first auction. Use it as an experiment, a way to observe and scout out how the professionals go about buying at an auction. When you decide to buy at an auction, please make sure you have attended one or more.

Now, you may wish to bid at your first auction, just to get over the experience of making that "first bid". Please make a low-ball offer, even if it means a little humiliation at the hands of the auctioneer or some embarrassment. People have found incredible bargains just by making a low-ball bid. The crowd might become puzzled but no one has laughed at me yet for making a low-ball offer. Once you've made your first bid and gotten that out of the way, you'll feel a little more comfortable, perhaps you'll even feel so confident you'll jump into the bidding full steam. Don't do that. See how high your low-ball bid went and for how much the item or merchandise sold. Observe how many bidders jumped and how it finally concluded with two or three bidders working against themselves for a 'knockdown price". You may even notice a few people who made one-time bids in the middle of the bidding and dropped out. They might have been first-timers as well.

Once you've gotten your feet wet, you might try that again on the next item. You might pop in a quick bid right after someone else made an opening, low-ball bid - say one guy bid $25 on a car. You might counter with $30. Do this just to get the feel of it and drop out once the bidding gets underway. Do this a few times after you've seen a number of items get sold in this way. You'll see that often the items get more than a dozen bids and you'll get the pace of the auction. Then you can bid less cautiously and still not buy anything.

After you've bid on a number of items and feel how the auction is progressing, you can, at least, write this off as an educational experience. If the auction is sloppily conducted or there is excess merchandise, you might even stick around and pick something up at a bargain price. At the very worst, you'll be more prepared for your next auction and have gained a little courage, a little experience and a pace on how to make bids on items. Nothing you can read in this book can act as a substitute for actual auction experience. Go to an auction and see what I mean by that.

Beginnings and Endings

For some strange reason I have noticed that the beginning and the ending of an auction often have better deals found than the greater bulk of the auction, the middle and longer part of it.

Common sense tends to dictate that one would find some speculative and high bidding at the beginning of the auction. On the other hand, the last part of the auction seems to afford those with a last chance to "just buy something" so the person wouldn't think he wasted time by going to the auction.

However, I have found that, except for auctions which sell junk at the very beginning, you are more likely to find a great bargain at the very beginning of an auction than in nearly any other part of it. People who go to their first auction are naturally frightened. On that same principle, people going to a particular auction may at first be disoriented by unfamiliar surroundings and by the auctioneer himself; therefore, they may hesitate in making a bid. If you notice any great reluctance to bid and you see something you really like, toss in a low-ball bid. There may be hesitation from the crowd, the auctioneer might not like it and you could walk off with a great bargain.

Similarly, at the end of the auction, much of the merchandise may have been sold and many of the auction-goers gone home. If there is still something at that auction you would like to purchase, you might also try the same technique as at the beginning of the auction. And you may find many participants already bored or simply so exhausted by the auction that you can walk off with a bargain.

That doesn't mean you should avoid bidding in the middle of the auction. You probably won't find the bargain-of-a-lifetime but you can still find a great deal. Sometimes, after a number of vehicles have been sold, you might see one car or boat that just doesn't get a lot of bidding or the struggle upward to that final price is difficult . At that time, unless you are bidding on a real goat (or it has exceeded its resale value) you might just drop in a final bid. I saw that happen at a particular vehicle auction. There was a tremendous struggle on the bidding and the auctioneer was fighting to get the vehicle to sell at a realistic (by his standards) price. One man popped in a final bid $200 above what others were willing to pay and bought a vehicle at more than 50% below Blue Book value while knocking out the competition.

At that very same auction, another gentleman found himself with an incredible bargain on a car he didn't want. Since he didn't have the sense to appreciate his great bargain, he left the auction. After about 20 more cars were sold and the auction-goers had the pace and feel of the auction, this very same car was put up for auction again. Previously the buyer had practically no competition and the car went for $1,100. In this second round the bidding was fast and furious, with several bidders competing and the winning bidder took the car for $1,900! Just an hour earlier he could have had it for better than 40% less.

Once the auction participants see that others are buying, then they'll assume it's safe for them to buy as well. In fact, at this very same auction (the bankruptcy of an auto dealer) bidders were so comfortable with the auctioneer they were suckered into paying more for the show-room models than the dealer himself had tried to sell them for a week earlier with expensive half-page newspaper advertising.

At a different auction, for computer dealers, I saw computers sold with quite a few bidders. However, when they got to the typewriters, very good ones, indeed, those sold for 50% of their retail value with only one or two bidders, as most of the participants had gone home.

Remember to be observant at the beginnings and endings of auctions. If the participants are slow to bid, jump in and get a bargain. When most have gone home, stick around and pick up the bargains that remain. Obviously, if the auction is nearly over and many still remain, they're also going to want to buy something, simply for having spent the time of being at the auction - they want something to show for it. Don't get caught in that trap and find yourself paying more than your set limit.

If you're going to be a professional at this game, you had better assume that frame of mind. The next chapter will also help you prepare for that.

Important Warning

This is a notice that has been circulated by the National Auctioneers Association. Please do not violate it. I have warned you, so please heed the advice given.

Bid Rigging is a Felony

"Agreements among buyers not to bid against each other for the purpose of purchasing goods at low and non-competitive prices can be a criminal violation of the federal antitrust laws, punishable by heavy fines and imprisonment."

Section 1 of the Sherman Act (15 U.S.C. #1) prohibits bid-rigging agreements among competitors if they affect or restrain interstate commerce. Upon conviction, individuals are subject to a maximum fine of $250,000 and/or three years imprisonment. Corporations are subject to a maximum fine of at least $1 million.

If you notice some people, used car dealers (for example), participating in this, please report it to the auctioneer and any security officers (or law enforcement officials) on the premises.

CHAPTER 4

Preparing Yourself for an Auction

Preparing Yourself for an Auction
Using a Professional

Preparing Yourself for an Auction

The professional auction-goer, computer dealer, car dealer, boat dealer and others have a tremendous advantage over the novice. These veterans know exactly what to look for in what they are buying and can rapidly appraise that item or merchandise for a set limit price. Unless you are going to tag along with them for the rest of your life or get lucky on occasion and strike it rich by being the one bold bidder at that auction filled with other amateurs, you should begin preparing yourself to compete with the "big boys".

A very wise man once told me that the difference between a professional and the amateur is his tools and that pro's use of his tools. Every professional, whether an attorney or a plumber, has not only experience behind him but training manuals and guides and other "second-hand information" that got him to his professional status.

Of course, an attorney has experience and that's why you hire an attorney to protect you, defend you or act as a buffer for you. That attorney got his experience first by reading his law books. He studied them and was tested on what he read and finally got started as an attorney. In the beginning he apprenticed under a more experienced attorney. Slowly, he was given experience. Eventually he attained a status of being very good in his chosen profession. But he first read his book. He referred to various cases. Along the way he accumulated various guides to assist him.

The various books I am going to refer you to in this chapter are excellent reference guides or appraisal manuals that professionals use to evaluate price. You are going to compete with the pros so you had better find out what standard they are using to reach their set limit.

Vehicles

The most frequently used guide in appraising cars up for auction is the National Automobile Dealer Association Official Used Car Guide. It is a market report of used car values and is sold by annual subscription. You'll hear about this booklet from used car dealers, new car dealers, banks, finance companies and various professionals who buy and sell cars. You may not necessarily need this guide to attend your first few auctions but if you ever get serious about buying a number of vehicles for resale or profit and hope to make this a viable career, then you had better order this subscription for your region of the country. Their 1989 subscription rates are $35 for each region of the country you wish to use. Just one region is fine unless you are a seasoned traveler or automobile wholesaler. You'll get 12 issues each year. Their listings include used cars for model years 1982-1989. To order, you may call or write as follows:

NATIONAL AUTOMOBILE DEALERS
USED CAR GUIDE COMPANY
8400 Westpark Dr.
McLean, VA 22102-9985
(703) 821-7193

National Toll-Free Number
(outside Virginia): 1-800-544-6232
(Inside Virginia): 1-800-523-3110

If you're really going to be a seasoned professional at this, you should also order the Official Used Car Trade-In Guide which lists wholesale prices derived from Auto Auction Sales and they are classified by car condition. The subscription is $37.00 and you'll get an update every other Monday, 26 times throughout the year.

Other such publications sold by NADA include guides for older cars (those for model years 1972-1981) which is available by annual subscription for $40.00 and gives you an update every four months; a guide of Recreational Vehicles (RV Guide) which sells annually for $80, with updates every four months; a guide for Motorcycles, Snowmobiles, ATV and personal watercraft which is on annual subscription for $45, also with updates every four months; a Boat Guide for $80 annually with updates every four months and an Official Mobile Home Guide for $80, with updates every four months. As you can see they've covered major vehicular purchases fairly well.

Yet another source of appraisal information is MacLean Hunter Market Reports, Inc. They are another recognized authority on this subject and have been publishing since 1911. Their used car guide is called The Automobile Red Book and also comes in regional editions, published eight times per year. A subscription costs $47. You can contact them as follows:

MacLean Hunter Market Reports, Inc.
P.O. Box 6500
Chicago, IL 60608
(312) 726-2802

National Toll-Free Number: 1-800-621-9907
Fax Number: (312) 726-2574

They also have a Canadian Red Book which you may order by contacting their Canadian Sales Agent:

> Canadian Red Book
> Imants Grotans
> MacLean Hunter Bldg.
> 777 Bay St.
> Toronto, M5W 1A7, Ontario
> (416) 596-5082

MacLean Hunter Market Reports has a number of specialty books for professionals in several different categories. They also have an Older Car Red Book for those cars before 1981 model year, costing $63 annually with three updates, a Motorcycle Red Book, for over 40 different manufacturers for model years 1979-1989 (it costs $52 and you get one update), and a Recreational Vehicle Blue Book, costing $94 with two updates, covering 1979 forward.

Other categories you'll be able to find with Maclean Hunter are these:

- Farm Tractor Blue Book. Cost: $80 for one annual edition. Covering tractors from 1980 forward.

- Van Conversion Blue Book. Cost: $47 annually with three updates. Includes original retail prices and gives three different valuations: Finance Value, Retail Value and As-is Value.

- Truck Blue Book. Cost: $98 annually with three updates. Gives values for all models of heavy, medium and light-duty trucks from 1981 forward with regional values.

- Trucks Blue Book. Lease Guide. Cost: $57 annually with three updates. Gives value projections for medium and heavy duty trucks for lease contracts of 12 months to 60 months.

Such information can be expensive at first glance but, if you wish to pursue this line of work professionally, you have to have the materials a professional will use. The savings you'll get by being informed are far greater than purchasing blindly.

Computers

You probably haven't escaped the computer age. Around you various people of all ages are using computers. Most have bought their computers in retail outlets or through computer magazines. However, there are an increasing number of computer auctions going on throughout the United States. And it is to your advantage to attend such auctions if you are looking for computers at your office or for your home. Frequently, computers sold at suggested retail prices are worth about 50% less when used. The only book I've seen computer dealers refer to at computer auctions is <u>The Sybex Computer Blue Book</u>, patterned after the various vehicle Blue or Red Books.

In the Computer Blue Book you'll find out the suggested list price of various computers, monitors, terminals, printers, modems, software and peripherals. The United States is divided into four different regions, with some regions having a higher cost than others for the various computer components. The Blue Book will give a suggested list price, a wholesale price, retail prices in various regions and a used price. To order please write to the following address:

SYBEX ASSOCIATION OF COMPUTER DEALERS
14925 Memorial Dr., Bldg. A
Houston, TX 77079-9979
1-800-223-5264

An annual subscription will cost $15.95. You'll receive an update with your order during the year. The book will also list over 200 used computer stores and rental agencies and give you various manufacturers' addresses and phone numbers. Later in this chapter we'll discuss the importance of contacting a speciality store for advice before attending an auction.

Electronics Merchandise

At various auctions you'll get the opportunity to pick up assorted electronics items. Some are very inexpensive and others require research. For instance, one of our employees picked up a very nice and functional radio at a police auction for only $1. I have attended electronics auctions where I would not bid on certain high-priced items because I didn't have their value appraised for me. If you're going to be a successful expert, you should find the Blue Books for the area on which you wish to bid. Buying various items from time to time, if they are low-priced, doesn't pose much of a challenge but, if you wish to make a business or career of it, you should get as much of an edge as possible. Here are some suggested books or guides you can use for evaluating the prices of electronics equipment at auctions you may attend in the future:

- <u>Audio Blue Book</u>. Lists 33,000 products from over 1400 manufacturers. Comes in hardbound, 672 pages. The 1989 annual edition costs $125 and lists the following products: cassettes, compacts, 8-track and 4-track cartridges, digital audio discs, equalizers, integrated amplifiers, mixing boards, mobile citizen bands, pre-amplifiers, power amplifiers, raw speakers, receivers, reel-to-reels, scanners, signal processors, speakers, turntables, tuners and walkie-talkies.

- <u>Camera Blue Book</u>. Lists 14,750 products from over 400 manufacturers. Comes in hardbound, 290 pages. The 1989 annual edition costs $99.50 and lists nearly every item needed in the camera field from 35mm cameras, lenses, projectors, slide viewers, single 8 movie cameras, super 8 movie cameras and 36mm movie cameras.

- <u>Car Stereo Blue Book</u>. Lists 9,000 products from over 200 manufacturers. Comes in hardbound, 190 pages. The 1989 annual edition costs $49.50 and lists car cassettes, car digital audio disc players, car power amplifiers, car equalizers and car speakers.

- <u>Guitar and Musical Instruments Blue Book</u>. Lists 26,000 products from over 500 manufacturers. Comes in hardbound, 450 pages. The 1989 annual edition costs $79.50 and lists accordions, banjos, brass winds, cellos, cymbals, drums, dulcimers, electric guitars, acoustic guitars, harps, keyboards, mandolins, marimbas, synthesizers, violins, woodwinds and xylophones.

- <u>Professional Sound Blue Book</u>. Lists 12,000 products from over 500 manufacturers. Comes in hardbound, 200 pages. The 1989 annual edition costs $59.50 and lists all professional sound equipment.

- <u>Video and Television Blue Book</u>. Lists 14,000 video products from over 450 manufacturers. Comes in hardbound, 384 pages. The 1989 annual edition costs $99.50 and lists over 8,000 TVs, broadcast cameras, professional recorders, VHS recorders, camcorders, large screen projectors and everything you can imagine under this subject.

You can order these various price guides from a private publisher in Colorado. You'll have to add $5 per book for shipping and handling. The entire set is $572, which is an unrealistic price except for the seasoned veteran who expects to attend many, many auctions in the coming year and who needs such information to guarantee a maximum profit margin. For these materials or other questions you may have contact:

ORION RESEARCH CORPORATION
1315 Main Ave., Ste. 230
Durango, CO 81301
(303) 247-8855
Fax: (303) 247-9783

Coins

If you are an avid coin collector, you may find postal auctions and state unclaimed property auctions that may have coins to suit you. If you are apt to turn "pro" in this endeavor, your best bet for coin evaluations is the Handbook of United States Coins, which is a dealer buying guide. Be sure you don't purchase the Guidebook of United States Coins as that will give retail prices. You want to buy the book which will show you the prices dealers may wish to pay you for coins you'll buy at auction. Specifically, that is the 1989 Handbook of United States Coins, 46th Edition. This will contain mint records and prices paid by dealers for all U.S. coins from 1616 to the present year. You may order this book by sending $3.95 to:

Western Publishing Company, Inc.
Racine, WI 53404

If you are going to make a good career with coins you should subscribe to various numismatic publications which will keep you up-to-date on various practices and prices in the coin business.
Such publications include the following:

Coinage Magazine
2660 E. Main St.
Ventura, CA 93003

Coin World
P.O. Box 150
Sidney, OH 45365

Numismatic Coin Weekly
700 E. State Street
Iola, WI 54990

Coin Magazine
700 E. State Street
Iola, WI 54990

The Numismatist
818 N. Cascade Ave.
Colorado Springs, CO 80903
(This is probably your best selection as it is published monthly by American Numismatic Association

If you wish current retail prices of various U.S. Coins, you can send $6.95 to: Western Publishing Company, Inc., Racine, WI 53404 and ask for their 1989 A Guidebook of United States Coins.

Antiques and Collectibles

The most frequently used book on appraising collectibles and antiques is Kovel's Antique and Collectible Price List which is appraiser-approved and contains over 50,000 appraiser-approved prices. It is published annually by Crown Publishers, Inc., 225 Park Ave. S., New York, NY 10003. You should be able to find it in any major bookstore chain in the "antique" or "collectible" section. The cost is $10.95. Ralph and Terry Kovel also publish other major books in this area, including books on: Collector plates, figurines, depression glass and American dinnerware, American art pottery, country furniture, American silver, pewter and silverplate. Depending on your area of interest or career pursuit, please examine these books free of charge in your library or local bookstore before determining whether or not you wish to use them.

Using A Professional

Having the important appraisal guides is very important in evaluating prices of various items up for auction. However, there are certain areas where you absolutely need a professional to assist you.

For example, let's go over these two areas: buying a house and buying a vehicle. Does the house have liens on the property? Has a title search been done? What local restrictions must you avoid? Can you build on that property? Is the car a lemon? Will it emit blue smoke? Does it need a new transmission? New brakes? What kind of resale value does your property or vehicle have?

When you are ready to buy at an auction or house sale, these are some of the fears that might come to mind. Otherwise, you can make a painful and expensive mistake which will be difficult to undo.

Real Estate

Unless you have been handed the most incredible deal of a lifetime, you absolutely must consult with an attorney. There are certain legal words, encumbrances and liens, which can mean additional money out of your pocket unless a title search is done. How would you like to buy a house at an incredible bargain, say $15,000 complete on a $50,000 home, only to discover that there are liens for which you are now responsible in excess of $40,000! Is that unlikely? Not necessarily, not always but don't be the one to write me and say you weren't warned about this problem. Consulting with an attorney, preferably a real estate lawyer, may cost you less than $200, perhaps less than $100. You may not need to hire that lawyer to do a title search for you but you should at first, just to help you get a feeling for what paperwork or research is required. Later on, you may have the hang of it and can save yourself that expense. At the very least you should have a title search done on any property you are going to purchase - unless it is a bank repossession or unless you are personally guaranteed that your property has no encumbrances or liens upon it and that, if it does, the seller will then pay all debts or costs on relieving that debt, only if your attorney approves of that deal. This is not an area where you want to be casual or amateurish. Real estate fortunes have been made by those who buy low and sell dear. How about those people who have bought dear and got stuck with losses? How about those people who have attended sheriff sales and found that property, on which they have placed a deposit, now requires additional funds to remove the liens.

Title searches are not that hard to do. Primarily, you wish to find out if there are Lis Pendens on the property. A Lis Pendens is filed by a creditor to warn purchasers that there is soon to be a judgment action filed against that debtor and that particular property is likely to have a lien against it. When a person has reached the point of foreclosure, in this day and age, that person has also accumulated numerous other debts, including car loans, credit card debt, finance company debt and other unspeakable problems. If liens are placed against that property and, if it goes to public auction, you many inherit numerous headaches. Avoid them by finding out what problems there are by doing a title search. If you don't know what this means, get a professional real estate attorney to show you and explain all the local and state complications you are likely to encounter. At sheriff sales, which are a great source of bargains on real estate, you should be especially careful to follow the above advice.

There are two other types of professionals which you could use for various reasons. A real estate broker is very good, when he or she is not selling you, in providing you with information about the area, including rumors or political decisions which could affect your property's value. However, a real estate broker works on a commission and his decision could be influenced by the value of the property you are going to buy. A 6% commission on a $200,000 property is $12,000; the same commission on a $100,000 property is $6,000. You can buy a lot of groceries with $6,000. Remember that when listening to the next real estate broker's pitch. He is the seller's representative, not yours and he is trying to get a good price for the property.

Now, I've said the bad things about real estate brokers. Here's the good information. He may have inside information on local development in the area you wish to buy. For instance, there may be light industrial development permitted near your real estate, which is bad if you wish to live there or a nuclear power plant may be getting underway a few miles away or even a crematorium may be getting set up in the next few months a block away. It could be as little as the two-lane highway in front of your house that has been projected by the State Department of Transportation to be expanded to four-lane divided highway. Who knows? Your local real estate broker might.

You are not obligated to buy from him to get advice. You might ask him about a certain area. He might not know the answer but he is a good source of information. When you are buying a VA or HUD home or even a Fannie Mae home or bank repossession, you may have to go through a real estate broker. Then, the government or bank is paying his commission and possibly even your closing costs so it is worth your while to ask him any questions under the sun. You may even ask his estimate for renovations or other improvement-type questions. Use that person. It doesn't cost you a penny.

A third person to consult on real estate purchases is a contractor. In many cities there are people struggling in this occupation and hungry for work. You can hire such a person for a day after you've eliminated most of your potential real estate purchases and have this person examine the various properties you are considering.

Find out how much it's going to really cost to renovate the house or building. He may point out to you that you need a new roof or will need one in a year or that your basement is damp and the structure is termite-ridden. That will, of course, affect your bidding price. Such people can be hired for under $100 per day and you can ask them for estimates on repairing the house. Will it need minor repairs or a complete overhaul?

By using a professional who is skilled in that area, you can save yourself headaches at a later date. And it's all part of the bargain-hunting game. However, there are certain inspection points you can personally make. By making such an inspection you can help eliminate various undesirable properties by qualifying them. If that property doesn't "cut the mustard" with you on these points, then you'll have saved time and money spent with a professional, who is also likely to bring up these points as well.

<u>Inspection Points</u>

The Outside

1.   Is the property located near a toxic waste dump, an abandoned mine or quarry or a polluted lake, pond or river?

2.   What is the general noise level of the property? Is the house behind a freeway, thruway or interstate highway?

3.   What is the traffic level in front of the property?

4.   On what kind of terrain is the property? Does the land slope down toward the house, causing a potential for water damage?

5.   Find out from the police department the approximate crime level of that property's area.

6.   How near are various key elements of the community: shopping, public transportation, a fire station, recreational or cultural facilities, religious institutions or schools, hospital?

7.   How private is the property and what are the neighbors like?

8.   Is the property likely to be in a radon zone?

9.   Check the roof (shingles) and the gutters for maintenance and repair.

Once you've gone through the above list and if the property is still to your satisfaction, you can now investigate the interior of the property to determine whether or not you wish to purchase it.

The Interior

1.   Check for stains or peeling on the walls or ceiling for possible water damage.

2.   Does the house have lead-based paint? With HUD homes special arrangements have to be made when purchasing those.

3.   Check the basement for dampness. Check the attic for water leaks.

4.   Investigate for rodent or insect infestation. Check around doors for unsightly rot. Check the attic or darker areas for mice droppings, dead insects or other pests.

5.   Examine the ceilings and wallboards for workmanship. If you see seams between the sheet rock panels, then the spackling job may need to be redone.

6.   Look at the floors. Are they level? Solid? In need of repair?

7.   Make a list of repairs you observe while scouting around the house. Determine what changes you'll want or need to make if you purchase the house and approximate square footage of various areas in need of a paint job. You can then use this when contacting a contractor for a rough estimate of costs.

Now, some government homes on which you wish to bid are going to be fixer-uppers. In your area you may need to buy a fixer-upper because of escalating housing costs. However, you should have a rough idea of the costs involved before contacting a contractor for his estimate.

You may also need to have an electrician or plumber investigate your property to determine just how extensive the repairs are going to be. However expensive these estimates are, they are best not avoided at this stage. If you are permitted such investigations of the real estate and property, it is to your advantage to do them. You may lose $200-$300 in such costs but it would be better to find out this information before making your bid. This data can help you in placing your bid, as opposed to discovering *after* making the purchase that you are now going to have to spend an additional $15,000 to make your residence liveable.

Your last resort and one you should consider if you are especially new in this, is to use the services of a home inspector, whose fees are $100 or more. It is recommended that he be a member of the American Society of Home Inspectors, to avoid those people who may have a side business of recommending contractors to you after you've also paid them to help you. He may find damage or problems which your inexperienced eye has missed.

If you insist on evaluating and appraising the property yourself then get a professional home inspection manual. The best one I've seen on the subject is: <u>What's It Worth? A Home Inspection and Appraisal Manual</u> by Joseph V. Scaduto (published by TAB BOOKS). You can probably find this book in a large bookstore chain or your library. If you can't and wish to do home inspecting yourself or you're a do-it-yourselfer, then please order it from:

> Tab Books, Inc..
> Blue Ridge Summit, PA 17294-0214

The cost is $12.95 and it has over 230 pages. It contains a full home inspection worksheet which you can use from time to time in appraising homes and other properties.

<u>Vehicles</u>

It is very important to use a mechanic when you are previewing a vehicle up for auction. There are so many little mistakes you can make that add up to heartache and headache that even the best books you can read on the subject won't replace his expertise. In many cities and towns, you can hire a mechanic for $50 a day to assist you in attending an auction.

At many of the large auctions you can bring a mechanic along for just a few hours and have him scout through various vehicles with you and point out their defects. Of course, many vehicle auctions require that you buy the car "as-is, where-is". That simply means you can't test drive it. At some auctions, the auctioneer may point out the defects of the vehicle. But even that advice can't be trusted as he is not bound to buy back the vehicle after the hammer has come down.

There are several points to include on a checklist when previewing a vehicle. At various auctions you can have the car started up. They may even have it run for a while with the hood up. You might even have several experts make comments or jiggle with various components. These activities don't replace a mechanic.

<u>Inspection Points</u>

The Outside

1.   One of the very first things you can easily and should, examine is the paint job of the car you'll be trying to buy. This will give you an indication of the "character" of that car as left behind by the previous owner. A sloppy paint job is going to point out some history of that car.

There may be other things wrong with it. Inspect for these items to determine just how bad or good the paint job is: paint on the chrome or around the rubber moldings of the car or if the trim on the inside of the car door doesn't match the car's exterior and is entirely a different color. Your general rule of thumb is, just stay away from cars with a new paint job. If you can easily tell that the car just had a new paint job, it's probably hiding rust or some other defect.

2.   Just as you should beware the "sudden" paint job of this car, you should also look out for bodywork. Some people recommend a small magnet run around fenders and other areas of possible damage requiring repair work. You can determine metal from body filler with the magnet, because the magnet will adhere to the metal but not to the body filler. A simpler way, which you can use in a pinch, is to knock with your knuckles against the various areas and see if you get a hollow or a solid sound. If it's hollow, that's metal. If it's a solid sound, then it could be body filler.

3.   Looking under the car will not only show you rusted areas but you can also notice leaks (puddles on the ground). If you notice anything but clear water (from the air-conditioner), it could mean problems.

4.   Without even starting the car, you can observe several key problems with the car just by looking inside the tail pipe. If you've rubbed your finger on the inside and come away with a black and gummy slime, the car may need a ring or valve job. If it's black and sooty, you'll need a tune-up.

5.   Look around the car for rust problems: window moldings, door frames, inside the wheel wells. If it has severe rust, you may have a hard time re-selling it for a profit.

6.   Bounce the car. Once it starts bouncing, it should not do so more than once after you've stopped. If it does, you'll need new shocks.

7.   Tires. If the tires are not worn uniformly, then you'll have other replacements to make. A car that looks very old with brand new tires, is to be as seriously taken as a car with a brand-new paint job. Something is being withheld from you.

8.   Look through the window at the odometer. Multiply the age of the car by 12,000. A six-year-old car multiplied by 12,000 would equal 72,000 miles. If this car has an odometer reading of far less than the total you've just come up with, someone may have "adjusted" the odometer in his favor. The 56,000 miles on the odometer of that eight-year-old car may have been driven by "a little old lady who only took it to Church on Sunday" but more than likely someone has a friend who knows how to set back odometers.

At many police auctions you are not permitted to test drive the car but you can't even open the car and a locksmith has to be called in to open it for you and present you with brand-new keys. The above checklist will help you in those circumstances. If, however, the car is started up for you, there are other things you can look for which will help you determine a set limit price.

The Inside

1.   Look for tell-tale signs of rust once you open the doors. Take a peek at the bottom of the door frame. Look under the mats to see if the floorboards are weak (or even have holes in them).

2.   Open the door and move it up and down. Is it weak? Does that door drop or fall? It may have had an extra workout that isn't easily apparent, which you can use to lower your price or even complain about out loud.

3.   At some auctions they'll even start up the car for you. Look for two very important items: How easily does the car start up (a new starter, new battery), and what kind of smoke comes out when the guy floors it in Park or Neutral? (Blue smoke means engine problems).

4.   If possible, have the guy who starts up the car run it through the gears. If it "clunks" between gears in an automatic car, you may need transmission band adjustment or even a new transmission.

5.   Look at the car's engine while it's in idle. Is the motor shaking? It could need new motor mounts or some adjustments.

6.   Look at the fan belts. Do they have cracks or are they shredding? Are they loose?

7.   At some auctions you'll even find the hoods up for inspection. While the car is still cool, open the radiator cap and take a look. If the water is rusty, the radiator may need to be replaced. If you see a shiny oily film on the water, engine oil may be leaking into the cooling system. You could have a huge engine repair bill to contend with.

8.   After the car has been started and shut off and just before the bidding gets underway, pull out the dipstick and look at the oil. If it looks gummy or gritty, you may have a poorly maintained car. This may mean other problems. If the oil is milky brown or gray, there are expensive repairs forthcoming. If you notice a very thick oil, realize that some owners will use a heavier oil to quiet the valve lifters and cover up other engine problems. Be sure to bring rags or paper towels to these auctions for these inspections.

Be sure to have the above checklist used at auctions you'll be attending. There are numerous other problems one can encounter with a car. Not being able to test drive the car makes an auction purchase more difficult. You should use the above points as a yardstick to determine a set limit and your likelihood of bidding on that car! Buying a car at auction for 50% off Blue Book can be a disappointment if you then have to spend four times that amount to make it work.

If you wish a more detailed education on used cars I recommend the most thorough book on the subject, one that has been quoted extensively in various information books:

The Used Car Books by Jack Gillis
Harper & Row Publishers
10 E. 53rd St.
New York, NY 10022

It has 160 pages and costs $8.95. You'll find it in most bookstores or your local public library. You'll not only find all the important points one should look for in buying a used car but which used cars to avoid and why and various repair ratings. Jack Gillis has spent three years with the U.S. Department of Transportation and was responsible for developing the government's automotive information program. You may have seen him on various popular talk shows or quoted in numerous business publications.

Other Merchandise

If you are going to buy something at an auction, you should first ascertain what is going to be sold at a particular auction. You may find typewriters at a computer auction. You might find office furniture at at that same auction. You might find any number of various items at a bankruptcy auction or postal auction. If there is not a catalog or brochure you'll receive to review, then simply call the auction house or government agency which is having the auction and inquire. Ask about unusual items up for auction. Once you've discovered just what is going to be auctioned, here are a few hints and tips on gathering data to help you at your auction.

One of the fastest places to refer to for comparably priced auction merchandise is the household section, the office equipment section or other similar sections of your local newspaper's classified advertising section. So make a price-comparison on various items. If you know that office furniture is going to be auctioned off, scan through and find similar items in the classifieds that are being offered and at what prices. The same goes for practically anything that may be auctioned. You can also do this with automobiles, boats and real estate. It will give you a ball-park figure on which you can establish your set limit.

Call the professionals. If you are going to a jewelry or antique auction, call ahead to various antique stores or jewelry stores and find out if the market is weak or strong. Find out what is hot-selling, what is slow-selling and what there is a surplus of in that marketplace at that particular point in time. You can also do this with car dealers and boat shops.

When calling the professionals, find out about out-dated equipment, such as computers, typewriters and other office equipment. A few years ago a fax machine cost many thousands of dollars; now many sell for under a thousand. Find out what equipment has been discontinued and from what to stay away.

Contact pawnbrokers in your area and find out what they're overstocked with. These items might be good to avoid at an auction.

Go through the yellow pages and find someone who matches up with the specialty of the item you are seeking to purchase. If it's a slow period and you are friendly, he may give you a lesson or two about what to be on the look-out for or what not to purchase.

Go to your local library and flip through various consumer report magazines or studies to determine what is highly or poorly rated (call ahead and find out if they have them first). It seems that each profession has its own specialized magazine, also known as a trade paper or magazine. Find out what that magazine is and go through it. Accumulate as much data as you can from these sources as they may have the latest developments and can prepare you well for the auction.

If you have extra time or are making this a full-blown career, you should get the "books" on the subject. I have listed one for real estate and one for cars. There are others for every subject under the sun. For example, here are two different specialty books for appraising common auction items: jewelry and antiques/collectibles.

Gems and Jewelry Appraising:
Techniques of Professional Practice by Anna M. Miller.
Van Nostrand Reinhold
115 Fifth Ave.
New York, NY 10003

Schroeder's Antique Price Guide, 1989 Edition.
Collector's Books
P.O. Box 3009
Paducah, KY 42002-3009
(It costs $12.95, plus $2.00 postage)

Meet with your local librarian and ask his advice on which books are the best on the subject. Ask your local bookstore which ones are the best to use to get started in this area. Many have spent countless thousands of hours preparing you for expertise in each area. All it takes on your part is interest, ambition and a willingness to set aside several hours each week to learn about the subject.

You may not need all of this material to get started at an auction. Doing a few points will help you compete with the professionals in each area. However, if you do feel you can make a full-time career and enjoy dealing with certain items of merchandise, you need only find the tools to help you get started. Many have made profitable careers by just getting the basics. I hope I've helped point you in the right direction with this advice. It is by no means complete. It'll get you to the starting line and may even help you succeed where, before, you may have hesitated or failed. Please re-read those parts of this chapter where you felt confused or uncertain as it will help give you greater confidence when you next attend an auction.

The next chapter will give you financial information which you can use to help you buy your auction merchandise. Sit back and relax because we're going to talk for a while on a subject that nearly everyone on the planet is both interested in and worried about...money.

CHAPTER 5

Financing Your Auction Purchases

Ways of Raising Cash
Non-traditional Sources of Financing

Financing Your Auction Purchase

There aren't many people in this world who can easily purchase anything their heart desires with cash out of their savings account and continue to do so throughout their entire lifetime. If you feel you have all the money in the world and don't need to explore ways of raising finances, then please skip this chapter.

For those of us who must borrow, I've tried to seek and find as many financing techniques as one can use in raising money for an auction purchase. I hope this information helps you at auctions because you're going to need it.

At nearly every auction you will attend, aside from many real estate auctions, you're going to have to pay for the entire purchase with some form of cash vehicle: cash, money orders, traveler's checks, certified checks or something along those lines. That's not always easy to do, nor is it desirable for many of us who would like to pay in installments. Let's look over the obvious ways one can raise cash for auction purchases and then move into the more sophisticated, non-traditional sources of financing.

Ways of Raising Cash

Common Methods

Two of the most common methods by which people obtain cash are the most obvious. "Rainy day" funds are wise to have all of the time. You may have stored up money for something special. That's one way to find cash. Take it out of your savings account. The other way is to take a cash advance from your credit card(s). Many people in the United States seem to have as many as ten different credit cards. Some are up to their limit. Others have just had their limits raised. And still others are not being used. If you find a really great deal or opportunity, you can always take a cash advance and replace it if you don't make the auction purchase. Just be sure to avoid spending it on the way back to the bank simply because it's now in your hands.

Banks

In many cases a bank or finance company will lend you money through either a credit account, an outright loan for a certain amount of money or an overdraft on your checking. These are unsecured loans, which means you do not put up any collateral. Such loans generally charge several interest points more than the prime rate, which is used to determine the interest rate to the most credit worthy customers, usually major corporations. These loans are usually paid back over a period of one to five years. There are various companies that will advertise through the mail or in newspapers which will lend you various sums of money, on a three to five year basis, at very high interest rates. These all may be sources for you, depending on your financial condition.

Most people misunderstand bankers because bankers are so conservative in their lending practices. Not many borrowers understand that a lending officer has to contend with federal and state banking regulations, the bank's own policy on lending standards and the desire to control what they are lending out to you.

There are many different ways you can borrow money from a bank as an existing businessman. On the short-term, you can establish a line of credit with the bank which may be extended to you from 30 days to 2 years. There are various options on this with most requiring you to pay monthly installments on that line of credit. If you have an established business you may be eligible for an "inventory loan" which permits you to borrow against your inventory and pay the bank back as you sell the merchandise to consumers. Most banks recognize a 6-9 month period for such loans. Most businesses, for bookkeeping purposes, will take out a commercial loan which is repaid in one lump sum, after 3-6 months.

Also on the short-term, one could borrow money against his accounts receivables with either banks, finance companies or even factoring companies. It is one of the more difficult forms of financing but I have known friends in the NYC garment industry to use such loans to help them through their "cash-poor" stages.

There are also medium-term loans which are used to finance various fixed assets, such as office equipment, machinery and various tangible expansion plans for the business. Such loans are generally over five-year periods but in some cases they may be for longer stretches of time if the asset purchase has a longer useful life. You'll find banks will lend up to 80% or 90% of the amount needed. And repayment will be on a monthly or quarterly basis with varying sizes of payment schedules, depending upon your bank.

The hardest loans to get are long-term loans. Many want them, few get them. Those, in the past, who have been given these loans, used them to purchase real estate or hard assets for big plants. Realize that a bank will probably give you only about 70-75% of the appraised value of the real estate you wish to purchase or the asset you wish to obtain.

Because many banks are now saddled with foreclosed real estate properties, you'd think that such loans are impossible to obtain. Right? Wrong! Just this week someone approached me abut buying a foreclosed bank property which has a potential value of over $1 million in my area. The bank will loan up to 75% of the appraised value of that property to us to buy their own building back from them. They're appraising this building at $650,000 and selling it to us for less than $425,000, which means we'll make a profit just by buying this building from them!

Your job is easier if you already have assets to borrow against but that doesn't mean the door is closed to you if you don't. The SBA frequently loans money to those who don't have assets in the form of guarantees. It works this way: You find a local bank (of which there are 500) which participates in the SBA's Certification Program. If you are able to assemble partners and others who are willing to put money into your venture, the SBA may loan you the money on a term-loan basis. The one catch is that they'll guarantee up to 90% of the total amount. That means you'll have to raise 10% on your own, which isn't that hard a task if your idea is good and you've done your basic homework in order to convince others to work with you. It may mean delays and frustrations which is typical in these matters but even those can be overcome if you are persistent.

So, now, how do you borrow money from a bank? How can they trust you? The bank's primary tool in determining whether or not you will be loaned money is your loan proposal. Most people don't know the first thing about packaging this loan proposal and often just think dim thoughts about getting money from a bank. And when that fails they blame the bank or someone else. Here is your chance to write a correct loan proposal. It does not guarantee your success. It does, however, increase your chances to succeed in getting a loan approved. You may not be able to use it now. You may still not be approved, for various reasons, even if you do use it. However, it may get you started on the right road. And, with your banker's advice and other professional counseling, it may open the door to you more quickly than without it. Please use it.

Writing Your Loan Proposal

The first thing you're going to do is work backwards. Write your summary first and put it at the top of your proposal. Your summary should include these elements: Your name, title you hold in the company and the name of the company and the company's address, the amount you seek from the bank, what you plan to do with this money after you get it and how you plan to pay it back.

The next thing the bank is going to want to look at is you and your associates or partners. This should be done on a separate page which gives a profile on you and your management team. In a few brief paragraphs you have to show the bank who you and your partners are and why they should trust you. You should give a convincing background on your educational past, your current (or relevant past) experience, key skills that you possess related to this business venture, accomplishments or achievements that are noteworthy and your strengths. No matter how solid that venture looks to you, the bank is going to want to know how good you are in pulling off this project. Have you succeeded in similar endeavors in the past? Does your experience, education or skills show that you are capable of succeeding and repaying the money you plan to borrow or not? Do not go into an over-sell on this point. Do not list every high school or college award you've won. If you belonged to some national fraternity and you know the lending officer or member of the loan committee did also, then you might include that. But don't get carried away.

You're now going to have to give a business description of your company. How long have you been around? Is there a parent company which owns all the stock? Who are the board of directors? Who is your attorney? How many employees do you have? Does your company have any tangible, negotiable assets? What are you selling? To whom? What kinds of customers? Who are your competitors? What are you doing that's going to increase your market share from those competitors? What's the size of your inventory? How fast does the inventory turn over? Is there inventory which does not? Is it steady or just a fad? What do your accounts receivables look like? Are they more than 60 days old? Do you have many customers or just a few big ones you're living off? What kinds of liabilities do you have? How are you protected? Are you involved in any lawsuits, personally or corporately? These are the basic questions to which your banker must have the answers. Simply do a question and answer sheet and be specific. Give the banker solid, hard facts, not an opinion. Be thorough in your research and investigation for these answers. Don't just guess, as that is sloppy and a cursory investigation by the bank will catch your errors. Many businessmen fail simply because they don't have the answers to the above questions. They merely continue on in business until the cash dries up and ask: What happened? Better instead you should answer the above questions now for yourself, even if you aren't going to ask for a loan, as a minor safeguard in protecting your livelihood.

Once you've correctly described your business and its operations, you must now give projections. You should give at least two projections but not more than four, based on the following: You get no money from the bank - then what happens. You get the full amount you are requesting from the bank - here's what happens. You get half the amount you need from the bank - here's what happens.

You should describe your existing production. What is your current market share? For instance, does your garage service 20% of the business in the area or only 3%? How did you get to be that big? Or why are you still that small? If you have a taxicab company, how many cabs are there in your city? How many of those cabs do you own? It may only be 10-20 but that could be 10% of the cabs in your area. That's market share.

As part of your projections, you must show why you plan to grow. Would adding another 20 taxicabs just mean you've got 20 new empty taxicabs or will they be fully utilized? Answer *why* to that by showing there may likely be an increase in the population in the next 18 months. You might get research figures from your local newspaper or library showing that growth has been 15% annually for the past five years AND that growth is expected to continue or increase beyond that pace for the next ten years! There may have been articles written about it, newsletters promoting the areas, etc. All this should be part of your projections. Bankers are influenced by reputable projections. Such projections exist. Use the newspapers or libraries to find them.

Also, as part of your projections, you should show how you, personally, plan to take advantage of this growth. You'll have to show who is going to be your consumer and how you plan to satisfy that person's needs. For instance, you may have a new slant or "niche" discovered in the taxicab market: more older people are going to be coming into your area; the current service is geared toward yuppies; your company is going to market for the older people. This is not an easy task but if the amount of money involved is substantial, you are advised to do this step thoroughly.

You should include a page on what alternatives you are going to pursue if the bank does not loan you the money. Are you just going to give up? The bank wants to see your enthusiasm for this project, despite any economic cynicism or even a recession. How do you plan to grow without the money? At what pace? Will you fail without their money? These are questions which must be answered on this page. What happens if there is an economic downturn? Will people still come to this area? If so, how will that affect current projections?

Now comes the hardest and most unpleasant part. Without it being in order, no bank is likely to lend you money. You are going to have to gather up your balance sheets, tax forms and income statements for the past few years. Some banks will want to see two years; others will demand three years. When contacting your bank about making a loan proposal, ask them how many years of financials they wish to see. You should then make projections from those financials for the next 3-5 years. Ideally, you'll have a full audit done on those financials. Otherwise, have your accountant assemble unaudited financial statements on your past years.

At this time you are going to have to provide the bank with your tax returns for the past few years as well, along with the tax returns of any others signing on the loan. The bank is going to use these to run a credit check on you, as well as your company and look for discrepancies if any. Hopefully, there will not be any.

Please make your projections realistic. Everyone embarking on an entrepreneurial path, at one time or another, is convinced that he or she has got the panacea to that industry's problems or has filled the perfect niche on that market. One can get out of hand in their future projections. Banks will compare what your industry is likely to do. Exaggerations and hyperbole at this stage may label you as an unreliable character. Understate your projections and overestimate your costs to be on the safe side. The bank will probably do so in analyzing your loan request.

You have now accomplished the hard part, if you've reached this point at all. You've now faced the most difficult complexities in a loan proposal. The rest is downhill and so simple that many often overlook the most fundamental problems: the purpose of your loan, the exact amount of the loan needed and how you plan to repay this amount.

Many people in giving the purpose of their loan will just state: "to tide us over" OR "need working capital". Believe it or not, bankers have told me and others that these are probably the most often made requests. Another one is to "build up inventory". These are not the purposes your banker wants to hear. He wants specifics. You'll either make his job easier and speed up your loan request or you'll slow your request down until he gets his answers. Or he'll put you out of your misery and shoot the loan down. Give an exact use for your loan. "To buy used automobiles at public auction and put them on the road, after 'prepping', for use as taxicabs." If you've done your homework properly in the projections stage of the proposal, you'll have shown how the following ten cars with a Blue Book value of "X" amount sold for 50% less than that Blue Book value and that they required "y" amount in repairs and preparation to become serviceable taxicabs. Be certain you educate your banker at the projection stage and, again, at this stage. He'll have an increased confidence in you.

Once you've described your purpose fully and comfortably to him, you should give the exact amount you need. Don't fluff this up to an unrealistic level. If you need $19,876 for what you need, don't ask for $35,000 to be on the safe side. Bankers also go to auctions to buy cars, not just used car dealers. They'll ask around, find someone who's opinion they can trust and ask the right questions. If your amount is too high, you may be told this and advised to ask for less or explain yourself. If you lie at this stage, forget the loan. Remember that most bankers are well-educated, intelligent people. As lenders, it is their job to protect the bank's interests and their job as well. Don't assume you can easily fool the banker and the loan committee. Be specific and be exact. Give a breakdown on your loan amount, outlining where this loan money is going and to whom and when. That all helps in the final analysis.

This is the last leg in a long journey: repayment. How do you plan to repay this amount? Everything may look solid up to this stage but the lender is going to want to know how, exactly, he is getting his money back. Obviously, the asset is expected in some way or another to generate income so that you can repay the loan. The asset should last, at least, as long as the loan payment period; bankers expect it to last longer than that. And your projections must show how you plan to fit in the interest and principal payments. If you're running on a shoestring, you must show how cutting costs (in one way or another) is going to fit that repayment in *and* on time.

What happens if your company can't pay it back? Banks want an alternative. Since businesses fail at an alarming rate, bankers want some assurance from you or someone else that the loan will be repaid. You may be counting on that business; your banker is counting on getting the loan and interest repaid. In practically all loan cases I've had or known others to have had, a personal guarantee is going to be needed. You should be able to show what assets you have and be able to back it up in a personal guarantee. One person's signature may be worth $1 million on that personal loan guarantee; another's may be worth $5,000. If you can't personally guarantee the loan for the repayment amount, you'll have to find another to do that for you or with you. This is where friends, relatives and business associates come in.

Your lending officer is going to find ways to restructure the payment schedule, which may or may not be helpful to you. Your presentation of your financials and your projections will help in his decision-making. There are various ways to pay off a loan: equal monthly payments, which include principal and interest, graduated repayments over the loan period (with either escalating or decelerating payments of interest and principal), or even lump sum payments - often called a balloon payment - with either a regular schedule of interest payments along the way or interest and principal all at one time.

Here's the summary, plus advice at the end for your review:

- A summary of the loan proposal.
- Highlights of the management team's background and profiles of the members.
- A description of the business.

- Financial projections, with the research to back up those projections.
- Corporate and personal financial statements.
- An explanation of the exact purpose of the loan request.
- The exact amount of the loan requested.
- A suggested repayment schedule.

Please save yourself and the banker or lender a lot of time and tell the truth. Be honest about your business and your personal finances as well as your projections and cost estimates. The chief lending officer for small businesses in NYC (at one of the country's largest banks) once told me that they'll review the loan proposal and analyze it but before giving over the check, they'll want to inspect the business, just to be sure that everything connects properly. This may or may not happen to you. Be on the safe side and be completely honest in your dealings.

If you don't qualify, the bank may recommend other solutions for you, at that time or be helpful to you. If the lender feels you're running a con on him, you might not get that assistance. There are many other types of lenders other than banks. That person might more readily help you find them if you are friendly, honest and you ask about them.

Another pointer is this: Deposit with that bank. That bank may view you more surely if they feel you are already their customer. The lender may require you begin banking with them if they are ready to lend you the money. After all, you're practically partners in that venture and they wish to see the money coming through their accounts. And, if the occasion arises, it is easier to seize your company's money if it is already there.

Here is one last note on the loan application: Many businessmen don't understand that many of their "retail" banking outlets aren't prepared to process loan requests. You may just have the right bank but the wrong person. Please ask your local banker where their "small business loan division" is located. It may be at a different banking location in the same city than where you normally bank. Unless you've found the right division, you'll probably hear all kinds of stories like, "we don't lend money" or something similar to that. Be sure you get the right person in the division as well.

Mortgages

There have been for a number of years a financial instrument called the second mortgage. Now it's called a home equity loan. This is only valid if you already have a home and have built equity within it. However, if you are able to buy a VA-repossessed home, a HUD-repossessed home or a bank repossession, either directly from the bank or from FSLIC or Fannie Mae, you may be able to take out a home equity loan against the property, depending on how good a deal you got on the property. Home Equity Loans are often just above the prime rate since you've used your home as collateral with which to borrow the money.

Home Equity Loans

You, personally, may not be eligible for such a loan, because you do not have a home. However, you may have a parent or relative who is willing to participate for you. Banks have various requirements on their home equity loans. Generally, they want to lend between 70% and 80% of the home's appraised value minus the outstanding mortgage. With relatives who've owned homes for many years and have seen those homes appreciate greatly, this is an excellent way to raise cash. However, you do have to pay that money back. And if you are able to launch a worthy career (or buy an excellent piece of property at a great discount), then it may be to your advantage to do so.

Banks will ask for up-front fees, including points on the "second mortgage", and these will include applications, appraisals and title searches. On repayment, some will ask that you repay the money within five years while some will extend repayment up to 15 years. Repayment can be structured, in some cases, to either include interest and principal repayment during the life of the loan or interest payments only with the principal due at the end.

Be certain you are going to find an excellent auction opportunity before risking a relative's or friend's home in such a speculation.

This is not gambling; it is investing. Investing demands you be prudent in your decisions.

Friends and Relatives

This is a delicate way to borrow money. It requires salesmanship on your part and that salesmanship can be reinforced by your having previously gone to several auctions and discovered what great bargains can be found. Borrowing money from someone else, whether it is a bank or someone you know, requires confidence. And that confidence demands that you actually attend auctions and develop a comfort level at those auctions so that you can honestly persuade someone to lend you the money for such purposes. Many people borrow money from relatives or others in order to raise the down payment on a first home. However, in many cases, one, through proper research and hard work, could acquire various properties throughout the United States for very little down, in some cases as little as $100 down or even no money down. Such are the opportunities one can find through the government!

Some people have, in the past, suggested acknowledging a family member or friend's help by guaranteeing their loan to you with a U.S. Savings Bond. Since you buy the bond at 1/2 face value, the person after a period of time can redeem it for full value. The person would get the Bond and you would get the difference between the Bond's Face Value and the amount it cost you. You'd then keep half the amount of the money lent to you and the person would get the Bond as collateral.

However, you could also do the same financing with a "zero coupon bond". In this case you would buy a $1,000 bond for about $200 or less. The person would still have to wait until maturity to get their money back if your project failed. You would get to keep greater than half-dollar amount for yourself for use in your venture. Zero coupon bonds have been very reliable if bought on companies that are highly rated. Don't buy zero coupon junk bonds or the person will risk never seeing their money back. Make sure your bond has a "non-callable" feature, which means that it won't get called in for less before its due date.

There are also various government-issued zero coupon bonds which your broker will be happy to tell you about. They are obviously safer than corporate zero coupon bonds, since the U.S. Government is not likely to default before our major corporations do.

You should shop around for these, as there are various commissions tacked on in different, hidden ways from broker to broker. There could be quite a spread between brokers when you buy them, so be cautious and get several estimates. Even the best brokers have been reported by the Wall Street Journal as taking more than they should. Many top-name houses can easily make extra money by selling you the same product lesser houses will. The name doesn't mean anything here, just the bond.

Government Financing

You may qualify on certain real estate purchases to have the government lend you the money with which to pay for your home. The VA and FHA have various programs to help homeowners use government money as part of the financing package. There may be some tightening up because of budget difficulties but there hasn't been a month that's gone by yet that I haven't seen VA listings for homes which give financing even if you are not a U.S. Veteran or HUD homes which are sold for $100 down to owner-occupants.

There are certain limits to the financing, particularly from FHA but even those limits are being investigated for possible upward adjustment by Congress because homes are getting very expensive for the first-timer.

Another method you may use for your real estate purchase is state financing by your state's housing financing authority. If you qualify, both for the acquisition cost of your home purchase and for your income level - which is generally required to be "moderate" -you can have your state government's money finance your home purchase. Many states have pools of federal money running into the tens of millions of dollars available for your use. Many people don't use this obvious financing because they think they don't qualify or because you'll only get the worst homes. That's not true. Use that money; it's coming from your taxpaying dollars.

(Regulations vary from state to state, so refer to **Section Three** for the numbers to call for details.)

Speciality Financing By The Government

Some people are opting for mobile or manufactured homes. Under Title II of the National Housing Act, if the homeowner also owns the land and the home is on a permanent foundation, he can get an FHA loan for up to 30 years for mortgages in the range of $67,000 to $90,000. FHA insures the loan for up to 97% of the first $25,000 and 95% of the balance. Because of the high price of conventional homes, for many first-timers, such housing now comprises over 20% of all homes!

Another form of specialty financing is through the Farmer's Home Administration. There are a total of 46 state offices located throughout the United States; their listings include single family homes, apartments, hospitals and businesses. The FmHA can give loans only to individuals who have tried but cannot get a loan from another source. The property must be located in a rural area (defined by them as open country and places with populations of 20,000 or less).

Loans from FmHA can be for up to 100% of their appraised value of the home with repayment periods of between 33 years and 38 years. Addresses on how to contact one in your area are found in **Section Three**. They'll finance home building, existing homes and manufactured homes. And you can even use them for financing the expansion of your current home.

Advertising For Investment

This may not be as bizarre or unreliable as it sounds. There are many, many people who have sums of cash who wish to invest it in sound projects. If you find an incredible real estate purchase which requires cash at some near-future date, this is one act of desperation that may and can pay off for you. Many accountants and other financial men advertise in the Wall Street Journal in order to raise capital. I personally knew one tax attorney who used to raise nearly all the money he needed for his projects and projects for his clients using this method.

Another man, a best-selling author of No Money Down fame, encouraged his readers to use such a method. From time to time I would see classified ads of such people in major circulation newspapers. Some succeeded while others failed.

Those who succeeded had found a credible and legitimate bargain. This is not the kind of work where you sit back on your sofa and "will" checks to come in the mail to you. It does require work.

None of these techniques are that unusual nor unacceptable in this society. You should not use any of these techniques, which require borrowing, until you have gone to several auctions and discovered what kinds of bargains are available on the merchandise you wish to purchase in your area. Successes are often made by people who wish to put a good idea to use and by those who work very hard and work for many hours, not by people with hot-air dreams.

Non-Traditional Sources Of Financing

I use this term with tongue in cheek because these are frequently used techniques by major corporations. If you think these ideas are offbeat or unusual, you should visit the inner workings of a major corporation or the federal government's Budget Management Office to fully understand how truly simplistic these techniques are.

It has been said that the more unprepared or disorganized a person is, the more frantic will be his endeavor to complete a project. If someone has suddenly won a lottery and is a new millionaire, he will be completely unprepared to deal with the various promoters, schemers and scammers. Likewise, a college star turning pro is often bombarded from all sides with numerous offers. There is a sort of panic that person undergoes before he has organized a structure (sometimes just a business manager) to deal with such people.

In the same light, if you have never had wealth or even a very high-paying job, you may be unprepared for the amount of effort you are going to have to expend in acquiring our auction bargains. We can't all be Donald Trump who can buy a bankrupt airline for about 40¢ on the dollar. Another company was in the bidding but failed because they couldn't find a lender. However, he was able to put very little of his own money into the purchase, depending on other peoples' confidence in him to make this airline work well. Others lent him the money to buy an airline and at the price he desired. He was prepared.

Now, how can you get others to lend you the kind of money you may need to finance your auction purchases? On a smaller scale, you can use some of the obvious methods. On a larger scale, you'll have to use the ones below. Others are using those methods, so why shouldn't you?

Equity Sharing

This was developed or promoted, by a real estate guru in California a number of years ago. In fact, it has been around since the beginning of time. It works like this: You don't have the money. You have found something worth buying (a car, property, a home). You will do everything necessary to see this project through to completion. The other person will provide all or most of the financing. True, you do not own the property or home entirely. However, if your purchase is done at a low enough price and if the property is likely to appreciate, you will benefit from this and have more money to pursue other projects at a later date.

I know one woman who was able to buy her first home using this method. Her home appreciated by 50%. She was able to buy out her partner and she now owns the home herself (and is ready to get involved in other real estate projects). It does require work. You may encounter frustration and rejection but there are many people who are actually doing it and there are many people who are looking for ways to invest their money for a greater return. You just need to find them. You can do this by advertising, networking or just by being persistent in asking people and never giving up.

Investment Clubs

There are so many investment clubs abounding throughout the United States in the field of stock-investing. Why can this principle not be applied to auctions? Surely, there are numerous people who wouldn't mind chipping in dollars from time to time if the bargain is good. This could apply to cars and boats and a time-sharing sort of use could be made of them. Years ago, when I was concerned about buying a car in NYC and couldn't just buy one, I went "halves" with a friend on the purchase of a clunker. We would use it on various days.

People do this sort of thing, whether or not they are aware of it, when they buy shares in a company through a stock exchange. The company may invest, using your money as a stockholder, in a Rembrandt (bought at an auction) or in property. They are called things other than Investment Clubs. But you can still do this thing and call it an Investment Club or an Auction Club or anything at all.

Partners sometimes pool their resources in order to buy buildings. With the prices of some commercial real estate, versus its rate of return, many people find safety in numbers. And you can, too. Just because you don't know someone today, doesn't mean you will always be disadvantaged and never own property yourself. If you have confidence (developed by actual experience and not lies) and energy and enthusiasm, there are many opportunities for you to succeed. This also requires work and trust among the club's members.

I have read about various Oriental clubs throughout the United States, where each member deposits a monthly sum regularly. Each person is then able to take from the "pot" a certain amount and use it for investing in a business. These are loans among each member of the community. Members share an ethnic common denominator and there are varying degrees of trust by each group member of the other, which is why this method seems to work. You can find people with common interests and do the same. And you can reap the harvest of knowing you've also helped your friends make money while you are making money.

Real Estate Clubs

I've only seen these in major cities but they may exist in various places. Many have come about through their interest in the field and/or through connections with various radio real estate talk show hosts or as an outgrowth of real estate conferences that have been held currently or in the past about buying real estate "creatively". At such places there are usually a handful of "money men or women" and a surplus of people who have ideas but no money. Obviously, the most persuasive person and/or the person with the better deal is going to be most successful. You might try these clubs as a way to raise money for your purchases.

One way of finding out about these people is listening to the talk show stations in your area. Call the radio station and ask the show's producer or host if he is aware of any real estate investment clubs. In some cases, these clubs advertise on these shows for members (or to sell them literature). Some of the more aggressive talk shows, at least two that I know of, have been known to help send members to the club for a piece of the action - or make their money by having these clubs put on seminars (for which they are paid a gargantuan fee in order to appear). Join the clubs but don't be the guy who supports them by buying everything they try to sell you.

Sweat Equity

This is an old term, which may go back to sharecropping from post-Civil War times, perhaps earlier, if you look at the medieval feudal states throughout Europe. Basically, you are putting your construction skills into a property while buying something for less value and making it valuable, using someone else's money to buy something for a price you couldn't afford and making it more valuable, through your work, a combination of the above or buying something less valuable and hiring others to upgrade it and make it more valuable, also making a profit on the appreciation and upgrade.

Many people buy "fixer-uppers" or "handy-man specials". Many more should, if the structure is sound and it is within their means and wherewithal to renovate the property. There is an astounding amount of surplus government and bank property at this time throughout the United States. A large amount needs renovations. Why not put effort and skill into buying something for a little money and selling it for a lot more?

Limited Partnerships

These require the use of an attorney and no one should ever establish one without an attorney overseeing the paperwork. But did you know that over $10 Billion is raised annually for public limited partnerships? And that about $25 Billion is invested in private limited partnerships. That is a lot of money. Movies, Broadway shows, real estate, equipment leasing and an enormous amount of research and development for new technology would never come about or be bought without limited partnerships.

Behind every limited partnership is an individual or two with a superhuman amount of energy and self-confidence in his or her project. Face it. No one ever made it with a great idea if that person wasn't abounding with a divine belief in their service or product and a willingness to overcome every obstacle posed in raising the money. Raising money requires those two commitments. If you do not have them, then there is an incorrect premise you are working on. You may not really believe you've found an incredible bargain. You may not have the vision to see your purchase through to the end. You may have failed at something earlier.

If you've failed in the past, you are not alone. Practically every great investor or businessman has met with a major failure at one time or another. The founder of Macy's Department Store, which occupies a large block in New York City, had been bankrupted seven times before finally making his big smash success. Nearly every great religious leader in the past 2500 years has been, at one time or another, condemned or vilified by his contemporaries. Many scoffers are people who aren't trying. They are not content with what little they have and are usually very bitter about it. Those same people will convince you, from time to time, that every attempt you make to better yourself is doomed to failure and they'll be right there to say, "I told you so".

But you can't kill a great idea. Eventually, it surfaces somewhere else through the efforts of someone who is willing and knows how to overcome the obstacles. At an auction, someone is going to buy that Rolls Royce, that ten-story building or that undeveloped land. That someone is going to do what ever it takes to succeed and overcome the bad advice of the scoffers and doomsayers and get the job done or will raise the money necessary for that condo project that was auctioned at 50% of its market value. It could be you.

Your best advice on limited partnerships is to find a lawyer and ask him about the various regulations and restrictions you are going to face in assembling this creature. Once you've done that (raising "seed money" from friends and relatives), you're going to embark on a trek which is seemingly impossible but probably very rewarding. You may need to contact an investment banker or accountant or tax attorney who has clients willing to invest money in this project. You may need to advertise in various major papers under "Business Opportunities Sections" which are found in nearly every city. You may face humiliation, contempt and rejection. But if you do raise the money and if you do find the auction bargains, then they'll write about you in the business sections of the local newspapers, stating what a great person you are or what an astute businessman you have become. What those reporters don't ever grasp is that it simply takes a great idea, belief in that idea and willingness to overcome the nonsense of rejection to see your plan through.

But don't start on such a project until you've consulted an attorney and attended a few auctions or contacted several government agencies for their brochures or catalogs to see just what is available.

<u>Money</u>

The subject of money is probably as confusing as the other great sins that abound. What most people don't understand about money is that it is simply a medium of exchange. In a barter society, we might pay with things like eggs, bread or something else that is physically tangible and immediately consumable.

Somewhere along the way, we moved into a paper money society and now into a plastic money society...away from tangible objects like gold coins, silver bars and eggs. Money is nothing more than a representative of how good your ideas are and how hard you are willing to work for those ideas. Far too many people are willing to settle for an hourly wage; others, without any ambition, for a steady salary.

I hope I've provided you with some good ideas on financing to help you get started. The various government agencies have diverse merchandise and an abundance of vacant real estate available to you if you wish to reach out and get some of it. You will be required to work. At times you may give up. Don't let the lack of money stop you. There are trillions of dollars available throughout the world. And there are many, many eager investors looking for the right person with the right idea. I hope that person could be you!

CHAPTER 6

Claiming Your Auction Purchase

Claiming Your Auction Purchase

Buying something at auction is one thing. You have to take possession of that merchandise or real estate as well. The auction stops, on your particular item, the moment the auctioneer has accepted your bid. Now you've got another problem to worry about: what to do with it.

Payment

Once you've been recognized by the auctioneer as the successful bidder on that merchandise, you are now logged in by the auctioneer's clerk onto a triplicate sheet of paper with the item number, your bidder's number and the purchase price. Unless you have other items to purchase, you can proceed to the cashier with your bidder's number and item number you have just purchased. In some cases the clerk, auctioneer or another assistant may even give you a sheet of paper with that information on it. If not, you should write down that information into your notebook and keep track of it, just in case the clerk makes a mistake.

Now that you have the item number (and you should also jot down a brief description of the merchandise on your note pad, such as: "Chevy Caprice, 1985, blue", and the purchase price), you proceed to the cashier and discuss payment procedures. At various auctions you may be able to extend your payment beyond the date of the auction, perhaps as much as two weeks. At others you must pay by a certain time on the same date of your purchase or you lose possession of the merchandise. Some are flexible, others are not.

Rejection Of The Merchandise

If the merchandise has been damaged from the point you've inspected it until after you've purchased it, you may file a complaint. Your offer will be withdrawn and the merchandise removed from the auction. This is rare but it has happened.

Similarly, with a sealed bid, if you've once inspected the merchandise and then purchased it by sealed bid, it's yours - unless you find a change in the condition of that merchandise from the point of inspection until it has come time for you to remove it from the premises. If that's the case, file a complaint and state why there is a problem. It will then be withdrawn from that auction. It may reappear later at a different auction with the damages listed.

Please keep in mind that with nearly all of these auctions, the merchandise comes with the warning: as-is, where-is. That can mean only one thing: If it doesn't work, you have to repair it and once you've bought it, you are responsible for its removal. Please understand that various auctioneers make every effort to provide you with correct information about the merchandise. If you have properly inspected it in the manner described in **Chapter Four**, then you should not have a problem with it. If you merely take the auctioneer's word, you may have complications; whether intentional or not, there are no warranties on these auctioned items, unless specified. And usually conditions of sale specify that there are no warranties on the merchandise.

Removal Of The Merchandise

Just as you have been advised to prepare well for the auction by doing your homework on the merchandise, you should also be prepared for removal of it. This can be as simple as arranging with a friend or neighbor to borrow a pick-up truck to cart off a desk or it can be as complicated as having to arrange for an 18-wheeler and moving people to remove a truckload of men's shirts from a Customs Auction.

It can also mean hiring a towing company to tow off your newly-purchased clunker if you don't inspect properly. Whatever you do buy, please keep in mind that you will have to take it away or drive it away and you should be prepared.

For instance, if you go to a car auction, you must bring your driver's license (even if you attend an auction in another state) and you must bring a proof of insurance card so you can drive away your purchase. Failure to bring these along may prevent you from registering at the auction and will definitely obstruct your removal of the vehicle, except by a towing company, if at all, for that day.

While you are appraising the merchandise, keep in mind that you will have to remove these items once you've bought them. You can do homework in preparing for the auction by flipping through the yellow pages of your telephone book and finding moving companies, if you attend larger office equipment or furniture auctions. Use common sense here.

Bait And Switch

I hate to even bring this up but some unscrupulous auctioneers have done this in the past. They are in the minority so don't become overly mistrustful.

If you buy something, do make sure that the item you remove is the item you bought. At various times an auctioneer has sold you one item and delivered to you another. You can overcome this by quick removal of the merchandise and detailing your purchase in your note pad.

If you feel that this has occurred, complain loudly to the cashier or the auctioneer and then follow this up in writing to your state's Consumer Protection Agency (located in your state capital).

Definitely do not pay for the merchandise. Do not remove it from the premises. If you happen to have a camera, photograph the item you bought and the item which was switched onto you. Use that as evidence when notifying your state's consumer protection agency.

Sometimes, honest mistakes are made. Confusions can occur. Merchandise can look "alike" and be mistaken for something else. The auctioneer's clerk can write down the item number incorrectly or illegibly. Purchase prices can be confused, and so forth. First, give these people the benefit of the doubt. If the problem persists, act accordingly as advised above.

Buyer's Premium

When you purchase auction merchandise, you will have to pay state sales tax, at the applicable level. You will have to pay that at the time of the purchase. However, there may be an additional premium you might have to pay which will be stated in the flier announcing the auction and it will also be stated in the conditions of sale. This is another important reason to read those conditions of sale. A buyer's premium comes about because the seller and the auctioneer have agreed to it as part of the auction. Generally, at various auctions the government will contract out the auction to a private auctioneer - Bankruptcy Trustees almost always use private auctioneers for their auctions. Sometimes, SBA auctions will have a buyer's premium (they use private auctioneers).

The amount of the buyer's premium varies. Usually, you'll find a buyer's premium of between 5% and 10% of the amount of your purchase. This means that something you've just bought for $100 may cost you as much as $110 plus sales tax. Please calculate that into your bidding. Many people fail to do so and feel a bit "taken" afterwards.

GSA Sealed Bid Auctions

These sealed bid auctions work in this way, most times. You'll send in your bid (with or without a deposit depending on the conditions of sale). At a certain date - the deadline - they'll open the sealed bids and notify the winners. You'll usually have about ten calendar days after the award announcement to pay for the merchandise. This will either be by mail (certified or otherwise, depending on the conditions of sale) or in person (as specified once again in the conditions of sale).

You will then have an additional ten days to remove the merchandise. That means within 20 days after the award announcement you must remove the item or merchandise from wherever the custodian is keeping it. You will be entirely responsible for the removal of that merchandise. It may take packing and crating it. It may require a moving company or just the back seat of your car. Whatever it takes, it is your responsibility to remove it by the time limit. If you fail to do so, you are likely to be charged for storage costs on that merchandise on a daily basis until you do remove it. The conditions of sale are to be read very carefully to eliminate any possible future problems.

Twists And Turns

This happens primarily with real estate auctions, specifically foreclosure or bankruptcy auctions. You can find something withdrawn from auction or given to someone else simply because of a right of precedence. The legal definition used here is:

PRECEDENCE: "The right of being first placed in a certain order."
(Black's Law Dictionary, Fifth Edition)

Let's say a bankrupt individual or company somehow manages to assemble the funds to satisfy his creditors. If this is done before the auction takes place, he can get his property back.

The right of precedence gives that company or individual the last opportunity he has to retain ownership. It closes the auction at that time and removes the item being auctioned. The person also gets the opportunity, under some circumstances, to bid against you at that auction and retain ownership.

Bulk Bidding

Another way you can lose something which you thought you'd won can occur at certain IRS or bankruptcy auctions. After each item has been sold at an auction individually, some courts or government agencies may accept a bulk bid on the entire lot of items up for auction. The grand total of all bids is tallied and announced. Someone may then offer this bulk bid, which nullifies your purchase and awards the winning bulk bid possession of the entire lot.

This is not very common at many auctions but has been known to occur. You're not likely to find it at various Customs auctions, real estate auctions, police sales, GSA auctions, Marshal's auctions, postal auctions and others. It is most commonly found in bankruptcy auctions or sheriff sales (where more than one item is up for auction).

Guarantees

As mentioned earlier, there are no warranties at most auctions. However, another problem you may encounter is liens against property and merchandise. For instance, at some county and city marshal auctions (held primarily in New York City and Los Angeles) there may be liens against the car, boat or other merchandise. This may not be disclosed to you and you can be held liable for those liens.

Similarly, you could possibly end up having to pay liens on property bought at a sheriff's auction. You must be certain there are no liens on the property, either through conditions of sale or by having a title search done. Although there are incredible bargains in these areas, caution is advised.

CONCLUSION

At this point you have been given some practical tips for auction-going. Please go over the rules for auction-goers at the beginning of this section and know them well before you go to an auction. You'll probably be tempted to make one of those mistakes while at your first few auctions. Be advised that those mistakes have been made for you by many people which is why they've become rules.

The entire point of this **Section Two** has been to educate you rapidly on the subject of auctions so that you can succeed when you begin going to them. Realize that thousands (or more) of people have made full-time careers by going to auctions and have led profitable lives. You can, too but you won't do it overnight. You won't make millions all at once. Very few people have made millions at this. This is a vehicle you may use, along with hard work, to make a very comfortable living *or* to find a series of bargains on things you might ordinarily pay full price for.

This is just a guide, not the ultimate word on the subject. Much of this guide has been gathered together from professional advice and practical experience. You must persist at this to succeed. Nothing magical is likely to occur if you don't fully understand what has been written and then apply it in real life. If you do make the necessary phone calls and attend the auctions the various government agencies and private auctioneers hold, I am certain that you will find bargains at these auctions. I have. Many others have. People do nearly every day. You can, too but first you must try.

"The journey of a thousand miles begins with the first step."

--Ancient Chinese proverb

SECTION THREE

Directory of Government Agencies

INTRODUCTION

    Section Three is composed of a vast number of hard to find phone numbers, addresses and inside information about our government agencies and their auctions. All information requiring a phone number or address previously mentioned in **Sections One** or **Two** will be found in this section.

    When calling a particular government agency, please be polite and understanding. For many of the government agencies, the auction part of the business is generally an unwanted job. Many wish they didn't have to do auctions, let alone have to continue answering phone calls, sending out fliers for requests and other unnecessary traffic. This varies from person to person, the whole part of it being human nature. Good manners and persistence will go a long way toward being helped.

    Please don't be rude or unfriendly when dealing with these people, even if they are that way with you. As a result of our book, the amount of phone traffic into their offices has increased dramatically. They would prefer to have more staff to handle your calls and answer your questions but they don't. Some agencies are just not geared toward so many requests. However, you can make their job easier by just being friendly.

    I wish you great luck on this new venture you have undertaken and I hope you will be successful. We found, through our research, that many government agencies are very willing to answer our questions. Some have even made possible many parts of this book that would have been difficult or impossible without their help. A few government agencies in some parts of the country did make our task more difficult. I do warn people that various GSA offices around the country have been upset that people attend their auctions; many don't even want to be bothered, let alone answer their phones or their mail. Other GSA offices have offered assistance to our research team by volunteering new phone numbers and addresses for this edition. Their auctions, most will find, are not a very good source of bargains. If you wish to contact them out of curiosity or attend their auctions as a way of practicing or preparing for other auctions, then please do so.

    Have fun contacting the various government agencies in this section. Be prepared to take notes in case they have any advice or further information which we have not covered for you already.

HOTLINE NUMBERS

U.S. Marshals:

Los Angeles	(213) 894-2495
San Diego	(619) 233-8924
Houston	(713) 229-2806
Chicago	(312) 353-0101
Newark	(212) 264-4823
Philadelphia	(215) 597-7253
San Antonio	(512) 229-6537
Honolulu	(808) 541-3610

G.S.A.:

San Francisco	(415) 974-9189
Miami (Kennedy Space Center)	(404) 331-5177
Tampa/St. Petersburg	(404) 331-5177
New York City	(212) 264-4823
Chicago	(312) 353-0246
Detroit	(215) 597-7253
Atlanta	(404) 331-5177
Washington, D.C. area	(202) 557-7796

I.R.S.:

San Francisco	(415) 556-5021
Seattle	(206) 442-0703
Los Angeles	(213) 894-5777
New York City	(718) 780-4020

Police Department:

New York City	(212) 406-1369
Boston	(617) 247-4579
San Francisco (vehicles)	(415) 553-9751
San Diego	(619) 531-2767

The General Services Administration

```
┌─────────────────────────────────────────────────────────┐
│                   HOTLINE  NUMBERS                        │
│                                                           │
│  San Francisco                         (415) 974-9189     │
│  Miami (Kennedy Space Center)          (404) 331-5177     │
│  Tampa/St. Petersburg                  (404) 331-5177     │
│  New York City                         (212) 264-4823     │
│  Chicago                               (312) 353-0246     │
│  Detroit                               (215) 597-7253     │
│  Atlanta                               (404) 331-5177     │
│  Washington, D.C. area                 (202) 557-7796     │
│                                                           │
└─────────────────────────────────────────────────────────┘
```

Federal Service Supply Bureau

There are 10 different Supply Service Bureau regions throughout the United States and the National Capitol Region in the United States. If you wish to find out about or get on the GSA's free mailing lists for surplus merchandise or seized merchandise auctions, then you should call the phone numbers or write the addresses on the following pages for the region under which you fall.

NATIONAL CAPITOL REGION:

Washington, D.C. and the metropolitan areas

Federal Supply Service Bureau (GSA)
6808 Loisdale Rd.
Bldg. A
Springfield, VA 22150
(703) 557-0384
HOTLINE: (703) 557-7796

REGION ONE:

Connecticut, Maine, Massachusetts, New Hampshire, Rhode Island, and Vermont

Federal Supply Service Bureau (GSA)
10 Causeway St.
#2FBP-1
Boston, MA 02222
(617) 565-7317

REGION TWO:

New Jersey, Puerto Rico, Virgin Islands, and New York

Federal Supply Service Bureau (GSA)
26 Federal Plaza
#2FB-2
Rm. 20-100D

173

New York, NY 10278
(212) 264-3592
HOTLINE: (212) 264-4823

REGION THREE:

Delaware, Pennsylvania, Virginia, West
Virginia, and Maryland

General Services Administration (GSA)
Personal Property Sales Section
9th & Market Sts.
Rm. 5156
Philadelphia, PA 19107
(215) 597-5674/ 597-1889
HOTLINE: (215) 597-7253

REGION FOUR:

Alabama, Florida, Georgia, Kentucky,
Mississippi, North Carolina, South Carolina,
and Tennessee

General Services Administration (GSA)
Sales Branch
75 Spring St.
#4FBS
Atlanta, GA 30303
(404) 331-3064 OR
(404) 331-0972

REGION FIVE:

Illinois, Indiana, Michigan, Minnesota, Ohio,
and Wisconsin

General Services Administration (GSA)
Federal Supply Service Bureau
Sales Services, Mail Staff 34-5
230 S. Dearborn St.
Chicago, IL 60604
(312) 353-5375/353-6064
or
Assistant Regional
Administrator's Office (312) 353-5504
HOTLINE: (312) 353-4242

REGION SIX:

Iowa, Kansas, Missouri, and Nebraska

Excess Properties Sales
GSA Federal Supply Bureau
#6FB-P
4400 College Blvd.
Ste. 175
Overland Park, KS 66211
(913) 236-2525

REGION SEVEN:

Arkansas, Louisiana, New Mexico,
Oklahoma, and Texas

General Services Administration
819 Taylor St.
Fort Worth, TX 76102
(817) 334-2352/334-2353

REGION EIGHT:

Colorado, Montana, North Dakota, South
Dakota, Utah, and Wyoming

General Services Administration
Federal Supply Service Bureau
Bldg. 41
Denver Federal Ctr.
Denver, CO 80226
(303) 844-6575

REGION NINE:

Arizona, California, Guam, Hawaii, and
Nevada

General Services Administration
Federal Supply Service Bureau
525 Market St.
San Francisco, CA 94105
(415) 974-9179
HOTLINE: (415) 974-9189

REGION TEN:

Idaho, Oregon, and Washington

General Services Administration
Excess Personal Property Sales
GSA Center Rm. 1478
Auburn, WA 98001
(206) 931-7566

Federal Property Resources Service

There are four Regional centers for this service which handle the surplus Federal real estate. If you wish to contact them about their sales listings or to receive their quarterly brochure, please call the appropriate phone number for your region below or write to their address. A postcard will be attached to the back of the brochure which will, when mailed, continue to get you future mailings or be notified of upcoming property auctions. The GSA plans to issue their brochures on a bi-monthly basis in the very near future.

To get the GSA's Real Estate Bidder's Package, simply call 1-800-GSA-1313 or you may write to them at:

> GSA Central Mailing Lists Service IRMS-9KS
> 525 Market St.
> San Francisco, CA 94105
> or
> Consumer Information Center
> P.O. Box 100
> Pueblo, CO 81002

THE FPRS sales force of realty specialists is divided among regions of the country.Below are the addresses and phone numbers of each region and the states each one covers:

OFFICE OF REAL ESTATE SALES (2DR-1)

Federal Property Resources Service
U.S. General Services Administration
10 Causeway Street, Room 1075
Boston, MA 02222
(617) 565-5700

CHICAGO FIELD OFFICE

Office of Real Estate Sales (2DR-1C)
Federal Property Resources Service
U.S. General Services Administration
230 S. Dearborn Street Room 3756
Chicago, IL 60604
(312) 353-6045

Maryland, Pennsylvania, Virginia, West Virginia, Alabama, South Carolina, Tennessee, Mississsippi, North Carolina, Delaware, Kentucky, Georgia, Florida and the District of Columbia

OFFICE OF REAL ESTATE SALES (4DR)

Federal Property Resources Service
U.S. General Services Administration
75 Spring Street, SW Room 818
Atlanta, GA 30303
(404) 331-5133

Colorado, Montana, North Dakota, South Dakota, Utah, Wyoming, Iowa, Kansas,

Missouri, Nebraska, Louisiana, New Mexico,
Oklahoma and Texas

OFFICE OF REAL ESTATE SALES
(7DR)

Federal Property Resources Service
U.S. General Services Administration
819 Taylor Street Room 11A26
Fort Worth, TX 76102
(817)334-2331

Arizona, California, Hawaii, Nevada,
American Samoa, Guam, the Pacific Trust
Territories, Alaska, Idaho, Oregon and
Washington

OFFICE OF REAL ESTATE SALES
(9DR)

Federal Property Resources Service
U.S. General Services Administration
525 Market Street
San Francisco, CA 94105
(415) 974-9086

AUBURN FIELD OFFICE

Office of Real Estate Sales (9DRF)
Federal Property Resources Service
U.S. General Services Administration
GSA Center Room 2476
Auburn, WA 98002
(206) 931-7550

SECTION THREE - U.S. Customs

U.S. Customs

U.S. Customs auctions are conducted, at this time, through a subsidiary of Northrop World-Wide Aircraft. They charge between $25 and $60 annually for their frequent brochures and fliers to be mailed to you. If you wish to purchase their service immediately, it is broken down as follows:

OPTION #1

Nationwide, including Puerto Rico and
Hawaii
Cost: $50
Add $10 for Foreign delivery

OPTION #2

Eastern United States,
including Puerto Rico

Cost: $25
Add $10 Foreign Delivery

OPTION #3

Western United States,
including Hawaii
Cost $25
Add $10 Foreign Delivery

Auctions are conducted in these cities of the United States as well as by sealed bid through their Lawton, Oklahoma headquarters:

NORTHEASTERN REGION

Jersey City, NJ
Chicago, IL

SOUTHEASTERN REGION

Miami, FL
San Juan, PR

NORTHWESTERN REGION

Los Angeles, CA
Calexico, CA
San Diego, CA

SOUTHWESTERN REGION

Texas: Laredo, Brownsville, Del Rio,
Houston, Edinburgh
Nogales, AZ

U.S. Marshals

HOT LINE NUMBERS

Los Angeles	(213) 894-2495
San Diego	(619) 233-8924
Houston	(713) 229-2806
Chicago	(312) 353-0101
Newark	(212) 264-4823
Philadelphia	(215) 597-7253
San Antonio	(512) 229-6537
Honolulu	(808) 541-3610

The U.S. Marshal's Offices do not maintain a mailing list. They have four avenues of conducting auctions:

1. They conduct the auctions themselves, without contracting a private auctioneer or another governmental agency, such as the GSA. These auctions are referred to as "in house auctions."

2. They turn over merchandise to GSA.

3. The Marshal's Office will use various private auction companies, however these change frequently.

4. Or you may encounter any combination of the above.

They advertise in daily newspapers and/or legal publications. If you are interested in the U.S. Marshal's auctions, refer to the area(s) listed to obtain up-to-date information on upcoming auctions. There is no need to call the U.S. Marshal's Office for auction update.

Generally, real estate is handled by brokers within the area. No one broker handles all real estate, as properties are usually given to an approved list of brokers on an even basis.

Keep in mind that the information listed on the following pages are subject to change. The rule of thumb, however, is:

• To get on the mailing list for GSA and the private auction companies listed. Even if the private auction company's contract is not renewed, you still have the advantage of being on their mailing list. And you can certainly take the initiative to consult the yellow pages in the desired area to contact all private auction companies about their auctions.

• Check all local papers for auction in classified and legal sections. Don't forget the County papers as well.

• Check legal publications in the area.

Below are the complete listings of U.S. Marshals' offices and how they go about disposing of their merchandise.

ALABAMA - BIRMINGHAM

General Merchandise: Acton & Associates-Auctioneers (205) 823-2336
Real Estate: Private realtors within area.
Advertises in County paper where auctions are to be held. Also, check the offical County newspapers and any local law journals.

ALABAMA - BIRMINGHAM

General Merchandis: Acton & Associates Auctioneers (205) 823-2336
Real Estate: Private realtors within area.
Advertises in County paper where auctions are to be held.
Also check official County newspapers and any local law journals.

ALABAMA - MOBILE

General Merchandise: In house.
Autos: GSA.
Real Estate: Private realtors within area.
Other U.S. Marshal in Atlanta.
Advertises in MOBILE PRESS REGISTER.
Also, check the offical County newspapers and any local law journals.

ALABAMA - MONTGOMERY

General Merchandise: Sends to other agencies.
Auto: Used car lots on consignment.
Real Estate: Private realtors within area, also In house.
Advertises in local newspapers.
Also, check the offical County newspapers and any local law journals.

ALASKA - ANCHORAGE

General Merchandise: Grubstake Realty and Auction Co., (907) 274-9269.
Autos: in house.
Real Estate: Private realtors within area.
Advertises in ANCHORAGE TIMES and ANCHORAGE DAILY NEWS. Also, check offical County newspapers and any local law journals.

ARKANSAS - FORT SMITH

General Merchandise/Autos: GSA in Fort Smith.
Real Estate: Private realtors within area, also In house.
Advertises in local news papers. Also, check the official County newspapers and any local law journals.

ARKANSAS - LITTLE ROCK

179

U.S. Marshal handles the two annual auctions unless they are.big enough to hire professional auctioneers.
Real estate: Private realtors within area.
Advertises in ARKANSAS DEMOCRAT and ARKANSAS GAZETTE.
Also, check the offical County newspapers and any local law journals.

ARIZONA - PHOENIX

General Merchandise: Different auctioneers from yellow pages.
Autos: AAA Galleries
Real Estate: Private realtors within area.
Advertises in ARIZONA BUSINESS GAZETTE.
Also, check the offical County newspapers and any local law journals.

COLORADO - DENVER

General Merchandise: In house; hires an auctioneer.
Autos: In house.
Real Estate: In house.
Private Realtors within area.
Advertises in ROCKY MOUNTAIN POST
Also, check the offical County newspapers and any local law journals.

CONNECTICUT - HARTFORD

Autos: Wholesale dealer or used by other agencies.
Real estate: NASAF and Private realtors within area.
Advertises in largest County newspapers and local law journals.

CALIFORNIA - LOS ANGELES

Some merchandise sent to GSA; some auctioned.
Check local newspapers and local law journals.

CALIFORNIA - SAN DIEGO

General Merchandise: Butterfield and Butterfield Auctioneers and Appraisers, (213) 850-7500.

Autos/Boats: Fischer Auction Service (619) 233-1851; one or two per month.
Real Estate: Private realtors within area.
General Merchandise: Advertised in SAN DIEGO UNION.
Auto auctions advertised in UNION TRIBUNE on Sunday, two weeks prior to auction.
Also, check the offical County newspapers and any local law journals..

CALIFORNIA - SAN FRANCISCO

All handled through GSA.
Check local newspapers and local law journals for advertising.

CALIFORNIA - SACRAMENTO

Auctions very rarely held; larger lots handled by GSA in Sacramento.
General Merchandise/Auto: All American Auction Co.
Advertises in local and offical County newspapers and any local law journals.

CONNECTICUT - NEW HAVEN

General Merchandise/Autos: GSA in Boston, private auctioneers and Southern Auto Sales.
Real Estate-Private realtors within area.
Other: jewelry, to New Jersey or Chicago.
Advertises in legal notices of newspapers.
Also, check offical County newspapers and any local law journals.

DELAWARE - WILMINGTON

General Merchandise/Autos: has had neither in five years.
Real Estate: Private realtors within area.
Advertises in DAILY NEWS JOURNAL and SEAFORD LEADER, legal notices.
Also, check the offical County newspapers and any local law journals.

FLORIDA - KENNEDY SPACE CENTER

General Merchandise: Private auctiioneer.
Autos: GSA at Kennedy Space Center
Real Estate: Private realtors within area.
Advertises in MIAMI HERALD.

180

Also, check the offical County newspapers and any local law journals.

FLORIDA - TALLAHASSEE

General Merchandise/Autos: GSA Office
Real Estate: Private realtors within area.
Other: aircraft, Stambaugh Aviation, Brunswick, GA
Advertises in TALLAHASSEE DEMOCRAT, legal section.
Also, check the offical County newspapers and any local law journals.

FLORIDA - TAMPA

General Merchandise: Private auctioneers
Autos: Cyprus Aviation Boats/Planes
Real Estate: Private realtors within area; In house also.
Advertises in TAMPA TRIBUNE, County newspapers or boating, aviation, etc. magazines.
Also, check the ofical County newspapers and any local law journals.

GEORGIA - ATLANTA

General Merchandise/Autos: Private auctioneers.
Real Estate: Private realtors within area.
Advertises in MACON NEWS and TELEGRAPH.
Also, check the offical County newspapers and any local law journals

GEORGIA - SAVANNAH

General Merchandise/Autos: In house
Real Estate: Private realtors within areas.
Advertises in SAVANNAH MORNING NEWS.
Also, check the offical County newspapers and any local journals.

HAWAII - HONOLULU

General Merchandise: Private auctioneers.
Autos: GSA does advertising; Marshal holds auction; *high quality.**
Real Estate: Private realtors within area.
Advertises in major newspapers.

Also, check the offical County newspapers and any local law journals.
20-30 autos a year, mostly very expensive, exotic cars and 40-50 properties a year (most from drug seizures).

IDAHO - BOISE

General Merchandise/Autos sent to auctioneers.
Real Estate: Private realtors/brokers within area.
Advertises in BOISE STATE.
Also, check the offical County newspapera and any local law journals.

ILLINOIS - CHICAGO

General Merchandise: In house
Autos: Auto Pound; 200 vehicles seized in April!
Real Estate: Private realtors within area.
Advertises in CHICAGO SUNDAY TIMES, CHICAGO TRIBUNE and CHICAGO DAILY LAW BULLETIN.
Also, check the offical County newspapers.

ILLINOIS - EAST ST. LOUIS

General Merchandise/Autos: In house.
Real Estate: Private realtors within area.
Advertises in BELLEVILLE NEWS DEMOCRAT, Legal notices.
Also, check the offical County newspapers and any law journals.

ILLINOIS - SPRINGFIELD

General Merchandise/Autos: In house.
Real Estate: Private realtors within area.
Advertises in County where seized.
Also, check the offical County newapapers and any local law journals.

INDIANA - HAMMOND

General Merchandise/Autos: Private auctioneers.
Real Estate: Private realtors within area.
Advertises in LAKE COUNTY STAR and VERDETTE.
Also, check the offical County newspapers and any local law journals.

INDIANA - INDIANAPOLIS

Autos: GSA
Advertises in County where auction will occur.
Also, check the offical County newpapers and any local law journals.

IOWA - CEDAR RAPIDS

Autos/Real Estate: In house.
Advertises in CEDAR RAPIDS GAZETTE.
Also, check the offical County newsapers and any local law journals.

IOWA - DES MOINES

General Merchandise/Autos: Greenfield Auctions
Real Estate: Private realtors within area.
Advertises in County newspaper where auction will occur and in DES MOINES REGISTER.
Also, check the offical County newspaper and any local law journals.

KANSAS - KANSAS CITY

General Merchandise: In house.
 Autos: In house.
Real Estate: In house
Advertises in County newspaper where auction will occur.
Also, check the offical County newspapers and any local law journals..

KENTUCKY - LEXINGTON

Autos: Greater Lexington Auto Auction (Lexington covers 60 counties)
Real Estate: Private realtors within area, (8-10 houses foreclosed per month).
Advertises in local newspaper where property is located; notices posted in Post Office lobbies.
Also, check the offical County newspapers and any local law journals.

KENTUCKY - LOUISVILLE

General Merchandise/Autos: private auctioneers.
Real Estate: In house (about three per week; more expected in the future). Private realtors within area.
Advertises in TIME GAZETTE, COURIER-JOURNAL.
Also, check the offical County newspapers and any local law journals.

LOUISIANA - BATON ROUGE

Real Estate: In house.
Other jewelry: Private auctioneer.
Advertises in STATE TIMES, legal journal (for the district).
Also, check the offical County newspapers

LOUISIANA - NEW ORLEANS

General Merchandise/Autos/Real Estate: In house.
Advertises in TIMES PICAYUNE, classified section.
Also, check the offical County (Parish) newspapers and any local law journals.

LOUISIANA - SHREVEPORT

Autos/Real Estate: In house.
Advertises in MONROE MORNING STAR, legal section, also SHREVEPORT TIMES.
Also, check the offical (Parish) newspapers and any local law journals.

MAINE - PORTLAND

General Merchandise/Autos/Real Estate: In house.
Real estate will be turned over to FHA.
Advertises in PORTLAND PRESS HERALD.
Also, check the offical newspapers and any local journals.

MARYLAND - BALTIMORE

General Merchandise/Autos/Real Estate: In house.
Check all daily newapapers, legal and classified sections as well as County newspaper and any local law journals.

MASSACHUSETTS - BOSTON

Autos: American Auto Auction Co. (sells only to dealers)
Real Estate: By open house.
Advertises statewide; in BOSTON GLOBE or BOSTON HERALD on Tues. or Thurs. in legal notices.
Also, check the offical County newspapers and any local law journals.

MICHIGAN - DETROIT

General Merchandise: In house.
Autos: Midwest Auto.
Real Estate: PHC of Michigan.
Advertises in DETROIT FREE PRESS and DETROIT LEGAL NEWS/PUBLICATION.
Also, check the offical County newspaper.

MICHIGAN - GRAND RAPIDS

General Merchandise: Depends on Court Order.
Autos: Auctioneers.
Real Estate: Private realtors within area.
Advertises in DETROIT PRESS, classified section, GRAND RAPIDS PRESS and DETROIT FREE PRESS.
Also, check the offical County newspapers and any local law journals.

MINNESOTA - MINNEAPOLIS

General Merchandise/Autos: In house (jewelry only), furs to charity.
Real Estate: In house and to Private Realtors within area.
Advertises in ST. PAUL LEDGER, MINNEAPOLIS STAR and TRIBUNE. Also in finance and commerce newspapers, and in the offical County newspapers and any local law journals.

MISSISSIPPI - JACKSON

Autos: Miss. South Auction (Dealer auction/dealer trade-ins)
Real Estate: Private realtors within area.
Other: Government surplus-GSA.
Advertises in County/District
Also, check the offical County newspapers and any local law journals.

MISSISSIPPI - OXFORD

General Merchandise/Autos/Real estate: In house. Other: depends on Court Order
Advertises in TUPELO JOURNAL, WASHINGTON COUNTY TIMES, legal notices; COMMERCIAL APPEAL, specialized publications.
Also, check the offical County newspapers and any local law journals.

MISSOURI - KANSAS CITY

General Merchandise/Autos: DeWeese Auction Company.
Real Estate: Private realtors within area.
Advertises in DAILY RECORD one day a week for three weeks; ads posted at County Courthouse.
Also, check the offical County newspapers and any local law journals.

MISSOURI - ST. LOUIS

General Merchandise/Autos/jewelry: In house
Real Estate: Private realtors within area.
Advertises in ST. LOUIS POST, legal section.
Also, check the offical County newspapers and any local law journals.

MONTANA - BILLINGS

Real Estate: Private realtors within area.
Advertises in the BILLINGS TIMES.
Also, check the offical County newspapers and any local law journals.

NEBRASKA - OMAHA

General Merchandise/Autos: GSA
Real Estate: In house or private realtors within area.
Advertises in OMAHA WORLD HERALD and in legal papers of County where property foreclosed.
Also, check the offical County newspapers and any local law journals.

NEVADA - LAS VEGAS

General Merchandise: Butterfield & Butterfield.
Real Estate: Private realtors within area.
Advertises in REVIEW JOURNAL.
Also, check the offical County newspapers and any local law journals.

NEW HAMPSHIRE - CONCORD

General Merchandise/Autos/Real Estate: In house.
Advertises in MANCHESTER UNION LEADER.
Also, check the offical County newspapers and any local law journals.

NEW JERSEY - NEWARK

General Merchandise: Private auctioneers.
Autos: GSA.
Real Estate: Private realtors within area.
Advertises in STAR LEDGER. Also, check the offical County newspapers and any local law journals.

NEW MEXICO - ALBUQUERQUE

Advertises in DAILY NEWS
Also, check the offical County newspapers and any local law journals.

NEW YORK - BROOKLYN

General Merchandise/Autos: Private auctioneers.
Real Estate: Private realtors within area.
Advertises in BROOKLYN TIMES, HOME REPORTER, and BROOKLYN SPECTATOR.
Also, check the offical County newspapers and any local law journals.

NEW YORK - BUFFALO

General Merchandise: In house.
Real Estate: Private realtors within area.
Advertises in BUFFALO NEWS.
Also, check the offical County newspapers and any local law journals.

NEW YORK - NEW YORK CITY

General Merchandise/Autos (75 per auction):
Private auctioneers.
Real Estate: Private realtors within area. (Will auction home only by Court Order.)
Advertises in NEW YORK TIMES or NEW YORK JOURNAL.
Also, check the offical County newspapers and any local law journals.

NEW YORK - SYRACUSE

General Merchandise: In house.
Autos: Kept for Marshal's use or divided with DEA.
Real Estate: Private realtors within area; random auctions.
Advertises in HERALD JOURNAL or POST STANDARD.
Also, check the offical County newspapers and any local law journals.

NORTH CAROLINA - ASHEVILLE

Real Estate: Private realtors within area.
Advertises in ASHEVILLE CITIZEN TIMES and local newspapers where property is seized.
Also, check the offical County newspapers and any local law journals.

NORTH CAROLINA - CHARLOTTE

Autos: Statesville Auction Company.
Real Estate: Private realtors within area.
Advertises in MACKLENBERG TIMES legal press; posted in County Court.
Also, check the offical County newspapers and any local law journals.

NORTH CAROLINA - RALEIGH

General Merchandise: Rogers Auctions, Mount Airy.
Autos: Private auctioneers.
Real Estate: Private realtors within area.
Advertises in RALEIGH NEWS AND OBSERVER.
Also, check the offical County newspapers and any local law journals.

NORTH DAKOTA - FARGO

General Merchandise: In house.
Autos: GSA, Denver region.
Real Estate: NASAF Program, (National Asset & Forfeit Program)
Advertises in County newspaper where property is located.
Also, check the offical County newspapers and any local law journals.

OHIO - CLEVELAND

Autos: Bankers Motor Vehicle Inc., Cleveland, Ohio.
Real Estate: Private realtors within area.
Advertises in CLEVELAND PLAIN DEALER, classified.
Also, check the offical County newspapers and any local law journals.

OHIO - CINCINNATI

Autos: Ron's Pre-owned Cars, Blue Ash, Ohio, a storage facility for U.S. Marshal.
Real Estate: Private realtors within area.
Also, check the offical County newspapers and any local law journals.

OKLAHOMA - MUSKOGEE

General Merchandise/Autos/Real Estate: In house or private auctioneer.
Advertises in DAILY OKLAHOMAN and posted on property.
Also, check the offical County newspapers and any local law journals.

OKLAHOMA - OKLAHOMA CITY

General Merchandise: GSA
Autos: GSA, in house.
Real Estate: In house, private realtors within area.
Advertises in DAILY OKLAHOMAN, and legal papers where property is.
Also, check the offical County newspapers and any local law journals.

OKLAHOMA - TULSA

Autos: Private auctioneer.
Real Estate: Williams & Williams Auctioneers
Advertises in TULSA WORLD and TULSA TRIBUNE.

Also, check the offical County newspapers and any local law journals.

OREGON - PORTLAND

General Merchandise: In house.
Real Estate: Private realtors within area.
Advertises in PORTLAND TIMES and SALEM.
Also, check the offical County newspapers and any local law journals.

PENNSYLVANIA - PHILADELPHIA

General Merchandise/Autos: GSA
Real Estate: GSA and Private realtors within area.
Advertises in PHILADELPHIA LEGAL NEWS.
Also, check the offical County newspapers and any local law journals.

PENNSYLVANIA - PITTSBURGH

General Merchandise: In house
Autos: GSA.
Real Estate: Private realtors within area.
Advertises in PITTSBURGH PRESS.
Also, check the offical County newspapers and any local law journals.

PENNSYLVANIA - SCRANTON

General Merchandise: Private Auctioneers. (Recently auctioned entire airport and equipment.)
Autos: Combines with other agency auctions.
Real Estate: Private realtors within area.
Advertises in newspaper in County of auction or property; posted in Courthouse and Post Office.
Also, check the offical County newspapers and any local law journals.

RHODE ISLAND - PROVIDENCE

Autos: Dealers only auction or used by local law enforcement.
Real Estate: Private realtors within area.
Other, boats: In house.
Advertises in PROVIDENCE JHOURNAL, legal notices.

Also, check the offical County newspapers and any local law journals.

SOUTH CAROLINA - COLUMBIA

Advertises in County where auction occurs. Also, check the offical County newspapers and any local law journals.

SOUTH DAKOTA - SIOUX FALLS

General Merchandise: To local police.*
Autos/Real Estate: In house.
Advertises in ARGUS LEADER.
Also, check the offical County newspapers and any local law journals.
*In 1984 seized in a drug deal: airplanes, ranch, cars and guard dogs - one of the biggest ever at the time!

TENNESSEE - KNOXVILLE

Autos/Real Estate: In house.
Advertises in KNOXVILLE NEW SENTINEL.
Also, check the offical County newspapers and any local law journals.

TENNESSEE - MEMPHIS

Autos: In house.
Real Estate: Private realtors within area.
Advertises in COMMERCIAL APPEAL or DAILY NEWS.
Also, check the offical County newspapers and any local law journals.

TENNESSEE - NASHVILLE

General Merchandise/Autos: GSA.
Real Estate: Private realtors within area.
Advertises in local newspapers or elsewhere according to Court Order.
Could be USA TODAY.
Also, check the offical County newspapers and any local law journals.

TEXAS - BEAUMONT

Autos: Used by state or federal agencies.
Real Estate: private realtors within area.
Advertises in BEAUMONT ENTERPRISE, legal publication..

Also, check the offical County newspapers and any local law journals.

TEXAS - DALLAS

General Merchandise/Autos:
Used by agencies.
Real Estate: Private realtors within area.
Advertises in DALLAS MORNING NEWS or in newspapers where property was seized.
Also, check the offical County newspapers and any local law journals.

TEXAS - FORT WORTH

General Merchandise/Autos: In house.
Real Estate: Private realtors within area.
Advertises in DALLAS MORNING NEWS, TIMES HERALD.
Also, check the offical County newspapers and any local law journals.

TEXAS - HOUSTON

General Merchandise: In house.
Autos: Private Auctioneers.
Real Estate: Private realtors within area.
Advertises in POST and CHRONICLE.
Also, check the offical County newspapers and any local law journals.

TEXAS - SAN ANTONIO

General Merchandise/Autos/Real Estate:
Private auctioneers.
Advertising by private auctioneer in their local papers.
Also, check the offical County newspapers and any local law journals.

UTAH - SALT LAKE CITY

General Merchandise/Autos: In house.
Real Estate: Private realtors within area.
Advertises in SALT LAKE TRIBUNE or DESERT NEWS.
Also, check the offical County newspapers and any local law journals.

VIRGINIA - ALEXANDRIA

General Merchandise/Autos: In house.

Real Estate: Private realtors within area.
Advertises in WASHINGTON POST.
Also, check the offical County newspapers and any local law journals.

VIRGINIA - ROANOKE

General Merchandise/Autos: Private auctioneers.
Real Estate: Private realtors within area.
Auction companies advertise in classified section of newspapers 30 days prior to auction.
Also, check the offical County newspapers and any local law journals.

VIRGINIA - BURLINGTON

Autos: Private auctioneers.
Real Estate: Private realtors within area.
Advertises in BURLINGTON FREE PRESS, also fliers and brochures.
Also, check the offical County newspapers and any local law journals.

WASHINGTON - SEATTLE

General Merchandise: Private auctioneer.
Autos: James Murphy Auction Company, Kenmore, Washington.
Real Estate: Private realtors within area.
Advertises in DAILY JOURNAL OF COMMERCE.
Also, check the offical County newspapers and any local law journals.

WASHINGTON - SPOKANE

General Merchandise/Autos: Auctions take place on steps of Courthouse where property was seized.
Real Estate: Government agents-FHA (randomly sold off).
Advertises in DAILY JOURNAL OF COMMERCE- SEATTLE.
Also, check the offical County newspapers and any local law journals.

WASHINGTON, D.C.

General Merchandise: In house/Adam A. Weschler & Son, Washington, D.C.

Autos: In house/Adam & Winer Auctioneers, Baltimore, Maryland.
Real Estate: Private realtors within area.
Advertises in BALTIMORE SUN, WASHINGTON POST, WASHINGTON TIMES, community and special interests publications (art, horses).
Also, check the offical County newspapers and any local law journals.

WEST VIRGINIA - CHARLESTON

General Merchandise: In house.
Autos: In house, GSA.
Real Estate: In house, private realtors within area.
Advertises in CHARLESTON DAILY MAIL and BAREFIELD DAILY TELEGRAPH
Also, check the offical County newspapers and any local law journals.

WEST VIRGINIA - ELKINS

Autos: In house.
Real Estate: In house, private realtors within area.
Advertises in DOMINION POST and FAIRMOUNT TIMES and newspapers where auctions are held.
Also, check the offical County newspapers and any local law journals.

WEST VIRGINIA - WHEELING

Real Estate: Private realtors within area.
Advertises in local newspapers.
Also, check the offical County newspapers and any local law journals.

WISCONSIN - MADISON

General Merchandise/Autos: GSA.
Real Estate: Private realtors within area.
No advertising indicated.
Also, check the offical County newspapers and any local law journals.

WISCONSIN - MILWAUKEE

General Merchandise: Hanzel Gallery, Chicago, Illinois.
Autos: Liquitec Industries, Milwaukee.
Real Estate: Private realtors within area.

Advertises in MILWAUKEE JOURNAL,
Sunday edition, BROOKFIELD NEWS.
Also, check the offical County newspapers
and any local law journals.

WYOMING - CHEYENNE

Real Estate: Western Auction.
Also, check the offical County newspapers
and any local law journals.

U.S. Postal Service - Merchandise

United States Postal Auctions are conducted in five different regions of the country with undeliverable and unclaimed merchandise from within the region being offered. You may contact them at the following addresses:

ATLANTA

730 Great SW Parkway
Atlanta, GA
(404) 344-1625

PHILADELPHIA

2970 Market St., Rm. 531-A
Philadelphia, PA
(215) 895-8140

ST.PAUL/MINNEAPOLIS

443 Fillmore St.
St. Paul, MN
(612) 293-2931

SAN FRANCISCO

1300 Evans Ave.
San Francisco, CA
(415) 550-5400

NEW YORK CITY

380 W. 33rd St.
New York City, NY
(212) 330-2931

U.S. Postal Service - Vehicles

From time to time various Postal Offices have surplus vehicles which they wish to sell to you. Here are some of the postal offices contacted and updates on what they have available and how frequently they have auctions.

ALABAMA

U.S. Postal Service
708 E. South Blvd.
Montgomery, AL 36119
(205) 244-7500

ALASKA

Postal Service Supply Office
Vehicle Maintenance
8221 Petersburg
Anchorage, AK 99507-3132
(907) 349-8900

ARIZONA

U.S. Postal Service
Vehicle Maintenance Facility
4949 E. Van Buren
Phoenix, AZ 85026
(602) 225-3341

ARKANSAS

General Mail Facility--Fleet
4700 E. McCain Blvd.
N. Little Rock, AR 72231
(501) 945-6710

CALIFORNIA

Fleet Maintenance Division
1300 Evans Ave.
San Francisco, CA 94105-9603
(415) 550-5212

COLORADO

U.S. Postal .Service
915 S. Logan
Denver, CO 80209
(303) 297-6730

CONNECTICUT

U.S. Post Office
Vehicle Maintenance Service
85 Weston St.
Hartford, CT 06101
(203) 524-6240

DELAWARE

U.S. Post Office
Vehicle Maintenance
147 Quigley Blvd.
Wilmington, DE 19850
(302) 323-2237

FLORIDA

U.S. Post Office
2800 S. Adams
Tallahassee, FL 32301-9998
(904) 878-7268

GEORGIA

U.S. Post Office
Vehicle Maintenance Facility
3900 Crown Rd.
Atlanta, GA 30304-9721
(404) 765-7735

HAWAII

U.S. Postmaster
c/o Mgr., Fleet Maintenance

89 Sand Island Rd.
Honolulu, HI 96819
(808) 845-1026

IDAHO

U.S. Post Office Garage
770 S. 13th
Boise, ID 83707
(208) 383-4225

ILLINOIS

Main Post Office Garage
2105 E. Cook
Springfield, IL 62703
(217) 788-7241

INDIANA

U.S. Post Office Garage
615 S. Capitol Ave.
Indianapolis, IN 46225-9721
(317) 464-6081

IOWA

U.S. Post Office
1165 Second Ave.
Des Moines, IA 50318-9121
(515) 283-7720

KANSAS

U.S. Post Office Garage
424 S. Kansas Ave.
Topeka, KS 66603
(913) 295-9167

KENTUCKY

U.S. Postal Service
1420 Gardiner Lane
P.O. Box 3111
Louisville, KY 40232-9111
(502) 454-1891

LOUISIANA

Main Post Office Garage
Vehicle Maintenance Dept.

750 Florida Blvd.
Baton Rouge, LA 70021
(504) 381-0388

MAINE

Main Post Office
68 Sewell St.
Augusta, ME 04330
(207) 871-8467

MARYLAND

U.S. Postal Service
6 Waelchli Ave.
Baltimore, MD 21227
(301) 625-8931

MASSCHUSETTS

U.S. Postal Service
25 Dorchester Ave.
Boston, MA 02205
(617) 654-5771 or 654-5292

MICHIGAN

U.S. Post Office
4800 Collins Rd.
Lansing, MI 48924
(517) 337-8736

MINNESOTA

U.S. Postal Service
1144 Fillmore
St. Paul, MN 55107
(612) 349-3082

MISSISSIPPI

U.S. Post Office
350 E. Silas Brown St.
Jackson, MS 39301-5201
(601) 968-5784

MISSOURI

U.S. Postal Service
Vehicle Maintenance Facility
3535 Katherine Rd.

191

Quincy, IL 62301-9998
(217) 224-4950

MONTANA

No auctions--see San Francisco
& Salt Lake City

NEBRASKA

U.S. Postal--Bldg. Maintenance
700 R. St.
Lincoln, NE 68501
(402) 473-1630

NEVADA

U.S. Post Office
2000 Vassar St.
Reno, NV 89510-9997
(702) 788-0626

NEW HAMPSHIRE

U.S. Post Office
Vehicle Maintenance Facility
955 Goffs Falls Rd.
Manchester, NH 03100-7221
(603) 644-4022

NEW JERSEY

Main Post Office
Vehicle Maintenance Facility
680 State Hwy. 130
Trenton, NJ 08650
(609) 581-3089

NEW MEXICO

U.S. Post Office
1135 Broadway, NE
Albuquerque, NM 87101
(505) 848-3887

NEW YORK

U.S. Postal Garage
201 11th Ave.
New York City, NY 10199-9721
(212) 330-4830

NORTH CAROLINA

U.S. Postal Office
310 Newborne Ave.
Raleigh, NC 27611
(919) 831-3661

NORTH DAKOTA

U.S. Post Office
220 E. Rosser Ave.
Bismarck, ND 58501
(701) 221-6517

OHIO

U.S. Postal Service
850 Twin River Dr.
Columbus, OH 43216
(614) 469-4255

OKLAHOMA

Main Post Office
Vehicle Services
320 S.W .Fifth St.
Oklahoma City, OK 73125-9105
(405) 278-6159 or 278-6154

OREGON

U.S. Post Office
Vehicle Maintenance Facility
918 NW Park Ave.
Portland, Oregon 97208
(503) 294-2444

U.S. Post Office
1050 25th SE
Salem, OR 97301
(503) 370-4700

PENNSYLVANIA

Philadelphia Post Office Garage
30th and Chestnut
Philadelphia, PA 19104
(215) 895-9290

RHODE ISLAND

192

No auctions--see New York City

SOUTH CAROLINA

U.S. Post Office
1601 Assembly St.
Columbia, SC 29201-9122
(803) 733-4692

SOUTH DAKOTA

U.S. Postal Service
Vehicle Maintenance Facility
500 E. Boulevard
Rapid City, SD 57701-5709
(605) 394-8648

TENNESSEE

U.S. Post Office Garage
707 Chestnut St.
Nashville, TN 37229-9721
(615) 885-9275

TEXAS

U.S. Postal Service
10410 Perrin Beitel
San Antonio, TX 78284
(512) 657-8300

UTAH

U.S. Post Office
Vehicle Maintenance Dept.
1760 W. 2100 S.
Salt Lake City, UT 84199-9721
(801) 974-2350

VERMONT

U.S. Postal Service
Vehicle Maintenance Facility
1800 Page Blvd.
Springfield, MA 01152-9721
(413) 785-6383

VIRGINIA

U.S. Post Office Garage

1801 School St.
Richmond, VA 23232
(804) 775-6159

WASHINGTON, D.C.

U.S. Postal Service
Fleet Operations
980 V. St., NE
Washington, D.C. 20018-9601
(202) 832-0158

WASHINGTON

U.S. Postal Service
3825 S. Warren
Tacoma, WA 98409
(206) 756-6140

WEST VIRGINIA

U.S. Post Office
Vehicle Maintenance Facility
602 Donnelly St.
Charleston, WV 25301-9721
(304) 357-4158

WISCONSIN

U.S. Postal Service
3902 Milwaukee St.
Madison, WI 53703
(608) 246-1249

Internal Revenue Service

HOT LINE NUMBERS

San Francisco   (415) 556-5021
Seattle   (206) 442-0703
Los Angeles   (213) 894-5777
New York City   (718) 780-4020

In order to get on the mailing list for the IRS auctions, please contact the IRS offices below by phone or in writing. The national 800 number, which will ring to your state's IRS office, is 1-800- 829-1040. When you call, you should ask for notices on upcoming public auctions. You should also ask for FORM 2222 which is the sealed bid form for placing your sealed bid for those auctions.

ALABAMA
2121 8th Ave. N.
Birmingham, AL 35203

ALASKA

P.O. Box 1500
Anchorage, AK 99510

ARIZONA

P.O. Box 2350
Phoenix, AZ 85002

ARKANSAS

P.O. Box 3778
Little Rock, AR 72203

CALIFORNIA

300 N. Los Angeles
Los Angeles, CA 90012
or
450 Golden State Ave.
San Fransisco, CA 94102

COLORADO

1050 17th St.
Denver, CO 80265

CONNECTICUT

P.O. Box 2555
Hartford, CT 06101

DELAWARE

P.O. Box 28
Wilmington, DE 19899

**DISTRICT OF COLUMBIA/
MARYLAND**

P.O. Box 1018
Baltimore, MD 21203

FLORIDA

P.O. Box 35045
Jacksonville, FL 32202

GEORIGA

P.O. Box 875
Atlanta, GA 30301

HAWAII

P.O. Box 50088
Honolulu, HI 86850

IDAHO

550 W. Fort St.
Box 041
Boise, ID 83724

ILLINOIS

P.O. Box 1192
Chicago, IL 60690

INDIANA

P.O. Box 44687
Indianapolis, IN 46244

IOWA

P.O. Box 313
Des Moines, IA 50305

KANSAS

P.O. Box 400
Witchia, KS 67201

KENTUCKY

P.O. Box 1735
Louisville, KY 40201

LOUISANA

P.O. Box 30608
New Orleans, LA 70190

MAINE

P.O. Box 1020
Augusta, ME 04330

MASSACHUSETTS

P.O. Box 9087 9088
JFK Post Office
Boston, MA 02203

MICHIGAN

P.O. Box 32500
Detroit, MI 48232

MINNESOTA

P.O. Box 3450
St. Paul, MN 55165

MISSISSIPPI

P.O. Box 370
Jackson, MS 39205

MISSOURI

P.O. Box 1487
St. Louis, MO 63188

MONTANA

Second Fl., Federal Bldg.
Helena, MT 59601

NEBRASKA

P.O. Box 1052
Omaha, NE 68101

NEVADA

P.O. Box 4200
Reno, NV 89504

NEW HAMPSHIRE

275 Chestnut St.
Manchester, NH 03103

NEW JERSEY

P.O. Box 1269
Newark, NJ 07101

NEW MEXICO

P.O. Box 1967
Alburquerque, NM 87103

NEW YORK

P.O. Box 60 G. P.O.
Brooklyn, NY 11202
or
P.O. Box 2200
Church Street Station,
NY 11202

NORTH CAROLINA

P.O. Box 20541
Greensboro, NC 27420

OHIO

P.O. Box 1579
Cincinnati, OH 45201
or
P.O. Box 99183
Cleveland, OH 44199

OKLAHOMA

P.O. Box 66
Oklahoma City, OK 73101

OREGON

P.O. Box 3341
Portland, OR 97208

PENNSYLVANIA

P.O. Box 12898
Philadelphia, PA 19106
or
P.O. Box 2488
Pittsburgh, PA 15230

RHODE ISLAND

P.O. Box 6867
Providence, RI 02940

SOUTH CAROLINA

P.O. Box 407
Columbia, SC 29202

SOUTH DAKOTA

P.O. Box 370
Abredeen, SD 57401

TENNESSEE

P.O. BOX 1107
Nashville, TN 37202

TEXAS

P.O. Box 250
Austin, TX 78767
or
1100 Commerce Street
Code 401
Dallas, TX 75242

UTAH

P.O. BOX 2196
Salt Lake City, UT.84110

VERMONT

11 Eimwood Ave.
Burlington, VT 05401

VIRGINA

P.O. Box 10025
Richmond, VA 23240

WASHINGTON

Call only:(206) 442-0703
Seattle, WA

WEST VIRGINA

P.O. Box 1907
Parkersburgh, WV 26101

WISCONSIN

P.O. Box 493
Milwaukee, WI 53201

WYOMING

P.O. Box 1829
Cheyenne, WY 82001

Defense Reutilization and Marketing Service

The United States Defense Reutilization and Marketing Service (DRMS) is an agent of the Department of Defense and sells surplus government personal property previously owned by the Defense Logistics Agency, Army, Navy, Air Force, Marine Corps and other components of the Department of Defense.

They have headquarters in Battle Creek, Michigan and field offices located in 50 states and 20 foreign countries. They're divided into five regions, which are headquartered in:

Columbus, OH
Memphis, TN
Ogden, UT
Hawaii
West Germany

The National Bidder's List for wholesale items is located at this address. You may call the phone number to get their sealed bid lists for wholesale, bulk items and large equipment:

National Bidder's List
Defense Reutilization and Marketing Sales Office
P.O. Box 1370
Battle Creek, MI 49016-1370
(616) 961-4000, Ext. 7331

If you wish to go to retail sales or public auctions, they are held on a frequent basis at the following locations. You may call and get on their mailing lists for upcoming auctions.

DRMO - United States

ALABAMA

DRMO--Anniston
Anniston Army Depot
Anniston, AL 36201-5090
(205) 235-7733/7133

DRMO--Fort McClellan (ZWSE)
Bldg. T342
Anniston, AL 36205-5000
(205) 235-7133

DRMO--Huntsville
Bldg. 7408
Redstone Arsenal, AL
35898-7230
(205) 876-9634

DRMO--Montgomery
Bldg. 900/Gunter AFS
Montgomery, AL 36114-5000
(205) 279-4194

DRMO--Rucker
Bldg. 1313
Fort Rucker, AL 36362-5286
(205) 255-2275/5263

ALASKA

DRMO--Anchorage
P.O. Box 866
Bldg. 34-600
Elmendorf AFB, AK
99506-0866
(907) 552-3911

DRMO--Fairbanks
P.O. Box 35028
Fort Wainwright, AK
99703-0028
(907) 353-7334/6318

ARIZONA

DRMO-HUACHUCA
P.O. Box 104
Fort Huachuca, AZ 85613-0104
(602) 533-2074

DRMO--SZT
Luke AFB
Glendale, AZ 85309-5000
(602) 856-7144

DRMO--Tucson
P.O. V Box 15011
Tucson, AZ 85708-0011
(602) 750-5041

DRMO--Yuma
MCAS, P.O. Box 12397
Yuma, AZ 85364-5000
(602) 726-2748

ARKANSAS

DRMO--Eaker AFB
Bldg. 427
Eaker AFB, AR 72317
(501) 762-7479

DRMO--Fort Chaffee (ZMFC)
Bldg. 339
Fort Smith, AR 72905-5000
(501) 484-2862

DRMO--Little Rock
Little Rock AFB
Jacksonville, AR 72099-5000
(501) 988-6782

CALIFORNIA

DRMO--Alameda
Warehouse 5
Ziss Mariner Square Loop
Alameda, CA 94501-1022
(415) 869-8309

DRMO--Barstow
Marine Corps Logistic Base
Bldg. 226
Barstow, CA 92311-5045
(619) 577-6561

DRMO--Edwards
P.O. Box 308
Edwards AFB, CA 93523-5000
(805) 277-2209

199

DRMO--El Toro
P.O. Box 21
East Irvine, CA 92650-0021
(714) 726-4924

DRMO--Mare Island
Code 1005
Bldg. 655, Door 18
Vallejo, CA 94592-5021
(707)646-3235

DRMO--McClellan
Bldg. 700
McClellan AFB. CA
95652-6448
(916) 643-3830

DRMO--Moffett
Bldg. 127
Naval Air Station
Moffett Field,CA 94035-5127
(415) 966-5368

DRMO--North Island
P.O. Box 337
Imperial Beach, CA
92032-0337
(619) 545-8055

DRMO--Norton Bldg. 948
Norton AFB. CA 92409-6488
(714) 382-6164

DRMO--Ord
P.O. Box 810
Marina, CA 93933-0810
(408) 242-7189

DRMO--Pendleton
SZ 3139
P.O. Box 1608
Oceanside, CA 92054-0291
(619) 725-4331

DRMO--Port Hueneme
NCBC Bldg. 513
Port Hueneme, CA 93043-5015
(805) 982-5636/5637/5638

DRMO--San Diego
P.O. Box 337
Imperial Beach, CA
92032-0337
(619) 437-9456/9439/9440

DRMO--Stockton
Bldg. 1004

Rough & Ready Island
Stockton, CA 95203-4999
(209) 944-0267/0268/0260

DRMO--Travis
Bldg. 724
Travis AFB. CA 94535-7100
(707) 424-3137

DRMO--Vandenburg
Box 5127
Vandenburg AFB, CA
93437-6100
(805) 866-9852

COLORADO

DRMO--Colorado Springs
Fort Carson Bldg. 318
Colorado Springs, CO
80913-5670
(719) 579-4355

DRMO--Denver
Bldg. 621
Rocky Mountain Arsenal
Commerce City, CO
80022-2180
(303) 289-0378

Pueblo Army Depot
Bldg. 163
Pueblo, CO 81001-5000
(719) 549-4111

CONNECTICUT

DRMO--Groton
Naval Submarine Base
New London Box 12
Groton, CT 06349-0012
(203) 449-2866/3523/3524

DELAWARE

DRMO--Dover
Bldg. 114
Dover AFB, DE 19902-6468
(302) 678-6165/6166

FLORIDA

DRMO--Eglin
DRMO (ZJE) Bldg. 525

Eglin AFB, FL 32542-5280
(904) 882-2822/2823/2824

DRMO--Homestead
Bldg.607
Homestead AFB, FL
33039-5000
(305) 257-7425/7426

DRMO--Jacksonville
P.O. Box 82
Jacksonville, FL 32212-0082
(904) 772-9248/9249

DRMO--Key West
NAS Harry S. Truman
Annex Bldg. 795
Key West, FL 33040-0006
(305) 292-5271/5272

DRMO--Patrick
Bldg. 1391
Patrick AFB, FL 32925-7469
(407) 494-6507/7912

DRMO--Pensacola
U.S. Naval Air Station
Pensacola, FL 32508-7404
(904) 452-2451

DRMO--Tampa
Bldg. 1110
P.O. Box 6838
MacDill AFB, FL 33608-0838
(813) 830-2871/2872/2873

GEORGIA

DRMO--Albany
Marine Corps Logistic Base
Albany, GA 31704-5045
(912) 439-5966/5967/5969/5970

DRMO--Benning
P.O. Box 3760
Columbus, GA 31903-0760
(404) 545-7206/3497/7214

DRMO--Forest Park (ZWAF)
Fort Gillem
Bldg. 310-B
Forest Park, GA 30050-5000
(404) 363-5117/5118

DRMO--Gordon
Bldg. 19601
Fort Gordon, GA 309-05-5667

(404) 791-3749/2487

DRMO--Stewart
P.O. Box 10
Hinesville, GA 31313-0010
(912) 767-8863/8878/8893/8899

DRMO--Valdosta (ZWAE)
Bldg. 997
Moody AFB, GA 31699-5260
(912) 333-3349/4667

DRMO--Warner-Robins (ZWA)
Bldg. 1602
Robins AFB, GA 31098-5000
(912) 926-2164/3159/4541

IDAHO

DRMO--Mountain Home
P.O. Box 4068
Mountain Home AFB, ID
83648-4068
(208) 828-2306

ILLINOIS

DRMO--Chanute
Bldg. 734
Chanute AFB, IL 61868-5000
(217) 495-2701/3131

DRMO--Great Lakes
Naval Training Center
Bldg. 3212A
Great Lakes, IL 60088-5798
(312) 688-3655/3656

DRMO--Rock Island
Rock Island Arsenal
Bldg. 154
Rock Island, IL 61299-7030
(309) 782-1617/1618/1619

DRMO--Scott
Bldg. 4141
Scott AFB, IL 62225-5000
(618) 256-3105/4497/5964

INDIANA

DRMO--Crane
Naval Weapons Support Center
Crane, IN 47522-5091
(812) 854-3442/1554/1728

DRMO--Indianapolis
Bldg. 124
Fort Benjamin Harrison, IN
46216-7400
(317) 543-6615/6616

KANSAS

DRMO--Leavenworth
Bldg. 269
Fort Leavenworth, KS
66027-6500
(913) 684-2878/2383

DRMO--McConnell
Bldg. 1349
McConnell AFB, KS
67221-6100
(316) 652-4098/4099/4101

DRMO--Riley
P.O. Box 2490
Fort Riley, KS 66442-2490
(913) 239-6202/6203/6204/6205

KENTUCKY

DRMO--Campbell (ZMJ)
P.O. Box 2555
Fort Campbell, KY 42223-5000
(502) 798-4762

DRMO--Knox
Bldg. 2962
Fraizer Rd.
Fort Knox, KY 40121-5640
(502) 624-5755/1328

DRMO--Lexington (ZMH)
Lexington--Blue Grass Depot
Lexington, KY 40511-5108
(606) 293-3436/3543/3405/4125

LOUISIANA

DRMO--Barksdale (ZWS)

Bldg. 4964
Barksdale AFB, LA
71110-6100
(318) 456-4898/3216/3309

DRMO--Polk
P.O. Box 901
Fort Polk, LA 71459-0901
(318) 535-4068/4609/2401

MAINE

DRMO--Brunswick
Naval Air Station
Bldg. 584
Brunswick, ME 04011-5000
(207) 921-2627/2452

DRMO--Limestone
P.O. Box 1021
Loring AFB, ME 04751-6100
(207) 999-6193/2464/7134

MARYLAND

DRMO--Aberdeen
Aberdeen Proving Ground
Aberdeen, MD 21005-5001
(301) 278-2235/4785/2435

DRMO--Meade
P.O. Box 388
Fortmeade, MD 20755-0388
(301) 677-6366

DRMO--Patuxent
Bldg. 604
Naval Air Station
Patuxent River, MD 20670
(301) 863-3316

MASSACHUSETTS

DRMO--Devens
P.O. Box 69
Fort Devens, MA 01433-5690
(508) 796-2418

DRMO--Westover
Bldg. 1604
Westover AFB, MA
01022-5000
(413) 557-3904/3939

MICHIGAN

DRMO--Sawyer
Bldg. 417
K. I. Sawyer AFB, MI
49843-6100
(906) 346-2254/2432

DRMO--Selfridge
Bldg. 590
Selfridge ANG Base, MI
48045-5003

DRMO--Wurtsmith
P.O. Box 3001
Wurtsmith AFB, MI
48753-6100
(517) 747-6332/6357

MINNESOTA

DRMO--Duluth
c/o 148th Tactical
Reconnaissance GP
Minnesota Air National Guard
Duluth International Airport
Duluth, MN 55811-5000
(218) 723-7441/7452/7453

MISSISSIPPI

DRMO--Columbus (CMAF)
Bldg. 152
Columbus AFB, MS
39701-5000
(601) 434-7463/7464/7465

DRMO--Keesler
Bldg. 4422
Keesler AFB, MS 39534-5000
(601) 377-2505/2393

MISSOURI

DRMO--Leonard Wood
Gas St. Bldg. 2391
Fort Leonard, MO 65473-5820
(314) 368-7101

DRMO--Whiteman
P.O. Box 6010
Whiteman AFB, MO
75305-6100
(816) 687-3308/3521

MONTANA

DRMO--Great Falls
Bldg. 1531
Malmstrom AFB, MT
59402-6100
(406) 731-6346/6347

NEBRASKA

DRMO--Offcutt
P.O. Box 13292
Omaha, NE 68113-6100
(402) 294-2425/4964

NEVADA

DRMO--Nellis
Bldg. 838
Nellis AFB, NV 89191-5000
(702) 652-2002

NEW HAMPSHIRE

DRMO--Portsmouth
Portsmouth Naval Shipyard
P.O. Box 2028
Portsmouth, NH 03801-2028
(207) 438-2282

NEW JERSEY

DRMO--Bayonne
Military Ocean Terminal
Bldg. 63
Bayonne, NJ 07002-5301
(201) 823-7541/7209/5996/5997

DRMO-Lakehurst
Naval Air Engineering Ctr
Bldg. 75
Lakehurst, NJ 08733-5010
(201) 323-2661/2669/7373/7374

DRMO--XPOS
U.S. Ardec
Bldg. 314
Pickatinny Arsenal, NJ
07806-5000
(201) 724-4219/4747

NEW MEXICO

DRMO--Cannon
Bldg. 215
Cannon AFB, NM 88103-5000
(505) 784-2436

DRMO--Holloman
Bldg. 112
Holloman AFB. NM 87117-6001
(505) 479-3747/2213

DRMO--Kirtland
Bldg. 1025
Kirtland AFB. NM 87117-6001
(505) 844-0125

NEW YORK

DRMO--Plattsburgh
Plattsburgh AFB
P.O. Box 864
Plattsburgh, NY 12901-0864
(518) 565-5778/5779/5431

DRMO--Rome
Bldg. T-8
Griffis AFB, NY 13441-6100
(315) 330-3400/4822

DRMO--Romulus
Seneca Army Depot
Romulus, NY 14541-5011
(607) 869-1236

DRMO--Wateruliet
Wateruliet Arsenal
Bldg. 145
Wateruliet, NY 12189-5000
(518) 266-4112/5126

NORTH CAROLINA

DRMO--Bragg
Bldg. J
1334 Knox St
Fort Bragg, NC 28307-5000
(919) 396-5222

DRMO--Cherry Point
PSC 4298
MCAS Cherry Point, NC
28533-4298
(919) 466-2743/5905/3338

DRMO--Lejeune
Louis Rd. Bldg. 906

Camp Lejeune, NC 28542-5000
(919) 451-5613/5652/2302

NORTH DAKOTA

DRMO--Grand Forks
Grand Forks AFB
Bldg. 432
Grand Forks, ND 58206-6100
(701) 747-3780/3781/
3782/3783/3784

DRMO--Minot
Bldg. 531
Minot AFB, ND 58705-5000
(701) 723-6120

OHIO

DRMO--Columbus
3990 E. Broad St.
P.O. Box 13297
Columbus, OH 43213-5000
(614) 238-3244

DRMO--Wright-Patterson
Bldg. 89 Area C
Wright-Patterson AFB, OH
45433-5000
(513) 257-4291/4203/7823

OKLAHOMA

DRMO--McAlester (ZOAE)
U.S. Army Ammunition Plant
McAlester, OK 74501-5000
(918) 421-2248/2249

DRMO--Oklahoma City (ZOA)
Tinker AFB/L-11
Oklahoma City, OK 73145-5000
(405) 739-7135

DRMO--Sill (ZOB)
Bldg. 3373 Naylor Rd.
Fort Sill, OK 73503-6900
(405) 351-4703/3415/3295

OREGON

OSB Umatella Oregon
Umatella Army Depot
Hermiston, OR 97838
(503) 564-8632, Ext. 5273

PENNSYLVANIA

DRMO--Chambersburg
Letter Kenny Army Depot
P.O. Box 229
Chambersburg, PA
17201-0229
(717) 267-5425/8852

DRMO--Mechanicsberg
5450 Carlisle Pike
P.O. Box 2020
Mechanicsberg, PA
17055-0788
(717) 790-3325/3135

DRMO--Philadelphia
2800 S. 20th St.
Bldg. 26-C
Philadelphia, PA 19101-8419
(215) 952-5914

DRMO--Tobyhanna
P.O. Box 366
Topbyhanna, PA 18466-0366
(717) 894-7455

RHODE ISLAND

DRMO--Davisville
Naval Construction
Battalion Ctr.
Davisville, RI 02854-0795
(401) 267-2294/2213

SOUTH CAROLINA

DRMO--Charleston
P.O. Box 5716
North Charleston, SC
29406-0715
(803) 743-5176/5177

DRMO--Jackson
Bldg. 1902
Fort Jackson, SC 29207-6050
(803) 751-7716/3271

DRMO--Shaw(ZWLF)
Bldg. 26
Shaw AFB, SC 29152-0890
(803) 668-3556

SOUTH DAKOTA

DRMO--Ellsworth
Ellsworth AFB
Bldg. 1801
Rapid City, SD 57706-6100
(605) 385-1021

TENNESSEE

DRMO--Memphis
2163 Airways Blvd.
Memphis, TN 38114-5297
(901) 775-6155/4987

DRMO--Naval Air Station
(ZMAE)
Bldg. S. 6
Millington, TN 38054-5027
(901) 775-4896/4897

TEXAS

DRMO--Bliss
P.O. Box 8029
El Paso, TX 79908-9991
(915) 568-8503

DRMO--Carswell
P.O. Box 27177
Carswell AFB, TX 76127-5000
(817) 782-5321/5748

DRMO--Corpus Christi
Bldg. 22
Naval Air Station
Corpus Christi, TX 78419-5600
(512) 939-2936/2933/3359

DRMO--Hood
Bldg. 4289 (80th) St.
P.O. Drawer 6
Fort Hood, TX 76544-0210
(817) 287-4770/
8824/8822/3315

DRMO--San Antonio
Bldg. 3050 E. Kelly
Kelly AFB, TX 78241-5000
(512) 925-7766/6167/6168/6169

DRMO--Sheppard
DRMO 37, Bldg. 2135
Sheppard AFB, TX 76311-5000
(817) 676-2712/4933

DRMO--Texarkana
P.O. Box 1330
Hooks, TX 75561-1330
(214) 334-3177/3178

UTAH

DRMO--Hill
Attn: DRMO--YOA
Bldg. 890
Hill AFB, UT 84056-5000
(801) 777-6557

Defense Depot Ogden
500 W. 12th St.
Ogden, UT 81001
(801) 399-7281

DRMO--Tooele
Tooele Army Depot
Bldg. 2010
Tooele, UT 84074-5019
(801) 833-3571

VIRGINIA

DRMO--Belvoir
Stop 566/SX 151 W
Bldg. 2517
Fort Belvoir, VA 22060-0566
(703) 664-6551/6553/6554

DRMO--Camp Allen
Salvage Yard
Bldg. CAO 429 Annex
Norfolk, VA 23511-0060
(804) 444-5689/5366

DRMO--Norfolk
Norfold Naval Station
Post Office
P.O. Box 15068
Norfolk, VA 23511-0068
(804) 444-5366/5472

DRMO--Richmond
P.O. Box 34448
Richmond, VA 23234-0448
(804) 275-4407/4943

DRMO--Williamsburg
Cheatham Annex Bldg. 16
Naval Supply Ctr.
Williamsburg, VA 23187-8792
(804) 887-7289/7164

WASHINGTON

DRMO--Fairchild
P.O. Box 1321
Fairchild AFB, WA
99011-1321
(509) 247-2350

DRMO--Lewis
P.O. Box 56
Tillicum, WA 98492-0056
(206) 967-4890

DRMO--Whidbey Island
NAS Whidbey Island
Oak Harbor, WA 98278-5100
(206) 257-2501

WISCONSIN

DRMO--Sparta
Fort McCoy--Bldg. 2184
Sparta, WI 54656-6002
(608) 388-3718

WYOMING

DRMO--Warren
Bldg. 808
Francis E, Warren AFB
WY 82005-6100
(307) 775-3959/3970

DRMO - Europe

DRMO Giessen, Germany
APO NY 09169
641-42678

DRMO Keflavik, Iceland
APO NY 09571
00354-25-7092/7307

DRMO Lajes, Azores

APO NY 09406
351-95-53001

DRMO Livorno, Italy
APO NY 09019
586-943272

OSB Naples, Italy
APO NY 09520
539-81-724 Ext. 5218/5282

DRMO Molesworth, England
APO NY 09238
480-432117

DRMO Nurenburg, W. Germany
APO NY 09696
49-911-713935

OSB Augsburg, Germany
APO NY 09178
49-821-524685

OSB Grafenwoehr, Germany
APO NY 09114
49-9721-88960 Ext. 7146

OSB Schweinfurt, Germany
APO NY 09702
49-9721-88960

DRMO Seckenheim, W. Germany
APO NY 09081
49-621-473231

DRMO Ankara, Turkey
APO NY 09254
90-41-255100

OSB Incirlik, Turkey
APO NY 09289
009071-14228 Ext.3155/6037

DRMO Athens, Greece
APO NY 09223
003001-9815-830

DRMO Aviano, Italy
APO NY 09293
39-434-31393

OSB Vicenza, Italy
APO NY 09221
39-444-517651/517275

DRMO Berlin, Germany
APO NY 09742
49-30-819-3174

DRMO Hanau, W. Germany
APO NY 09165
49-6181-55614

DRMO Laiserlautern,
W. Germany
APO NY 09227
49-631-40307, Ext. 8692/7416

OSB Baumholder, W. Germany
APO NY 09034
49-6783-7219

OSB Bitburg, W. Germany
APO NY 09132
49-6561-2484

OSB Chievres, Belgium
APO NY 09088
0032-68-223171, Ext. 5484

DRMO Kastel W. Germany
APO NY 09633
6134-63713, Ext. 5484

OSB Bremerhaven, Germany
APO NY 09069
49-471-415351

OSB Germersheim, Germany
APO NY 09114
49-9641-83-2947, Ext.7146

OSB Germersheim, Germany
APO NY 09095
49-7274-2947

OSB Ludwigsburg, Germany
APO NY 09279
49-7141-44675

DRMO Torrejon, Sopain
APO NY 09283
00341-665-7637

OSB Rota, Spain
FPO NY 09540
003456-862780,
Ext. 2489/2091

OSB Zaragoza, Spain
APO NY 09286
003476-326711,
Ext. 2166/2331

DRMO - Pacific

DRMO Hawaii
Box 580
Pearl City, HI 96782-0580
Ext. (808) 474-6872

DRMO Okinawa
Box 4497
APO San Francisco 96331-3008
011-81-98938-1111
(Telex) 695-526

DRMO Pusan
APO San Francisco 96259-0269
011-82-51-801-3413/3801/3472
011-82-51-807-1338

DRMO Sagami
APO San Francisco 96343-0063
011-81-0427-59-4148

DRMO Sagami (Site B)
OSB Yokota
APO San Francisco 96328-5000
Ext: 255-8633/8413

DRMO Sagami (Site C)
OSB Yokosuka
P.O. Box 161
FPO Seattle 98762-2980
Ext. 234-5806/7519

DRMO Sagami (Site D)
OSB Misawa
APO San Francisco 96519-5000
Ext. 226-4052/3448

DRMO Sagami (Site E)
OSB Iwakuni
FBO Seattle 98764-5017

Ext. 236-3982/4008

DRMR Pacific
Sales Field Office Korea
APO San Francisco 96483-0120
Telex: 787 22 88 6 DPDRKS

DRMR Pacific
Sales Field Office Philippines
Box 40
FPO San Francisco 96651-1523
011-63-89-882-3167
Telex: 14534

DRMO Australia
American Embassy
APO San Francisco 96404-5000
011-61-62-472-568
Telex: 790 AA62096 WESTEN

DRMO Australia
(Exmouth Site)
FPO San Francisco 96680-2920
011-61-99-491-352
Ext: 3265

DRMO Bupyong
APO San Francisco 96483-0120
011-82-32-524-047262

DRMO Clark
APO San Francisco 96274-5000
011-6352-47240/47262

DRMO Guam
Box 190
FPO San Francisco 96630-3000
011-(671)-339-5198/5227
Telex: 723634174

Veteran's Administration

There are over 18,000 properties available to purchase from the Veteran's Administration. For more information as to the specific homes available, qualifications and steps you need to take in order to purchase these properties, please contact the V. A. office in your area.

ALABAMA

474 S. Court St.
Montgomery, AL 36104
(205) 832-7025

ALASKA

235 E. Eighth Ave.
Anchorage, AK 99501
(907) 271-2215

ARIZONA

3225 N. Central Ave.
Phoenix, AZ 85012
(602) 241-2748

ARKANSAS

P.O. Box 1240
North Little Rock, AR 72115
(501) 370-3800

CALIFORNIA

Federal Bldg.
11000 Wilshire Blvd.
(213) 209-7175
or
211 Main St.
San Francisco, CA 94105
(415) 495-8900

COLORADO

44 Union Blvd.
Box 25126
Denver, CO 80225
(303) 980-1300

CONNECTICUT

450 Main St.
Hartford, CT 06103
(203) 278-3230

DELAWARE

1601 Kirkwood Hw
Wilmington, DE 19
(302) 998-0191

DISTRICT OF C

941 N. Capitol St.,
Rm. 90-1-12
Washington, DC
(202) 275-1325 or

FLORIDA

144 First Ave. S.
St. Petersburg, FL 33731
(813) 898-2121

GEORGIA

730 Peachtree St. N. E.
Atlanta, GA 30365
(404) 881-1776

HAWAII

PJKK Federal Bldg.
300 Ala Moana Blvd.
Honolulu, HI 96813
(808) 541-1476

IDAHO

550 W. Fort St.
Box 044
Boise, ID 83724
(208) 334-1900

ILLINOIS

VA Section 265
P.O. Box 4841
Chicago, IL 60680
(312) 353-2049

IOWA

210 Walnut St.
Rm .985
Des Moines, IA 50309
(515) 284-4675

KENTUCKY

600 Federal Plaza
Rm .473
Louisville, KY 40202
(502) 584-2231

LOUISIANA

701 Loyola Ave.
New Orleans, LA 70113
(504) 589-6459

MAINE

VA Medical Ctr.
Loan Guarantee Division
Togus, ME 04330
(207) 623-8411

MARYLAND

31 Hopkins Plaza
Baltimore, MD 21202
(301) 962-4466

MASSACHUSETTS

Government Ctr.

JFK Blvd.
Rm. 312
Boston, MA 02205
~~(617) 565-3027~~
(617) 227-4600

MICHIGAN

477 Michigan Ave.
Detroit, MI 48226
(313) 226-4200

MINNESOTA

Federal Bldg, Rm. 128
Fort Snelling
St. Paul, MN 55111
(612) 725-3870

MISSISSIPPI

100 W. Capitol St.
Jackson, MS 39269-0199
(601) 965-4840

MISSOURI

Federal Bldg, Rm 4705
Rm. 4705
1520 Market St.
St. Louis, MO 63103
(314) 539-3144

MONTANA

Property Management (261)
Ft. Harrison, MT 59636
(406) 442-6410 Ext. 344/345

NEBRASKA

Federal Bldg.
100 Centennial Mall N.
Lincoln, NE 68508
(402) 437-5031

NEVADA

1201 Terminal Way
Reno, NV 89520
(702) 329-9244

NEW HAMPSHIRE

Federal Bldg.
275 Chestnut St.
Manchester, NH 03101
(603) 666-7654

NEW JERSEY

20 Washington Place
Newark, NJ 07012
(201) 645-2150

NEW MEXICO

Loan Guarantee
500 Gold Ave., SW
Albuquerque, NM 87102
(505) 766-3361

NEW YORK

111 W. Huron St.
Buffalo, NY 14202
(716) 846-5191

NORTH CAROLINA

Federal Bldg.
251 N. Main St.
Winston-Salem, NC 27155
(919) 761-3494

NORTH DAKOTA

655 First Ave., N.
Fargo, ND 58102
(701) 232-3241

OHIO

Federal Bldg.
240 E. Ninth St.
Cleveland, OH 44199
(216) 522-3583

OKLAHOMA

125 S. Main St.
Muskogee, OK 74401

(918) 687-2161

OREGON

1220 SW Third Ave.
Office 1420
Portland, OR 97204
(503) 326-2484

PENNSYLVANIA

P.O. Box 8079
5000 Wissahickon Ave.
Philadelphia, PA 19101
(215) 438-5225

RHODE ISLAND

321 S, Main St.
Providence, RI 02903
(401) 273-4910

SOUTH CAROLINA

1801 Assembly St.
Columbia, SC 29201
(803) 765-5154

SOUTH DAKOTA

Loan Property Management Division
P.O. Box 4046
Sioux Falls, SD 57117
(605) 336-3230

TENNESSEE
110 Ninth Ave., S.
Nashville, TN 37203
(615) 736-5241

TEXAS

2515 Murworth Dr.
Houston, TX 77054
(713) 664-4664
or
N. Valley Mills Dr.
Waco, TX 84147

UTAH

125 S. State St.
Salt Lake City, UT 84111
(801) 524-5986

VERMONT

White River Junction, VT
05001
(802) 295-9363

VIRGINIA

210 Franklin Rd. SW
Roanoke, VA 24011
(703) 982-6141 or 6149

WASHINGTON

915 Second Ave.
12th Fl.

Seattle, WA 98174
(206) 624-7200

WEST VIRGINIA

640 Fourth Ave.
Huntington, WV 25701
(304) 529-5046

WISCONSIN

Bldg. G
P. M. 266
Milwaukee, WI 53295
(414) 385-8680

WYOMING

2360 E. Pershing Blvd.
Cheyenne, WY 82001
(307) 778-7550

Department of Housing and Urban Development

HUD offices are located in nearly every city with 10 regional offices and 71 field offices. If you are interested in their larger properties, you may contact the regional office.

If you are interested in getting more information on HUD and how their home sales work, please contact one of the regional offices or field offices located below:

REGION I (BOSTON)

Boston Regional Office
Room 375
Thomas P. O'Neil, Jr.
Federal Bldg.
10 Causeway St.
Boston MA 02222-1092
(617)565-5234

Field Offices:

Hartford Office
First Floor
330 Main St.
Hartford, CT 06106-1860
(203) 240-4523

Manchester Office
Norris Cotton Federal Bldg.
275 Chestnut St.
Manchester, NH 03101-2487
(603) 666-7458

Providence Office
330 John O. Pastore
Federal Bldg.
U.S. Post Office-Kennedy Plaza
Providence, RI 02903-1785
(401) 528-5351

Bangor Office
Manchester, N.H. 03101-2487
(603) 666-7458

Burlington Office
Manchester, N.H. 03101-2487
(603) 666-7458

REGION II (NEW YORK)

New York Regional Office
26 Federal Plaza
New York, NY 10278-0068
(212) 264-8053

Field Offices:

Albany Office
Leo W. O'Brien Federal Bldg.
North Pearl St. and Clinton Ave.
Albany, NY 12207-2395
(518) 472-3567

Buffalo Office
465 Main Street
Lafayette Court Building - 5th Floor.
Buffalo, NY 14203
(716) 846-5755

Camden Office
The Parkade Bldg.
519 Federal St.
Camden, NJ 08103-9998
(609)757-5081

Caribbean Office
159 Carlos Chardon Ave.
San Juan, PR 00918-1804
(809) 753-4201

Newark Office
Military Park Bldg.
60 Park Place
Newark, NJ 07102-5504
(201) 877-1662

REGION III (PHILADELPHIA)

Philadelphia Regional Office
Liberty Square Bldg.
105 South Seventh St.

Philadelphia, PA 19106-3392
(215) 597-2560

Field Offices:

Baltimore Office
3rd Floor
The Equitable Bldg.
10 North Calvert St.
Baltimore, MD 21202-1865
(301) 962-2520

Charleston Office
Suite 708
405 Capitol St.
Charleston, WV 25301-1795
(304) 347-7036

Pittsburgh Office
412 Old Post Office Courthouse
7th and Grant Streets
Pittsburgh, PA 15219-1906
(412) 644-6388

Richmond Office
P.O. Box 10170
400 N. 8th Street - 1st Floor
Richmond, VA 23240-9998

Washington, D.C. Office
Room 3158
451 Seventh Street, SW
Washington, D.C. 20410-5500
(202) 453-4500

Willmington Office
Room 1304
J. Caleb Boggs Federal Bldg.
844 King St.
Wilmington, DE 19801-3519
(302) 573-6300

REGION IV (ATLANTA)

Atlanta Regional Office
Richard B. Russell Federal Bldg.
75 Spring St., SW
Atlanta, GA 30303-3388
(404) 331-5136

Field Offices:

Birmingham Office
600 Beacon Parkway W.
Suite 300
Birmingham, AL 35209

(205) 731-1617

Columbia Office
Strom Thurmond Federal Bldg.
1835-45 Assembly St.
Columbia, SC 29201-2480
(803) 765-5592

Coral Gables Office
Gables 1 Tower
1320 South Dixie Hghy.
Coral Gables, FL 33146-2911
(305) 662-4500

Greensboro Office
415 North Edgeworth St.
Greensboro, NC 27401
(919)333-5363

Jackson Office
Suite 910
Doctor A. H. McCoy
Federal Building
100 West Capitol St.
Jackson, MS 39269-1096
(904) 965-4738

Jacksonville Office
325 West Adams St.
Jacksonville, FL 32202-4303
(904) 791-2626

Knoxville Office
Third Floor
John J. Duncan Federal Bldg.
710 Locust St.
Knoxville, TN 37902-2526
(615) 549-9384

Louisville Office
601 W. Broadway
P.O. Box 1044
Louisville, KY 40201-1044
(502) 582-5251

Memphis Office
Suite 1200
One Memphis Place
200 Jefferson Ave.
Memphis, TN 38103-2335
(901) 521-3367

Nashville Office
Suite 200
251 Cumberland Bend Dr.
Nashville, TN 37228-1803
(615) 736-5213

Orlando Office Suite 270
Langley Bldg.
3751 Maquire Blvd.
Orlando, FL. 32803
(407) 648-6441

Tampa Office
Room 527
700 Twiggs St.
P.O. Box 172910
Tampa, FL 33602-4029
(813)228-2501

REGION V (CHICAGO)

Chicago Regional Office
626 W. Jackson Blvd.
Chicago, IL 60606
(312) 353-5680

Field Offices:

Cincinnati Office
Room 9002
Federal Office Bldg.
550 Main St.
Cincinnati, OH 45202-3253
(513) 684-2884

Cleveland Office
Room 420
One Playhouse Square
1375 Euclid Ave.
Cleveland, OH 44115-1832
(216) 522-4065

Columbus Office
200 North High St.
Columbus, OH 43215-1832
(614)469-7345

Detroit Office
Patrick V. McNamara
Federal Bldg.
477 Michigan Ave.
Detroit, MI 48226-2592
(313) 226-6280

Flint Office
Room 200
Gil Sabuco Bldg.
352 South Saginaw St.
Flint, MI 48502-1953
(313) 766-5109

Grand Rapids Office
2922 Fuller Ave., NE

Grand Rapids, MI 49505-3409
(616) 456-2137

Indianapolis Office
151 North Deleware St.
Indianapolis, IN 46204-2526
(317) 226-7034

Milwaukee Office
Suite 1380
Henry S. Reuss Federal Plaza
310 West Wisconsin Ave.
Milwaukee, MN 55403-2289
(414) 291-3214

Minneapolis-St. Paul
220 Second St., S
Minneapolis, MN 55401-2195
(612) 370-3000

Springfield Office Suite 672
Lincoln Tower Plaza
524 South 2nd St.
Springfield, IL 62701-1774
(217) 492-4085

REGION VI (FORT WORTH)

Fort Worth Regional Office
1600 Throckmorton
P.O. Box 2905
Fort Worth, TX 76113-2905
(817) 885-5505

Field Offices:

Albuquerque Office
625 Truman St., NE
Albuquerque, NM 87110-6443
(505) 262-6463

Dallas Office
Room 106
525 Griffin St.
Dallas, TX 75202-5007
(214) 767-8300

Houston Office
Suite 200
Norfolk Tower
2211 Norfolk
Houston, TX 77098-4096
(713) 653-3274

Little Rock Office
Suite 200

Lafayette Building
523 Louisiana St.
Little Rock, AR 72201-3707
(501) 378-5401

Lubbock Office
Federal Office Bldg.
1205 Texas Ave.
Lubbock, TX 79401-4093
(806) 743-7265

New Orleans Office
Fisk Federal Bldg.
1661 Canal St.
New Orleans, LA 70112-2887
(504) 589-7200

Oklahoma City Office
Murrah Federal Bldg.
200 N.W. Fifth St.
Oklahoma City, OK 73102-3202
(405) 231-4891

San Antonio Office
Washington Square
800 Dolorosa
San Antonio, TX 78207-4563
(512) 229-6806

Shreveport Office
New Federal Bldg.
500 Fannin St.
Shreveport, LA 71101-3077
(318)226-5385

Tulsa Office
1516 S. Boston
Suite 110
Tulsa, OK 74119-403
(918) 581-7435

REGION VII (KANSAS CITY)

Kansas City Regional Office
Professional Bldg.
1103 Grand Ave.
Kansas City, MO 64106-2496
(816) 374-6432

Field Offices

Des Moines Office
Room 259
Federal Bldg.
210 Walnut St.
Des Moines, IA 50309-2155
(515) 284-4512

Omaha Office
Braiker/Brandeis Bldg.
210 South 16th St.
Omaha, NE 68102-1622
(402) 221-3703

St. Louis Office
210 North Tucker Blvd.
St. Louis, MO 63101-1997
(314) 425-4761

Topeka Office
Room 370
Frank Carlson Federal Bldg.
444 SE Quincy
Topeka, KS 66683-0001
(913) 295-2652

REGION VIII (DENVER)

Denver Regional Office
Executive Tower Bldg.
1405 Curtis St.
Denver, CO 80202-2349
(303) 844-4513

Field Offices:

Casper Office
4225 Federal Office Bldg.
100 East B St.
P.O. Box 580
Casper, WY 82602-1918
(307) 261-5252

Fargo Office
Federal Bldg.
653 2nd Ave., N.
P.O. Box 2483
Fargo, ND 58108-2483
(701) 239-5136

Helena Office
Room 340
Federal Office Bldg.,
Drawer 10095
301 S. Park
Helena, MT 59626-0095
(406) 449-5205

Salt Lake City Office
Suite 220
324 S. State St.
Salt Lake City, UT 84111-2321
(801) 524-5237

Sioux Falls Office
Suite 116
"300" Bldg.
300 N. Dakota Ave.
Sioux Falls, AD 57102-0311
(605) 330-4223

REGION IX (SAN FRANSISCO)

San Francisco Regional Office
Phillip Burton Federal Bldg. and U.S. Courthouse
450 Golden Gate Ave.
P.O. Box 36003
San Francisco, CA 94102-3448
(415) 556-4752

Indian Programs Office
Suite 400
1 North First St.
Phoenix, AZ 85004-2360
(602) 261-4156

Field Offices:

Fresno Office
Suite 138
1630 E. Shaw Ave.
Fresno, CA 93710-8193
(209) 487-5036

Honolulu Office
Prince Jonah Federal Bldg.
300 Ala Moana Blvd.
P.O. Box 50007
Honolulu, HI 96850-4991
(808) 541-1343

Las Vegas Office
Suite 205
1500 E. Tropicana Ave.
Las Vegas, NV 89119-6516
(702) 388-6500

Los Angeles Office
1615 W. Olympic Blvd.
Los Angeles, CA 90015-3801
(213) 251-7122

Phoenix Office Third Fl.
1 North First St.
P.O. Box 13468
Phoenix, AZ 85002-3468
(602) 261-4434

Reno Office
1050 Bible Way

P.O. Box 4700
Reno, NV 89505-4700
(702) 784-5356

Sacramento Office
Suite 200
777 12th St.
Sacramento, CA 95814-1997
(916) 551-1351

San Diego Office
Room 5-S-3
Federal Office Bldg.
880 Front St.
San Diego, CA 92188-0100
(619) 557-5310

Santa Ana Office
Box 12850
34 Civic Center Plaza
Santa Ana, CA 92712-2850
(714) 836-2451

Tucson Office
Suite 410
100 North Stone Ave.
Tucson, AZ 85701-1467
(602) 629-5220

REGION X (SEATTLE)

Seattle Regional Office
Arcade Plaza Building
1321 Second Ave.
Seattle, WA 98101-2054
(206) 442-5414

Field Offices

Anchorage Office
Box 64
701 "C" St.
Anchorage, AK 99513-0001
(907) 271-4170

Boise Office
Federal Bldg. U.S. Courthouse
550 West Fort St.
P.O. Box 042
Boise, ID 83724-0420
(208) 334-1990

Portland Office
520 Southwest Sixth Ave.
Portland, OR 97204-1596
(503) 221-2561

217

Spokane Office
FarmCredit Bank Bldg.
8th Floor East
West 601 First Ave.
Spokane, WA 99204
(509) 353-2136

Bureau of Land Management

The Bureau of Land Management is a government agency which is involved in the sale of both undeveloped land and oil/gas leases. Call the numbers listed below for information on these sales.

ALASKA

Anchorage Federal Office Bldg.
222 W. 7th Ave., #13
Anchorage, AK 99513-7599
(907) 271-5555

ARIZONA

3707 N. 7th St., (85014)
P.O. Box 16563
Phoenix, AZ 85011
(602) 241-5504

CALIFORNIA

Federal Office Bldg.
2800 Cottage Way
Room E 2841
Sacramento, CA 95825
(916) 978-4754

COLORADO

2850 Youngfield St.
Lakewood, CO 80215
(303) 236-2100

IDAHO

3380 Americana Terrace
Boise, ID 83706
(208) 334-1414

MONTANA
(NORTH AND
SOUTH DAKOTA)

Granite Tower
222 N. 32nd St.
P.O. Box 36800
Billings, MT 59107
(406) 255-2913

NEVADA

Federal Bldg., Room 3123
850 Harvard Way
P.O. Box 12000
Reno, NV 89520
(702) 328-6300

NEW MEXICO
(Oklahoma,
Texas and Kansas)

Joseph M. Montoya Federal Bldg.
South Federal Place
P.O. Box 1449
Santa Fe, NM 87504-1449
(505) 988-6000

OREGON and WASHINGTON

825 N. E. Multnomah St.
P.O. Box 2965
Portland, OR 9
(503) 231-627

UTAH

Consolidated Fi
Suite 301
324 South Stat
Salt Lake City, L
(801) 539-4001

pending brochure) 9-30-91

WYOMING an

2515 Warren Av
P.O. Box 1828
Cheyenne, WY 8
(307) 772-2334

EASTERN STATES OFFICE
(All other states)

350 S. Pickett St.   (703) 461-1328
Alexandria, VA 22304

Federal Deposit Insurance Corporation

The FDIC rarely has auctions and advertises in the paper when they do. They do have property listings which they turn over to real estate brokers for resale. By contacting FDIC, you can get listings for your area or for the region in which you wish to buy property. Their regional addresses and phone numbers are as follows:

REGIONAL OFFICE:	STATES COVERED:
ATLANTA Telephone: (404) 522-1145 William M. Dudley Regional Director-Liquidation Federal Deposit Insurance Corporation Marquis One Building, Suite 1400 245 Peachtree Center Avenue N. Atlanta, GA 30303	Alabama Florida Georgia Louisiana Mississippi South Carolina
CHICAGO Telephone: (312) 207-0200 Thomas A Beshara Regional Director-Liquidation Federal Deposit Insurance Corporation 30 Wacker Drive, 32nd Floor Chicago, IL 60606	Illinois Iowa Minnesota N. Dakota S. Dakota Wisconsin
DALLAS Telephone: (214) 754-0098 G. Michael Newton Regional Director-Liquidation Federal Deposit Insurance Corporation 1910 Pacific Avenue, Suite 1600 Dallas, TX 75202	Arkansas Oklahoma Texas
KANSAS CITY (816) 531-2212 Carmen J. Sullivan Regional Director-Liquidation Federal Deposit Insurance Corporation 4900 Main St. 5th Floor Kansas City, MO 64112	Colorado Kansas Missouri Nebraska Wyoming

221

NEW YORK
Telephone: (212) 704-1200

Michael J. Martinelli
Regional Director-Liquidation
Federal Deposit Insurance Corporation
452 Fifth Avenue, 21st. Floor
New York, NY 10010

Connecticut	Massachusetts
Delaware	Puerto Rico
Pennsylvania	Rhode Island
Indiana	Tennessee
Kentucky	Vermont
Maine	Virginia
Maryland	Virgin Island
Michigan	District of
Ohio	Columbia
New York	New Jersey
N. Carolina	W. Virginia

SAN FRANCISCO
Telephone: (415) 546-1810

Lamar C. Kelly, Jr.
Regional Director-Liquidation
Federal Deposit Insurance Corporation
25 Ecker Street, Suite 1900
San Francisco, CA 94105

Alaska	Arizona
California	Guam
Hawaii	Idaho
Montana	Nevada
New Mexico	Oregon
Utah	Washington

222

Resolution Trust Corporation

This agency was formed to dispose of the assets of insolvent savings and loans. For information on available properties call the regional office closest to your home:

1-800-782-6326
Massachusetts area

EASTERN REGIONAL OFFICE

245 Peachtree Ctr. Ave.N. E.
Marquis Tower I, Suite 1100
Atlanta, GA 30303
(404)522-1145

EASTERN AREA OFFICE

10 South La Salle St.
Chicago, IL 60603
(312)419-3700

CENTRAL REGIONAL OFFICE

1910 Pacific Ave.
Suite 1700
Dallas TX 75201
(214)754-0098

WESTERN AREA OFFICE

1125 17th Street
Suite 700
Denver, CO 80202
(202)789-6313

REOs Direct

This is a partial list of major U.S. banks which may have REOs (Real Estate Owned properties):

ATLANTA

C & S National Bank
25 Broad Street
Atlanta, GA 30302-0000
(404) 581-2121

First National Bank of Atlanta
2 Peachtree Street
Atlanta, GA 30383-0001
(404) 332-5000

Trust Co. Bank of Georgia
25 Park Place
Atlanta, GA 30303-2900
(404) 588-7711

BOSTON

Bank of Boston
100 Federal Street
Boston, MA 02110-1898
(617) 434-2200

Shawmut Bank NA
1 Federal Street
Boston, MA 02211-0001
(617) 742-4000

Bank of New England NA
28 State Street
Boston, MA 02109-1784
(617) 742-4000

CHICAGO

Continental Bank NA
231 S. LaSalle Street
Chicago, IL 60697-0001
(312) 828-5740

First National Bank of Chicago
1 First National Plaza
Chicago, IL 60607-0001
(312) 372-4000

Chicago Bank of Commerce
200 G. Randolph Street
Chicago, IL 60601-6473

(312) 861-1000

CINCINNATI

Central Trust Co.
201 E. Fifth Street
Cincinnati, OH 45202-4117
(513) 651-8896

Fifth Third Bank
38 Fountain Square Plaza
Cincinnati, OH 45236-0001
(513) 579-5300

Provident Bank
1 E. Fourth Street
Cincinnati, OH 45202-3799
(216) 579-2000

CLEVELAND

Ameritrust Bank
900 Euclid Avenue
Cleveland, OH 44115-0000
(216)737-5000

Bank One Cleveland NA
1255 Euclid Avenue
Cleveland, OH 44115-1807
(216) 781-3333

National City Bank Cleveland
1900 E. Ninth Street
Cleveland, OH 44114-3484
(216) 575-2000

DALLAS

BancTexas Dallas NA
1601 Elm Street
Dallas, TX 75201-4793
(214) 969-6111

Deposit Guarantee
3300 Oak Lawn Avenue
Dalla, TX 75219-4216
(214) 521-4171

NCNB Texas National Bank

1707 Pacific Avenue
Dallas, TX 75201-4609
(214) 922-5000

DENVER

United Bank of Denver
1700 Broadway
Denver, CO 80274-0001
(303) 861-8811

Denver National Bank
1125 17th Street
Denver, CO 80202-2088
(303) 292-4000

Colorado State Bank of Denver
1600 Broadway
Denver, CO 80202-4999
(303) 861-2111

DETROIT

Manufacturers National Bank
100 Renaissance Center
Detroit, MI 48243-1085
(313) 222-4000

National Bank of Detroit NA
611 Woodward Avenue
Detroit, MI 48226-3497
(313) 225-1000

First of America Bank Detroit
645 Griswold Street
Detroit, MI 48226-4061
(313) 965-1900

HOUSTON

Bank of Houston
5115 Main Street
Houston, TX 77002-9754
(713) 529-4881

First City National Bank
1001 Main Street
Houston, TX 77002-6599
(713) 658-6011

Texas Commerce Bank, Houston
712 Main Street
Houston, TX 77002-3206
(713) 236-4865

INDIANAPOLIS

Indiana National Bank

1 Indiana Square
Indianapolis, IN 46266-0001
(317) 266-6000

Merchants National Bank & Trust Co.
of Indiana
1 Merchants Plaza
Indianapolis, IN 46255-0001
(317) 267-7000

Peoples Bank & Trust Co.
130 East Market Street
Indianapolis, IN 46204-3288
(317) 237-8000

KANSAS CITY

Commerce Bank of Kansas City NA
922 Walnut Street
Kansas City, MO 64106-1871
(816) 234-2000

Mercantile Bank of Kansas City
1101 Walnut Street
Kansas City, MO 64106-2169
(816) 842-2000

Merchants Bank
850 Main Street
Kansas City, MO 64105-2000
(816) 471-1700

LOS ANGELES

California Overseas Bank
3701 Wilshire Boulevard
Los Angeles, CA 90010-2870
(213) 736-9400

First Interstate Bank of California
707 Wilshire Boulevard
Los Angeles, CA 90017-3500
(213) 239-4000

Mercantile Bank
1840 Century Park East
Los Angeles, CA 90067-2101
(213) 277-2265

MIAMI

Barnett Bank of South Florida
701 Brickell Avenue
Miami, FL 33131-2822
(305) 825-5900

City National Bank of Florida
25 West Flagler Street

Miami, FL 33130-1785
(305) 577-7333

National Westminster Bank USA
700 Brickell Avenue
Miami, FL 33131-2804
(305) 789-3700

MINNEAPOLIS

First Bank of Minneapolis
120 South Sixth Street
Minneapolis, MN 55402-1803
(612) 370-4141

Independent State Bank of Minnesota
510 Marquette Avenue
Minneapolis, MN 55402-0000
(612) 333-4364

National City Bank of Minneapolis
75 South Fifth Street
Minneaplis, MN 55402-1195
(612) 340-3000

NEW YORK CITY

Chase Manhattan Bank
1 Chase Manhattan Plaza
New York, NY 10081-0001
(212) 552-2222

CitiBank NA
399 Park Avenue
New York, NY 10034-0001
(212) 559-1000

Royal Bank & Trust Co.
68 William Street
New York, NY 10005-1514
(212) 806-3000

PHILADELPHIA

First Pennsylvania Bank NA
15th & Chestnut Streets
Philadelphia, PA 19101-0000
(215) 786-5000

Mellon Bank
Seventh & Market Streets
Philadelphia, PA 19106-1516
(215) 553-3000

Philadelphia National Bank
Fifth & Market Streets
Philadelphia, PA 19110-0000
(215) 973-8400

PITTSBURGH

Equibank
2 Oliver Plaza
Pittsburgh, PA 15222-2705
(412) 288-5000

Mellon Bank
3 Mellon Bank Center
Pittsburgh, PA 15259-0001
(412) 234-5000

Pittsburgh National Bank
Fifth Avenue & Wood Street
Pittsburgh, PA 15222-0000
(412) 762-2000

PORTLAND

First Interstate Bank of Oregon
1300 SW Fifth Avenue
Portland, OR 97201-5699
(503) 225-2111

Oregon Bank
1001 SW Fifth Avenue
Portland, OR 97204-1147
(503) 222-7777

U.S. National Bank of Oregon
111 SW Fifth Avenue
Portland, OR 97204-3684
(503) 275-6111

SACRAMENTO

Bank of Alex Brown
1425 River Park Drive
Sacramento, CA 95815-4571
(916) 925-0572

Capitol Bank of Commerce
300 Capitol Mall
Sacramento, CA 95814-4393
(916) 449-8300

River City Bank
825 K Street
Sacramento, CA 95814-3590
(916) 441-4653

ST. LOUIS

American Bank of St. Louis
1731 South Broadway
St. Louis, MO 63104-4050
(314) 421-3200

Centerre Bank
1 Centerre Plaza
St. Louis, MO 63101-2602
(314) 554-6000

Mercantile Bank NA
721 Locust Street
St. Louis, MO 63101-1602
(314) 425-2525

SAN DIEGO

First National Bank
401 W. "A" Street
San Diego, CA 92101-7917
(619) 233-5588

San Diego Trust & Savings Bank
530 Broadway
San Diego, CA 92101-5209
(619) 238-4511

SAN FRANCISCO

Bank of America NT & SA
555 California Street
San Francisco, CA 94104-1590
(415) 622-3456

Security Pacific National Bank
201 California Street
San Francisco, CA 94111-5099
(415) 565-7200

Wells Fargo Bank NA
420 Montgomery Street
San Francisco, CA 94104-1298
(415) 983-2000

SEATTLE

Puget Sound Bank
815 Second Avenue
Seattle, WA 98104-1594
(206) 447-5700

SeaFirst Bank
1001 Fourth Avenue
Seattle, WA 98154-0001

(206) 358-0800

Security Pacific Bank
1301 Fifth Avenue
Seattle, WA 98101-2678
(206) 621-4111

TAMPA / ST. PETERSBURG

Barnett Bank of Tampa
101 E. Kennedy Boulevard
Tampa, FL 33602-5133
(813) 225-8111

NCNB National Bank of Florida
600 N. FLorida Avenue
Tampa, FL 33602-4524
(813) 882-1100

Sun Bank of Tampa Bay
315 E. Madison Street
Tampa, FL 33602-4898
(813) 224-2121

Chase Bank of Florida
111 Second Avenue NE
St. Petersburg, FL 33701-3451
(813) 823-5880

WASHINGTON, D.C./BALTIMORE

American Security Bank NA
1501 Pennsylvania Avenue NW
Washington, DC 20013-0000
(202) 624-4000

Riggs National Bank of Washington, D.C.
1503 Pennsylvania Avenue NW
Washington, DC 20006-3944
(202) 835-5400

Bank of Baltimore
1 East Baltimore Street
Baltimore, MD 21202-1670
(301) 244-3360

Chase Bank of Maryland
2 North Charles Street
Baltimore, MD 21201-3795
(301) 347-0900

Federal Savings and Loan Insurance Corporation

FSLIC has numerous properties of which they are eager to dispose. You may get a quarterly listing catalogue with detailed information on their properties and their contact points by contacting one of the offices below. You'll find they have hundreds and hundreds of listings.

FSLIC NATIONAL OFFICE

1730 Rhode Island Ave, N.W.,
Washingron, D.C. 20036
(202) 955-4530

WESTERN REGIONAL OFFICE

Serving: Alaska, Arizona, California, Hawaii, Idaho, Montana, Nevada, Oregon, Utah, Washington and Wyoming.

523 W 6th. St.
Los Angeles, CA 90014
(213) 623-7055

CENTRAL REGIONAL OFFICE

Serving: Colorado, Kansas, Nebraska, New Mexico, North Dakota, Oklahoma, South Dakota, and Texas

5080 Spectrum Dr.
Suite 105 W
Dallas, TX 75248
(214) 701-7200

EASTERN REGIONAL OFFICE

Serving: Alabama, Arkansas, Connecticut, Delaware, Florida, Georiga, Illinois, Indiana, Iowa, Kentucky, Louisiana, Maine, Massachuetts, Maryland, Michigan, Mississippi, Minnesota, Missouri, New Hampshire, New Jersey, New York, North Carolina, Ohio, Rhode Island, South Carolina, Tennessee, Vermont, West Virginia, and Wisconsin

9-30-91
Sending Catalogue

285 Peachtree Ave., N. E.
Suites 300, 400, 500
Atlanta, GA 30303
(404) 880-3000

Massachusetts office
1-800-283-3139

Savings and Loans Associations

The following list should be an excellent avenue for obtaining properties, listed in their REO departments. When calling these banks to inquire about real estate, it may be worth your time to ask about the auction of merchandise as well. Our research team brought to light an S&L auction which took place in Houston, Texas where a 1957 Bentley was sold for $10,050!!! (*See story on page 58.*)

ALABAMA

First FS & L Assn.
1100 E. Three-Notch St.
Andalusia, AL
(205) 222-8401

Birmingham FS & L Assn.
511 S. 20th St
Birmingham, AL
(205) 322-5601

City FS & L Assn.
2030 Second Ave., N.
Birmingham, AL
(205) 320-6309

Guaranty FS & L Assn.
2030 First Ave., N.
Birmingham, AL
(205) 320-6600

Jefferson FS & L Assn.
215 N. 21st St.
Birmingham, AL
(205) 731-8292

Secor Bank, FSB
201 Office Park Dr.
Birmingham, AL
(205) 877-0200

New South FSB
2000 Crestwood Blvd.
Irondale, AL
(205) 470-6254

Altus Bank, A FSB
851 S. Beltline Hwy.
Mobile, AL
(205) 470-6254

Phenix FS & L Assn.
910 13th St.
Phenix City, AL
(205) 297-3446

Baldwin County FSB
Corner of Hwys. 59 & 104
Robertsdale, AL
(205) 947-2522

ALASKA

First Federal Bank of Alaska, SB
813 W. Northern Lights Blvd.
Anchorage, AK
(907) 274-6565

Home Savings Bank
1001 E. Benson
Anchorage, AK
(907) 276-1451

ARIZONA

Sentinel S & L Assn.
5055 N. 32nd St.
Phoenix, AZ
(602) 957-9579

Southwest S & L Assn.
3101 N. Central Ave.
Phoenix, AZ
(602) 241-4400

Sun State S & L Assn.
4222 E. Camelback Rd.
Phoenix, AZ
(602) 224-1108

Security S & L Assn.

4110 N. Scottsdale Rd.
Scottsdale, AZ
(602) 946-4300

Universal S & L Assn., A FS & LA
4141 N. Scottsdale Rd.
Scottsdale, AZ
(602) 481-1000

Great American First SB, FSB
32 N. Stone Ave.
Tucson, AZ
(602) 792-0902

Pima S & L Assn.
4801 E. Broadway
Tucson, AZ
(602) 570-7100

ARKANSAS

Independence FS & L Assn.
Twelfth & Main Sts.
Batesville, AR
(501) 793-4123

First FS & L Assn.
235 Jackson St., SW
Camden, AR
(501) 836-6841

First Financial FS & L Assn.
315 W. Main St.
El Dorado, AR
(501) 863-7000

First FS & L Assn..
First Fed Bldg.
Fayetteville, AR
(501) 521-3424

First America FSB
Sixth & Garrison
Fort Smith, AR
(501) 782-8901

Superior Federal Bank, FSB
5000 Rogers Ave.
Fort Smith, AR
(501) 452-8900

First FS & L Assn. of Harrison
200 W. Stephenson
Harrison, AR
(501) 741-7641

Landmark Savings Bank, FSB

#1 Market Place
Hot Springs, AR
(501) 321-2511

Home FS & L Assn.
700 S. Main
Jonesboro, AR
(501) 932-1561

United FS & L Assn.
515 W. Washington
Jonesboro, AR
(501) 932-6663

Arkansas FSB
650 S. Shackleford Rd., Ste. 150
Little Rock, AR
(501) 227-7301

First Federal of Arkansas, FA
401 W. Capitol
Little Rock, AR
(501) 372-3200

Savers FS & L Assn.
320 W. Capitol Ave.
Little Rock, AR
(501) 372-2220

First FS & L Assn.
E. Page and Keith Sts.
Malvern, AR
(501) 332-5231

First State Savings Bank, FSB
650 South St.
Mountain Home, AR
(501) 425-5171

Home FS & L Assn.
100 S. Main St.
Mountain Home, AR
(501) 425-9100

Commonwealth S & L Assn.
750 W. Keiser
Osceola, AR
(501) 563-3232

First FS & L Assn.
300 W. Emerson
Paragould, AR
(501) 236-7623

Pocahontas FS & L Assn.
203 W. Broadway
Pocahontas, AR
(501) 892-4595

First Federal Savings Bank
500 W. Walnut St.
Rogers, AR
(501) 636-3441

Grant County S & L Assn.
120 S. Oak
Sheridan, AR
(501) 942-5105

First FS & L Assn.
216 E. Third St.
Texarkana, AR
(501) 773-1103

Texarkana FS & L Assn.
2200 State Line Ave.
Texarkana, AR
(501) 773-5571

CALIFORNIA

Progressive S & L Assn.
1415 Lake Ave.
Pasadena, CA
(818) 793-7500

Republic FS & L Assn.
6320 Canoga Ave.
Woodland Hills, CA
(818) 715-6000

United California SB
2000 E. McFadden
Santa Ana, CA
(714) 953-1800

Placer S & L Assn.
949 Lincoln Way
Auburn, CA
(916) 888-2822

First FS & L Assn.
1517 18th St.
Bakersfield, CA
(805) 324-4773

Paramount Savings Bank
1712 K St.
Bakersfield, CA
(213) 588-1171

Beverly Hills FSB
27271 Las Rambles
Mission Viejo, CA
(213) 275-4351

Columbia S & L Assn.
17911 Bon Karmon Blvd.
Irving, CA
(213) 657-6303

Gibraltar Savings
2800 N. Madeira Rd.
Simi Valley, CA
(213) 278-8720

Great Western Bank, A FSB
9301 Corbin Ave.
Northridge, CA
(213) 852-3951

Southern California S & L Assn.
9100 Wilshire Blvd.
Beverly Hills, CA
(213) 272-6200

Unity S & L Assn.
8501 Wilshire Blvd.
Beverly Hills, CA
(213) 854-0110

Pacific Savings Bank
1901 Newport Blvd.
Costa Mesa, CA
(714) 889-0231

Fidelity FS & L Assn.
600 N. Brand Blvd.
Glendale, CA
(818) 956-7100

Glendale FS & L Assn.
301 E. Olive, Ste. 300
Burbank, CA
(818) 842-0912

Westport Savings Bank
317 N. Douty
Hanford, CA
(209) 582-9096

Old Stone Bank of California,
A FSB
(Main)2700 Hesperian Blvd.
Hayward, CA
(415) 887-6000

Charter Savings Bank
17011 Beach Blvd.
Huntington Beach, CA
(714) 756-0666

Huntington S & L Assn.

231

6967 Warner Ave.
Huntington Beach, CA
(714) 842-8600

Mercury S & L Assn.
7812 Edinger Ave.
Huntington Beach, CA
(714) 848-2307

Antelope Valley S & L Assn.
831 W. Lancaster Blvd.
Lancaster, CA
(805) 945-3511

Bel Air S & L Assn.
11726 San Vicente
Los Angeles, CA
(213) 826-2300

Brookside S & L Assn.
1828 Sawtelle Blvd.
Los Angeles, CA
(213) 824-5335

California FS & L Assn.
5760 Wilshire Blvd.
Los Angeles, CA
(213) 932-4321

Coast S & L Assn.
2 N. Lake Ave., Ste. 300
Pasadena, CA
(213) 688-2000

First Network Savings Bank
10100 Santa Monica Blvd.
Los Angeles, CA
(213) 551-1500

Founders S & L Assn.
3910 W. Martin Luther King Jr. Blvd.
Los Angeles, CA
(213) 295-3161

Hancock S & L Assn.
3550 Wilshire Blvd.
Los Angeles, CA
(213) 383-2200

Home Savings of America, FA
4900 Rivergrade Rd.
Irwindale, CA
(213) 736-8604

Lincoln S & L Assn.
1913 E. 17th St., Ste. 119
Santa Ana, CA
(213) 628-4131

Southwest S & L Assn.
20061 Saticoy
Canoga Park, CA
(213) 938-7800

Union FSB
220 College Blvd.
Brae, CA
(213) 688-8555

Malibu Savings Bank
1700 Adams Ave.
Costa Mesa, CA
(213) 456-5579

Western Federal Savings S & L
13160 Mindanao Way
Marina Del Rey, CA
(213) 306-6803

Far West S & L Assn.
4001 MacArthur Blvd.
Newport Beach, CA
(714) 833-8383

Household Bank, FSB
2901 S. Pullmen
Santa Ana, CA
(714) 833-0367

Newport Balboa Savings, FA
1100
 Ave.
Newport Beach, CA
(714) 645-6505

Standard Pacific Savings, FA
4590 MacArthur Blvd., Ste. 125
Newport Beach, CA
(714) 955-0536

Unified Savings, A FS & L Assn.
9040 Tampa Ave.
Northridge, CA
(818) 993-4222

Equitec Savings Bank
7677 Oakport St.
Oakland, CA
(415) 430-9900

World S & L Assn., A FS & LA
1901 Harrison St.
Oakland, CA
(415) 446-3300

First California Savings, FSA

625 The City Dr., S., Ste. 450
Orange, CA
(714) 937-5600

Palm Springs Savings Bank
420 S. Palm Canyon Dr.
Palm Springs, CA
(619) 325-2021

Mutual S & L Assn.
315 E. Colorado Blvd.
Pasadena, CA
(818) 449-2345

Valley S & L Assn.
530 Main St.
Pleasanton, CA
(415) 462-7200

Pomona First FS & L Assn.
399 N. Garey Ave.
Pomona, CA
(714) 623-6511

Provident Savings Bank
3756 Central Ave.
Riverside, CA
(714) 686-6060

Commerce Savings Bank
1545 River Park Dr.
Sacramento, CA
(916) 922-9500

Sacramento S & L Assn.
424 L St.
Sacramento, CA
(916) 444-8555

Arrowhead Pacific SB
301
Way, Ste. 300
San Bernardino, CA
(714) 888-8870

Great American First SB
600 B. St.
San Diego, CA
(619) 231-1885

Home FS & L Assn.
615 Broadway
San Diego, CA
(619) 450-7000

Imperial Savings Assn.
8787 Complex Dr.
San Diego, CA

(619) 292-2000

Citicorp Savings, A FS & L Assn.
180 Grand Ave.
Oakland, CA
(415) 891-8600

Continental Savings of America
250 Montgomery
San Francisco, CA
(415) 398-1515

First Nationwide Bank, A FSB
700 Market St.
San Francisco, CA
(818) 546-3081

Gateway Savings Bank
393 13th St.
Oakland, CA
(415) 874-4900

Golden Coin S & L Assn.
170 Columbus Ave.
San Francisco, CA
(415) 362-8588

Hamilton Savings Bank, FSB
450 Sansome St.
San Francisco, CA
(415) 781-2600

Homestead Savings,
FS & L Assn.
979 Broadway
Milbrae, CA
(415) 692-9010

Pacific Coast
S & L Assn. of America
100 Pine St.
San Francisco, CA
(415) 397-1122

San Francisco FS & L Assn.
99 Post St.
San Francisco, CA
(415) 955-5970

United Savings Bank, FSB
711 Van Ness Ave.
San Francisco, CA
(415) 928-0700

Saratoga S & L Assn.
1960 Concourse Dr.
San Jose, CA
(408) 433-0110

Bay View FS & L Assn.
2121 S. El Camino Real,
Rm. 1104
San Mateo, CA
(415) 573-7300

Pan American Savings Bank
1300 S. El Camino Real St.
San Mateo, CA
(415) 345-1800

Butterfield S & L Assn., FSA
200 E. Sandpoint Dr.
Santa Ana, CA
(714) 725-0112

County Bank, SSB
3760 State St.
Santa Barbara, CA
(805) 682-2400

Santa Barbara S & L Assn.
1035 State St.
P.O. Box Drawer D-D
Santa Barbara, CA
(805) 682-5000

First FS Bank of California
401 Wilshire Blvd.
Santa Monica, CA
(213) 458-3011

Santa Paula S & L Assn.
725 E. Main St.
Santa Paula, CA
(805) 525-3377

New West FS & L Assn.
343 E. Main
Stockton, CA
(209) 546-3711

Washington S & L Assn.
526 W. Benjamin Holt Dr
Stockton, CA
(209) 952-1740

Tracy S & L Assn., FA
1003 Central Ave.
Tracy, CA
(209) 836-5111

Independence S & L Assn.
3271 Marin St.
Vallejo, CA
(707) 552-6664

Valley FS & L Assn.
6842 Van Nuys Blvd.
Van Nuys, CA
(818) 904-3000

Delta Savings Bank
8860 Bolsa Ave.
Westminster, CA
(714) 891-5711

Investment S & L Assn.
19935 Ventura Blvd.
Woodland Hills, CA
(818) 346-3920

Western Empire S& L Assn.
17951 Cowan St.
Irving, CA
(714) 660-9111

Sutter Buttes S & L Assn.
700 Plumas St.
Yuba City CA
(916) 673-7283

COLORADO

Capitol FS & L Assn.
3300 S. Parker Rd.
Aurora, CO
(303) 671-1000

American FS & L
Assn. of Colorado
5475 Tech Center Dr.
Colorado Springs, CO
(719) 599-7400

Otero Savings, A FS & L Assn.
1515 N. Academy Blvd.
Colorado Springs, CO
(719) 597-1011

Delta S & L Assn.
145 W. Fourth St.
Delta, CO
(303) 874-9755

Bank Western, A FSB
700 17th St.
Denver, CO
(303) 623-5100

Columbia, A FS & L Assn.
#14 Denver Tech Ctr.
Box 17127
Denver, CO

(303) 773-3444

Centennial Savings Bank, FSB
1101 Second Ave.
Durango, CO
(303) 247-4183

Colorado S & L Assn.
9250 E. Costilla Ave.
Englewood, CO
(303) 792-7200

Mesa FS & L Assn. of Colorado
131 N. Sixth
Grand Junction, CO
(303) 242-5211

Modern FS & L Assn.
235 N. Seventh St.
Grand Junction, CO
(303) 242-8142

Valley FS & LA,
Grand Junction
225 N. Fifth St.
Grand Junction, CO
(303) 242-1900

Gunnison S & L Assn.
303 N. Main St.
Gunnison, CO
(303) 641-2171

First FSB of Colorado
215 S. Wadsworth Blvd.
Lakewood, CO
(303) 232-2121

Heritage S & L Assn.
201 S. Fifth St.
Lamar, CO
(719) 336-7715

First America SB, FSB
400 Lashley St.
Longmont, CO
(303) 678-0826

Rio Grande S & L Assn.
901 First Ave.
Monte Vista, CO
(719) 852-5932

Sun S & L Assn.
11500 Sun Way
Parker, CO
(303) 841-0104

The Salida B & L Assn.
130 W. Second St.
Salida, CO
(719) 539-2516

Alpine FS & L Assn.
200 S. Lincoln
Steamboat Springs, CO
(303) 879-2450

Equitable S & L Assn.
2210 N. Third
Sterling, CO
(303) 522-6522

Century S & L Assn.
233 E. Main St.
Trinidad, CO
(719) 846-2257

Rocky Mountain S & L Assn.
701 Gold Hill Square S.
Woodland Park, CO
(719) 687-3061

CONNECTICUT

Bristol FSB
222 Main St.
Bristol, CT
(203) 589-4600

Northeast Savings, FA
50 State St.
Hartford, CT
(203) 241-8351

WASHINGTON, D.C.

Home Federal Savings Bank
5225 Wisconsin Ave., NW
Washington, D.C.
(202) 537-8828

Washington FSB
5101 Wisconsin Ave.
Washington, D.C.
(202) 471-9189

DELAWARE

Wilmington S. Fund Society, FSB
838 Market St.
Wilmington, DE
(302) 571-7116

FLORIDA

Southern FloridaBanc FS & LA
5255 N. Federal Hwy.
Boca Raton, FL
(407) 994-4605

Enterprise FS & L Assn..
2437 U.S. Hwy. 19 N.
Clearwater, FL
(813) 799-6880

Fortune Savings Bank
2120 U.S. Hwy. 19 S.
Clearwater, FL
(813) 536-1000

Life Savings Bank
301 U.S. Hwy. 19 N.
Clearwater, FL
(813) 796-5433

Pioneer Savings Bank
5770 Roosevelt Blvd.
Clearwater, FL
(813) 530-7672

Coral Gables FS & L Assn.
2511 Ponce De Leon Blvd.
Coral Gables, FL
(305) 529-6090

Professional Savings Bank
3001 Ponce De Leon Blvd.
Coral Gables, Fl
(305) 460-7000

Security First FS & L Assn.
501 N. Ave.
Daytona Beach, FL
(904) 274-1367

First FSB of De Funiak Springs
Corner of Hwy. 90
& Nelson Ave.
De Funiak Springs, FL
(904) 892-2141

Investors of Florida SB
1802 W. Hillsboro Blvd.
Deerfield Beach, FL
(305) 429-3800

Financial Security FS & L Assn.
7239 W. Atlantic Ave.
Delray Beach, FL

(407) 496-8900

First FS & L Assn. of Englewood
1200 S. McCall Rd.
Englewood, FL
(813) 474-3205

First Family FS & L Assn.
2801 S. Bay St.
Eustis, FL
(904) 589-7300

BankAtlantic, A FSB
1750 E. Sunrise Blvd.
Fort Lauderdale, FL
(305) 760-5000

Guardian S & L Assn.
6520 N. Andrews Ave.
Fort Lauderdale, FL
(305) 491-8400

First FS & L Assn.
2201 Second St.
Fort Myers, FL
(813) 336-0299

First Citizens FS & L Assn.
1600 S. Federal Hwy.
Fort Pierce, FL
(407) 464-4900

Harbor FS & L Assn.
100 S. Second St.
Fort Pierce, FL
(407) 461-2414

First FSB of NW Florida
198 Eglin Pkwy., NE
Ft. Walton Beach, FL
(904) 243-3148

New Metropolitan FS & LA
1291 W. 49th St.
Hialeah, FL
(305) 825-0400

Hollywood FS & L Assn.
1909 Tyler St.
Hollywood, FL
(305) 929-8614

Home Savings Bank of Florida
1720 Harrison St.
Hollywood, FL
(305) 925-3211

First FS & LA of Citrus County

800 Main St.
Inverness, FL
(904) 726-1237

Citizens FSB
930 University Blvd.
Jacksonville, FL
(904) 743-3100

Duval FS & L Assn.
One N. Hogan St.
Jacksonville, FL
(904) 398-6700

First FS & L Assn.
300 W. Adams St.
Jacksonville, FL
(904) 366-1757

Jacksonville FSB
2107 Hendricks Ave.
Jacksonville, FL
(904) 398-5633

Republic Savings Bank
675 W. Indiantown Rd.
Jupiter, FL
(407) 744-3500

First FS & LA,
Florida Keys
1010 Kennedy Dr.
Key West, FL
(305) 294-5113

First FS & L Assn.
205 E. Orange St.
Lakeland, FL
(813) 688-6811

First FS & L Assn.
100 Clearwater-Largo Rd.
Largo, FL
(813) 584-8141

Commonwealth S & L Assn.
1200 NS Road #7
Margate, FL
(305) 493-5100

United States of America, FA
502 E. New Haven Ave.
Melbourne, FL
(407) 984-1521

American S & LA of Florida
17801 NW Second Ave.
Miami, FL

(305) 654-2012

Amerifirst Bank, A FSB
One SE Third Ave.
Miami, FL
(305) 387-7800

Atico Savings Bank
101 SE Second Ave.
Miami, FL
(305) 377-6901

Brickell Banc SA
2666 Brickell Ave.
Miami, FL
(305) 285-5500

Centrust Savings Bank
101 E. Flagler St.
Miami, FL
(305) 376-5130

Chase Federal Bank, A FSB
7300 N. Kendall
Miami, FL
(305) 595-4200

Citicorp S. of Florida, A FS & L
1776-90 Biscayne Blvd.
Miami, FL
(305) 577-8951

Citizens Federal Bank, A FSB
999 Brickell Ave.
Miami, FL
(305) 577-0400

Flagler FS & L Assn.
101 NE First Ave.
Miami, FL
(305) 377-1711

General Bank, A FSB
3099 SW Eighth St.
Miami, FL
(305) 649-1670

Interamerican FS & L Assn.
9190 Coral Way
Miami, FL
(305) 223-1434

Lincoln S & L Assn.
18405 NW Second Ave.
Miami, FL
(305) 653-6500

Miami Saving Bank

261 NE First St.
Miami, FL
(305) 662-2887

Financial FS & LA,
Dade County
6625 Miami Lakes Blvd.
Miami Lakes, FL
(305) 827-7400

BancFlorida, A FSB
5801 Pelican Bay Blvd.
Naples, FL
(813) 597-1611

Liberty FS & L Assn.
7419 U.S. Hwy. 19
New Port Richey, FL
(813) 842-4242

First FS & LA of New Smyrna
900 N. Dixie Freeway
New Smyrna Beach, FL
(904) 428-2466

Mid-State FS & L Assn.
3232 SW College Rd.
Ocala, FL
(904) 237-1194

American Pioneer Savings Bank
135 W. Central Blvd., Ste. 700
Orlando, FL
(407) 896-2311

Beneficial Savings Bank, FSB
400 N. Brumby Ave.
Orlando, FL
(407) 896-0774

First Financial, A Savings Bank
255 S. Orange Ave., 12th Fl.
Orlando, FL
(407) 841-3333

The First, Federal Association
One Dupont Center
390 N. Orange Ave.
Orlando, FL
(407) 841-3430

Florida First FSB
144 Harrison Ave.
Panama City, FL
(904) 872-7000

Peoples First Financial
2305 Hwy. 77

Panama City, FL
(904) 769-5261

Security FSB of Florida
800 Harrison Ave.
Panama City, FL
(904)769-3232

Citizens & Builders FSB
33 W. Garden St.
Pensacola, FL
(904) 435-1100

First FSB of Perry
115 W. Green St.
Perry, FL
(904) 584-2057

Gold Coast Savings Bank
1801 N. Pine Island Rd.
Plantation, FL
(305) 476-0707

Community Savings, FA
2600 Broadway
Riviera Beach, FL
(407) 848-6661

Coast FS & L Assn.
1777 Main St.
Sarasota, FL
(813) 377-5731

First Home FS & L Assn.
126 W. Center Ave.
Sebring, FL
(813) 453-6992

Anchor Savings Bank
6850 Central Ave.
St. Petersburg, FL
(813) 347-7283

Florida FSB
Fourth St. & Central Ave.
St. Petersburg, FL
(813) 893-1131

Goldome Savings Assn.
2100 66th St. N.
St. Petersburg, FL
(813) 384-5000

Central S & L Assn.
2401 S. Kanner Hwy.
Stuart, FL
(407) 283-8100

238

California FS & LA-Broward
500 E. Broward Blvd.
Sunrise, FL
(305) 473-2666

Andrew Jackson State S & LA
2000 Apalachee Pkwy.
Tallahassee, FL
(904) 878-6105

Ambassador S & L Assn.
8201 N. University Dr.
Tamarac, FL
(305) 722-3330

Community FS & L Assn.
1493 Tampa Park Plaza
Tampa, FL
(813) 223-5643

Freedom S & LA, A FS & LA
200 Madison St.
Tampa, FL
(813) 870-5126

First Venice S & L Assn.
1320 Venice Ave. E.
Venice, FL
(813) 484-0461

First FS & LA
of The Palm Beaches
215 S. Olive Ave.
West Palm Beach, FL
(407) 655-8511

Royal Palm Savings Bank
100 Australia Ave., Ste. 400
West Palm Beach, FL
(407) 697-7300

Haven FS & L Assn.
250 Second St., NW
Winter Haven, FL
(813) 294-7511

Meritor Savings Bank, FSB
203 Avenue A NW
Winter Haven, FL
(813) 294-3101

GEORGIA

First FS & L Assn.
228 W. Lamar St.
Americus, GA
(912) 924-2725

Athens FSB
124 E. Hancock Ave.
Athens, GA
(404) 357-7000

Fulton FS & L Assn.
One Park Place S.
Atlanta, GA
(404) 586-7070

Georgia Federal Bank, FSB
20 Marietta St. NW
Atlanta, GA
(404) 330-2440

Habersham FSB
781 Marietta St. NW
Atlanta, GA
(404) 870-8300

Home FSB of Atlanta
79 W. Paces Ferry Rd. NW
Atlanta, GA
(404) 841-4650

Southern FS & LA of Georgia
712 W. Peachtree St. NW
Atlanta, GA
(404) 881-6879

Bankers First FS & L Assn.
985 Broad St.
Augusta, Ga
(404) 828-6410

First FSB of Brunswick Georgia
777 Gloucester St.
Brunswick, GA
(912) 265-1410

First Georgia SB, FSB
1703 Gloucester St.
Brunswick, GA
(912) 267-7283

Barnett FSB
1234 First Ave.
Columbus, GA
(404) 571-7800

First FS & L Assn.
129 E. Memorial Dr.
Dallas, GA
(404) 445-2143

Decatur FS & L Assn.
250 E. Ponce De Leon Ave.

Decatur, GA
(404) 371-4242

Dekalb FSB
116 Clairmont Ave.
Decatur, GA
(404) 377-0211

Mt. Vernon FS & L Assn.
2408 Mt. Vernon Rd.
Dunwoody, GA
(404) 396-3966

Home FSB of Georgia
104 Green St., NE
Gainesville, GA
(404) 535-7600

Liberty Savings Bank, FSB
201 Second St.
Macon, GA
(912) 743-0911

Home FS & L Assn.
307 E. Second Ave.
Rome, GA
(404) 291-4500

Great Southern FSB
132 E. Broughton,
Savannah, GA
(912) 944-6280

United FS & L Assn.
945 Windy Hill Rd.
Smyrna, GA
(404) 436-2421

Tucker FS & L Assn.
2355 Main St.
Tucker, GA
(404) 938-1222

First FS & L Assn.
1570 Watson Blvd.
Warner Robins, GA
(912) 923-7127

First FSB of Georgia
202 E. Athens St.
Winder, GA
(404) 867-3161

HAWAII

Honfed Bank, A FSB
188 Merchant St.

Honolulu, HI
(808) 546-2200

International S & L Assn. Ltd.
1111 Bishop St.
Honolulu, HI
(808) 547-5110

Territorial S & L Assn.
900 Bishop St.
Honolulu, HI
(808) 523-0211

IDAHO

First FS & L Assn.
401 Front St.
Coeur D'Alene, ID
(208) 667-2566

Home FS & L Assn.
500 12th Ave. S.
Nampa, ID
(208) 466-4634

ILLINOIS

GermaniaBank, A FSB
543 E. Broadway
Alton, IL
(618) 465-5543

Home Federal Savings
2410 State St.
Alton, IL
(618) 466-7700

Arlington Heights FS & LA
25 E. Campbell St.
Arlington Heights, IL
(312) 255-9000

Aurora FS & L Assn.
101 N. Lake St.
Aurora, IL
(312) 844-5200

Olympic Federal S & L Assn
6201 W. Cermak Rd.
Berwyn, IL
(312) 795-8700

Champion FS & L Assn.
115 E. Washington St.
Bloomington, IL
(309) 829-0456

Home FS & LA of Centralia
400 E. Broadway
Centralia, IL
(618) 533-2771

Calumet FS & L Assn.
8905 S. Commercial Ave.
Chicago, IL
(312) 768-6331

Citicorp Savings of Illinois, A FS
One S. Dearborn St.
Chicago, IL
(312) 263-6660

Enterprise Savings Bank, FA
200 S. Wacker Dr.
Chicago, IL
(312) 930-0900

First Cook Bank for Savings,
A FSA
2720 W. Devon Ave.
Chicago, IL
(312) 761-2700

First Security FSB
936 N. Western Ave.
Chicago, IL
(312) 772-4500

Illinois-Service FS & L Assn.
4619 S. Martin L. King Dr.
Chicago, IL
(312) 624-2000

Irving FS & L Assn.
3515 W. Irving Park Rd.
Chicago, IL
(312) 478-3131

Northwestern S & L Assn.
2300 N. Western Ave.
Chicago, IL
(312) 489-2300

Pathway Financial, A FA
100 N. State St.
Chicago, IL
(312) 346-4200

St. Paul FB for Savings
6700 W. North Ave.
Chicago, IL
(312) 622-5000

Standard FS & LA of Chicago

4192 S. Archer
Chicago, IL
(312) 847-1140

The Talman Home FS & LA
of Illinois
5501 S. Kedzie Ave.
Chicago, IL
(312) 434-3322

United Savings of America
4730 W. 79th St.
Chicago, IL
(312) 585-7700

Chillicothe FS & L Assn.
917 N. Fourth St.
Chillicothe, IL
(309) 274-2116

Mid-America FS & L Assn.
55th & Holmes, Ste. 300
Clarendon Hills, IL
(312) 325-7300

First FS & LA of Colchester
109 E. Depot St.
Colchester, IL
(309) 776-3225

First FS & LA of Macon Cty.
455 N. Main St.
Decatur, IL
(217) 429-2366

Mutual Home & SA
135 E. Main St.
Decatur, IL
(217) 429-2306

First FS & LA of East Alton
200 W. Main St., P.O. Box 240
East Alton, IL
(618) 259-7611

Community Savings Bank
1505 Seventh St.
E. Moline, IL
(309) 752-9200

Elgin Fed Financial Ctr., A FA
1695 Larkin Ave.
Elgin, IL
(312) 741-3900

Fidelity FS & L Assn.
Main & Cherry Sts.
Galesburg, IL

241

(309) 343-9181

United Federal SB
50 E. Main St.
Galesburg, IL
(309) 343-9131

Madison County FS & LA
3600 Nameoki Rd.
Granite City, IL
(618) 876-3800

Hinsdale FS & L Assn.
Grant Square
Hinsdale, IL
(312) 323-1776

Homewood FS & L Assn.
18300 Dixie Hwy.
Homewood, IL
(312) 798-4000

Union FS & L Assn.
104 N. Tremont St.
Kewanee, IL
(309) 853-3535

Concordia FB for Savings
2320 Thorton Rd.
Lansing, IL
(312) 474-1600

Lemont SA
1151 State St.
Lemont, IL
(312) 257-2281

Libertyville FS & L Assn.
354 N. Milwaukee Ave.
Libertyville, IL
(312) 367-0570

Midwestern SA
440 N. Lafayette St.
Macomb, IL
(309) 833-4534

Republic Savings Bank, FSB
4600 W. Lincoln Hwy.
Matteson, IL
(312) 481-7220

First FS & L Assn. of Moline
1616 Sixth Ave.
Moline, IL
(309) 764-8339

Security S & L Assn.

220 E. Broadway
Monmouth, IL
(309) 734-9333

Morton FS & L Assn.
150 S. Main St.
Morton, IL
(309) 263-8406

Citizens S & L
301 Broadway
Normal, IL
(309) 452-1102

Clyde FS & L Assn.
7222 W. Cermak Rd.
N. Riverside, IL
(312) 442-6700

Great American FS & L Assn.
1001 Lake St.
Oak Park, IL
(312) 383-5000

Olney S & L Assn.
240 E. Chestnut St.
Olney, IL
(618) 395-8676

Fin. FT & SB of Olympia Fields
Western Ave. & Lincoln Hwy.
Olympia Fields, IL
(312) 747-2000

First Savings of America,
A FS & LA
9031 W. 151st St.
Orland Park, IL
(312) 460-9411

First Federal Savings Bank
633 La Salle St.
Ottawa, IL
(815) 434-3500

Illinois Savings Bank, FA
1916 N. Knoxville Ave.
Peoria, IL
(309) 685-6560

River Valley SB, FSB
2232 SW Adams
Peoria, IL
(309) 674-3121

Security S & L Assn., FA
200 NE Adams St.
Peoria, IL

242

(309) 671-1700

Gem City S & L Assn.
636 Hampshire St., Box C-249
Quincy, IL
(217) 223-4983

River Valley Savings Bank
201 First Ave.
Rock Falls, IL
(815) 626-3000

Black Hawk FS & L Assn.
1600 Fourth Ave.
Rock Island, IL
(309) 793-4400

First FS & LA of Rockford
612 N. Main St.
Rockford, IL
(815) 987-3500

Skokie FS & L Assn.
4747 Dempster St.
Skokie, IL
(312) 674-3600

First S & LA of S. Holland
475 E. 162nd St.
S. Holland, IL
(312) 333-7400

Metro Savings Bank, FSB
1301 Edwardsville Rd.
Wood River, IL
(618) 259-5030

INDIANA

First S & LA of Central Indiana
33 West Tenth St.
Anderson, IN
(317) 649-5551

Hometown FSB
215 E. Main St.
Delphi, IN
(317) 564-2696

First United
One N. Locust St.
Greencastle, IN
(317) 653-9793

First Indiana Bank, A FSB
First Indiana Place
135 N. Pennsylvania

Indianapolis, IN
(317) 269-1200

Union FSB
7101 E. 56th St.
Indianapolis, IN
(317) 543-5800

First Federal SB of Kokomo
200 W. Mulberry St.
Kokomo, IN
(317) 457-5551

First Federal SB of Marion
100 W. Third St.
Marion, IN
(317) 664-0556

Muncie FS & L Assn.
120 W. Charles St.
Muncie, IN
(317) 288-0271

Mutual FSB
110 E. Charles St.
Muncie, IN
(317) 747-2800

Community First FS & LA
202 E. Spring St.
New Albany, IN
(812) 944-2224

Mutual FS & L Assn.
498 Ohio St.
Terre Haute, IN
(812) 234-4851

Valley FSB
350 Wabash Ave.
Terre Haute, IN
(812) 232-0311

IOWA

Home FS & L Assn.
220 E. State St.
Algona, IA
(515) 295-7251

Midwest FS & LA of East. Iowa
3225 Division St.
Burlington, IA
(319) 754-6526

Mississippi Valley S & L Assn.
321 N. Third St.

Burlington, IA
(319) 754-7517

First FS & L Assn. of Carroll
109 E. Seventh St.
Carroll, IA
(712) 792-4397

Banc Iowa Savings Bank
316 Second St. SE
Cedar Rapids, IA
(319) 364-0153

Perpetual Savings Bank
110 Second Ave., SE
Cedar Rapids, IA
(319) 366-1851

First Central Bank, A FSB
Main & Braden Sts.
Chariton, IA
(515) 774-2147

Sioux Valley S & L Assn.
401 W. Main St.
Cherokee, IA
(712) 225-6444

Clinton FS & L Assn.
340 Fifth Ave., S.
Clinton, IA
(319) 243-1512

First FS & LA, Council Bluffs
421 W. Broadway
Council Bluffs, IA
(712) 328-3803

First FS & L Assn. of Creston
301 N. Pine St.
Creston, IA
(515) 782-8482

Citizens FS & LA, Davenport
101 W. Third St.
Davenport, IA
(319) 322- 6237

First FSB of Iowa
131 W. Third St.
Davenport, IA
(319) 326-0121

American FS & L Ass. of Iowa
601 Grand Ave.
Des Moines, IA
(515) 244-9131

Midland Financial S & L Assn.
606 Walnut
Des Moines, IA
(515) 283-2151

United FSB of Iowa
Fourth & Locust
Des Moines, IA
(515) 247-4694

Harvest Savings Bank
2560 Dodge
Dubuque, IA
(319) 557-9000

First FS & L Assn. Estherville
& Emmetsburg
21 N. Sixth St.
Esterville, IA
(712) 362-2664

Grinnell FS & L Assn.
1025 Main St.
Grinnell, IA
(515) 236-3121

Home FS & LA of Harlan
712 Durant St.
Harlan, IA
(712) 755-2188

Metropolitan FB of Iowa
124 N. Washington Ave.
Mason City, IA
(515) 423-8611

Oskaloosa Home L & S Assn.
301 First Ave., E.
Oskaloosa, IA
(515) 673-8328

Peoples S & L Assn.
107 S. Court
Ottumwa, IA
(515) 683-1811

First FS & LA of Sioux City
329 Pierce St.
P.O. Box 897
Sioux City, IA
(712) 277-0200

Northwest FSB
101 W. Fifth St.
Spencer, IA
(712) 262-4100

MidAmerica SB, FSB

999 Home Plaza
Waterloo, IA
(319) 234-5523

Statesman Bank for Savings, FSB
Fourth at Mulberry
Waterloo, IA
(319) 234-7783

KANSAS

First FS & LA of Coffeyville
Eighth & Maple Sts.
Coffeyville, KS
(316) 251-2800

Landmark FSA
Central & Spruce
Dodge City, KS
(316) 227-8111

Mid-Continent FS & LA,
El Dorado
124 W. Central
El Dorado, KS
(316) 321-2700

Golden Belt S & L Assn.
901 Washington St.
Ellis, KS
(913) 726-3157

Columbia SA, FA
715 Merchant St.
Emporia, KS
(316) 342-1832

First of Kansas B & S Assn.
1200 E. 27th St.
Hays, KS
(913) 628-1004

First FS & LA, Hutchinson
825 Main
Hutchison, KA
(316) 669-0111

Valley FS & LA Hutchison
811 E. 30th
Hutchison, KS
(316) 663-6111

First FS & LA, Independence
112 E. Myrtle St.
Independence, KS
(316) 331-1660

Anchor SA
8200 State Ave.
Kansas City, KS
(913) 334-2000

Sun Savings Assn., FA
1300 N. 78th St.
Kansas City, KS
(913) 334-1800

Kingman S & L Assn.
401 N. Main St.
Kingman, KS
(316) 532-5135

Colonial SA of America
824 N. Kansas
Liberal, KS
(316) 624-7204

The Lyons S & L Assn.
200 E. Ave. S.
Lyons, KS
(316) 257-2316

The Barber County S & LA
120 E. Kansas
Medicine Lodge, KS
(316) 886-3

Mid-America FS & L Assn.
1909 Main St.
Parsons, KS
(316) 421-3500

Peoples S & L Assn.
87 Parsons Plaza
Parsons, KS
(316) 421-4600

First FS & LA of Pittsburg
306 N. Broadway
Pittsburg, KS
(316) 945-9600

Colonial Savings, A FA
4000 Somerset Dr.
Prairie Village, KS
(913) 648-6500

The Pioneer S & L Assn.
5400 W. 95th St.
Prairie Village, KS
(913) 381-0300

Peoples Heritage FS & L Assn.
1129 SW Wanamaker Rd.
P.O. Box 4600

Topeka, KS
(913) 273-5800

The Security S & L Assn.
317 S. Santa Fe
Salina, KS
(913) 825-8241

Capitol FS & L Assn.
700 Kansas Ave.
Topeka, KS
(913) 235-1341

Postal S & L Assn.
108 W. Eighth St.
Topeka, KS
(913) 354-7735

Shawnee FS & L Assn.
906 Kansas Ave.
Topeka, KS
(913) 357-1231

Topeka Savings, A FS & LA
800 Quincy St.
Topeka, KS
(913) 232-0402

First FSB of Kansas
403 N. Washington
Wellington, KS
(316) 326-7487

Fidelity SA of Kansas
100 E. English St.
Wichita, KS
(316) 265-2261

Mid Kansas FS & LA, Witchita
230 S. Market St.
Wichita, KS
(316) 269-4825

Railroad S & L Assn.
110 S. Main St.
Wichita, KS
(316) 269-0300

Wichita FS & L Assn.
340 S. Broadway
Wichita, KS
(316) 265-3151

KENTUCKY

Republic Savings Bank, FSB
507 Main St.

Benton, KY
(502) 527-3193

First Kentucky FS & L Assn.
214 N. First St.
Central City, KY
(502) 754-1331

Sunrise FS & L Assn.
2216 Dixie Hwy.
Fort Mitchell, KS
(606) 331-6565

Henderson Home FS & LA
240 Third St.
Henderson, KY
(502) 827-1841

First FS & L Assn.
1101 S. Main St.
Hopkinsville, KY
(502) 886-3341

Future FSB
3940 Grandview Ave.
Louisville, KY
(502) 896-5676

The Cumberland FSB
200 W. Broadway
Louisville, KY
(502) 562-5224

Family FSB of Paintsville
103 Main St.
Paintsville, KY
(606) 789-3541

Mutual FS & L Assn.
124 N. Main St.
Somerset, KY
(606) 679-4375

LOUISIANA

Capital-Union Savings FA
339 Florida Blvd.
Baton Rouge, LA
(504) 387-2112

First City S & L Assn.
of Baton Rouge Louisiana
9400 Old Hammond Hwy.
Baton Rouge, LA
(504) 923-0232

First FS & L Assn.

246

7990 Scenic Hwy.
Baton Rouge, LA
(504) 775-6133

River City FSB
10425 Airline Hwy.
Baton Rouge, LA
(504) 769-8860

Citizens S & L Assn.
of Washington Parish
201 Cumberland St.
Bogalusa, LA
(504) 735-6555

St. Tammany Hmstd Assn.
210 New Hampshire St.
Covington, LA
(504) 892-4565

Acadia S & L Assn., A FSA
576 N. Parkerson Ave.
Crowley, LA
(318) 783-0261

Crowley B & L Assn.
204 N. Parkerson Ave.
Crowley, LA
(318) 783-4121

Parish FSB
1509 S. Range
Denham Springs, LA
(504) 664-3280

First FS & L Assn.
151 S. Fourth St.
Eunice, LA
(318) 457-7334

Teche FS & L Assn.
211 Willow St.
Franklin, LA
(318) 828-3212

Jefferson S & L Assn.
1011 Fourth St.
Gretna, LA
(504) 363-7871

Lafayette S & L Assn.
1300 Stumpf Blvd.
Gretna, LA
(504) 362-4567

Commercial FSB
1745 SW Railroad Ave.
Hammond, LA

(504) 542-9770

Elmwood FS & L Assn.
5360 Mounes St.
Harahan, LA
(504) 733-3171

Terrebonne S & L Assn.
701 Barrow St.
Houma, LA
(504) 868-4700

Jennings FS & L Assn.
500 Cary Ave.
Jennings, LA
(318) 824-2105

Jonesboro FS & L Assn.
128 Allen Ave.
Jonesboro, LA
(318) 259-3009

Delta S & L Assn.
3540 Williams Blvd.
Kenner, LA
(504) 443-5110

First Savings of Louisiana, FSA
675 Airline Hwy.
La Place, LA
(504) 652-9541

Evangeline FS & L Assn.
3838 W. Congress
Lafayette, LA
(318) 988-1580

First Louisiana FSB
2014 Pinhook Rd.
Lafayette, LA
(318) 264-1200

Home S & L Assn.
523 Jefferson St.
Lafayette, LA
(318) 237-1960

Lafayette BA
107 W. Vermilion
Lafayette, LA
(318) 981-7300

First FS & L Assn.
1135 Lakeshore Dr.
Lake Charles, LA
(318) 433-3611

Louisana SA

901 Lakeshore Dr.
Lake Charles, LA
(318) 436-7283

Landmark Savings Bank, SSB
903 Belle Terre Dr.
La Place, LA
(504) 652-7002

Desoto FS & L Assn.
214 S. Washington Ave.
Mansfield, LA
(318) 872-4355

Enterprise FS & L Assn.
3900 La Place Blvd.
Marrero, LA
(504) 340-1337

Columbia Hmstd Assoc.
5300 Veterans Blvd.
Metairie, LA
(504) 885-8500

First FSB of New Orleans
3131 N. 110 Service Rd.
Metairie, LA
(504) 832-4000

French Market Hmstd, FSA
3900 Veterans Blvd.
Metairie, LA
(504) 454-1800

Greater N.O. Hmstd Assn.
1600 Veterans Memorial Blvd.
Metairie, LA
(504) 834-1190

Horizon FS & L Assn.
4545 Veterans Memorial Blvd.
Metairie, LA
(504) 454-5300

Louisiana FSB
3041 N. Causeway Blvd.
Metairie, LA
(504) 832-1985

Mutual S & L Assn.
4725 Veterans Blvd.
Metairie, LA
(504) 455-2444

Pelican Hmstd & SA
2121 Airline Hwy.
Metairie, LA
(504) 834-7283

Deposit Trust Savings Bank
1900 N. 18th St.
Monroe, LA
(318) 388-3610

People's Hmstd FS for Savings
1220 N. 18th St.
Monroe, LA
(318) 329-8500

Progressive FSB
700 Second St.
Natchitoches, LA
(318) 352-8148

Oak Tree Savings Bank, SSB
233 Carondelet St.
New Orleans, LA
(504) 588-9313

First FS & L Assn.
320 E. Main St.
New Iberia, LA
(318) 365-7373

Iberia S & L Assn.
301 E. St. Peter St.
New Iberia, LA
(318) 365-2361

American S & L Assn.
200 St. Charles Ave.
New Orleans, LA
(504) 581-4561

Carrollton Hmstd Assn.
2619 Canal St.
New Orleans, LA
(504) 821-1563

Central S & L Assn.
710 Canal St.
New Orleans, LA
(504) 581-7081

Citizens Hmstd Assn.
325 Carondelet St.
New Orleans, LA
(504) 586-1500

Commonwealth SA
140 Carondelet St.
New Orleans, LA
(504) 566-1661

Dryades S & L Assn.
814 Gravier St.

SECTION THREE - Savings and Loans Associations

New Orleans, LA
(504) 525-0577

Fifth District S & L Assn.
4000 General DeGualle Dr.
New Orleans, LA
(504) 362-7544

Home S & L Assn.
3625 Canal St.
New Orleans, LA
(504) 486-7791

Security Hmstd Assn.
221 Carondelet St.
New Orleans, LA
(504) 581-9361

Southern Savings Bank, SSB
135 St. Charles Ave.
New Orleans, LA
(504) 586-1776

United FS & L Assn.
1501 Canal St.
New Orleans, LA
(504) 525-5628

St. Laudry Hmstd Assn.
271 N. Court St.
Opelousas, LA
(318) 948-3033

Family FS & L Assn.
1701 N. Market
Shreveport, LA
(318) 227-0675

First FS & L Assn.
505 Travis St.
Shreveport, LA
(318) 221-7161

Home FS & L Assn.
624 Market St.
Shreveport, LA
(318) 222-1145

Fontainebleu FSB
770 Gause Blvd.
Slidell, LA
(504) 649-0378

South S & L Assn.
2250 E. Gause Rd.
Slidell, LA
(504) 643-1300

First FS & L Assn.
200 W. Second St.
Thibodaux, LA
(504) 446-5011

Peoples FS & LA, Thibodaux
210 N. Canal Blvd.
Thibodaux, LA
(504) 446-2196

First FS & L Assn.
118 W. Main
Winnfield, LA
(318) 628-3562

MAINE

First FS & L Assn.
Corner Canal & Chestnut Sts.
Lewiston, ME
(207) 784-7376

MASSACHUSETTS

Boston Five Cents SB FSB
10 School St.
Boston, MA
(617) 742-6000

Greater Boston Bank A Co-op Bk.
414 Washington St.
Boston, MA
(617) 782-5570

Home Owners FS & L Assn.
21 Milk St.
Boston, MA
(617) 695-4000

Sentry FSB
765 Main St.
Hyannis, MA
(508) 771-6800

Comfed Savings Bank
45 Central St.
Lowell, MA
(508) 256-3751

Home FSB
419 Main St.
Worcester, MA
(508) 799-0571

MARYLAND

Annapolis FSB
140 Main St.
Annapolis, MD
(301) 267-8686

First Annapolis SB, FSB
2024 West St.
Annapolis, MD
(301) 224-5500

Atlantic Federal SB
100 West Rd.
Baltimore, MD
(301) 938-8600

Baltimore Fed Fin, FSA
300 E. Lombard St.
Baltimore, MD
(301) 625-4600

Fairfax Savings, A FSB
7133 Rutherford
Woodlawn, MD
(301) 265-7900

Hamilton FS & L Assn.
5600 Harford Rd.
Baltimore, MD
(301) 254-9700

Harbor FS & L Assn.
3200 Eastern Ave.
Baltimore, MD
(301) 342-4060

Loyola FS & L Assn.
1300 N. Charles St.
Baltimore, MD
(301) 332-7000

John Hanson SB, FSB
11700 Beltsville Dr.
Beltsville, MD
(301) 572-2400

Chevy Chase SB, FSB
6200 Chevy Chase Dr.
Laurel, MD
(301) 953-8070

First FSB of West. Maryland
118 Baltimore St.
Cumberland, MD
(301) 724-3363

Fairview FS & L Assn.
9151 Baltimore Ntl. Pike

Ellicott City, MD
(301) 465-4800

Standard FSB
5280 Corporate Dr.
Gaithersburg, MD
(301) 696-4282

Home FSB
122-128 W. Washington St.
Hagerstown, MD
(301) 733-6300

Maryland FS & L Assn.
3505 Hamilton St.
Hyattsville, MD
(301) 231-5777

American FSB
1700 Rockville Pike
Rockville, MD
(301) 231-9199

Citizens Savings Bank, FSB
8458 Fenton St.
Silver Spring, MD
(301) 565-8900

MICHIGAN

Great Lakes Bancorp, A FSB
401 E. Liberty St.
Ann Arbor, MI
(313) 769-8300

Mutual S & L Assn., FA
623 Washington Ave.
Bay City, MI
(517) 892-3511

First Federal of Michigan
1001 Woodward Ave.
Detroit, MI
(313) 965-1400

D & N Savings Bank, FSB
400 Quincy St.
Hancock, MI
(906) 482-2700

Colonial Central SB, FSB
36800 Gratiot Ave.
Mount Clemens, MI
(313) 792-8055

First Federal SB & Trust
761 W. Huron St.

Pontiac, MI
(313) 333-7071

Sterling Savings Bank
28400 Northwestern Hwy.,
Ste. 400
Southfield, MI
(313) 355-9200

Guaranty FSB
23333 Eureka Rd.
Taylor, MI
(313) 855-4900

Heritage FSB
20600 Eureka Rd.
Taylor, MI
(313) 285-1010

Northwestern S & L Assn.
201 E. Front St.
Traverse City, MI
(616) 947-5490

Standard Federal Bank
2401 W. Big Beaver Rd.
Troy, MI
(313) 643-9600

MINNESOTA

Metropolitan FB of Minnesota
Eighth & Laurel Sts.
Brainerd, MN
(218) 829-1731

Lakeland FSB
928 Lake Ave.
Detroit Lakes, MN
(218) 847-3041

St. Louis County FS & LA
332 W. Superior St.
Duluth, MN
(218) 727-3533

American Federal SB
124 De Mers Ave.
E. Grand Forks, MN
(218) 773-9711

Fairmont FS & L Assn.
115 W. First St.
Fairmont, MN
(507) 235-5556

Community FS & L Assn.

of Little Falls Minnesota
35 E. Broadway
Little Falls, MN
(612) 632-5461

First Minnesota SB, FSB
1021 Tenth Ave. SE
Minneapolis, MN
(612) 623-7566

Investors SB, FSB
200 Dain Tower
Minneapolis, MN
(612) 371-2200

Midwest FS & LA, Minneapolis
801 Nicollet Mall
Minneapolis, MN
(612) 372-6123

TCF Banking and Savings, FA
801 Marquette Ave.
Minneapolis, MN
(612) 370-7000

Wells FS & L Assn.
53 First St., SW
Wells, MN
(507) 553-3151

United FSB
220 Eighth St.
Windom, MN
(507) 831-1006

MISSOURI

Jefferson S & L Assn.
4626 S. Kings Hwy.
St. Louis, MO
(314) 352-4135

The Cameron S & L Assn.
123 E. Third St.
Cameron, MO
(816) 632-2154

Colonial FS & L Assn.
2027 Broadway
Cape Girardeau, MO
(314) 334-3024

First FS & L Assn.
of Southeast Missouri
325 Broadway
Cape Girardeau, MO
(314) 335-8263

Roosevelt Bank, A FSB
900 Roosevelt Pkwy.
P.O. Box 1042
Chesterfield, MO
(314) 532-6200

Clayton S & L Assn.
135 N. Meramec
Clayton, MO
(314) 727-7400

Missouri Savings Assn.
10 N. Hanley Rd.
Clayton, MO
(314) 862-3300

Cass FS & L Assn.
1281 Graham Rd.
Florissant, MO
(314) 837-9100

North American SA
125th & S. 71 Hwy.
Grandview, MO
(816) 765-2200

Capital S & L Assn.
425 Madison St.
Jefferson City, MO
(314) 635-4151

Financial FS & L Assn.
701 Main St.
Joplin, MO
(417) 623-2115

Blue Valley FS & L Assn.
6515 Independence Ave.
Kansas City, MO
(816) 231-2883

First FS & L.A, Kansas City
919 Walnut St.
Kansas City, MO
(816) 842-8544

Home SA of Kansas City, FA
1006 Grand Ave.
Kansas City, MO
(816) 221-7100

Kirksville S & L Assn.
202 E. McPherson
Kirksville, MO
(816) 665-8374

United S & L Assn.
Jefferson at Second

Lebanon, MO
(417) 588-4111

The Lexington B & L Assn.
919 Franklin Ave.
Lexington, MO
(816) 259-2247

First S & LA of Mt. Vernon
109 N. Hickory St.
Mt. Vernon, MO
(417) 466-2171

Farm and Home SA
221 W. Cherry St.
Nevada, MO
(417) 667-3333

Home S & LA of Norborne
210 E. Second St.
Norborne, MO
(816) 594-3313

Palmyra S & B Assn.
123 W. Lafayette
Palmyra, MO
(314) 769-2134

Southern Missouri S & LA
531 Vine St.
Poplar Bluff, MO
(314) 785-1421

Great Southern S & L Assn.
1451 E. Battlefield Rd.
Springfield, MO
(417) 887-4400

Community FS & L Assn.
One Community Fed Ctr.
St. Louis, MO
(314) 822-5000

Heartland SB, FSB
312 N. Sixth St.
St. Louis, MO
(314) 621-2660

Pulaski S & L Assn.
12300 Olive Blvd.
St. Louis, MO
(314) 878-2210

United Postal SA
10015 Manchester Rd.
St. Louis, MO
(314) 966-2530

MISSISSIPPI

Mississippi Savings Bank
176 Hwy .51 N.
Batesville, MS
(601) 563-4772

First FS & LA Brookhaven
303 W. Cherokee St.
Brookhaven, MS
(601) 833-1821

Fidelity FSB
303 N. Madison
Corinth, MS
(601) 286-8417

Great American Fed S & LA
306 Cass St.
Corinth, MS
(601) 287-5211

Southern FB for Savings
3300 W. Beach Blvd.
Gulfport, MS
(601) 867-2004

Charter Bank, A FSB
700 Hardy St.
Hattiesburg, MS
(601) 544-2090

First Guaranty Bank for Savings
300 W. Hardy St.
Hattiesburg, MS
(601) 583-5000

Magnolia FB for Savings
130 W. Front St.
Hattiesburg, MS
(601) 545-4700

Eastover Bank for Savings
656 N. State St.
Jackson, MS
(601) 960-8000

Republic Bank for Savings, FA
6158 Old Canton Rd.
Jackson, MS
(601) 956-2550

Security S & L Assn.
200 S. Lomas
Jackson, MS
(601) 949-8000

Unifirst Bank for Savings, FA
525 E. Capotol St.
Jackson, MS
(601) 948-8700

Laurel FS & L Assn.
317 N. Fifth Ave.
Laurel, MS
(601) 649-4411

Southeastern Savings Bank
705 Sawmill Rd.
Laurel, MS
(601) 649-3921

Natchez First FS & L Assn.
115 S. Pearl St.
Natchez, MS
(601) 442-2733

MONTANA

First FS & L Assn.
2929 Third Ave. N.
Billings, MT
(406) 252-3823

Security FSB
219 N. 26th St.
Billings, MT
(406)259-4571

United Savings Bank, FA
601 First Ave. N.
Great Falls. MT
(406) 761-2200

Western FSB of Montana
100 E. Broadway
Missoula, MT
(406) 721-3700

NORTH CAROLINA

First Southern Savings Bank
115 S. Fayetteville St.
Asheboro, NC
(919) 625-5133

Watauga S & L Assn.
106 W. King St.
Boone, NC
(704) 264-8885

Brevard FS & L Assn.
132 S. Caldwell St.

Brevard, NC
(704) 884-2951

First FS & L Assn.
300 S. Tryon St.
Charlotte, NC
(704) 335-4480

Mutual S & L Assn, Inc.
330 S. Tryon St.
Charlotte, NC
(704) 379-1700

North Carolina FS & L Assn.
5416 N. Tryon St.
Charlotte, NC
(704) 335-5700

Southeastern SB, Inc.
First SE Ctr.,
112 S. Tryon St.
Charlotte, NC
(704) 379-1300

Clyde S & L Assn.
Corner Main & Carolina Blvd.
P. O. Box 988
Waynesville, NC
(704)456-9425

Cabarrus Savings Bank, Inc.
71 McCachern Blvd.
Concord, NC
(704) 782-1193

First Home FS & L Assn.
of the Carolinas
444 N. Elm St.
Greensboro, NC
(919) 373-5000

First American SB, FSB
4411 W. Market St.
Greensboro, NC
(919) 852-8410

Old Stone Bank of NC, A FSB
645 N. Main St.
High Point, NC
(919) 886-5191

Preferred S & L Assn.
600 N. Hamilton St.
High Point, NC
(919) 889-3132

Great Atlantic SB FSB
U.S. Hwy. 64

Manteo, NC
(919) 473-5871

Heritage FS & L Assn.
111 E. Jefferson St.
Monroe, NC
(704) 283-7431

Workmens FSB
541 N. Main St.
Mount Airy, NC
(919) 789-9526

Citizens Savings Bank, Inc.
12 N. Main Ave.
Newton, NC
(704) 464-1661

First FS & L Assn.
1157 Executive Cir.
Carey, NC
(919) 460-5780

Raleigh FSB
224 Fayetteville St. Mall
Raleigh, NC
(919) 833-7511

Pioneer SB, Inc.
224 S. Franklin St.
Rocky Mount, NC
(919) 446-0611

United FS & L Assn.
116 S. Franklin St.
Rocky Mount, NC
(919) 446-9191

Home FSB
500 E. Broad St.
Statesville, NC
(704) 873-4363

Carolina Savings Bank
202 N. Third St.
Wilmington, NC
(919) 341-3200

NORTH DAKOTA

First FS & L Assn.
of Bismarck
320 N. Fourth St.
Bismarck, ND
(701) 222-3300

Gate City FSB

500 Second Ave. N.
Fargo, ND
(701) 293-2400

Metropolitan FB, FSB
215 N. Fifth St.
Fargo, ND
(701) 293-2600

Northwestern FS & LA, Fargo
720 Main Ave.
Fargo, ND
(701)235-4248

Midwest FSB
123 First St. SW
Minot, ND
(701) 852-1161

NEBRASKA

Custer FS & L Assn.
341 S. Tenth Ave.
Broken Bow, NE
(308) 872-6486

Columbus FSB
1371 26th Ave.
Columbus, NE
(402) 563-3550

Equitable S & L Assn., FA
1369 25th Ave.
Columbus, NE
(402) 564-7181

Equitable FSB
400 E. Military Ave.
Fremont, NE
(402) 721-1211

Platte Valley FS & L Assn.
1740 Tenth St.
Gering, NE
(308) 436-3111

Home FS & LA, Grand Island
221 S. Locust St.
Grand Island, NE
(308) 382-4000

Home FS & LA of Nebraska
201 W. Seventh St.
Lexington, NE
(308) 324-2331

American Charter FS & LA

4000 S. 27th
Lincoln, NE
(402) 473-3707

First FS & LA of Lincoln
2101 S. 42nd St.
Omaha, NE
(402) 475-0521

Lincoln FS & L Assn.
1101 North St.
Lincoln, NE
(402) 474-1400

Midwest FS & L Assn.
920 Central Ave.
Nebraska City, NE
(402) 873-7702

Commercial FS & L Assn.
2120 S. 72nd St.
Omaha, NE
(402) 390-0135

Conservative SB
11207 W. Dodge Rd.
Omaha, NE
(402) 334-8475

Heritage FSB
10802 Farham Dr.
Omaha, NE
(402) 330-7474

Occidental Nebraska FSB
1108 W. Center Rd.
Omaha, NE
(402) 334-4609

Nile Valley FS & L Assn.
1701 First Ave.
Scottsbluff, NE
(308) 635-3666

First FS & L Assn.
100 E. Fourth St.
York, NE
(402) 362-7781

NEW HAMPSHIRE

Home Bank, FSB
Rt. 11
Guilford, NH
(603) 752-1330

Numerica SB, FSB

1155 Elm St.
Manchester, NH
(603) 624-2424

NFS Savings Bank
157 Main St.
Nashua, NH
(603) 880-2011

NEW JERSEY

Polifly S & L Assn.
730 River Rd.
New Milford, NJ
(201) 261-6900

Ocean FS & L Assn.
730 Brick Blvd.
Brick Town, NJ
(201) 477-5151

Center S & L Assn.
295 Clifton Ave.
Clifton, NJ
(201) 365-1717

Metropolitan FS & L Assn.
6 Bloomfield Ave.
Denville, NJ
(201) 625-3200

Crestmont FS & L Assn.
2035 Lincoln Hwy.
Edison, NJ
(201) 287-3838

Collective FSB
200 Philadelphia Ave.
Egg Harbor City, NJ
(609) 965-1234

City FSB
1141 E. Jersey St.
Elizabeth, NJ
(206) 453-2327

Glen Ridge S & L Assn.
329 Belleville Ave.
Bloomfield, NJ
(201) 743-8719

Haven Savings Bank, SLA
621 Washington St.
Hoboken, NJ
(201) 659-3600

AmeriFederal SB

Quakerbridge Executive Ctr.
Grovers Mill
Lawrenceville, NJ
(609) 275-1000

Shadow Lawn SB, SLA
Monmouth Rd.
West Long Branch, NJ
(201) 222-1000

Mutual Aid S & L Assn.
Hwy. 71 & Main St.
Manasquan, NJ
(201) 223-3434

Yorkwood S & L Assn.
One Fredrick Rd.
Warren, NJ
(201) 561-5900

Berkeley FS & L Assn.
of New Jersey
21 Brecker St.
Millburn, NJ
(201) 467-2800

First FS & LA of Montclair
N. Fullerton Ave.
Montclair, NJ
(201) 783-8336

Carteret Savings Bank, FA
10 Waterview Blvd.
Parsippany, NJ
(201) 623-7339

Penn FSB
622 Eagles Rock Ave.
West Orange, NJ
(201) 589-8616

Trident FS & L Assn.
504 Rt. 9
Lanoka Harbor, NJ
(201) 372-0303

North Jersey S & L Assn.
625 Main Ave.
Passaic, NJ
(201) 773-5900

Irving S & L Assn.
530 High Mountain Rd.
N. Haledon, NJ
(201) 423-2000, Ext. 2904

Lakeview S & L Assn.
1117-1119 Main St.

Paterson, NJ
(201) 742-3060

First Atlantic S & L Assn.
107 Park Ave.
Plainfield, NJ
(201) 769-0550

Cenlar FSB
101 Carnegie Ctr.
Princeton, NJ
(609) 987-0440

Nassau S & L Assn.
188 Nassau St.
Princeton, NJ
(609) 924-4498

Riverside SB, SLA
15-17 Scott St.
Riverside, NJ
(609) 461-0461

Pulawski S & L Assn.
6 Jackson Street
South River, NJ
(201) 572-4200

Jersey Shore S & L Assn.
36 Washington St.
Toms River, NJ
(201) 349-1000

Old Borough S & L Assn.
1434 S. Broad St.
Trenton, NJ
(609).393-4148

The United S & L Assn.
of Trenton NJ
70 N. Montgomery St.
Trenton, NJ
(609) 394-1100

Security Savings Bank, SLA
818 Landis Ave.
Vineland, NJ
(609) 696-8700

NEW MEXICO

Abuquerque Bank, FSB
6501 Americas Pkwy., NE
Albuquerque, NM
(505) 889-1110

American FS & L Assn.

2400 Louisiana Blvd. NE
Albuquerque, NM
(505) 881-6600

New Mexico Federal S & L
2900 Louisiana Blvd., NE
Albuquerque, NM
(505) 884-3000

Sandia FS & L Assn.
500 Marquette NW
Albuquerque, NM
(505) 848-7800

Sun Country SB
of New Mexico, FSB
423 Copper Ave., NW
Albuquerque, NM
(505) 764-3600

Security Savings Bank, FSB
212 N. Canal
Carlsbad, NM
(505) 885-4101

Home FSB of New Mexico
520 S. Gold
Deming, NM
(505) 546-2707

First FS & L Assn.
624 University St.
Las Vegas, NM
(505) 425-9354

First Federal Savings Bank
300 N. Pennsylvania Ave.
Roswell, NM
(505) 622-6201

Pioneer Savings & Trust, FA
306 N. Pennsylvania
Roswell, NM
(505) 624-5200

Valley Federal Savings Bank
Third & Main Sts.
Roswell, NM
(505) 622-8521

Charter Bank for Savings FSB
1881 St. Michaels Dr.
Santa Fe, NM
(505) 982-2534

First American SB, FSB
601 S. Santa Fe Hwy.
Taos, NM

(505) 758-1340

NEVADA

First Western Savings Assn.
2700 W. Sahara Ave.
Las Vegas, NV
(702) 871-2000

Frontier SA
801 E. Charleston Blvd.
Las Vegas, NV
(702) 796-4523

Primerit Bank, FSB
3300 W. Sahara
Las Vegas, NV
(702) 362-5555

American FSB
2330 S. Virginia St.
Reno, NV
(702) 785-8500

NEW YORK

Amsterdam SB, FSB
11 Division St.
Amsterdam, NY
(518) 842-7200

Yorkville FS & L Assn.
3030 Buhre Ave.
Bronx, NY
(212) 409-3000

Crossland Savings, FSB
189 Montague St.
Brooklyn, NY
(718) 780-0400

Nassau FS & L Assn.
2815 Atlantic Ave.
Brooklyn, NY
(718) 647-5300

The Lincoln SB, FSB
7427 Fifth Ave.
Brooklyn, NY
(718) 745-2000

Empire of America FSB
One Empire Tower
Buffalo, NY
(716) 845-7000

Long Island SB of Centereach
201 Old Country Rd.
Melville, NY
(516) 597-2000

Fidelity New York FSB
155 Jericho Turnpike
Floral Park, NY
(516) 488-2400

Dime SB of NY, FSB
975 Franklin Ave.
Garden City, NY
(516) 351-1550

Citizens Savings Bank FSB
118 N. Tioga St.
Ithaca, NY
(607) 273-7111

Central Federal Savings FSB
249 E. Park Ave.
Long Beach, NY
(516) 432-4000

Astoria FS & L Assn.
37-16 30th Ave.
Long Island City, NY
(718) 728-2500

American Savings Bank, FSB
1133 Ave. of the Americas
New York, NY
(212) 287-2641

Ensign Bank, FSB
345 Park Ave.
New York, NY
(212) 752-8282

Seamen's Bank for Savings, FSB
30 Wall St.
New York, NY
(212) 428-4500

Anchor Savings Bank, FSB
225 Main St.
Northport, NY
(516) 261-6000

Champlain Valley FS & LA
of Plattsburgh
9 Margaret St.
Plattsburgh, NY
(518) 563-1800

The Poughkeepsie SB, FSB
21 Market St.

Poughskeepsie, NY
(914) 431-6200

Columbia Banking FS & LA
31 E. Main St.
Rochester, NY
(716) 454-6780

First FS & LA of Rochester
One First Federal Plaza
Rochester, NY
(716) 238-2100

Monroe Savings Bank, FSB
300 E. Main St.
Rochester, NY
(716) 325-3250

Eastern FS & LA, Sayville
160 Main St.
Sayville, NY
(516) 589-5900

OHIO

Midland-Buckeye FS & LA
260 E. Main St.
Alliance, OH
(216) 823-6100

First American SB, FSB
400 Tuscarawas St., W.
Canton, OH
(216) 454-3272

The Citizens SB of Canton
100 Central Plaza S.
Canton, OH
(216) 489-3600

Charter Oak FSB
4445 Lake Forest Dr.
Cincinnati, OH
(513) 563-3300

Gateway FS & L Assn.
9650 Colerain Ave.
Cincinnati, OH
(513) 741-7980

Hunter SA
7840 Montgomery Rd.
Cincinnati, OH
(513) 745-8700

The Franklin S & LC
126 E. Sixth St.

Cincinnati, OH
(513) 721-0808

The Mercantile Savings Bank
8001 Kenwood Rd.
Cincinnati, OH
(513) 891-7711

Broadview Savings Bank
6000 Rockside Woods Blvd.
Cleveland, OH
(216) 447-1900

Cardinal FSB
150 Euclid Ave.
Cleveland, OH
(216) 623-6000

Cuyahoga Savings Assn.
One Erieview Plaza
Cleveland, OH
(216) 771-3550

Ohio Savings Bank
1801 E. Ninth St.
Cleveland, OH
(216) 696-2222

Superior Savings Assn.
798 E. 185th St.
Cleveland, OH
(216) 481-3008

The First FSB
1215 Superior Ave.
Cleveland, OH
(216) 566-5300

TransOhio Savings Bank
1250 Superior Ave
Cleveland, OH
(216) 579-7700

Women's FSB
120 Public Square
Cleveland, OH
(216) 687-8200

Buckeye FS & L Assn.
36 E. Gay St.
Columbus, OH
(614) 225-2126

Freedom FS & L Assn.
2939 Kenny Rd.
Columbus, OH
(614) 459-6100

Mid-America FS & L Assn.
4181 Arlingate Plaza
Columbus, OH
(614) 278-3401

State Savings Bank
20 E. Broad St.
Columbus, OH
(614) 460-6100

Citizens FS & L Assn.
8 N. Main St.
Dayton, OH
(513) 223-4234

Gem SA
Gem Plaza
Dayton, OH
(513) 224-6700

Potters S & L Co.
Washington & Broadway
East Liverpool, OH
(216) 385-0770

Diamond S & LC
500 S. Main St.
Findlay, OH
(419) 424-7500

Columbia FS & L Assn.
537 Park
Hamilton, OH
(513) 895-1326

Dollar FSB
Dollar Federal Bldg.
Hamilton, OH
(513) 895-1321

Home FS & L Assn.
Third & Court Sts.
Hamilton, OH
(513) 868-0100

Citizens L & B Co.
300 W. Market St.
Lima, OH
(419) 228-2734

First FS & L Assn.
3721 Oberlin Ave.
Lorain, OH
(216) 282-6188

First S & L Co.
153 Lincoln Way E.
Massillon, OH

(216) 832-1547

County Savings Bank
42 N. Third St.
Newark, OH
(614) 345-9751

Civic Savings Bank
507 Chillicothe St.
Portsmouth, OH
(614) 354-6611

Merchants & Mechanics FS & LA
20 S. Limestone St.
Springfield, OH
(513) 324-4141

World S & L Assn. of Ohio
500 Market St.
Stubenville, OH
(614) 283-4121

C S L Savings Bank
301 S. Main St.
Tiffin, OH
1-800-367-1194

First FS & L Assn.
701 First Federal Plaza
Toledo, OH
(419) 243-9100

United Home Federal
519 Madison Ave.
Toledo, OH
(419) 249-1000

Peoples Federal Savings Bank
121 N. Market St.
Wooster, OH
(216) 264-2641

American FS & L Assn. of Ada
606 E. Main
Ada, OH
(405) 332-2910

Home FSB & LA of Ada
301 S. Broadway Ave.
Ada, OH
(405) 332-2057

OKLAHOMA

Peoples FS & L Assn.
3309 E. Frank Phillips Blvd.
Bartlesville, OK

(918) 333-8300

Broken Arrow FS & L Assn.
311 S. Main St.
Broken Arrow, OK
(918) 251-2511

First FS & L Assn. of Chickasha
402 Chickasha Ave.
Chickasha, OK
(405) 224-6586

First FSB of Oklahoma
1698 S. Lynn Riggs Blvd.
Claremore, OK
(918) 341-7100

Clinton S & L Assn.
1101 Frisco
Clinton, OK
(405) 323-5442

The Duncan S & L Assn.
1006 Main St.
Duncan, OK
(405) 255-8187

The Globe Savings Bank, FSB
100 N. Rock Island Rd.
El Reno, OK
(405) 262-2345

Liberty FS & L Assn. of Enid
401 W. Broadway
Enid, OK
(405) 234-5313

Guthrie S & L Assn.
120 N. Division
Guthrie, OK
(405) 282-2201

Chisholm FS & L Assn.
801 S. Main
Kingfisher, OK
(405) 375-4201

Red River FS & L Assn.
One SW 11th
Lawton, OK
(405) 355-0253

Cimarron FS & L Assn.
619 N. Main St.
Muskogee, OK
(918) 683-6501

Continental FS & L Assn.

13801 Continental Dr.
Box 1491
Edmond, OK
(405) 348-4180

First Western FS & L Assn.
312 W. Commerce St.
Oklahoma City, OK
(405) 634-3331

Local FS & LA, Oklahoma City
3601 NW 63rd
Oklahoma, OK
(405) 841-2100

Heartland FS & L Assn.
400 E. Central Ave.
Ponca City, OK
(405) 765-2442

Family FSB
600 S. Main St.
Sapulpa, OK
(918) 224-4510

First FS & L Assn. of Seminole
229 N. Second St.
Seminole, OK
(405) 382-0690

The Stillwater S & L Assn.
601 S. Husband
Stillwater, OK
(405) 372-5782

Local American Bank
of Tulsa, A FSB
5801 E. 41st St.
Tulsa, OK
(918) 622-0000

Sooner FS & L Assn.
Brittany Square
Box 1004
Tulsa, OK
(918) 743-3700

State FS & L Assn.
502 S. Main Mall
Tulsa, OK
(918) 583-8111

Great Plains FS & L Assn.
of Weatherford
109 E. Franklin St.
Weatherford, OK
(405) 772-7441

OREGON

Family FS & L Assn.
689 Main St.
Dallas, OR
(508) 623-2361

Washington FSB
401 SW Fifth Ave.
Portland, OR
(503) 225-1574

Jackson County FS & L Assn.
2 E. Main St.
Medford, OR
(503) 776-0600

Far West Federal Bank, SB
421 SW Sixth Ave.
Portland, OR
(503) 224-4444

Benjamin Franklin FS & LA
501 SE Hawthorne Blvd.,
Ste. 600
Portland, OR
(503) 275-1234

Pacific First Bank, A FSB
580 State St.
Salem, OR
1-800-251-2111

PENNSYLVANIA

Liberty Bell SA
716 14th St.
Beaver Falls, PA
(412) 846-7200

Peoples Home SA
1427 Seventh Ave.
Beaver Falls, PA
(412) 846-7300

Greater Delaware Valley S & LA
541 Lawrence Rd.
Broomall, PA
(215) 353-2900

Ellwood FS & L Assn.
600 Lawrence Ave.
Ellwood City, PA
(412) 758-5584

Johnstown SB, FSB

Market at Main
Johnstown, PA
(814) 535-8900

Home Unity S & L Assn.
618 Germantown Pike
Lafayette Hill, PA
(215) 825-8900

Steitz S & L Assn.
547 S. Tenth St.
Lebanon, PA
(717) 272-7639

Mifflin County S & L Assn.
19 N. Brown St.
Lewistown, PA
(717) 248-5445

Colony Savings Bank, FSB
1202 State St.
Gerig, PA
1-800-444-6002

Community Savings Assn.
219 Grant St.
Turtle Creek, PA
(412) 829-1773

Concord-Liberty S & L Assn.
275 Center Rd.
Monroeville, PA
(412) 856-7510

Parkvale SA
4220 William Penn Hwy.
Monroeville, PA
(412) 373-7200

Dollar SA
Washington Centre
32 N. Mill St.
New Castle, PA
(412) 652-7741

Peoples FS & L Assn.
One Kensington Square
New Kensington, PA
(412) 335-4550

Commonwealth FS & L Assn.
70 Valley Stream Pkwy.
Valley Forge, PA
(215) 251-1616

Prime Savings Bank FSB
6425 Rising Sun Ave.
Philadelphia, PA

(215) 742-5300

Dollar Bank, FSB
3 Gateway Ctr.
Pittsburgh, PA
(412) 261-4900

First FS & L Assn. of Pittsburgh
180 Ft. Couch Rd.
Pittsburgh, PA
(412) 854-2800

First Home SA
501 Grant St., Ste. 775
Pittsburgh, PA
(412) 263-5069

Landmark SA
335 Fifth Ave.
Pittsburgh, PA
(412) 553-7719

Progressive-Home FS & L Assn.
820 Warrington Ave.
Pittsburgh, PA
(412) 344-9911

Hill Financial S & L Assn.
400 Main St.
Red Hill, PA
(215) 679-3131

Sewickley S & L Assn.
Broad St. & Centennial Ave.
Sewickley, PA
(412) 741-5000

First Federal of West. Penn.
1 E. State St.
Sharon, PA
(412) 981-1320

Horizon Financial, FA
735 Davisville Rd.
Southampton, PA
(215) 938-5783

Home SA of Penna
138 W. Broad St.
Tamaqua, PA
(717) 668-4670

Vanguard Federal Savings Bank
One Vanguard Ctr.
Vandergrift, PA
(412) 568-5541

Northwest Mutual SA

Second at Liberty
Warren, PA
(814) 726-2360

Washington FS & L Assn.
77 S. Main St.
Washington, PA
(412) 222-3120

Franklin First FS & L Assn.
44 W. Market St.
Wilkes-Barre, PA
(717) 821-7100

Penn Savings Bank FSB
1130 Berkshire Blvd.
Wyomissing, PA
(215) 320-8400

York FS & L Assn.
101 S. George St.
York, PA
(717) 846-8777

PUERTO RICO

Caguas-Central FSB of PR
Betances & Baldorioty, Esq. Jimenez
Caguas, PR
(809) 746-3388

Oriental Federal Savings Bank
2 Noya Y Hernandez Sts.
Humacao, PR
(809) 852-0378

Western FSB
19 W. McKinley St.
Mayaquez, PR
(809) 834-8000

First Federal Savings Bank
1519 Ponce De Leon Ave. Stop 23
Santurce, PR
(809) 721-6200

RHODE ISLAND

Old Stone Bank A FSB
86 S. Main St.
Providence, RI
(401) 278-2330

SOUTH CAROLINA

Palmetto FSB of SC
107 Chesterfield St., S
Aiken, SC
(803) 642-1400

First FS & L Assn.
34 Broad St.
Charleston, SC
(803) 745-5743

Cooper River FS & L Assn.
2170 Ashley Phosphate Rd.
Charleston Heights, SC
(803) 572-4600

First South Savings Bank
1300 Washington St.
Columbia, SC
(803) 733-5500

Security FS & L Assn.
1233 Washington St.
Columbia, SC
(803) 733-6624

South Carolina FS & L Assn.
1500 Hampton St.
Columbia, SC
(803) 254-1500

Peoples FS & L Assn.
1601 11th Ave.
Conway, SC
(803) 248-7550

American Federal Bank, FSB
300 E. McBee Ave.
Greenville, SC
(803) 255-7458

First FS & L Assn.
301 College St.
Greenville, SC
(803) 255-7819

United Savings Bank, Inc.
425 Main St.
Greenwood, SC
(803) 223-8686

Coastal FS & L Assn.
2619 N. Oak St.
Myrtle Beach, SC
(803) 448-5151

Union FS & L Assn.
203 W. Main St.
Union, SC

(803) 427-7692

SOUTH DAKOTA

First Federal Bank FSB
79 Second St. SW
Huron, SD
(605) 352-8601

First FSB of South Dakota
909 St. Joseph St.
Rapid City, SD
(605) 394-6800

First Western Federal Savings Bank
402 Main St.
Rapid City, SD
(605) 341-1203

Home FS & L Assn. of Sioux Falls
Main Ave. at 11th St.
Sioux Falls, SD
(605) 333-7638

First Federal Savings Bank
109 First Ave. SE
Watertown, SD
(605) 882-2090

TENNESSEE

First FS & L Assn.
601 Market Ctr.
Chattanooga, TN
(615) 756-1510

Cherokee Valley FSB
650 25th St.
Cleveland, TN
(615) 478-2265

Home FS & LA ,Upper E. Tenn.
2112 N. Roan St.
Johnson City, TN
(615) 282-6311

Heritage FS & L Assn.
110 E. Center St.
Kingsport, TN
(615) 378-8025

Security Trust FS & L Assn.
7005 Maynardville Hwy.
Knoxville, TN
(615) 922-2106

264

Lawrenceburg FS & L Assn.
118 W. Gaines St.
Lawrenceburg, TN
(615) 762-7571

Home FS & L Assn.
100 N. Main Bldg.
Memphis, TN
(901) 684-4690

Leader FB for Savings
158 Madison Ave.
Memphis, TN
(901) 578-2245

Lincoln FS & L Assn.
Kaywood & Main Sts.
Mt. Carmel, TN
(615) 357-4156

Fidelity FS & L Assn.
401 Union St.
Nashville, TN
(615) 726-4230

Investor FSB
2021 Richard Jones Rd.
Nashville, TN
(615) 298-9977

Metropolitan FS & L Assn.
230 Fourth Ave., N.
Nashville, TN
(615) 333-4293

Security FS & L Assn.
2700 Franklin Rd.
Nashville, TN
(615) 889-2255

First FSB of Tennessee
101 W. Lincoln St.
Tullahoma, TN
(615) 455-5411

TEXAS

Palo Duro S & L Assn.
3131 Bell St.
Amarillo, TX
(806) 374-1000

Andrews S & L Assn.
600 N. Main
Andrews, TX
(915) 523-2595

Centre Savings Assn.
410 W. Abrams St.
Arlington, TX
(817) 261-3099

Meridian Savings Assn.
611 Ryan Plaza, Ste. 1300
Arlington, TX
(817) 265-8822

The Savings Banc, AS & L Assn.
592 Orleans
Beaumont, TX
(409) 838-6391

Atlanta FS & L Assn.
201 N. Louise St.
Atlanta, TX
(214) 796-2811

American FSB
3013 Bee Caves Rd.
Austin, TX
(512) 328-3010

Austin Savings Assn.
1901 Capital Pkwy.
Austin, TX
(512) 328-2620

Capitol City SA
919 Congress Ave.
Austin, TX
(512) 478-1607

Fidelity Savings-Austin, FA
701 Brazos, Ste. 100
Austin, TX
(512) 320-5900

Franklin Federal Bancorp.,
A FSB
712 Congress Ave.
Austin, TX
(512) 477-5000

Southside S & L Assn.
4303 Victory Dr.
Austin, TX
(512) 443-8431

Windsor Savings Assn.
1601 W. 35th St.
Austin, TX
(512) 453-5554

Western Gulf S & L Assn.
2200 Seventh St.

Bay City, TX
(409) 245-5751

Century S & L Assn.
2615 Market St.
Baytown, TX
(713) 427-8585

Citizens of Texas S & L Assn.
401 W. Texas Ave.
Baytown, TX
(713) 427-8561

First FS & L Assn.
304 Pearl
Beaumont, TX
(409) 838-3901

Jefferson S & L Assn.
1025 Interstate 10 N.
Beaumont, TX
(409) 892-5915

Spindletop SA
3915 Phelan Blvd.
Beaumont, TX
(409) 835-0508

Bedford SA
1903 Central Ave.
Bedford, TX
(817) 571-1020

Continental Savings,
A FS & L Assn.
4500 Bissonnet Park,
Two Bissonnet Park
Bellaire, TX
(713) 665-8111

San Jacinto SA
6800 W. Loop SE Bldg.
Bellaire, TX
(713) 953-7000

First S & L Assn.
1300 W. Wilson
Borger, TX
(806) 274-7341

First SA of Brenhan
2000 S. Market
Brenhan, TX
(409) 836-6116

Golden Triangle S & L Assn.
150 E. Roundbunch
Bridge City, TX

(409) 735-5581

Southmost S & L Assn.
1623 Central Blvd.
Brownsville, TX
(512) 541-5211

First FS & L Assn.
2900 Texas Ave.
Bryan, TX
(409) 779-2900

Burleson County SA
300 W. Hwy. 21
Caldwell, TX
(409) 567-7848

Sabine Valley S & L Assn.
200 San Augustine St.
Center, TX
(409) 598-2434

Shelby County SA
111 Selma St.
Center, TX
(409) 598-5688

Trinity Valley S & L Assn.
1408 E. Houston St.
Cleveland, TX
(713) 592-8795

Homestead SA
3601 E. 29th St.
College Station, TX
(409) 779-3601

First FS & L Assn. of Conroe
400 W. Davis St.
Conroe, TX
(409) 539-1811

TexasBanc Savings Assn.
1110 Loop 336
Conroe, TX
(409) 756-0601

Pacific Southwest SB, FSB
5155 Flynn Pkwy.
Corpus Christi, TX
(512) 854-9090

Padre FS & L Assn.
4466 S. Staples St.
Corpus Christi, TX
(512) 992-9741

Golden Circle SA, FSB

109 N. Main
Corsicana, TX
(214) 872-8395

Cuero FS & L Assn.
218 N. Gonzales St.
Cuero, TX
(512) 275-2345

American Federal Bank FSB
5080 Spectrum, Ste. 1200 W.
Dallas, TX
(214) 980-2441

Bright Banc SA
2355 N. Stemmons, Ste. 400
Dallas, TX
(214) 638-9500

Consolidated FS & L Assn.
1845 Woodall Rodgers
Dallas, TX
(214) 871-0005

Guaranty FSB
10440 N. Central Expy, Ste. 700
Dallas, TX
(214) 360-3360

Metropolitan Financial S & L
6688 N. Central Expy., Ste. 1000
Dallas, TX
(214) 369-2700

Murray Savings Assn.
5580 LBJ Frwy., Ste. 255
Dallas, TX
(214) 851-6300

Park Cities Savings Assn.
8214 Westchester, Ste. 910
Dallas, TX
(214) 739-6300

Southwest SA
6029 Beltline Rd. (Residential)
Dallas, TX
(214) 788-0711

Sunbelt Savings FSB
14755 Preston Rd.
Dallas, TX
(214) 386-4074

Texas Mercantile Savings Assn.
5757 Alpha Rd., Ste. 100
Dallas, TX
(214) 386-9958

Southeastern SA
209 W. Hwy. 90
Dayton, TX
(409) 258-7611

Resource SA
1001 W. Main St.
Denison, TX
(214) 465-6717

Denton SA
300 N. Elm St.
Denton, TX
(817) 387-3505

North Texas S & L Assn.
Oak & Hickory at Piner
Denton, TX
(817) 382-9676

North Plains S & L Assn.
600 E. First St.
Dumas, TX
(806) 935-4184

HeritageBanc SA
600 E. Camp Wisdom Rd.
Duncanville, TX
(214) 298-0505

Hidalgo S & L Assn.
300 S. Closner
Edinburg, TX
(512) 383-1676

El Paso FS & L Assn.
517 N. Kansas
El Paso, TX
(915) 532-3941

Surety SA
6044 Gateway Blvd. E.
El Paso, TX
(415) 778-9933

Remington SA
2500 Fondern St.
Houston, TX
(713) 977-4700

Bankers S & L Assn.
601 Tremont
Galveston, TX
(409) 763-3411

BannerBanc Savings Assn.
801 W. Garland Ave.

Garland, TX
(214) 272-1511

Certified SA
1111 Austin Ave.
Georgetown, TX
(512) 863-5567

Graham S & L Assn.
745 Elm St.
Graham, TX
(817) 549-2066

Centennial Savings Bank, FSB
2900 Lee St.
Greenville, TX
(214) 455-6122

Hearne B & L Assn.
802 Market St.
Hearne, TX
(409) 279-5388

First FSB of Hempstead
840 13th St.
Hempstead, TX
(409) 826-8071

General SA
1610 Hwy. 79 S.
Henderson, TX
(214) 657-7566

Henderson S & L Assn.
130 N. Marshall St.
Henderson, TX
(214) 657-2577

Gill SA
1401 19th St.
Hondo, TX
(512) 222-2434

Ameriway Savings
615 Soledad
Houston, TX
(713) 783-2000

Benjamin Franklin SA
5444 Westheimer
Houston, TX
(713) 940-6700

Coastal Banc Savings Assn.
8 Greenway Plaza, Ste. 100
Houston, TX
(713) 623-2600

Commonwealth Savings Assn.
10000 Memorial Dr., Ste. 600
Houston, TX
(713) 683-1212

First Capital SA of Texas
11251 NW Freeway
Houston, TX
(713) 680-2600

First Gibraltar Bank, FSB
13401 N. Freeway
Houston, TX
(713) 872-3100

Commercial Bank, FSA
2700 Post Oak Blvd., Ste. 600
Houston, TX
(713) 623-9331

Heights of Texas, FSB
3401 Allen Pkwy.
Houston, TX
(713) 867-2200

Houston, SA
1919 Allen Pkwy., Ste. 100
Houston, TX
(713) 522-9073

Liberty Savings Assn.
3501 Fannin St.
Houston, TX
(713) 524-3118

Preferred SA
11757 Katy Frwy., Ste. 100
Houston, TX
(713) 556-6443

Spring Branch S & L Assn.
17314 FM 149
Houston, TX
(713) 469-3055

Standard SA
4310 Dowling St.
Houston, TX
(713) 529-9133

United SA of Texas FSB
3200 SW Freeway, Ste. 2000
Houston, TX
(713) 963-6500

Universal SA
10310 E. Freeway
Houston, TX

(713) 956-9797

University SA
1160 Dairy Ashford
Houston, TX
(713) 596-1000

Village Savings, FSB
11 Greenway Dr., Ste. 200
Houston, TX
(713) 850-8900

Humble S & L Assn.
19502 Eastex Frwy.
Humble, TX
(713) 446-8133

Jacksonville S & L Assn.
Commerce & Neches Sts.
Jacksonville, TX
(214) 586-9861

Savings of Texas Assn.
602 S. Jackson St.
Jacksonville, TX
(214) 586-1561

Deep East Texas SA
660 S. Wheeler
Jasper, TX
(409) 384-5406

Jasper FS & L Assn.
271 E. Lamar St.
Jasper, TX
(409) 384-2594

Atascosa SA
1001 Oak St.
Jourdanton, TX
(512) 769-3535

Karnes County S & L Assn.
200 E. Calvert
Karnes City, TX
(512) 780-3384

Permian S & L Assn.
202 S. Poplar
Kermit, TX
(915) 586-6691

Guadalupe S & L Assn.
624 Jefferson St.
Kerrville, TX
(214) 984-4924

Kilgore FS & L Assn.

1200 N. Kilgore St.
Kilgore, TX
(214) 984-2506

Vision Banc Savings Assn.
1830 S. Brahma Blvd.
Kingsville, TX
(512) 595-5567

Bayshore SA
1102 S. Broadway
La Porte, TX
(713) 471-5550

American S & LA of Brazoria
131 Oyster Creek Dr.
Lake Jackson, TX
(409) 297-8021

Excel Banc Savings Assn.
5219 McPherson
Laredo, TX
(512) 723-9235

First FS & L Assn.
900 Houston St.
Laredo, TX
(512) 723-2075

City SA
600 W. Main St.
League City, TX
(713) 332-9595

Liberty County FS & L Assn.
400 Main St.
Liberty, TX
(409) 336-6403

Texas Trust Savings Bank FSB
102 E. Young
Llano, TX
(915) 247-4177

First FS & L Assn.
116 E. South St.
Longview, TX
(214) 758-6144

Caprock S & L Assn.
7619 S. University
Lubbock, TX
1-800-874-2245

First Federal Savings Bank
1300 Broadway St.
Lubbock, TX
(806) 762-0491

269

Lufkin FS & L Assn.
211 Shepherd St.
Lufkin, TX
(409) 639-2121

Marshall FS & L Assn.
501 S. Washington
Marshall, TX
(214) 935-7955

Valley FS & L Assn.
#1 S. Broadway
McAllen, TX
(512) 686-0263

First Bankers Trust & SA
500 W. Wall
Midland, TX
(915) 683-5681

Mineola FS & L Assn.
215 W. Broad
Mineola, TX
(214) 569-2602

First FS & L Assn.
320 North St.
Nacodoches, TX
(409) 564-1116

Superior FSB
118 E. Hospital St.
Nacodoches, TX
(409) 564-8323

Timberland SA
3010 N. University Dr.
Nacodoches, TX
(409) 560-1401

Columbia Savings Assn.
18001 Upper Bay Rd.
Nassau Bay, TX
(713) 335-1111

First FS & L Assn.
199 Main Plaza
New Braunfels, TX
(512) 625-8001

New Braunsfels S & L Assn.
1093 W. San Antonio St.
New Braunfels, TX
(512) 625-9131

Olney S & L Assn.
300 E. Main

Olney, TX
(817) 564-5502

First FS & L Assn.
630 Clarksville St.
Paris, TX
(214) 784-0881

Bancplus Savings Assn.
1200 Smith, Ste. 2600
Pasadena, TX
(713) 651-9595

Interstate S & L Assn.
301 S. Main St.
Perryton, TX
(806) 435-4071

Hallmark Savings Assn.
2301 Ohio Dr.
Plano, TX
(214) 596-8300

Plano S & L Assn.
550 15th St.
Plano, TX
(214) 423-3591

Fidelity S & L Assn.
4749 Twin City Hwy.
Port Arthur, TX
(409) 727-6428

First South SA
2550 Gray Falls, Ste. 200
Port Neches, TX
(409) 722-4316

Fort Bend FS & L Assn.
1011 Millie St.
Rosenberg, TX
(713) 342-5571

Rusk FS & L Assn.
107 E. Sixth St.
Rusk, TX
(214) 683-2208

Alamo SA of Texas
901 NE Loop 410
San Antonio, TX
(512) 828-7171

Bexar Savings Assn.
1777 NE Loop 410
San Antonio, TX
(512) 820-8100

Citisavings & L Assn.
5300 Walzen Rd.
San Antonio, TX
(512) 650-3735

Commerce SA
111 Soledad, Ste. 600
San Antonio, TX
(512) 271-9700

First FS & L Assn.
1100 NE Loop 410
San Antonio, TX
(512) 828-7121

First State SA
530 NE Loop 410
San Antonio, TX
(512) 824-9099

La Hacienda Savings Assn.
11330 IH - 10 W.
San Antonio, TX
(512) 697-3070

Mission SA of Texas
10205 Oasis Dr., Ste. 100
San Antonio, TX
(512) 342-3161

N. American Savings Assn.
7900 Callahan
San Antonio, TX
(512) 366-2323

San Antonio SA
601 NW Loop 410, #31
San Antonio, TX
(512) 340-7272

Suburban SA
1735 S. WW White Rd.
San Antonio, TX
(512) 337-7100

Travis Savings & Loan
9311 San Pedro Ave.
San Antonio, TX
(512) 349-9311

Victoria SA
8023 Vantage Dr.
San Antonio, TX
1-800-444-1772

Balcones Banc Savings Assn.
Ranch Rd. 12-N
Wimberly, TX

(512) 847-5504

First Savings Assn.
of SE Texas
451 Hwy. 96 S.
Silsbee, TX
(409) 385-5211

Smithville S & L Assn.
1403 E. Third
Smithville, TX
(512) 237-2482

Sulphur Springs L & B Assn.
306 N. Davis St.
Sulphur Springs, TX
(214) 885-2121

TaylorBanc SA
316 N. Main St.
Taylor, TX
(512) 352-3623

First FS & L Assn.
18 W. Ave. A.
Temple, TX
(817) 773-5241

Security Savings Assn., FSA
2000 Richmond Rd.
Texarkana, TX
(214) 832-2000

First Equity SA
1111 W. Main
Tomball, TX
(713) 351-7283

East Texas S & L Assn.
6101 S. Braodway at Grande
Tyler, TX
(214) 534-6400

Uvalde S & L Assn.
605 E. Main St.
Uvalde, TX
(512) 278-4458

South Texas SA
1205 N. Navarro
Victoria, TX
(512) 573-5241

Central Texas S & L Assn.
5400 Bosque Blvd.
Waco, TX
(817) 776-4660

First FS & L Assn.
1224 Austin Ave.
Waco, TX
(817) 753-2411

Mutual B & L Assn.
133 College St.
Weatherford, TX
(817) 594-3855

First FS & L Assn.
915 Ninth St.
Wichita Falls, TX
(817) 766-0123

North Texas FS & L Assn.
2733 Midwestern Pkwy.
Wichita Falls, TX
(817) 691-0230

UTAH

Mountainwest S & L Assn.,
A FS & LA
2406 Washington Blvd.
Ogden, UT
(801) 621-6060

Ogden First FS & L Assn.
2425 Washington Blvd.
Ogden, UT
(801) 621-0100

United Savings Bank
4185 Harrison Blvd.
Ogden, UT
(801) 626-2200

American S & L Assn., A FA
77 W. 200 S.
Salt Lake City, UT
(801) 531-5621

Crossland Savings, FSB
41 E. First S.
Salt Lake City, UT
(801) 350-9600

Deseret FS & L Assn.
54 S. Main St.
Salt Lake City, UT
(801) 521-9726

First FS & L Assn.
505 E. Second S.
Salt Lake City, UT
(801) 531-7800

Home Savings & Loan
130 E. 3300 S.
Salt Lake City, UT
(801) 486-3600

Williamsburg Savings Bank
401 E. Second S.
Salt Lake City, UT
(801) 364-1116

VIRGINIA

AmeriBanc Savings Bank
7620 Little River Turnpike
Annandale, VA
(703) 658-1000

Columbia First FS & L Assn.
1560 Wilson Blvd.
Arlington, VA
(703) 247-5000

Charter FSB
110-112 Piedmont St.
Bristol, VA
(703) 669-5101

Continental Federal Savings Bank
4020 University Dr.
Fairfax, VA
(703) 733-3900

NVR Federal Savings Bank
Dolly Madison Blvd.
Mclean, VA
(703) 847-8900

Perpetual Savings Bank, FSB
1750 Old Meadow Rd.
Mclean, VA
(703) 556-3500

Newport News Savings Bank
301 Hidden Blvd.
Newport News, VA
(804) 599-1400

Atlantic Permanent SB, FSB
740 Boush St.
Norfolk, VA
(804) 446-0500

Cenit Bank for Savings, FSB
745 Duke St.
Norfolk, VA
(804) 446-6640

Virginia First Savings, FSB
Corner Franklin & Adams Sts.
Petersburg, VA
(804) 733-0333

Vista Federal Savings Bank
11515 Sunrise Valley Dr.
Reston, VA
(703) 620-6510

Coreast Savings Bank, FSB
808 Moorefield Park Dr.
Richmond, VA
(804) 323-7200

Heritage Savings Bank, FSB
500 Forest Ave.
Richmond, VA
(804) 282-8100

Investors Savings Bank
9201 Forest Hill Ave.
Richmond, VA
(804) 323-4500

Virginia FSB
224 E. Broad St.
Richmond, VA
(804) 649-1201

Trust Bank Savings
7799 Leesburg Pike
Tysons Corner, VA
(703) 848-3000

Seaboard S & L Assn.
501 S. Independence Blvd.
Virginia Beach, VA
(804) 490-3181

Virginia Beach Federal Savings Bank
210 25th St.
Virginia Beach, VA
(804) 428-9331

Jefferson S & L Assn.
Northern VA Shopping Ctr.
Warrenton, VA
(703) 347-3531

WASHINGTON

Aberdeen FS & L Assn.
120 N. Broadway
Aberdeen, WA
(206) 532-6222

Gibraltar Savings, FA
11000 NE 33rd Place
Bellevue, WA
(206) 581-7190

Summit Savings Assn.
11711 SE Eighth St.
Bellevue, WA
(206) 451-3585

Great Northwest FS & L Assn.
500 Pacific Ave.
Bremerton, WA
(206) 479-1551

Riverview Savings Bank
700 NE Fourth
Camas, WA
(206) 834-2231

Timberland FS & L Assn.
624 Simpson Ave.
Hoquiam, WA
(206) 533-4747

First FSB Northwest
1338 Commerce
Longview, WA
(206) 423-9333

World S & L Assn. of America
4001-200 St. SW
Lynnwood, WA
(206) 771-7283

Interwest Savings Bank
1259 W. Pioneer Way
Oak Harbor, WA
(206) 675-0788

Heritage FS & L Assn.
201 W. Fifth
Olympia, WA
(206) 943-1500

First FS & L Assn.
141 W. First St.
Port Angeles, WA
(206) 452-5305

Continental Savings Bank
720 Third Ave.
Seattle, WA
(206) 621-0100

Family S & L Assn.
2111 N. Northgate Way

Seattle, WA
(206) 542-0482

Metropolitan FS & L Assn.
1100 Olive Way
Seattle, WA
(206) 625-1818

Washington FS & L Assn.
425 Pike St.
Seattle, WA
(206) 624-7930

Sterling Savings Assn
N. 120 Wall St.
Spokane, WA
(509) 624-4121

Pacific First FSB
1145 Broadway, Ste. 1200
Tacoma, WA
(206) 383-7505

Vancouver FSB
1205 Broadway
Vancouver, WA
(206) 694-1234

First FSB of Washington
10 S. First St.
Walla Walla, WA
(509) 527-3636

Frontier FS & L Assn.
16 S. Second
Walla Walla, WA
(509) 527-3300

Washington Mutual, A FSB
18 S. Mission Ave.
Wenatchee, WA
(509) 662-3641

WISCONSIN

Home Savings Bank, SA
320 E. College Ave.
Appleton, WI
(414) 734-1483

North Land S & L Assn.
221 Fourth Ave. W.
Ashland, WI
(715) 682-9371

Monycor Savings Bank, FSB
410 E. La Salle Ave.

Barron, WI
(715) 537-3145

North Shore Bank, SSB
15700 Blue Mound Rd.
Brookfield, WI
(414) 797-3807

Federated Financial S & L
13195 W. Hampton Ave.
Butler, WI
(414) 251-7700

Durand FS & L Assn.
308 Third Ave. W.
Durand, WI
(715) 672-8055

First FS & L Assn. of Eau Claire
319 E. Grand Ave.
Eau Claire, WI
(715) 834-7741

Community S & L Assn.
8 S. Main St.
Fond Du Lac, WI
(414) 923-8016

Equitable S & L Assn.
5225 S. 108th St.
Hales Corners, WI
(414) 781-6805

First FS & L Assn. of La Crosse
605 State St.
La Crosse, WI
(608) 784-8000

Anchor S & L Assn.
25 W. Main St.
Madison, WI
(608) 252-8700

First FS & L Assn. of Madison
202 State St.
Madison, WI
(608) 256-2265

Continental S & L Assn.
1930 E. North Ave.
Milwaukee, WI
(414) 224-0700

Great American S & L Assn.
10400 W. North Ave.
Milwaukee, WI
(414) 259-8150

Mutual SB of Wisconsin
510 E. Wisconsin Ave.
Milwaukee, WI
(414) 272-8000

Republic S & L Assn.
of Wisconsin
500 W. Brown Deer Rd.
Milwaukee, WI
(414) 352-4085

Security S & L Assn.
184 W. Wisconsin Ave.
Milwaukee, WI
(414) 277-8610

Universal Savings Bank FA
754 N. Fourth St.
Milwaukee, WI
(414) 273-1776

Republic Savings Bank, SA
500 Brown Deer Rd.
Milwaukee, WI
(414) 352-4080

Central FS & L Assn.
125 Watson St.
Ripon, WI
(414) 748-2852

South Milwaukee S & L Assn.
1015 Marquette Ave.
South Milwaukee, WI
(414) 762-7600

St. Francis S & L Assn.
3545 S. Kinnickinnic Ave.
St. Francis, WI
(414) 747-6518

First Financial Bank, FSB
1305 Main St./Box 225
Stevens Point, WI
(715) 341-0400

Hopkins S & L Assn.
2600 N. Mayfair Rd.
Wauwatosa, WI
(414) 475-5595

Wauwatosa S & L Assn.
7500 W. State St.
Wauwatosa, WI
(414) 258-5880

WEST VIRGINIA

First FS & L Assn.
501 Federal St.
Bluefield, WV
(304) 327-8141

Atlantic Financial Federal
One Piedmont Rd.
Charleston, WV
(304) 347-9600

Evergreen FSB
200 Bradford St.
Charleston, WV
(304) 344-3424

First Empire FS & L Assn.
227 Capitol St.
Charleston, WV
(304) 340-4600

First Standard Savings FA
First Federal Plaza,
Merchant St.
Fairmont, WV
(304) 366-3650

Shenandoah FSB
617 Winchester Ave.
Martinsburg, WV
(304) 263-8901

Fed One Savings Bank, FSB
12th & Main Sts.
Wheeling, WV
(304) 234-1100

WYOMING

Buffalo FS & L Assn.
106 Fort St.
Buffalo, WY
(307) 684-5591

Provident FS & L Assn.
400 E. First St.
Casper, WY
(307) 237-8481

Rocky Mountain FSB
2020 Carey Ave.
Cheyenne, WY
(307) 634-2101

First Guaranty S & L Assn.
249 Kendrick
Gillette, WY

(307) 682-7244

Westland FS & L Assn.
501 W. Buffalo St.
Rawlins, WY
(307) 328-9600

Tri-County FS & L Assn.
2201 Main St.
Torrington, WY
(307) 532-2111

Federal Asset Disposition Association

FADA has been a marketing arm for FSLIC over the past four years. They may or may not be around, because of the Resolution Trust Corporation coming into existence after 1989. You may now contact them for one free directory of their properties which comes out bi-monthly. If you wish to re-contact them at a later date, you will likely receive another catalogue. However, if you wish to stay on their mailing lists and continue to receive catalogues on a regular, uninterrupted basis, you'll have to pay a semi-annual fee of $30 for three catalogues or $50 annually for 6 catalogues.

FADA has five regional offices: Atlanta, Dallas, Denver, Los Angeles, and Washington D.C. You may reach them as follows:

If you wish to receive further information on the properties contained in the catalogue, you'll call:

1-800-225-3968 (within the U.S.)
1-800-621-1219 (within Texas)
(214) 450-0777 (outside the U.S.)

1-800-527-0146

Will send a
listing of properties
9-30-91

277

Federal National Mortgage Association

Fannie Mae will send you listings in the specific area of your choice. You'll get a computer printout of the city or town you wish to explore or in which you want to buy property.

Contact them by phone by calling 1-800-553-4636 or write them directly at:

Fannie Mae Properties
P.O. Box 13165
Baltimore, MD 20203

HOME OFFICE
3900 Wisconsin
Washington Ave., N. W.
Washington, DC 20016-2899
(202) 752-7000

NORTHEASTERN REGION:
Connecticut, Delaware, District of Columbia, Maine, Maryland, Massachusetts, New Hampshire, New Jersey, New York, Pennsylvania, Puerto Rico, Rhode Island, Vermont, Virginia, and West Virginia.

Office:
510 Walnut St., 16th Floor
Philadelphia, PA 19016-3697
(215) 574-1400

SOUTHEASTERN REGION:
Alabama, Florida, Georgia, Kentucky, Mississippi, North Carolina, South Carolina, and Tennessee.

Office:
950 E. Paces Ferry Rd., Suite 1900
Atlanta, GA 30326-1161
(404) 365-6000

MIDWESTERN REGION:
Illinois, Indiana, Iowa, Michigan, Minnesota, Nebraska, North Dakota, Ohio, South Dakota, and Wisconsin.

Office:
One South Wacker Dr., Suite 3100
Chicago, IL 60606-4667

(312) 641-0740

SOUTHWESTERN REGION:
Arkansas, Colorado, Kansas, Louisiana, Missouri, New Mexico, Oklahoma and Texas.

Office:
Two Galleria Tower
13455 Noel Rd., Suite 600
Dallas, TX 75240-5003
(214) 991-7771
Mailing Address:
P.O. Box 650043
Dallas, TX 75265-0043

WESTERN REGION:
Alaska, Arizona, California, Guam, Hawaii, Idaho, Montana, Nevada, Oregon, Utah, and Washington.

Office:
P.O. Box 24019
10920 Wilshire Blvd., Suite 1800
Los Angeles, CA 90024-6519
(818) 568- 5000)

278

RHODE ISLAND

380 Westminster Mall 5th Fl.
Providence, RI 02903
(401) 528-4586

Auctioneers:
Write for list c/o Anthony Ricci

VERMONT

P.O. Box 605
Montpelier, VT 05602
(802) 828-4422

Auctioneers:
Write for list c/o Pete Downey

REGION II

NEW JERSEY

2600 Mt. Ethrin Ave.
Camden, NJ 08104
(609) 757-5183
or
60 Park Place, 4th Floor
Newark, NJ 07102
(201) 645-2434

Auctioneers:
Call for information.

Auctioneers: No list.
Look for advertisements
in Sunday Editions, NEWARK
STAR LEDGER.

NEW YORK

26 Federal Plaza, Rm. 3100
New York, NY 10278
(212) 264-4355

Auctioneers:
Look for advertisements in
NEW YORK TIMES.

100 S. Clinton St., Rm. 1071
Syracuse, NY 13260
(315) 423-5383

Auctioneers: Write to be put on
mailing list.
Attn: Don Prokop,
Chief of Liquidations

445 Broadway, Rm. 222
Albany, NY 12207
(518) 472-6300

Auctioneers: Write to be put on
mailing list.
Attn: Don Prokop,
Chief of Liquidations

100 State St., Rm. 601
Rochester, NY 14614
(716) 263-6700

Auctioneers: No list.
Look for advertisements
in Sunday Editions of TIMES
UNION and DEMOCRAT AND
CHRONICLE.

333 E. Water St., 4th Floor
Elmira, NY 14901
(607) 734-8130/734-2673

Auctioneers: Call for information.
Attn: Richard Wishneski

35 Pinelawn Rd., Rm. 102E
Melville, NY 11747
(516) 454-0750

Auctioneers: Write to be put on
mailing list.
Attn: Jim Ward

281

VIRGIN ISLANDS

U.S. Courthouse and Federal Bldg.
2nd Floor, Rm. 210
St. Thomas, VI 00801
(809) 774-8530

Auctioneers: Write for information.

REGION III

DELAWARE

1 Rodney Square
920 N. King, Ste. 412
Wilmington, DE 19801
(302) 513-6294

Auctioneers: All auctions handled by King of Prussia office. Leave message: (215) 962-3843 or call (215) 962-3839 to be put on the mailing list.

PENNSYLVANIA

475 Allendale Rd., Ste. 201
King of Prussia, PA 19406
(215) 962-3839

Auctioneers: Call Henry Nemrod (215) 627-6100 to be put on mailing list.

960 Penn Ave., 5th Floor
Pittsburgh, PA 15222
(412) 644-5429

Auctioneers: Call to be put on mailing list.

Harrisburg, PA
(717) 782-3840

Auctioneers: Call for information.

Wilkes-Barre, PA
(717) 826-6497

Auctioneers: Call for information.

MARYLAND

Auctioneers: Call for information.

10 N. Calvert St., 3rd Floor
Baltimore, MD 21202
(301) 962-2268/962-4392

WASHINGTON, D.C.

Auctioneers:
Adam A. Weschler
(202) 628-1281

1111-18th St. NW, 6th Flooror
Washington, DC 20036
(202) 634-6319
or
P.O. Box 19993
Washington, DC 20036

Write and ask to be put on the mailing list.

WEST VIRGINIA

P.O. Box 1608
Clarksburg, WV 26302-1608
(304) 623-5631

Charleston, WV 26302-1608
(304) 347-5220

<u>Auctioneers:</u> Call or write for information and to be put on the mailing list.

<u>Auctioneers:</u>
Jim McCutcheon Auctioneering
(304) 485-6561

REGION IV

ALABAMA

(205) 731-1344

<u>Auctioneers:</u>
Hudson & Marshall Auctioneers
(205) 546-1667
Bunch Auction & Real Estate
(205) 957-2310
Fowler Auction & Real Estate
(205) 420-4454
Griffith Recovery & Auction
(205) 289-0801
John A. Huton Real Estate &
Auction (205) 536-7497
Ludlum Auction Co.
(205) 794-3000

FLORIDA

700 Twiggs St., Rm. 607
Tampa, FL 33602
(813) 228-2594

<u>Auctioneers:</u>
Edward Bilbruk
(813) 791-9541
Randall Auction Co.
(813) 855-9580

400 W. Bay St.
Jacksonville, FL 32207
(904) 791-3782

<u>Auctioneers:</u> Call for information.

1320 S. Dixie Hwy., Ste. 501
Coral Gables, FL 33146
(305) 536-5521

<u>Auctioneers:</u>
Auction Company of America
(305) 651-0500
Harry P. Stamples Auctioneers
(305) 761-8744

GEORGIA

1720 Peachtree Rd., NW, 6th Fl.
Atlanta, GA 30309
(404) 347-2441
or
(404) 347-7361

<u>Auctioneers:</u>
Jim Rouse
(404) 622-4455
The Dobbins Company
(404) 352-2638

<u>Auctioneers:</u> No list, call monthly.

KENTUCKY

<u>Auctioneers:</u> Call for information.

600 Federal Place, Rm. 188
Louisville, KY 40202
(502) 582-5976

283

MISSISSIPPI

100 W. Capitol St. Ste. 322
Jackson, MS 39269
(601) 965-4378

1 Hancock Plaza, Ste. 1001
Gulfport, MS 39501
(601) 863-4449

NORTH CAROLINA

222 S. Church St., Ste. 300
Charlotte, NC 28202
(704) 371-6563

SOUTH CAROLINA

1835 Assembly St., 3rd Fl.
Columbia, SC 29202
(803) 765-5376

TENNESSEE

404 James Robertson Pkwy.,
Ste. 1012
Nashville, TN 37219
(615) 736-5881

Auctioneers:
McCool Auction Co.
(601) 362-1022
Osborne Auction Co.
(601) 859-3845
Sunbelt Auction Co.
(601) 536-2243/469-2966
Auctioneer:
Mozingo Realty
(601) 896-3400

Auctioneers: Call for information.

Auctioneers:
P.O. Box 2786
Columbia, SC 29202
Write for list

Auctioneers: Call for information.

REGION V

ILLINOIS

219 S. Dearborn St., Rm. 437
Chicago, IL 60604
(312) 353-4528

511 W. Capitol, Ste. 302
Springfield, IL 62704
(217) 492-4416

INDIANA

575 N. Pennsylvania St., Rm. 578
Indianapolis, IN 46204-1584
(317) 226-7272

Auctioneers:
Dynamic Auction Co.
(312) 599-9348
Marshal Natchbar
(312) 539-7460
Don Dodge Auction Services, Inc.
(312) 666-7777
AUCTION SERVICES INC.
(312) 631-2255

Auctioneers: Call for information.

Auctioneers: Call for information.

MICHIGAN

477 Michigan Ave., Rm. 515
Detroit, MI 48226
(313) 226-6075

Auctioneers: All sales handled through sealed bids. Call for information.

MINNESOTA

100 N. 6th St., Ste. 610C
Minneapolis, MN 55403
(612) 370-2324

Auctioneers: 90% of all auctions handled by banks. Call or write for information.
Kurt Kiefer Auctioneers
1-800-435-2726

OHIO

1240 E. 9th St., Rm. 317
Cleveland, OH 44199
(216) 522-4180

Auctioneers:
Rosen & Co.
(216) 621-1860
Grossman, Inc.
(216) 932-0777
Donn & Associates
(216) 331-5505
Paul Bambeck Auctions
(216) 343-1437

85 Marconi Blvd.
Columbus, OH 43215
(614) 469-6860

Auctioneers: Call for information.

WISCONSIN

212 E. Washington Ave., Rm. 213
Madison, WI 53703
(608) 264-5261

Auctioneers: No list. Look for advertisements in major newspapers.

310 W. Wisconsin Ave., Rm. 400
Milwaukee, WI 53203
(414) 291-3941

Auctioneers:
Liquitec
(414) 963-1799
Joe Mason Inc. (507) 285-1444
Gerlach Freund, Inc.
(414) 367-4950
Gronik
(414) 241-8300

500 S. Barstow St., Rm 37
Eau Claire, WI 54701
(715) 834-9012

Auctioneers: No mailing list. Look for advertisements in local newspapers.

REGION VI

ARKANSAS

320 W. Capitol Ave., Rm. 601
Little Rock, AR 72201
(501) 378-5871

Auctioneers: Call for information.

LOUISIANA

500 Fannin St., Rm. 8A08
Shreveport, LA 71101
(318) 226-5196

1661 Canal St.
New Orleans, LA 70112
(504) 589-2716

NEW MEXICO

SBA Liquidations Division
5000 Marble Ave. NE
Albuquerque, NM 87110
(505) 262-6026

TEXAS

1100 Commerce St., Rm. 3C36
Dallas, TX 75242
(214) 767-0605

2525 Murworth, Rm. 112
Houston, TX 77054
(713) 660-4401

North Star Executive Center
7400 Blanco Rd., Ste. 200
San Antonio, TX 78216
(512) 229-4535

10737 Gateway W., Ste. 320
El Paso, TX 79935
(915) 541-7586

300 E. 8th St., Rm. 526
Austin, TX 78701
(512) 482-5288

222 E. Van Buren, Ste. 500
Harlingen, TX 78550
(512) 427-8625

819 Taylor, Rm. 8A32
Ft. Worth, TX 76102
(817) 334-3777

<u>Auctioneers:</u> No list. Call for information.

<u>Auctioneers:</u> Call for information.

<u>Auctioneers:</u> Call for information.

<u>Auctioneers:</u>
Federal Auction
(713) 688-6688
Windsor Auction
(713) 680-8001

<u>Auctioneers:</u> Call for information.

<u>Auctioneers:</u> Call for information.

<u>Auctioneers:</u> Call for information.

<u>Auctioneers:</u>
James Dunn
(512) 464-3344
Also look for advertisements in
The Valley Morning Star and
Mc Callen Monitor.

<u>Auctioneers:</u> Call for information.

286

400 Mann St., Ste. 403
Corpus Christi, TX 78401
(512) 888-3331

Auctioneers:
Adams & Adams
(512) 857-2213
Larry Latham
(602) 998-1168

1611-10th St., Ste. 200
Lubbock, TX 79401-2693
(806) 743-7462

Auctioneers: Call for information.

505 E. Travis, Rm. 103
Marshal, TX 75670
(214) 935-5257

Auctioneers:
Ray Collins
1100 Commerce
Dallas, TX 75242
(214) 767-0483

REGION VII

IOWA

210 Walnut St., Rm. 749
Des Moines, IA 50309
(515) 284-4422

Auctioneers: Banks handle 80% of auctions. Advertisements do not specify "SBA" auctions. Call for information.

373 Collins Rd. NE, Rm. 100
Cedar Rapids, IA 52402
(319) 399-2571

Auctioneers: Call or write for information.

KANSAS

110 E. Waterman
Wichita, KS 67202
(316) 269-6571

Auctioneers: Call for information.

MISSOURI

1103 Grand, Sixth Fl.
Kansas City, MO 64106
(816) 374-6752/6754

Auctioneers: Call for information.

815 Olive St., Rm. 242
St. Louis, MO 63101
(314) 539-6600

Auctioneers: Call for information.

620 S. Glenstone, Ste. 110
Springfield, MO 65802-3200
(417) 864-7670

Auctioneers: Write to Carol Jones Auctioneers
3630 S. Campbell
Springfield, MO 65807
Attn: Steve Freeman

REGION VIII

COLORADO

999 18th St., Ste. 701
Denver, CO 80202
(303) 844-3673

Auctioneers:
Dave Roller & Assoc.
(303) 427-1600
W.J. Warren & Assoc.
(303) 791-2757
Radcliff Auctioneers
(303) 428-7568

MONTANA

301 S. Park, Rm. 528
(Drawer 10054)
Helena, MT 59626
(406) 449-5381

Auctioneers: Call for information.

NORTH DAKOTA

657 Second Ave. N., Rm. 218
Fargo, ND 58102
(701) 239-5131

Auctioneers: Call for information.

SOUTH DAKOTA

101 S. Main, Ste. 101
Sioux Falls, SD 57102
(605) 330-4231

Auctioneers:
Duane Strand
(605) 337-3182

UTAH

125 S. State St., Rm. 2237
Salt Lake City, UT 84138
(801) 524-5800

Auctioneers: Call or write for
information.

WYOMING

100 E. B St., Rm. 4001
Casper, WY 82601
(307) 261-5671

Auctioneers: Call for information.

REGION IX

ARIZONA

2005 N. Central, 5th Fl.
Phoenix, AZ 85004
(602) 261-3732

Auctioneers: Call for information.

300 W. Congress
Box FB-33
Tucson, AZ 85701
(602) 629-6715

Auctioneers: Call for information.

288

CALIFORNIA

211 Main St., 4th Fl.
San Francisco, CA 94105
(415) 974-0649

Auctioneers:
A.R.S. Auctioneers
(415) 566-6464
Ashman Company Auctioneers &
Appraisers, Inc.
(415) 682-8100

350 S. Figueroa St., 6th Fl.
Los Angeles, CA 90071
(213) 894-2956

Auctioneers:
Kohn-Megibow Co., Inc.
(213) 624-8401
Gamson & Flans
(818) 784-3200
Kennedy Wilson
(213) 452-6664

660 J St., Ste. 215
Sacramento, CA 95814
(916) 551-1426

Auctioneers:
Nelson Geiger Auctions
(916) 368-0130

880 Front St., Rm. 4-S-29
San Diego, CA
(619) 557-5440

Auctioneers:
McCormick Auction Co.
(619)447-1196
H & M Goodies Family Auction
(619) 474-8296

901 W. Civic Center, Ste. 160
Santa Ana, CA 92703
(714) 836-2494

Auctioneers: Call for information.

HAWAII

Auctioneers: Call for information.

300 Ala Moana, Rm. 2213
Honolulu, HI 96850
(808) 541-2979

NEVADA

P.O. Box 7527
Las Vegas, NV 89125
(702) 388-6611

Auctioneers:
Dan Watson
(702) 451-1822
George Chadwick
(702) 387-8980

REGION X

ALASKA

Auctioneers: Call for information.

222 W. 8th Ave., #67
Mail Code 1084
Anchorage, AK 99513-7559
(907) 271-4022

IDAHO

1020 Main St., Ste. 290
Boise, ID 83702
(208) 334-1696

Auctioneers:
Harold Stelling
(208) 278-3001
Bob Anneker
(208) 362-3917
Musick Auction Service
(208) 362-0687
Bill Vickers
(208) 237-5700
Bill Downs
(208) 466-5650

OREGON

1220 S. W. Third Ave., Rm. 676
Portland, OR 97204
(503) 221-2682

Auctioneers:
Steve Van Gordon Auctioneers
(503) 266-1551

WASHINGTON

915 Second Ave., Rm. 1792
Seattle, WA 98174
(206) 442-1420

Auctioneers:
James G. Murphy
(206) 486-1246
Auctions, Inc.
(206) 771-4232
Harris & Harris
(206) 451-8922

W. 920 Riverside Ave., Rm. 651
Spokane, WA 99201
(509) 456-3783

Auctioneers: Call for information.

Farmers Home Administration

FmHA is in the business of loaning out money and providing services to their lenders. When property is foreclosed they either turn it over to a real estate broker, hold it in their inventory (temporarily), or turn it over to private auctioneers. You may contact one of their 46 state offices for further information on how you can buy one of their homes, farms, or properties.

ALABAMA

Aronov Bldg., Room 717
474 South Court St.
Montgomery, AL 36104

ALASKA

634 S. Bailey, Suite 102
Palmer, AK 99645

ARIZONA

210 E. Indianola, Suite 275
Phoenix, AZ 85012

ARKANSAS

Federal Bldg., Room 5529
700 W. Capitol, P.O. Box 2778
Little Rock, AR 72203

CALIFORNIA

194 West Main St., Suite F
Woodland, CA 95695

COLORADO

2490 W. 26th Ave., Room 231
Denver, CO 80211

DELAWARE/MARYLAND

2319 South Dupont Hwy.
Dover, DE 19901

FLORIDA

Federal Bldg., Room 214
401 S. E. 1st Ave.
P.O. Box 1088
Gainesville, FL 32601-6805

GEORGIA

Stephens Federal ~~~
355 E. Hancock ~
Athens, GA 3061~

HAWAII

Federal Bld., Roo~
154 Waianuenue ~
Hilo, HI 96720

IDAHO

3232 Elder St.
Boise, ID 83705

ILLINOIS

Illini Plaza, Suite 103
1817 S. Neil St.
Champaign, IL 61820

INDIANA

5975 Lakeside Blvd.
Indianapolis, IN. 46278

IOWA

Federal Bldg., Room 873

did not have any farms or homes under foreclosure - when available advertised in the local papers.

9-30-91

291

210 Walnut St.
Des Moines, IA 50309

KANSAS

444 S. E. Quincy St., Room 176
Topeka, KS 66683

KENTUCKY

333 Waller Ave.
Lexington, KY 40504

LOUISIANA

3727 Government St.
Alexandria, LA 71302

MAINE

USDA Office Building
Orono, ME 04473

MASSACHUSETTS/RHODE ISLAND/CONNECTICUT

451 West St.
Amherst, MA 01002
(413) 584-7992

MICHIGAN

1405 S. Harrison Rd., Room 209
East Lansing, MI 48823

MINNESOTA

410 Farm Credit Building
375 Jackson St.
St. Paul, MN 55101

MISSISSIPPI

Federal Bldg. Suite 831
100 W. Capitol St.
Jackson, MS 39269

MISSOURI

555 Vandiver Drive

Colombia, MO 65202

MONTANA

Federal Bldg., Room 210
10 E. Babcock St.
P.O. Box 850
Bozeman, MT 59771

NEBRASKA

Federal Bldg., Room 308
100 Centennial Mall N
Lincoln, NE 68508

NEW JERSEY

100 High St., Suite 100
Mt. Holly, NJ 08060

NEW MEXICO

Federal Bldg., Room 3414
517 Gold Ave., SW
Albuquerque, NM 87102

NEW YORK

James Hanley Federal Bldg.,
Room 871
100 South Clinton St.
Syracuse, NY 13260

NORTH CAROLINA

4405 Bland Road, Suite 252
Raleigh, NC 27609

NORTH DAKOTA

Federal Bldg., Room 208
Third and Rosser
P.O. Box 1737
Bismark, ND 58502

OHIO

200 North High St.
Columbus, OH 43215

OKLAHOMA

USDA Agricultural Center Bldg.
Stillwater, OK 74074

OREGON

Federal Bldg., Room 1590
1220 S.W. 3rd. Ave.
Portland, OR 97204

PENNSYLVANIA

Federal Bldg., Room 730
P.O. Box 905
Harrisburg, PA 17108

PUERTO RICO

Room 501
New San Juan Center Bldg.
159 Carlos Chardon St.
Hato Rey, PR 00918

SOUTH CAROLINA

Strom Thurmond Federal Bldg.,
Room 1007
1835 Assembly St.
Columbia, SC 29201

SOUTH DAKOTA

Huron Federal Bldg., Room 308
200 4th St., SW
Huron, SD 57350

TENNESSEE

538 Federal Bldg.
801 Broadway
Nashville, TN 37203

TEXAS
101 S. Main
Federal Bldg., Suite 102
Temple, TX 76501

UTAH/NEVADA

Federal Bldg., Room 5438
125 South State St.
Salt Lake City, UT 84138

VERMONT/NEW HAMPSHIRE

141 Main St.
P.O. Box 588
Montpelier, VT 05602

VIRGINIA

Federal Bldg., Room 8213
400 N. Eight St.
P.O. Box 10106
Richmond, VA 23240

WASHINGTON

Federal Bldg., Room 319
P.O. Box 2427
Wenatchee, WA 98807

WISCONSIN

1257 Main St.
Stevens Point, WI 54481

WEST VIRGINIA

75 High St.
P.O. Box 678
Morgantown, WV 26505

WYOMING

Federal Building Room 1005
100 East B
P.O. Box 820
Casper, WY 82602

293

State Surplus Auctions

There are various state surplus auctions one can go to for vehicles, equipment, merchandise, and assorted items. Each area may have a different department to contact. Those to be contacted with information about them are as follows:

ALABAMA

State Agency for Surplus Properties
4401 North Blvd.
Montgomery, AL 36121
(205) 277-5866
Contact: Charles Bush

ALASKA

Dept. of Administration
Division of General Services
and Supply
2400 Viking Dr.
Anchorage, AK 99501
(907) 465-2172
Contact: Roy Stevens or
Mark Ford

ARKANSAS

D. F. & A.
Marketing and Redistribution
P.O. Box 2940
Little Rock, AR 72203
(501) 565-8645
Contact: Carol Ann Eichelmann

ARIZONA

State of Arizona
Surplus Property
Management Office
1533 W. Jackson St.
Phoenix, AZ 85007
(602) 542-5701
Contact: Jan Pixley

CALIFORNIA

Dept. of General Services
State Garage
1416 Tenth St. S.
Sacramento, CA 95814
(916) 445-4851
Contact: Norma Wood

COLORADO

State Fleet Management
1001 W. 62nd Ave.
Denver, CO 80216
(303) 287-7940
Contact: Paul Jensen

CONNECTICUT

Surplus Center
Call Only
(203) 566-7018
Contact: Jacqueline Dion

DELAWARE

Dept. of Administrative
Services, Division of Purchasing
P.O. Box 299
Delaware City, DE 19706
(302) 834-7081
Contact: Yvonne Gregg

WASHINGTON D.C.

Call Only
(202) 576-7850
Contact: Raymond Terry

FLORIDA

Dept. of General Services
Bureau of Motor Vehicles
and Watercraft
Rm. B-69, Larson Bldg.
Tallahassee, FL 32399-0950
(904) 488-4290
Contact: Ed Underwood

GEORGIA

Dept. of Administrative Services
Surplus Properties
1050 Murphey Ave., Bldg. 1A
Atlanta, GA 30310
(404) 756-4800

HAWAII

Call Only
(808) 523-4871 or 4874
Auctions for City and
County of Honolulu ONLY

IDAHO

Dept. of Transportation
3311 W. State St.
Boise, ID 83703
(208) 334-8082
Contact: Buz Shelton

ILLINOIS

Dept. of Central
Management Services
Property Control Division
3550 Great Northern Ave.
Springfield, IL 62707
(217) 793-1813
Contact: Dolores Walden

INDIANA

State Surplus Property
545 W. McCarty St.
Indianapolis, IN 46225
(317) 232-1365
Contact: Patty Bauguess

IOWA

State Vehicle Dispatcher Division

301 E. Seventh
Des Moines, IA 50319
(515) 281-5121
Contact: Deb Bales

KENTUCKY

Dept. of Finance
Division of Personal Property
501 Holmes St.
Frankfort, KY 40601
(502) 564-2213
Contact: Doug Lathram

LOUISIANA

Louisiana Division of Administration
Property Assistance Agency
P.O. Box 94095
Baton Rouge, LA 70804
(504) 342-6861
Contact: Clinton Thompson

MAINE

Surplus Properties
Station 95
Augusta, Maine 04333
(207) 289-5750
Contact: David Patterson

MARYLAND

Call Only
(301) 799-0440
Contact: Al Jackson

MASSACHUSETTS

State Surplus Properties Office
1 Ashburton Place, Rm. 1009
Boston, MA 02108
(617) 727-2920
Contact: Peter Ray or
Frank Kelly

MICHIGAN

State of Michigan Department
of Management and Budget
Office Services Division
3353 N. Logan

295

Lansing, MI 48913
(519) 334-6858
Contact: Doug Dodge

MINNESOTA

Materials Management Division
Materials Service
and Distribution,
Surplus Operation
5420 Hwy. 8 Arden Hills
New Brighton, MN 55112
(612) 296-5177
Contact: Gene Glaeser
Special Hotline: (612) 296-1056

MISSOURI

State Surplus Properties
P.O. Box 1310
Jefferson City, MO 65102
(314) 751-3415
Contact: Ed Goff

MONTANA

Property Supply Bureau
Capitol Station
930 Lyndale
Helena, MT 59620
(406) 444-4514
Contact: Terrie Howell

MISSISSIPPI

Dept. of Public Safety
P.O. Box 958
Jackson, MS 39205
(601) 987-1212 or
987-1453(direct)
Contact: James W. Bennett

Governor's Office of General Services
Bureau of Surplus Properties
P.O. Box 5778
Jackson, MS 39208
(601) 939-2050
Contact: Tracy Byas

Mississippi Wildlife
Conservation Dept.
c/o Ken Dukes
P.O. Box 451

Jackson, MS 39205
(601) 961-5300 or
961-5245(direct)
Contact: Ken Dukes

NEBRASKA

Materials Division
Mall Level--State Office Bldg.
301 Centennial Mall S.
P.O. Box 94847
Lincoln, NE 68509
(402) 471-2401 or
479-4890(direct)

NEW HAMPSHIRE

State Surplus Property
78 Regional Dr.
Bldg. 3
Concord, NH 03301
(603) 271-2126
Contact: Armand Verville

NEW MEXICO

New Mexico Hwy. and
Transportation Dept.
Equipment Section, SB-2
P.O. Box 1149
Santa Fe, NM 87504
(505) 827-5580
Contact: Mike Maes

NEVADA

State Purchasing Division
Capitol Complex
505 E. King, Rm. 400
Carson City, NV 89701
(702) 885-4070, Ext. 57
Contact: Betty Shewlett
Call or write for sealed bid
forms and information.
Open bid is held in Reno annually.

NEW JERSEY

State of New Jersey
Distribution Center
1620 Spuyvesant Ave.
Trenton, NJ 08628
(609) 530-3300

Contact: Frank Rich

NEW YORK

Surplus
Albany, NY 12226
(518) 457-6335
Contact: Harry Feisthamel

NORTH CAROLINA

State Surplus Property
P.O. Box 33900
Raleigh, NC 27636
(919) 733-3889
Contact: Jessie Murphy
$15 fee to be on the mailing list
for residents.
$25 for non-residents.

NORTH DAKOTA

Highway Department
Airport Rd.
Bismarck, ND
NO MAILING LIST
Call Only
(701) 224-2543

OHIO

Administrative Services
2260 N.Fifth St.
Columbus, OH 43266-0584
(614) 466-2850
Contact: Harold Davis

OKLAHOMA

Central Purchasing
State Capitol Bldg., Rm. B4
Oklahoma City, OK 73105
(405) 521-2206 or 521-2126
Contact: Steve Dwyer
To get on the mailing
list by mail, address letters to Mr. Bob Lister

OREGON

Surplus Properties
1655 Salem Industrial Dr., NE
Salem, OR 97310

(503) 378-4714
Contact: Cheryl Winn
If writing to be
put on the mailing list, send a business-sized
envelope,
SASE

PENNSYLVANIA

Dept. of General Services
Bureau of Vehicle Management
2221 Foster St.
Harrisburg, PA 17125
(717) 783-3132 or 787-3162
Contact: Frank Belty

RHODE ISLAND

No Auctions

SOUTH CAROLINA

Dept. of Hwys. and
Public Transportation
Procurement Office
191 Park St.
Columbia, SC 29202
(803) 737-6635
Contact: G. C. Cross
Motor Pool Vehicles

South Carolina
Surplus Properties
1441 Austin Ave.
West Columbia, SC 29169
(803) 734-4335 or 734-1000
Contact: Tom Rayfield

SOUTH DAKOTA

State Property Management
701 E. Sioux
Pierre, SD 57501
(605) 773-4935
Contact: Rick Boorhes

TENNESSEE

No mailing list (Nashville Only)
Call Only
(615) 741-4896
Contact: Brenda Grant

TEXAS

State Purchasing and
General Services Commission
P.O. Box 13047, Capitol Station
Austin, TX 78711-3047
(512) 463-3381
Contact: Marilyn Grimes

UTAH

Utah State Surplus
522 S. 700 W.
Salt Lake City, UT 84101
(801) 533-4616
Contact: Troy Manwaring

VERMONT

Central Surplus
Properties Agency
RR2, Box 350
Montpelier, VT 05602
(802) 828-3394
Contact: Lee Wallace

VIRGINIA

Division of Purchases
and Supply
P.O. Box 1199
Richmond, VA 23209
(804) 786-3876
Contact: Marquis Bolton

WASHINGTON

Dept. of General Administration
State Office of Commodities
Redistribution
2805 'C' St., SW
Door 49, Bldg. 5
Auburn, WA 98001
(206) 931-3944
Contact: Darrel Green

WEST VIRGINIA

West Virginia State Agency
for Surplus Property
P.O. Box 9

Dunbar, WV 25064
(304) 768-7303
Contact: George Agglerback or
Ken Frye

WISCONSIN

State Property Program
P.O. Box 7867
Madison, WI 53707
(608) 266-8024
Contact: Rex Owens

WYOMING

State Motor Vehicle
Management Services
723 W. 19th St.
Cheyenne, WY 82001
(307) 777-6855
Contact: George Tsuda

298

State Unclaimed Properties Auctions

For various reasons people leave behind unclaimed money in banks which is then turned over to states for recovery. In other cases people leave behind valuable jewelry and coins in safe deposit boxes which is then turned over to various Finance Departments in state governments. For further details of what is available and how you may claim such money or property, please contact the applicable agency.

Please note that some sates have various restrictions on making money on other people's unclaimed money or property. Most states will charge you a fee for renting or buying their lists. Occasionally states have auctions on such unclaimed property. Please read the information about the agency, address and telephone number before contacting them.

ALABAMA

Montgomery
Department of Unclaimed Property
P.O. Box 327580
Montgomery, AL 36132

Please write for information. No auctions held but the possiblity is being considered. No license is required; the finders fee is negotiable (paid by owner). List is updated and published twice a year but is not for sale. No public viewing.

ALASKA

Juneau
Revenue Unclaimed Properties
P.O. SA Juneau
Juneau, AL 99801

Write for information. No license required; the finders fee is negotiable. Files updated quarterly; list costs $101.50. Can view at State Archives.

ARIZONA

Phoenix
Department of Revenue
1600 W. Monroe
Phoenix, AZ 85007

Must go to office for information; one auction held each year; no calls--no letters. License required; 30% maximum finders fee (paid by owner). Files updated once a year and published in the Arizona Reporter. List is not for sale; viewing by appointment only.

ARKANSAS

Little Rock
Department of Unclaimed Property
Auditor of State Office
230 State Capitol
Little Rock, AR 72201

Must go to office for information; state residents only do not need licenses; 10% maximum finders fee (paid by owner). Files updated once a year, list available only to state residents at no cost. Viewing by appointment only.

CALIFORNIA

Sacramento
Controller, Unclaimed Property
300 Capital Mall, Ste. 801
Sacramento, CA 95814

Write for information and to get on the mailing list. There is one auction a year. No license is required; 10% finders fee (paid by owner). Files updated each month.

Information list costs $25.00; Alphabetical list costs $200.00; Accountable list costs $300.00. Viewing by appointment only.

COLORADO

Denver
Department of Treasury-Unclaimed Property
1560 Broadway, Rm. 630
Denver, CO 80202

Must go to office for information; no auctions held and no license required. Finders fee is negotiable (paid by owner). File is updated quarterly; list costs $10.00. Viewing by appointment.

CONNECTICUT

Hartford

State of Connecticut
Office of Treasury
Unclaimed Property Division
55 Elm St.
Hartford, CT 06106

Write for information; no auctions held and no license required (subject to change). Finders fee 20% up to 2 years; 50% finders fee thereafter (paid by owner). File updated annually and published in major newspapers. List costs $800 plus postage. Viewing by appointment only.

DELAWARE

Wilmington
State of Delaware
Department of Revenue
Unclaimed Property Division
P.O. Box 8931
Wilmington, DE 19899

Write for information; no auctions held and no license required. No limit to fee (paid by owner). File updated every September. List is not for sale. Viewing by appointment only.

FLORIDA

Tallahassee
State of Florida
Abandoned Property Division
State Capitol Bldg.

Tallahassee, FL 32399-0350

Write for information; auctions held once every three years. Must be a private investigator; finders fee is negotiable (paid by owner). File updated twice a year. List costs $30.00. Viewing by appointment, open to the public.

GEORGIA

Atlanta
State Department of Revenue
Property Tax Division
Unclaimed Property
270 Washington St., Rm. 405
Atlanta, GA 30334

Write for information; auctions held as needed. No license required but there is a 10% maximum finders fee (paid by owner). File updated once a year and published in August. List costs $22.50. Viewing by appointment.

HAWAII

Honolulu
Unclaimed Properties
Department of Budget & Finance
Finance Division
P.O. Box 150
Honolulu, HI 96810

Write for information; auctions held as needed. There is no mailing list; no license is required. There is a 20% finders fee (paid by owner). File is updated twice a year and costs $50.00; file not open for viewing.

IDAHO

Boise
Unclaimed Properties
State Tax Commission
700 State St.
Boise, ID 83722

Write for information and to be put on the mailing list; auctions held as needed. No license is required; finders fee is negotiable (paid by owner). File updated annually and published August 1. List costs $90-$200. The file is open to the public at $15.00 an hour.

300

ILLINOIS

Chicago
Department of Financial Institutions
Unclaimed Property Division
100 W. Randolph, 15th Fl.
Chicago, IL 60601
(217) 782-8607

Springfield
Department of Financial Institutions
Division of Unclaimed Properties
421 E. Capitol, Ste. 700
Springfield, IL 62706

Write for information; auctions are held as needed. No license required but there is a 50% finders fee under $1,000, and a 10% finders fee over $1,000 (both paid by owner). File updated in January and July; published in July. List costs $500 plus postage. Viewing by appointment.

KANSAS

Topeka
Kansas State Department
of Transportation
Unclaimed Property Division
900 Jackson, Ste. 201
Topeka, KS 66612-1235

Write for information; no auctions held. and no license required. Finders fee is 15% maximum (paid by owner). File updated daily and published in February. List costs $45-$500. Viewing by appointment only.

INDIANA

Indianapolis
State of Indiana
Office of Attorney General
State House, 2nd Fl.
Indianapolis, IN 46204
(317) 232-6348

Call for appointment; auctions held every 10 years--last held 2 summers ago. No license is required but there is a 10% finders fee over $1,000, and a negotiable finders fee under $1,000 (both paid by owner). Files updated twice a year but the list is not for sale. Viewing by appointment only.

IOWA

Des Moines
Unclaimed Properties Division
Great Iowa Treasurer Department
Hoover Hunt Bldg.
Des Moines, IA 50319

Write for information; next auction to be held in 1990. No license required and no limit on finders fee (paid by owner). File updated regularly and published May/June. List costs $600 plus postage. Viewing by appointment only.

KENTUCKY

Frankfort
State of Kentucky
Miscellaneous & Excise Tax Section
Abandoned Property, 4th Fl.
209 St. Clair St.
Frankfort, KY 40601

Write for information; no auctions held and no license required. Finders fee is negotiable with no requirements. File updated annually and published October 1. List costs $32.50. Viewing by appointment only.

LOUISIANA

Baton Rouge
Unclaimed Properties
P.O. Box 91010
Baton Rouge, LA 70821

Write for information; no auctions held and no license is required. Finders fee is 10% (paid by owner). File updated quarterly and no list is for sale. Viewing by appointment only.

MAINE

Augusta
State of Maine
Treasurer Department
Abandoned Property Division
State Office Bldg.
Station 39
Augusta, ME 04333

301

(207) 289-2771

Call for information about finders fee. Auction held every 3-4 years. No license is required: there is a 15% finders fee over first three years (paid by owner). File updated every six months and published in PORTLAND TELEGRAM and BANGOR DAILY NEWS; advertising monthly at end of month. List not for sale; viewing by appointment only.

MASSACHUSETTS

Boston
Commonwealth of Massachusetts
State Treasury Department
50 Franklin St., 2nd Fl.
Boston, MA 02110

Write for information; auction held June 27 each year. Auctioneer is Frank McDermit. No license is required; 35% maximum finders fee (paid by owner). File updated and published annually. List costs $10.00. Viewing by appointment.

MARYLAND

Baltimore
State of Maryland
Unclaimed Property Section
301 W. Preston St.
Baltimore, MD 21201

Write for information; two auctions held each year. No license is required; there is a 20% maximum finders fee (paid by owner) for first two years and no regulations after those two years. File updated yearly and published in local newspapers every 6 months. Lists cost $300-$400. Viewing by appointment.

MICHIGAN

Lansing
State of Michigan
Michigan Department of Treasurer
GSH Division
Code of Escheates
Lansing, MI 48972

Write for information; auction held every 3 years. A license is required and finders fee is negotiable (paid by owner). File updated

regularly and posted at Probate Court. List is not for sale. Viewing by appointment only.

MINNESOTA

St. Paul
Department of Unclaimed Properties
500 Metro Square
St. Paul, MN 55101
(612) 296-2568

Call regarding a single property; otherwise, write for information. Auction held every 10 years. A license is required; 10% finders fee (paid by owner). Files updated annually; list not for sale. Viewing by appointment only.

MISSISSIPPI

Jackson
Unclaimed Properties
P.O. Box 138
Jackson, MS 39205

Write for information; no auctions held and no license required. Finders fee is 33 1/3% maximum (paid by owner). Files updated and published every three years. List available free. Viewing by appointment only.

MISSOURI

Jefferson City
Department of Unclaimed Property
Harry S. Truman Blvd.
Jefferson City, MO 65102

Write for information; auctions held infrequently. No license required; 10-15% finders fee (paid by owner). File updated regularly and published every two weeks. List costs $200-$500. Viewing by appointment.

MONTANA

Helena
State of Montana
Department of Revenue
Abandoned Property Division
Mitchell Bldg.
Helena, MT 59620

Write for information; one or two auctions held each year. No license is required; negotiable finders fee (paid by owner). File updated and published annually. List not for sale. Viewing by appointment.

NEBRASKA

Lincoln
State Treasurer
Rm. 2003
State Capitol
Lincoln, NE 68509

Write for information; auction held each year in November. No license required; however finder must fill out "Nomination Form" for state approval to view. There is no finders fee but a 10% fee is proposed and would be paid by owner. File updated annually and must be hand-copied. Viewing by appointment.

NEVADA

Las Vegas
State of Nevada
Department of Commerce
Unclaimed Property Division
State Mail Room
Las Vegas, NV 89158

Write for information; auction is held once a year. License is required; there is a 10% finders fee (paid by owner). File updated regularly and published twice a year in newspapers. List costs $35. Viewing by appointment.

NEW HAMPSHIRE

Concord
State of New Hampshire
State Treasurer Office
House Annex, Rm. 121
Concord, NH 43301

Write for information; no auctions are held. No license is required; finders fee is negotiable (paid by owner). File updated twice a year; list not for sale. Viewing by appointment only. Out of state finders discouraged.

NEW JERSEY

Trenton
Department of Unclaimed Properties
Financial Management Division
1 W. State St.
3rd Fl. CNZ14
Trenton, NJ 08625

Write for information; no auctions held and no license required. Finders fee negotiable (paid by owner). File updated once a year and published in large newspapers each February. List is not for sale. Viewing not open to public; write to ask in which newspapers list is published.

NEW MEXICO

Santa Fe
State of New Mexico
Taxation and Revenues Department
Manuel Lujan Office Bldg.
Santa Fe, NM 87503

Write for information; an auction is held every 25 years and licenses are required. Finders fee is negotiable (paid by owner). Files updated and published twice each year. List and price available by summer, 1989. Viewing by appointment.

NEW YORK

Albany
Department of Unclaimed Funds
Department of Audit and Control
Governor Smith State Office Bldg.
Albany, NY 12236

Write for information; no auctions held. No license is required if you think you are rightful owner or heir--if you are a 'tracer'-- 15% finders fee (paid by owner). Files updated and published every six months. List costs $20-$25. Viewing by appointment only.

NORTH CAROLINA

Raleigh
Department of State Treasury
325 N. Salisbury St.
Raleigh, NC
(919) 733-3951

(919) 733-6876/7/8 (Unclaimed Property Dept.)

Call for information; auctions held as needed and license is required. Finders fee maximum 25% (paid by owner). File updated annually and published first of year. Lists cost $7.40 plus postage. Viewing by appointment for license holders only.

NORTH DAKOTA

Bismarck

Deputy Administrator
Unclaimed Property Division
Bismarck, ND 58505
(701) 224-2805

Write or call for information; no auctions held and no license required. Finders fee 25% (paid by owner). Files updated May 1 and November 1; published in newspapers in February. List is not for sale. Viewing by appointment only.

OHIO

Columbus

State of Ohio
Division of Unclaimed Funds
2 Nationwide Plaza
Columbus, OH 43266
(614) 466-4433

Call for appointment only; no auctions held in past six years. No license is required; there is a 10% maximum finders fee (paid by owner). Files updated and published annually. List is not for sale. Viewing by appointment only.

OKLAHOMA

Oklahoma City

Unclaimed Properties
919 NW 23rd, 2nd Fl.
Oklahoma City, OK 73106
(405) 521-4280

Write for information; auctions held every one to three years. No license is required; finders fee is negotiable (paid by owner). Files updated annually; list costs depend on how far back you request. Call for specifics. Viewing by appointment.

OREGON

Salem

Division of State Land
1600 State St.
Salem, OR 97310

Write for information; no calls accepted. License is required depending on county and city. Finders fee is negotiable (paid by owner). Files updated as needed. List costs $10.00 a year plus postage. Viewing by appointment only.

PENNSYLVANIA

Middleton

Pennsylvania Department of Revenue
Bureau of Administrative Services
Abandoned and Unclaimed Properties Section
2850 Turn Pike--Industrial Park
Middleton, PA 17057

Write for information; auction held each year. No license required; finders fee negotiable (paid by owner). File updated and published annually. List is not for sale. Viewing by appointment only.

RHODE ISLAND

Providence

Department of Revenue
Division of Unclaimed Properties
P.O. Box 1435
Providence, RI 02901

Write for information; auction held every two years. No license required; finders fee is negotiable (paid by owner). Files updated and published twice a year in PROVIDENCE GENERAL, EVENING BULLETIN and all local newspapers. List is not for sale; there is no public viewing, see newspapers.

SOUTH CAROLINA

Columbia

South Carolina Tax Commission
(Abandoned Property)
301 Gervais
Columbia, SC 29214

304

Write for information; no auctions held and no license required. Finders fee 5-15% (paid by owner). File updated once a year. List is not for sale. Viewing by appointment.

SOUTH DAKOTA

Pierre
State Treasurer's Office
Unclaimed Properties
500 E. Capitol
Pierre, SD 57501

Write for information; no auctions held and no license required. Finders fee 25% maximum (paid by owner). File updated annually and each new entry is published in the county of last known address. List is not for sale. Viewing by appointment only.

TENNESSEE

Nashville
Department of Treasury
Unclaimed Property
Andrew Jackson Bldg.
11th Fl.
Nashville, TN 37219

Write for information; no auctions held and no license required. Finders fee 10-15% (paid by owner). Files updated as needed; list is not for sale. Viewing by appointment only.

TEXAS

Austin
Heir Finders Co-Ordinator
Theino Unclaimed Properties
P.O. Box 17728
Austin, TX 78760
(512) 444-7833

Write or call for information; auctions held every two years. License is required; there is 10% finders fee (paid by owner). File updated and published once a year. List costs $160; viewing by appointment.

UTAH

Salt Lake City

State of Utah
Office of the State Treasurer
Unclaimed Property Division
Salt Lake City, UT 84114

Write for information; no auctions held and no license required. There is no set fee paid only for claims a minimum of two years old. File updated twice a year and published in legal section of SALT LAKE TRIBUNE and DESERT NEWS the last two Mondays in February and August. List costs $10-$16. Call for specific stipulations for viewing.

VERMONT

Montpelier
Vermont State Treasury
Recovery Department
133 State St.
Montpelier, VT 05602
(802) 828-2301

Write or call for information; no auctions held and no license required. Finders fee is negotiable (paid by owner). File updated as needed and published once a year in local newspapers. List costs $90 plus postage. Viewing by appointment.

VIRGINIA

Richmond
Department of Treasury
Division of Unclaimed Property
Post Office 3R
Richmond, VA 23207
(802) 225-2393

Write for information; auction held every two years. No license is required; 10% finders fee (paid by owner). Files updated twice a year and published in February and August in local newspapers. List is not for sale. No public viewing; call to ask in which newspapers list is published.

WASHINGTON

Olympia
Department of Revenue and Unclaimed Properties
State of Washington
Olympia, WA 98507
(206) 586-2736

305

Write or call for information; auctions held as needed. License is required; finders fee is negotiable (paid by owner). File updated and published every six months. List is not for sale. Viewing by appointment.

WISCONSIN

Madison
Unclaimed Properties Division
Office of State Treasurer
P.O. Box 2114
Madison, WI 53701

Write for information; auctions held every five to ten years. No license required; finders fee is negotiable (paid by owner). File updated every two years. List costs $95 Viewing by appointment.

WEST VIRGINIA

Charleston
Division of Unclaimed Properties
E-B-96
State Capitol
Charleston, WV 25305
(304) 343-4000

Write or call for information; auction held every two to three years. Business license required; finders fee is negotiable (paid by owner). File updated twice a year and published in local newspapers. List is not for sale. Viewing by appointment.

WYOMING

Cheyenne
State Treasurer's Office
State Capitol Bldg.
Cheyenne, WY 82002

Write for information; no auctions held and no license required. Finders fee is negotiable (paid by owner). File updated monthly. List costs $60. Viewing by appointment.

WASHINGTON D.C.

Department of Finance and Revenue
Small Claims Property Division
300 Indiana Ave.
Washington, D.C. 20001

Write for information; auction held every five years. No license required; 10% finders fee (paid by owner). File updated twice a year and published in the WASHINGTON POST and WASHINGTON TIMES in August and February. List is not for sale. Viewing by appointment.

U.S. Trustees

U.S. Trustees do not have auctions. They are the starting point for many people who wish to track down bankruptcy auctions. The various U.S. Trustees Offices maintain lists of bankruptcy trustees whom you may wish to contact for yet another trek to the correct person. Some people may wish to avoid this by calling auctioneers directly out of the phone book and asking to be placed on their mailing lists. However, this does not always give you all the different types of bankruptcy auctions.

To thoroughly research this please contact the U.S. Trustees offices below. Some will be helpful and mail you lists of bankruptcy trustees (some of which we have included in this section) while others will demand you visit them and hand-write down the names during your visit. Bankruptcy trustees will either mail you names of auctioneers they use or refer you to an auctioneer who will place you on their mailing lists.

Please choose the method with which you feel most comfortable. If one method doesn't work, then try the other.

DISTRICT ONE

United States Trustee
Rm. 472
10 Causeway St.
Boston, MA 02222
(617) 565-6360
NOTE: Has about 20 bankruptcy trustees.
Call or write to ask for the list.

DISTRICT TWO

United States Trustee
Rm. 534
1 Bowling Green
New York, NY 10004
(212) 668-7663
NOTE: Has about 30 bankruptcy trustees.
Call or write to ask for the list

DISTRICT THREE

United States Trustee
Rm. 210
60 Park Place
Newark, NJ 07102
(201) 645-3014

NOTE: Has about 60 bankruptcy trustees. You must go in person and hand-copy the list.

DISTRICT FOUR

United States Trustee
Rm. 410
421 King St.
Alexandria, VA 22314
(703) 557-0746
NOTE: Has about 30 bankruptcy trustees. You must go in person and hand-copy the list.

DISTRICT FIVE

United States Trustee
Ste. 211
500 S. 22nd St.
Birmingham, AL 35233
(205) 731-1705
NOTE: Has about 20 bankruptcy trustees.Call or write to ask for the list.

DISTRICT SIX

United States Trustee
U.S. Courthouse
Rm. 9C60
1100 Commerce
Dallas, TX 75242
(214) 767-8967
NOTE: Has about 25 bankruptcy trustees.
Send self-addressed, stamped envelope to
receive list.

DISTRICT SEVEN

United States Trustee
Rm. a-1335
175 W. Jackson Blvd.
Chicago, IL 60604
(312) 886-5785
NOTE: Has about 60-65 bankruptcy
trustees. Call or send self-addressed,
stamped envelope to receive list.

DISTRICT EIGHT

United States Trustee
U.S. Courthouse
Rm. 550
110 S. Fourth St.
Minneapolis, MN 55401
(612) 348-1900
NOTE: Has about 15-20 bankruptcy
trustees. Call or send self-addressed,
stamped envelope to receive list.

DISTRICT NINE

United States Trustee
Federal Bldg.
Rm. 3101
300 N. Los Angeles St.
Los Angeles, CA 90012
(213) 894-6387
NOTE: Send self-addressed,stamped
envelope to receive list.

DISTRICT TEN

United States Trustee
Columbine Bldg.
Ste. 300
1845 Sherman St.
Denver, CO 80203
Attn: Ms. Susan Parker
(303) 844-5188

NOTE: Send self-addressed, stamped
envelope to receive list.

308

Police Auctions

In every city and town there is likely to be a police station. Many of the larger cities police will have auctions on regular or infrequent schedules. For the local police number which is your contact number for finding out about auctions, please call the following applicable numbers. Please do not call the number listed in your phone book as it may delay the police department from doing its normal business or may prevent you from speedily getting to the proper department within the police office.

HOT LINE NUMBERS

New York City	(212) 406-1369
Boston	(617) 247-4579
San Francisco (vehicles)	(415) 553-9751
San Diego	(619) 531-2767

ATLANTA

Merchandise
Vehicles
(404) 658-6876
(404) 658-6717

BOSTON

Auction Hotline
(617) 247-4579

CHICAGO

Merchandise
(312) 744-6224

CINCINNATI

Merchandise
Vehicles
(513) 352-6480
(513) 352-6371

CLEVELAND

Merchandise
Some Vehicles
(216) 623-5366

DALLAS

Merchandise
Vehicles
(214) 670-3350

DENVER

Vehicles
(303) 295-4361

DETROIT

Merchandise
Vehicles
(313) 596-2092
(313) 267-7174

HOUSTON

309

Merchandise
Vehicles
(713) 247-5806

INDIANAPOLIS

Merchandise
Vehicles
(317) 236-3474

KANSAS

Merchandise
Vehicles
(816) 234-5000

LOS ANGELES

Merchandise
(213) 485-3196

MIAMI

Merchandise
Vehicles
(305) 579-6455
(305) 579-6111

MINNEAPOLIS

Merchandise
Vehicles
(612) 348-2932
(612) 348-2991

NEW YORK

Auction Hotline
(212) 406-1369

PHILADELPHIA

Vehicles
(215) 686-1776

PITTSBURGH

Vehicles
(412) 355-5683

PORTLAND

Merchandise
(503) 248-4395

SACRAMENTO

Merchandise
Vehicles
(916) 449-5316

SAN FRANCISCO

Auction Hotline
(415) 553-9751

ST. LOUIS

Merchandise
(314) 444-5540

SAN DIEGO

Auction Hotline
(619) 531-2767

SEATTLE

Merchandise
Vehicles
(206) 386-1234

TAMPA

Merchandise
Vehicles
(813) 893-7555
(813) 225-5880

WASHINGTON, D.C.

Merchandise
Vehicles
(202) 767-7586

Sheriff's Auctions

Sheriff's departments in many counties around the United States have auctions. Please contact the county sheriff in your area from the list below.

ALABAMA

Mobile County Commissioners
P.O. Box 1443
Mobile, AL 36633
(205) 690-8615

ARIZONA

Sheriff of Maricopa
102 W. Madison
Phoenix, AZ 85003
(602) 256-1000

Pima County Sheriff's Dept.
Civil Processing Unit
P.O. Box 910
Tucson, AZ (602) 798-5510

CALIFORNIA

Orange County Sheriff's Dept.
Orange County Register
1141 E. Chestnut
Santa Ana, CA 92705
(714) 568-4359
or
Orange County Sheriff
P.O. Box 449
Santa Ana, CA 92702
(714) 647-7000

Kern County Sheriff's Dept.
Civil Division
P.O. Box 2208
Bakersfield, CA 93303
(805) 861-7653
or
Ed Rogers Enterprises
3737 Gilmore
Bakersfield, CA 93308
(805) 322-2192

Fresno County Sheriff's Dept.
Fresno County Bldg.

2200 Fresno St.
Fresno, CA 93724
(209) 488-3939

Los Angeles County
Vehicle Auction
2500 S. Garfield
City of Commerce, CA 90040
(213) 720-6952 or 720-6951

Riverside County Garage
4293 Orange St.
Riverside, CA 92501
(714) 787-2186

Sacramento County Sheriff
6670 Elvas Ave.
Sacramento, CA 95819
(916) 732-3841
or
Roger Ernst & Associates
Auctioneer
P.O. Box 3251
Modesto, CA 95353
(209) 527-7399

San Diego Public Administrator's Office
5201-A Ruffin Rd.
San Diego, CA 92123
(619) 694-3500
or
U.S. Marshal Civil
940 Front St., LLB-71
San Diego, CA 92189
(619) 565-5200 or 557-6620
or
Fisher Auto Auctions
614 Fifth Ave., Ste. A
San Diego, CA 92101
(619) 233-1851

San Francisco Sheriff's Dept.
Civil Division, 333 City Hall
Federal Bldg., Hall of Justice
(Adjacent, Rm. 101)
San Francisco, CA 94102
(415) 554-7230

Santa Clara County
San Jose Sheriff's Dept.
Purchasing Dept.
1608 Las Plumas
San Jose, CA 91533-1695
Contact: Ms. Nancy
(408) 277-4413

COLORADO

Denver Sheriff's Dept.
Civil Division, Rm. 507
City & County Bldg.
Denver, CO 80202
(303) 575-5192

CONNECTICUT

Fairfield County Sheriff's Dept.
1061 Main St.
Bridgeport, CT 06604
(203) 579-6239

Hartford County Sheriff's Dept..
P.O. Box 6302
Hartford, CT 06106
(203) 566-4930

DELAWARE

New Castle County
Sheriff's Dept.
11th & King Sts.
Wilmington, DE 19801
(302) 571-7568

FLORIDA

Duval County
Office of Sheriff
(Jacksonville Police)
501 E. Bay St.
Jacksonville, FL 32202
(904) 630-2215

Dade County
Metro Dade Police Dept.
Sheriff's Services
Civil Process Bureau, 13th Fl.
Dade County Courthouse
Miami, FL 33130
(305) 375-5100

Orange County Sheriff's Dept.
P.O. Box 1440
Orlando, FL 32802
(407) 657-2500

Sarasota County Sheriff's Dept.
P.O. Box 4115
Sarasota, FL 34237/34230
(813) 951-5800

Hillsborough County
Sheriff's Dept.
Fiscal Division
P.O. Box 3371
Tampa, FL 33601
(813) 247-8031 or 247-8033
or
Tampa Machinery & Auction
P.O. Box 16000-B
Tampa, FL 33687
(813) 986-2485

Palm Beach County
Sheriff's Dept.
3228 Gun Club Rd.
Palm Beach, FL 33406
(407) 471-2000

GEORGIA

Fulton County Sheriff
136 Pryor St., Rm. 108
Atlanta, GA 30303
(404) 730-5100

HAWAII

Honolulu County
Sheriff's Dept.
2nd Fl, 1111 Alakea St.
Honolulu, HI 96813
(808) 548-4019 or 548-2284

ILLINOIS

Cook County Sheriff's Office
Real Estate Division
50 W. Washington, Rm. 701-A
Chicago, IL 60602
Personal Property:
(312) 443-3345
Real Estate:
(312) 443-3341
or

Sheriff's Dept. Auto Pound
3146 S. Archer Ave.
Chicago, IL 60608
(312) 890-3355

INDIANA

Allen County Sheriff's Dept.
Civil Division
Courthouse, Rm. 100
Fort Wayne, IN 46802
(219) 428-7632

Marion County Sheriff's Dept.
822 City-County Bldg.
Indianapolis, IN 46204
Merchandise & Vehicles:
(317) 231-8415
Real Estate:
(317) 231-8412
or
Steve Wildermuth
Property Room
40 S. Alabama
Indianapolis, IN 46204
(317) 231-8294

KENTUCKY

Jefferson County Police Garage
3528 Newburg Rd.
Louisville, KY 40218
(502) 452-2671

LOUISIANA

E. Baton Rouge Parish
(County) Sheriff's Office
Foreclosure Dept., Rm., 229
P.O. Box 3277
Baton Rouge, LA 70821
(504) 389-4818

Orleans Parish (County)
Civil Sheriff's Dept.
Moveables Dept. or
Real Estate
421 Loyola Ave.
New Orleans, LA 70112
(504) 523-6143

MARYLAND

Baltimore City Sheriff's Office

104 Courthouse
Baltimore, MD 21201
(301) 396-5826

MASSACHUSETTS

Suffolk County Sheriff's Dept.
Civil Process Division
11 Beacon St., Ste. 1300
Boston, MA 02108
(617) 227-2541

MICHIGAN

Washtenaw County
Dept. of Management & Budget
Warehouse Services Section
7461 Crowner Dr.
Lansing, MI 48913
(517) 322-1901
or
Washtenaw County
Sheriff's Dept.
2201 Hogback Rd.
Ann Arbor, MI 48107
(313) 971-3911

Stanton Real Estate & Auctioneers
144 S. Main
Vermontville, MI 49096
(517) 726-0181

Wayne County Sheriff's Dept.
1231 St. Antoine
Detroit, MI 48226
(313) 494-3060

Kent County Purchasing Dept.
Comptroller's Office
300 Monroe, NW
Grand Rapids, MI 49503
(616) 774-3500

MINNESOTA

Ramsey County
Sheriff's Dept., Civil
14 W. Kellog Blvd.
St. Paul, MN 55102
Civil Process:
(612) 292-6030
Legal Ledger:
(612) 222-0059

313

MISSOURI

St. Louis County Sheriff's Dept.
7900 Carondelet
Clayton, MO 63105
(314) 889-7502 or 889-2711

Jackson County
Purchasing & Supply Division
City Hall Bldg.
414 E. 12th, 3rd Fl.
Kansas City, MO 64106
City:
(816) 274-2325
Impounded:
(816) 274-1631

Sheriff's Dept.
City of St. Louis,
Civil Court Bldg.
11 N. 11th St., 1st Fl., N.
St. Louis, MO 63101
(314) 622-4851

NEBRASKA

Douglas County
Purchasing Dept., Rm. 902
Civic Ctr.
Omaha, NE 68183
(402) 444-7158

NEVADA

Clark County
Sheriff's Civil Bureau
309 S. 3rd St., Ste. 230
Las Vegas, NV 89155
(702) 455-4237

NEW JERSEY

Mercer County Sheriff's Dept.
209 S. Broad St.
Trenton, NJ 08650
(609) 989-6100

NEW MEXICO

Bernalillo County Sheriff's Dept.
Court Services Division
P.O. Box 1829
Albuquerque, NM 87103
(505) 768-4140

NEW YORK

Albany County Sheriff's Office
Albany County Courthouse
Albany, NY 12227
(518) 445-7515

Erie County (New York)
Sheriff's Dept.
Civil Process Division
134 W. Eagle St.
Buffalo, NY 14202
(716) 858-7606

Manhattan County
Sheriff's Office
31 Chambers St.
New York, NY 10007
(212) 374-8223

Monroe County Sheriff's Dept.
Civil Division
236 Hall of Justice
Rochester, NY 14614
(716) 428-2320

Onondaga County
Dept. of Purchase
6230 E. Molloy Rd.
East Syracuse, NY 13057
Materials Management Area:
(315) 463-8880

NORTH CAROLINA

Mecklenburg County
Sheriff's Dept.
800 E. Fourth St.
Charlotte, NC 28202
(704) 336-2543

Wake County Sheriff's Office
P.O. Box 550
Raleigh, NC 27602
(919) 755-6924

OHIO

Summit County Sheriff's Dept.
209 S. High St.
Akron, OH 44308
(216) 379-2278 or 379-2150

Hamilton County

Sheriff's Dept.
1000 Main St.
Cincinnati, OH 45202
(513) 825-1500

Cuyahoga County Sheriff's Dept.
1215 W. Third St.
Cleveland, OH 44113
(216) 443-6000

Franklin County Sheriff's Dept.
369 S. High St.
Columbus, OH 43215
(614) 462-4118

Montgomery County
Purchasing Dept.
41 N. Perry St.
Dayton, OH 45422
(513) 225-6464 or 225-4357

Lucas County Courthouse
Civil Division
700 Adams & Eric St.
Toledo, OH 43624
(419) 245-4000 or 245-4480

Mahoning County Sheriff's Dept.
Court Services Office
21 W. Broadman St.
Youngstown, OH 44503
(216) 740-2388

OKLAHOMA

Oklahoma County Sheriff's Dept.
321 Park Ave.
Oklahoma City, OK 73102
(405) 236-1717
          or
Oklahoma City Auctioneer
Oklahoma City Sheriff's Dept.
2932 SW 52nd Place
Oklahoma City, OK 73119
(405) 685-1621

Tulsa County Sheriff's Dept.
500 S. Denver
Tulsa, OK 74103
(918) 585-3811

OREGON

Multnomah County
Sheriff's Dept.
2505 SE 11th Ave.

Portland, OR 97202
(503) 248-5111

PENNSYLVANIA

Lehigh County Sheriff's Dept.
P.O. Box 1548
Allentown, PA 18105
(215) 820-3175

Philadelphia County
Municipal Service Bldg.
Rm. 1310
5th St & JFK Blvd.
Philadelphia, PA 19102-1685
(215) 686-4765

Allegheny County
Sheriff's Dept.
111 Courthouse
Pittsburgh, PA 15219
(412) 355-4704 or 355-4700

Luzern County Courthouse
North River St.
Wilkes-Barre, PA 18711
(717) 825-1651

RHODE ISLAND

Sheriff's Office
of Providence County
250 Benefit St.
Providence, RI 02903
(401) 277-3510

SOUTH CAROLINA

Charleston County
Sheriff's Office
2 Courthouse Square
Charleston, SC 29401
(803) 723-6710

Pitt County Sheriff's Dept.
Main County Office Bldg.
1717 W. Fifth St.
Greenville, SC 27834
(919) 830-6302 or 830-6306

TENNESSEE

Knox County Sheriff's Dept.
400 Main St.

315

Knoxville, TN 37902
(615) 521-2432

Shelby County
Memphis Police Dept.
Property & Evidence Division
201 Poplar
Memphis, TN 38103
Property:
(901) 576-2550
Vehicles:
(901) 452-2810

Davidson County
Madison Sheriff's Dept.
506 Second Ave., N.
Nashville, TN 37201
(615) 862-8174

TEXAS

Travis County
Travis County Sheriffs Dept.
P.O. Box 1748
Austin, TX 78767
(512) 322-4610 or (512) 322-4615

Dallas County Sheriff's Dept.
Civil Section
600 Commerce
Dallas, TX 75202
(214) 653-6531

El Paso County Sheriff's Dept.
601 E. Overland St.
El Paso, TX 79901
(915) 858-3903

Harris County
Sheriff Purchasing
1001 Preston
Show Room 670
Houston, TX 77002
(713) 221-5035

Bexar County Chourthouse
Purchasing Dept.
San Antonio, TX 78205
(512) 220-2211
        or
Bexar County Sheriff's Dept.
200 N. Comal
San Antonio, TX 78207
(512) 270-6020

UTAH

Salt Lake County
Sheriff's Office
Civil Division
437 S. 200 East
Salt Lake City, UT 84111
(801) 535-5441 or
468-2556 or 535-5425

VIRGINIA

Richmond's Sheriff's Dept.
800 E. Marshall St.
Richmond, VA 23219
(804) 780-6600

Norfolk's Sheriff's Dept.
P.O. Box 3908
Norfolk, VA 23514
(804) 441-2341

WASHINGTON

Dept. of Public Safety
King County Police
513 Third Ave., Rm. W150
Seattle, WA 98104
(206) 296-3800
        or
King County Sheriff's Dept.
516 Third Ave.
Seattle, WA 98104
(206) 296-4078

WISCONSIN

Milwaukee County
Sheriff's Dept.
821 W. State St.
Milwaukee, WI 53233
(414) 278-4907

City and County Marshals

Some cities and counties have marshals which carry out some of the functions of the local sheriff's department. These are not United States Marshals. Some have great auction bargains. Please contact from the list below for your area. If your area does not appear, it is because your area does not have such an agency.

CALIFORNIA

Los Angeles County Marshal
110 N. Grant, Rm. 525
Los Angeles, CA 90012
(213) 974-6311

Riverside County Marshal
4200 Orange St.
Riverside, CA 92501
(714) 788-8956

San Diego County Marshal
220 W. Broadway
San Diego, CA 92101
(619) 531-3995

Orange County Marshal
700 Civic Ctr. Dr. W., K-100
Santa Ana, CA 92701
(714) 834-5293

GEORGIA

City Marshal
55 Trinity Ave., SW, Ste. 1350
Atlanta, GA 30335
(404) 330-6270
Auctioneer: Arwood Auction Co.
(404) 352-0110

MISSOURI

City Marshal's Office
14th & Market, Rm. 200
St. Louis, MO 63103
(314) 622-4168

NEVADA

Las Vegas City Marshal
400 E. Stewart

Las Vegas, NV 89101
(702) 386-6637

NEW YORK

City Marshal's Office
City Hall, Rm. 215
Albany, NY 12207
(518) 434-5106

New York Dept.
of Investigations
City of New York
Marshal's Bureau
(212) 825-5953

Buffalo City Marshal
50 Delaware
Buffalo, NY
(716) 847-8430

City Marshal's Office
Public Safety Bldg., Rm. 508
511 S. State St.
Syracuse, NY 13202
Contact: Onondaga County
Sheriff's Dept.
425-3044

OKLAHOMA

City Marshal's Office
200 N. Shartol
Oklahoma City, OK 73102

Barry Jones Auction Co.
2132 SW 52nd Place
Oklahoma City, OK 73119
(405) 685-1621

TEXAS

City Marshal's Office

317

715 E. Eighth St.
Austin, TX 78701

Personal Goods Auctioned by:
Cleghorn Associates
7301 Camp Cove
Austin, TX 78749
(512) 892-0109

Autos (Confiscated & City Vehicles)
Auctioned by:
Rene Bates Auctioneers
Route 4
McKinney, TX 75070
(214) 548-9636

City Marshal's Office
811 Westheimer
Houston, TX 77006

Probate Departments

You may contact the following probate departments for information leading to the acquisition of property or merchandise, either at auction or before it gets to auction. They will give you further information about how to find out about such auctions or direct you to the person who can help you further.

ALABAMA
Mobile County
Chief Clerk (205) 690-8505

ARIZONA

Pheonix
Maricopa County
Chief Clerk (602) 497-4310

Tuscon
Pima County
Registrar (602) 740-8727

CALIFORNIA

Sacramento
Sacramento County
Examiner (916) 440-5621

San Jose
Santa Clara County
Filings (408) 299-2971

San Diego
San Diego County
(916) 236-3781

San Fransisco
San Francisco County
(415) 554-5073

Riverside
Riverside County
(714) 787-6362

Anaheim/Santa Ana
Orange County
(714) 834-2237

Fresno

Fresno County
(209) 488-3618

Los Angeles
Los Angeles County
(213) 974-1234

Bakersfield
Kern County
(805) 861-2044

COLORADO

Denver
Denver County
(303) 575-2263

CONNECTICUT

Hartford
Hartford County
(203) 722-6550

Bakersfield
Fairfield County
(203) 255-8226

DELAWARE

Wilmington
New Castle County
(302) 571-2380

FLORIDA

West Palm Beach
Palm Beach County
(407) 355-2900

319

Orlando
Orange County
(407) 244-2058

Sarasota
Sarasota County
(813) 951-5368

Jacksonville
Duval County
(904) 630-2053

Tampa
Hillsborough County
(813) 223-7811

Miami
Dade County
(305) 375-5978

GEORGIA

Atlanta
Fulton County
(404) 730-4070

HAWAII

Honolulu
Honolulu County
(808) 548-5441

ILLINOIS

Chicago
Cook County
(312) 443-6470

INDIANA

Indianapolis
Marion County
(317) 236-4718

Fort Wayne
Allen County
(219) 428-7543

KENTUCKY

Louisville
Jefferson County
(502) 588-4434

LOUISIANA

New Orleans
Orleans County
(504) 536-1633

LOUISANA

Baton Rogue
Parish County
(504) 389-3950

MARYLAND

Baltimore
NOT IN A COUNTY
(301) 752-5131

MASSACHUSETTS

Boston
Suffolk County
(617) 725-8300

MICHIGAN

Lansing
Washtenaw County
(517) 676-0288

Ann Arbor
Washtenaw County
(313) 994-2476

Detroit
Wayne County
(313) 224-5707

Grand Rapids
Kent County
(616) 774-3639

MINNESOTA

St. Paul
Ramsey County
(612) 298-4436

MISSOURI

Kansas City
Jackson County
(816) 881-4552

Clayton
St. Louis County
(314) 889-2629

ST. Louis
NOT IN A COUNTY
(314) 889-2629

NEBRASKA

Omaha
Douglas County
(402) 444-7152

NEVADA

Las Vegas
Clark County
(702) 455-4675

NEW JERSEY

Trenton
Mercer County
(609) 989-6321

NEW MEXICO

Albuquerque
Bernalillo County
(505) 768-4247

NEW YORK

Albany
Albany County
(518) 445-7618

Buffalo
Erie County
(716) 854-7867

New York
Manhattan County
(212) 374-8233

Rochester
Monroe County
(716) 428-5200

Syracuse
Onondaga County
(315) 253-1383

NORTH CAROLINA

Charlotte
Mecklenburg County
(704) 342-6800

Raleigh-Durham
Wake County
(919) 733-2782

OHIO

Akron
Summit County
(216) 379-2350

Cinncinati
Hamilton County
(513) 632-8269

Cleveland
Cuyahoga County
(216) 443-8764

Columbus
Franklin County
(614) 462-3894

Dayton
Montgomery County
(513) 225-4640

Toledo
Lucas County
(419) 245-4775

Youngstown
Mahoning County
(216) 740-2314

OKLAHOMA

Tulsa
Tulsa County
(918) 584-0471 Ext. 2020

Oklahoma City
Oklahoma County
(405) 278-1728

OREGON

Portland
Multnomah County
(503) 248-3016

PENNSYLVANIA

Allentown
Lehigh County
(215) 820-3000

Philadelphia
Philadelphia County
(215) 686-6255

Pittsburgh
Allegheny County
(412) 355-4180

Wilkes-Barre
Luzern County
(717) 822-0764

RHODE ISLAND

Providence
Providence County
(401) 421-7740

SOUTH CAROLINA

Charleston
Charleston County
(803) 723-6783

Greenville/
Spartanburg
Pitt County
(919) 830-6400

TENNESSEE

Knoxville
Knox County
(615) 521-2389

Memphis
Shelby County
(901) 576-4040

Nashville
Davidson County
(615) 259-6091

TEXAS

Austin
Travis County
(512) 473-9258

Dallas
Dallas County
(214) 653-7236

El Paso
El Paso County
(915) 546-2072

Houston
Harris County
(713) 221-6425

San Antonio
Bexar County
(512) 220-2241

UTAH

Salt Lake City
Salt Lake County
(801) 535-5551

VERMONT

Montpelier
Washington County
(802) 223-3405

VIRGINIA

Richmond
NOT IN A COUNTY
(804) 780-4683

Norfolk
NOT IN A COUNTY
(804) 441-5191

WASHINGTON

Seattle
King County
(206) 296-9300

322

WISCONSIN

Milwaukee
Milwaukee County
(414) 278-4444

Urban Homesteading Programs

Some cities have urban homesteading programs, not all do. Those we found that do are as follows. Please contact those that do for further information. Do not get discouraged if something is not available at this time; programs change and positive developments may occur at a later date. Many do have programs and some people are taking advantage of them.

ALABAMA

Mr. William Lindsay
Urban Homesteading Coordinator
Department of Community Development
and Housing
710 N. 20th St.
Birmingham AL 35203
(205) 254-2316

ARIZONA

Mr. Charlie Cochran
Homestead Coordinator
Urban Development and Housing
Department
920 E. Madison, Suite E
Phoenix AZ 85034
(602) 256-3115

COLORADO

Ms. Susan Spinell
Community Development Agency
1425 Kalamath
Denver CO 80204
(303) 572-8121

CONNECTICUT

Mr. William Gardiner
Housing Services Manager
Housing Department
990 Wethersfield Ave
Hartford CT 06114
(203) 722-6400

DELAWARE, Wilmington

Mr. Richard Heffron
Director of Housing Services
Department of Real Estate and Housing
City/County Building
800 French Street, 7th Fl
Wilmington DE 19801
(302) 571-4057 (not active)

FLORIDA, Broward County

Ms. Edna M Frazier
Urban Homesteading Coordinator
Community Development Division
Broward County Board of

County Commissioners
PO Box 14668
115 S Andrews Ave, Rm 3350
Ft. Lauderdale FL 33301
(305) 357-6762

FLORIDA, Dade County

Ms. Gwen Covington
Urban Homesteading Coordinator
Community & Economic Development
140 W Flagler St
Miami FL 33130
(305) 375-3409

FLORIDA, Ft. Lauderdale

Mr. Charles Adams
Community Development Coordinator
Department of Planning and Community
Development
101 N Andrews Ave
Ft. Lauderdale FL 33302
(305) 761-5281

FLORIDA, Hillsborough County

Mr. Vincent Lupo, Director
Office of Community and
 Economic Development
County of Hillsborough
700 Twiggs St, Suite 102
PO Box 1110
Tampa FL 33602
(813) 272-5330

FLORIDA, Jacksonville

Mr. Clifford D. Taffet
Director of Rehabilitation
Department of Housing and
 Urban Development
820 Laura St
Jacksonville FL 32202
(904) 630-3400

325

FLORIDA, Palm Beach County

Ms. Cynthia Matthews
Manager, Housing Section
Division of Community Development
Palm Beach County
801 Evernia St
West Palm Beach FL 33401
(305) 820-3852

FLORIDA, Pompano Beach

Mr. James Hudson
Director of Community Development
City of Pompano Beach
 Planning Department
Community Development Division
PO Drawer 1300
Pompano Beach FL 33061
(305) 786-4068

FLORIDA, St. Petersburg

Mr. Ben Meece
Urban Homesteading Coordinator
PO Box 2842
St. Petersburg FL 33731
(813) 893-7218

FLORIDA, Tampa

Mr. Fernando Noriega
Director of Rehabilitation
1514 Union St
Tampa FL 33607
(813) 223-8920

GEORGIA, Atlanta

Mr. Robert Sumbry, Director
Housing & Physical Development
Department of Community and
 Human Development
878 York Ave SW
Atlanta GA 30310
(404) 658-6664 (not active)

IDAHO, Boise

Mr. Timothy J. Hogland
Director, Boise City Bldg. Dept.
PO Box 500
Boise ID 83701
(208) 384-4272

ILLINOIS, Chicago

Ms. Loistene Roundtree
Homesteading Coordinator
318 S Michigan Ave
Chicago IL 60604
(312) 922-7922

ILLINOIS, Decatur

Ms. Laura Carstens
Homesteading Coordinator
Department of Community Development
One Civic Center Plaza
Decatur IL 62521
(214) 424-2777

ILLINOIS, East St. Louis

Ms. Carolyn Brooks
Division Administrator for Urban
Conservation
Regis Building
320 N 10th St
East N 10th St
East St. Louis IL 62201

ILLINOIS, Harvey

Mr. William Jones
Deputy Director of Rehabilitation
Department of Building & Planning
15320 Broadway Ave
Harvey IL 60426
(312) 339-4200

ILLINOIS, Joliet

Mr. Ernest Richardson
Director Neighborhood Service Div.
Department of Community Development
City Hall
150 West Jefferson St
Joliet IL 60431
(814) 740-2405

ILLINOIS, Rock Island

Ms. Rae Mary
Housing Coordinator
Redevelopment Division
Community Development Department
1528 3rd Ave
Rock Island IL 61201
(309) 793-3350

ILLINOIS, Rockford

Ms. Vicki L. Manson
Neighborhood Development Coordinator
Department of Community Development
City Hall
425 East State St
Rockford IL 61104
(815) 987-5690

INDIANA, Gary

Mrs. Nancy Valentine
Chief Homestead Officer
Department of Housing Conservation
824 Broadway
Gary IN 46402
(219) 883-3102

INDIANA, Indianapolis

Ms. Janet Cline
Assistant Manager
Housing Operations
Economic & Housing Development
Department of Metropolitan Development
148 E Market St, 6th Fl
Indianapolis IN 46204
(317) 663-3480

INDIANA, South Bend

Mrs. Theodore Leverman
Assistant Director
Urban Homesteading
Bureau of Housing
520 N Eclipse Pl
South Bend IN 46628
(219) 284-9475

INDIANA, Terre Haute

Mr. Dean Branson
Real Estate Administrator
Department of Redevelopment
301 City Hall
17 Harding Ave
Terre Haute IN 47807
(812) 232-0018

IOWA, Davenport

Ms. Pat Shean
Finance Specialist
City of Davenport
City Hall
226 W Fourth St
Davenport IA 52801
(319) 326-7748

IOWA, Des Moines

Ms. Nancy Granquist
Executive Director
Des Moines Housing Council, Inc.
1151 24th St
Des Moines IA 50311
(502) 277-6649

IOWA, Sioux City

Ms. Louie Anderson
Rehab. Loan Officer
Community Development Department
PO Box 447
Sioux City IA 51102
(712) 279-6277

KANSAS, Kansas City

Mr. Ed Smith
Community Development Director
One Civic Center Plaza
Kansas City KS 66101
(913) 573-5100

KANSAS, Topeka

Mr. Al Bailey, Director
Department of Community Development
820 S Quincy, Suite 501
Topeka KS 66612
(913) 234-0072

KENTUCKY, Jefferson County

Mr. Fred McMahon
Land Development Supervisor
Community Development of Jefferson
County
719 W Main St
Louisville KY 40202
(502) 625-6550

KENTUCKY, Louisville

Ms. Marcia Miller
Urban Homesteading Coordinator
Department of Housing
727 W Main St
Louisville KY 40202
(502) 587-3736

MARYLAND, Prince Georges County

Mr. Leroy Brown
Department of Housing & Community
Development
Landover Mall East,
Promenade One, Suite 300
3103 Brightseat Rd
Landover MD 20785
(301) 386-5073

MICHIGAN, Detroit

Mr. Russel White
Urban Homesteading Coordinator
Community & Economic Development Dept.
City of Detroit
150 Michigan Ave, 5th Fl
Detroit MI 48226
(312) 224-4943

MICHIGAN, Flint

Mr. Ed Custer
Project Manager
Planning and Development Section
Department of Community and Economic
Development
City of Flint
1101 South Saginaw
City Hall
Flint MI 48502
(313) 766-7410

MICHIGAN, Genesee County

Mr. Thomas A Roach
Homesteading Coordinator
County of Genesee
1101 Beach St, Rm 214
Flint MI 48502-1470
(313) 257-3010

MICHIGAN, Grand Rapids

Ms. Elizabeth Byron
Development Officer
City of Grand Rapids
City Hall, Room 408
300 Monroe Ave NW
Grand Rapids MI 49503
(619) 456-3396

MICHIGAN, Highland Park

Ms. Carrie Davis
Deput Program Manager
City of Highland Park
16480 Woodward Ave
Highland Park MI 48203
(313) 252-2763

MICHIGAN, Inkster

Mr. Clarence Oden
Deputy Director
Community Development Department
2121 Inkster Road
Inkster MI 48141
(313) 565-4100

MICHIGAN, Jackson

Mr. Duane Miller
Urban Homesteading Coordinator
City of Jackson
161 W Michigan Ave
Jackson MI 49201
(517) 788-4187

328

MICHIGAN, Kalamazoo

Ms. Peggy Giem
Grants Program Specialist
Housing and Programs Division
241 West South St
Kalamazoo MI 49007-4796
(616) 385-8225

MICHIGAN, Lansing

Ms. Sandra Hearns
Development Division
Department of Planning & Municipal
Development
City of Lansing
119 Washington Sq
City Hall Annex
Lansing MI 48933
(517) 483-4040

MICHIGAN, Saginaw

Ms. Rosetta Harrell
Urban Homesteading Coordinator
Dept of Neighborhood Services
City of Saginaw
1315 South Washington Ave
City Hall
Saginaw MI 48601
(517) 776-1530

MINNESOTA, Anoka County

Ms. Jo Ann Wright
CDBG Coordinator
Anoka County
Anoka County Courthouse
325 E Main St
Anoka MN 55303
(612) 421-4760 Ext 1178
(Serves Anoka and Columbia Heights)

MINNESOTA, Dakota County

Mr. Mark Ulfers
Executive Director
Dakota County HRA
2496-145th Street W
Rosemont MN 55068
(612) 423-4800
(Serves Farmington, Hasings, Lakeville,
Rosemount, and West St. Paul)

MINNESOTA, Duluth

Mr. Dennis Zimmerman
Rehabilitation Director of Duluth
Housing Redevelopment Authority
PO Box 16898
301 E 2nd St
Duluth MN 55816-0898
(218) 762-2876

MINNESOTA, Minneapolis

Mr. Bill Konrak
Project Coordinator
Minneapolis Community
Development Agency
331 2nd Avenue, 9th Fl
Minneapolis MN 55415
(612) 342-1354

MINNESOTA, St. Cloud

(Vacant)
Community Development Coordinator
St. Cloud Housing and Redevelopment
Authority
619 Germain Mall, Suite 212
St. Cloud MN 56301
(612) 252-0880

MINNESOTA, St. Paul

Mr. Warren Frost
Project Manager
Department of Planning and Economic
Development
25 West Fourth St
City Hall Annex, 12th Fl
St. Paul MN 55102
(612) 228-3354

MISSOURI, Berkeley

Mr. Bill Luchini
Assistant to City Manager
Community Development
City of Berkeley
6140 North Hanley Rd
Berkeley MO 63134
(314) 524-3313 Ext 129

329

MISSOURI, Ferguson

Ms. Deane Wagner, Director
Community Development
City of Ferguson
110 Church St
Ferguson MO 63135
(314) 521-7721

MISSOURI, Hillsdale

(Also serves Northwoods, Pagedale, Velda
Village, Vinita Park)
Mr. Tim Fischesser
Executtive Director
Normandy Municipal Council
7717 Natural Bridge Rd
St. Louis MO 63121
(314) 381-0066

MISSOURI, Jennings

Ms. Jan Winfield
Housing Coordinator
City of Jennings
2120 Hord Ave
Jennings MO 63136
(314) 388-1164

MISSOURI, Kansas City

Mr. James M Vaughn, Director
Department of Housing and Community
Development
City Hall, 14th Fl
414 E 12th Street
Kansas City MO 64106
(816) 274-2201

MISSOURI, St. Joseph

Ms. Sue Johnson
Community Development Director
11th and Frederick
St. Joseph MO 64501
(816) 271-4642

MISSOURI, St. Louis County

Mr. Sam Green
Director
St. Louis County Housing Authority
8865 Natural Bridge Rd
PO Box 23886
St. Louis MO 63132
(314) 428-3200

NEBRASKA, Omaha

Mr. Michael Saklar
Chief Acquisition & Relocation Officer
Housing & Community Development
Omaha-Douglas Civic Center
1819 Farnam St, Rm 401
Omaha NE 68103
(402) 444-5170

NEW JERSEY, Bridgeton

Mr. Raymond H. Maier
Assistant Director for Community
Development
City of Bridgeton
City Hall Annex
Office of Community and Economic
Development
Bridgeton NJ 08302
(609) 455-3230 Ext 266

NEW JERSEY, Camden

Mr. Joe Di Taranto
Housing Coordinator
Division of Housing Services
Camden City Hall, Room 222
Market St
Camden NJ 08102
(609) 757-7344

NEW YORK, Babylon

Ms.Sybil Mizzi
Manager, Community Development
Town of Babylon
Pan Tech Management Corporation
100 W Main St
Babylon NY 11702
(516) 661-6200

NEW YORK, Brookhaven

Ms. Geraldine Sheridan
Commissioner of Housing, Community
Development and Intergovernmental Affairs
Town of Brookhaven
3233 Route 112
Medford NY 11763
(516) 736-8400
(Mr. Jesus Garcia, Homesteading
Coordinator)

NEW YORK, Freeport (Village of)

Mr. Eric Hemphill, Director
Planning and Community Development
Freeport Community Development Agency
Village Hall,
46 N Ocean Ave
Freeport NY 11520
(516) 378-4000 Ext 203

NEW YORK, Hempstead (Town of)

Mr. Robert Francis
Commissioner
Department of Planning and Economic
Development
200 N Franklin St
Hempstead NY 11550
(516) 538-7100

NEW YORK, Hempstead (Village of)

Mr. Alan Schuman
Commissioner
Community Development Agency
Incorporated Village of Hempstead
202 Jackson St
Hempstead NY 11550
(516) 485-5737

NEW YORK, Islip (Town of)

Mr. Howard Quinn
Executive Director
Community Development Agency
15 Shore Lane, PO Box 587P
Bay Shore NY 11706
(515) 665-1185

NEW YORK, Niagara Falls

Mr. William K. Clark
Acting Community Development Director
City of Niagara Falls
City Hall, 745 Main St
Niagara Falls NY 14302
(716) 278-8261

OHIO, Canton

Ms. Sheila Barrino
Program Coordinator
218 Cleveland Ave SW
Canton OH 44702
(216) 489-3040

OHIO, Cincinnati

Mr. Mike Hunley
Homesteading Coordinator
HURC
415 West Court St
Cincinnati OH 45203
(513) 352-3473

OHIO, Cleveland

Ms. Barbara Hayes
Urban Homestead Coordinator
Rehabilitation Division
601 Lakeside Ave
Cleveland OH 44114
(216) 664-2869

OHIO, Columbus

Mr. Fred Dean
Department of Development
Division of Community Development
140 Marconi Blvd, 7th Fl
Columbus OH 43215
(614) 222-6059

OHIO, Cuyahoga County

Ms. Mary Jo Rawlins
Assistant Manager Rehabilitation
Cuyahoga County Department of
Community Development
112 Hamilton
Cleveland OH 44114
(216) 443-7543

OHIO, Dayton

Mr. Jim Martone
Director of Housing Services
City-Wide Development Corporation
40 West Fourth, Suite 1400
Miami Valley Towers
Dayton OH 45402
(513) 226-0457

OHIO, Franklin County

Ms. Kathy McCready
Urban Homesteading Coordinator
Mid-Ohio Regional Planning Commission
385 East Main St
Columbus OH 43215
(614) 228-2663

OHIO, Lima

Richard S Schroeder
Director of Planning
City of Lima
219 E Market St
Lima OH 45801
(419) 228-5462 Ext 250

OHIO, Montgomery County

Ms. Judy Beasley
Loan Officer
Montgomery County Corporation
1700 Miami Valley Tower
40 West Fourth St
Dayton OH 45402
(513) 225-6328

OHIO, Springfield

Mr. Joe Harner
Rehabilitation Coordinator
76 E High St
Springfield OH 45502
(513) 324-7368

OHIO, Toledo

Mr. Edward Sherman
Project Administrator
Department of Community Development
1 Government Center, Suite 1800
Toledo OH 43604
(419) 245-1400

OHIO, Warren

Mr. John Foley
Community Development Director
Community Development Department
525 Pine Ave SE
Warren OH 44483
(216) 841-2595

OHIO, Youngstown

Mr. Joe Allesl
Acting Director, Urban Homesteading
Community Development Agency, Millcreek
496 Glenwood Ave
Youngstown OH 44502
(216) 746-8416

OKLAHOMA, Lawton

Mr. Frank Robinson
Homesteading Coordinator
103 Fourth St
Lawton OK 73501
(405) 581-3375

OKLAHOMA, Tulsa

Ms. Bobbie Cunningham
Housing Assistance Administrator
Department of City Development
1436 N Cincinnati
Tulsa OK 74106
(918) 588-9088

OREGON, Eugene

Mr. Wayne Bumgarner
Development Department
72 West Broadway, Suite 200
Eugene OR 97401
(503) 687-5443

OREGON, Malheur County

Ms. Merlene Bourasa
Urban Homesteading Coordinator
Housing Authority of Malheur County
959 Fortner St
Ontario OR 97914
(503) 889-9661

OREGON, Multnomah County

Ms. Jane Burda
Urban Homesteading Coordinator
Community Development Division
Multnomah County
2115 SE Morrison St
Portland OR 97214
(503) 248-3631

OREGON, Portland

Ms. Trish Brown
Project Coordinator
Portland Development Commission
1120 SW Fifth Ave, Suite 1102
Portland OR 97204-1968
(503) 796-5304

PENNSYLVANIA, Allentown

Mr. Raymond Polaski
Director, Bureau of Code Enforcement and
Rehabilitation
Public Safety Building, Room 20
425 Hamilton St
Allentown PA 18101
(214) 437-7690

PENNSYLVANIA, Chester

Mr. Robert J. Kafalos
Director of Redevelopment
Chester Redevelopment Authority
401 Avenue of the States
PO Box 437
Chester PA 19016
(215) 447-7850

PENNSYLVANIA, Harrisburg

Mr. Dan Leppo
Bureau of Neighborhood Development
Department of Community and Economic
Development
City Government Center
10 N Second St
Harrisburg PA 17101
(717) 255-6433

PENNSYLVANIA, Lebanon

Mr. Melvin Caplan, Director
Department of Community Development
303 Chestnut St
Lebanon PA 17042
(717) 274-1401

PENNSYLVANIA, Philadelphia

Mr. Kenneth Woodson
Administrator
Home Improvement Programs
Philadelphia Housing Development Corp.
1234 Market St, 10th Floor
Philadelphia PA 19107
(215) 686-9371

PUERTO RICO, Bayamon

Ms. Jacqueline Matos
Planning Office
Municipality of Bayamon
Box 1588
Bayamon PR 00619
(809) 787-0451

PUERTO RICO, Ceiba

Mr. Francisco Nieves
Municipality of Ceiba
Box 224
Ceiba PR 00635
(809) 885-3020

PUERTO RICO, Ponce

Mr. Thamar Carrasquillo
Rehabilitation Housing Division
Municipality of Ponce
PO Box 1709
Ponce PR 00731
(809) 840-4141 Ext 251

PUERTO RICO, San Juan

Mr. Francis Gonzalez
Office of Housing and Community
Development
Municipality of San Juan
PO Box 2138
San Juan PR 00936
(809) 756-7300 Ext 3423

PUERTO RICO, Toa Alta

Mr. Hector M Vazquez
Municipality of Toa Alta
Box 82
Toa Alta PR 00758
(809) 870-1350

SOUTH CAROLINA, Anderson

Mr. Jerry Knighton, Jr.
Director of Community Development
City of Anderson
PO Box 2827
Anderson SC 29622
(803) 231-2230

SOUTH CAROLINA, Columbia

Mr.Darryl Bullock
Acquisition and Relocation Officer
Community Development Department
City of Columbia
PO Box 147
Columbia SC 29217
(803) 733-8311

SOUTH CAROLINA, Greenville County

Mr. Troy Newman
Acquisition and Relocation Specialist
Greenville County Redevelopment Authority
NCNB Plaza, PP54
Greenville SC 29601
(803) 242-9801

TENNESSEE, Knoxville

Ms. Diana Gerard
Housing Rehabilitation Manager
Department of Housing and Urban Affairs
PO Box 1631
Knoxville TN 37901
(615) 521-2120

TENNESSEE, Shelby County

Mr. Tim Bolding, Administrator
Department of Neighborhoods, Housing
and Economic Development
204 N 2nd Street-Basement
Memphis TN 38105
(901) 576-4523

TEXAS, Fort Worth

Mr. Will Williamson
UH Coordinator
Housing & Human Services Department
1000 Throckmorton
Fort Worth TX 76102
(817) 870-7331

TEXAS, Houston

Ms. Margaret Wallace
Program Coordinator
Department of Planning and Development
PO Box 1562
900 Babgy Street, Suite 4100
Houston TX 77251
(713) 247-1000

VIRGINIA, Danville

Mr. Lars Laubinger
Urban Homesteading Coordinator
Department of Community Development
City of Danville
PO Box 3300
Danville VA 24543
(804) 799-5260

VIRGINIA, Newport News

Mrs. Gerald Hickman
Urban Homesteading Coordinator
Newport News Development and Housing
Authority
PO Box 77
Newport News VA 23607
(804) 247-9701

VIRGINIA, Portsmouth

Mr. Charles R. Johnson
Community Planning Analyst
City of Portsmouth
PO Box 820
Portsmouth VA 23705
(804) 393-8356

VIRGINIA, Richmond

Mr. Duane Finger
Urban Homesteading Coordinator
Richmond Redevelopment and Housing
Authority
Box 26887
Richmond VA 23261
(804) 644-9881

VIRGINIA, Roanoke

Mr. James Bean
Urban Homesteading Coordinator
Roanoke Redevelopment and Housing
Authority
PO Box 6359
Roanoke VA 24017
(703) 342-4561

WASHINGTON, Spokane

Mr. Michael Adolfae
Manager, Community and Economic
Development Department
Municipal Building
808 Spokane Falls Blvd
Spokane WA 99201-3333
(509) 456-4306

WASHINGTON, Yakima

Ms. Dixie Kracht
CDBG Manager
Office of Housing and Neighborhood
Conservation
112 South 8th Street
Yakima WA 98901
(509) 575-6101

WISCONSIN, Kenosha

Ms. Donna Dawson
Urban Homesteading Coordinator
Department of City Development
812 56th Street
Kenosha WI 53140
(414) 656-8055

WISCONSIN, Milwaukee

Ms. Kris Martinsek
Urban Homesteading Coordinator
Department of City Development
809 No. Broadway
Milwaukee WI 53201
(414) 223-5600

WISCONSIN, Racine

Mr. Richard Linsmeier
Assistant Director of City Development
City of Racine
730 Washington Ave
Racine WI 53403
(414) 636-9151

STATE Offices:

MINNESOTA, State of

Ms. Judi Bruggeman
Program Director
Northwest Minnesota
Multi-County HRA
PO Box 128
Mentor MN 56736
(218) 637-2431
(Serves Fosston, Argyle, Fertile,
Alvarado,Ada, Crookston, Red Lake Falls,
and Pennington County)

OHIO, State of

Mr. Greg Capers
Program Coordinator
Spring, Inc.
Acrue Building, Suite 707
6 West High Street
Springfield OH 45502
(513) 323-7997
(Serves Zenia and Fairborn in Greene
County, and Bethel Township in Clark
County)

VIRGINIA, State of

Mr. David McKelvy
Planning and Research Program Manager
Virginia Housing Development Authority
13 South 13th Street
Richmond VA 23219
(804) 782-1986
(Serves Suffolk, Brunswick/
Dinwiddie, Tazewell)

Tax Sales

Tax Certificate sales occur in some states. You can also purchase property through these county tax offices at their auctions. Please contact those you wish whose auctions you want to attend:

ALABAMA

Jefferson County Tax Sales
Tax Collector's Office
716 North 21st St.
Birmingham, AL 35263-0010
(205) 325-5500

ARIZONA

Pima County Tax Sales
Treasurer's Office
Attn: Delinquent Taxes Dept.
115 North Church Ave.
Tucson, AZ 85701
(602) 792-8342

CALIFORNIA

Kern County Tax Sales
Real Estate
Tax Collector's Office
Redemption Division
1415 Truxton Avenue
Bakersfield, CA 93301
(805) 861-2357

Los Angeles County Tax Sales
Tax Collector
225 North Hill
Los Angeles, CA 90012
(213) 974-2045

San Diego County Tax Sales
1600 Pacific Hgwy.
San Diego, CA 92101
(619) 236-3121

El Paso County Tax Sales
Treasurer's Office
27 East Vermijo Avenue
Colorado Springs, CO 80903
(719) 520-6666

COLORADO

Denver County Tax Sales
Delinquent Real and Personal Property
Treasury Division
144 West Colfax Avenue
Denver, CO 80202
(303) 575-3458

CONNECTICUT

Hartford County Tax Sales
Tax Collector's Office
550 Main Street
Hartford, CT 06103
(203) 722-6096

New Haven County Tax Sales
Real Estate Services
209 Orange St.
New Haven, CT 06510
(203) 787-7094

Fairfield County Tax Sales
Tax Collector
888 Washington Blvd.
Stamford, CT 06901
(203) 977-4089

Waterbury County Tax Sales
Tax Collector's Office
235 Grand Street
Waterbury, CT. 06702
(203) 574-6811

DELAWARE

New Castle County Tax Sales
Sheriff's Office
11th & King Street
Wilmington, DE 19899
(302) 571-7564

DISTRICT OF COLUMBIA

337

Washington D.C. County Tax Sales
Real Property Tax Office
300 Indiana Avenue, N.W.
Washington, DC 20001
(202) 727-6441

FLORIDA

Broward County Tax Sales
Revenue Collector
Delinquent Real Estate
501 South East 6th Street
Fort Lauderdale, FL 33301
(305) 765-4604

Duval County Tax Sales
Circuit Court Clerk's Office
330 East Bay Street
Jacksonville, FL 32202
(904) 630-2059

Dade County Tax Sales
Tax Collection Division
Delinquent Real Estate Tax
140 West Flagler Street
Miami, FL 33130
(305) 375-5455

Ocelot County Tax Sales
Attn: Collection Division
Florida Department of Revenue
541 S. Orlando Avenue, Suite 301
Maitland, FL 32751
(407) 644-3133

Pinellas County Tax Sales
Tax Collector's Office
315 Court Street
Courthouse, 3rd Fl.
Clearwater, FL 34616
(813) 462-3383

Hillsborough County Tax Sales
Tax Collector
Hillsborough County Courthouse
Tampa, FL 33602
Attn: Delinquent Real Estate Tax (813) 272-6070

GEORGIA

DeKalb County Tax Sales
Tax Commissioner's Office
Delinquent Tax Office

120 West Trinity Place, Rm. 110
Decatur, GA 30030
(404) 371-2107

HAWAII

Honolulu County Tax Sales
Department of Taxation
830 Punchbowl Street
Honolulu, HI 96813
(808) 523-4972

ILLINOIS

Cook County Tax Sales
Cook County Collector's Office
118 North Clark
Chicago, IL 30344
(312) 443-6234

Peoria County Tax Sales
Peoria County Clerk
Peoria County Courthouse
324 Main Street, Room 109
Peoria, IL 61620
(309) 672-6059

Winnebago County Tax Sales
Winnebago County Treasurer
400 West State Street
Courthouse, Room 122
Rockford, IL 61105
(815) 987-3010

INDIANA

Vanderburgh County Tax Sales
Vanderburgh County Treasurer's Office
Civic Center Complex, Room 210
Evansville, IN 47708
(812) 426-5248

Lake County Tax Sales
Lake County Treasurer's Office
11 East 4th Avenue
Gary, IN 46402
(219) 881-6302

Marion County Tax Sales
Marion County Treasurer's Office
City/County Building, Room 1060
Indianapolis, IN 46204
(317) 236-4040

South Bend County Tax Sales

338

County/City Building
227 W. Jefferson
South Bend, IN 46601
(219) 284-9528

IOWA

Cedar Rapids county Tax Sales
Tax Assessor's Office
930 1st Street, S.W.
Cedar Rapids, IA 52404
(319) 398-3464

Davenport County Tax Sales
County Treasurer's Department
416 West 4th
Davenport, IA 52801
(319) 326-8670

Polk County Tax Sales
Polk County Treasurer's Office
111 Court Avenue
Des Moines, IA 50309
(515) 286-3060

KANSAS

Topeka County Tax Sales
County Counselor
200 East 7th, Room 203
Topeka, KS 66603
(913) 291-4042

Sedgwick County Tax Sales
Foreclosure Department
Sedgwick County Courthouse
525 North Main Street
Wichita, KS 67203
(316) 268-7482

KENTUCKY

Fayette County Tax Sales
Master Commissioner's Office
Fayette County Court Clerk
910 1st National Building
167 West Main, Suite 910
Lexington, KY 40507
(606) 254-1637

Jefferson County Tax Sales
Jefferson County Courthouse
Room 100A
Louisville, KY 40202
(502) 625-6016

LOUISIANA

Baton Rouge County Tax Sales
Baton Rouge Sheriff's Department
Civil Division, Property Tax Office
P.O. Box 3277
Baton Rouge, LA 70821
(504) 389-4810

Jefferson Parish County Tax Sales
Jefferson Parish Sheriff's Office
Tax Department
P.O. Box 130
Gretna, LA 70054
(504) 363-5714

Shreveport County Tax Sales
Sheriff's Office Tax Department
501 Texas Street, Room 101
Shreveport, LA 71101-5410
(318) 226-6538

MARYLAND

Baltimore County Tax Sales
Tax Sales Division
200 North Holiday Street, Room 1
Baltimore, MD 21202
(301) 396-3981

MASSACHUSETTS

Boston County Tax Sales
Deputy Commissioner
Department of Revenue
100 N. Cambridge Street
Boston, MA 02204
(617) 727-4201

Springfield County Tax Sales
Redevelopment Authority
73 State Street
Springfield, MA 01103
(413) 787-6538

Worcester County Tax Sales
Bureau of Land Use Control
Francis Donahue, Tax Title Custodian
City Hall, Room 209
455 Main Street
Worcester, MA 01608
(508) 799-1146

MICHIGAN

Washtenaw County Tax Sales
County Treasurer's Office
101 East Huron
Ann Arbor, MI 48104
(313) 994-2520

Wayne County Tax Sales
Department of Treasury
400 Monroe, Suite 520
Detroit, MI 48226
(313) 224-5990

Genesee County Tax Sales
County Treasurer's Office
1101 Beach Street
Flint, MI 48502
(313) 257-3054

Kent County Tax Sales
County Treasurer's Office
P.O. Box Y 300 Monroe Avenue
Grand Rapids, MI 49501
(616) 774-3641

Ingram County Tax Sales
Treasurer's Office, Courthouse
P.O. Box 215
Mason, MI 48854
(517) 676-0251

MINNESOTA

Hennepin County Tax Sales
Forfeited Property Department
300 South 6th Street, Room 603A
Minneapolis, MN 55487
(612) 348-3734

MISSISSIPPI

Hinds County Tax Sales
County Tax Collector
429 S. West Street
Jackson, MS 39215
(601) 968-6587

MISSOURI

Jackson County Tax Sales
County Manager of Revenue
Property Tax Division
415 East 12th Street, Room 100

Kansas City, MO 64106
(816) 881-3232

Greene County Tax Sales
Tax Collector
940 Boonville
Springfield, MO 65802
(417) 868-4036

St. Louis County Tax Sales
Tax Collector's Office
41 South Central
St. Louis, MO 63105
(314) 889-2208

Lewis & Clark County Tax Sales
Department of Treasury
City County Building
316 North Clark
Helena, MT 59620
(406) 443-1010

NEBRASKA

Lancaster County Tax Sales
County Treasurer's Office
City-County Building
555 South 10th
Lincoln, NE 68508
(402) 471-7425

Douglas County Tax Sales
County Treasurer's Office
Real Estate Division
Civic Center
1819 Farnam
Omaha, NC 68183
(402) 447-7272

NEVADA

Clark County Tax Sales
Treasurer's Office
225 Bridger
Las Vegas, NV 89155
(702) 455-4323

Washoe County Tax Sales
Washoe County Treasurer's Office
P.O. Box 11130
Reno, NV 89520
(702) 328-2510

NEW JERSEY

340

Union County Tax Sales
Tax Collector's Office
50 Winfield Scott Plaza
Elizabeth, NJ 07201
(201) 820-4115

Hudson County Tax Sales
County Tax Lien Department
280 Grove Street
Jersey City, NJ 07302
(201) 547-5125

Essex County Tax Sales
Property Tax Division
920 Broad Street, Room 104
Newark, NJ 07102
(201) 733-8060

Passaic County Tax Sales
Tax Assessor's Office
City Hall
155 Market Street
Paterson, NJ 47505
(201) 881-3484

NEW MEXICO

Albuquerque County Tax Sales
Taxation & Revenue Department
First National Bank Building, East
5301 Central Avenue, N.W.
Albuquerque, NM 87108
(505) 827-0881

NEW YORK

Albany County Tax Sales
Real Property Tax Service Agency
112 State Street, Room 820
Albany, NY 12207
(518) 447-7050

Erie County Tax Sales
Real Property Taxation
95 Franklin Street
Buffalo, NY 14202
(716) 858-8333

New York County Tax Sales
Department of General Services
Department of Real Estate
2 Lafayette Street
New York, NY 10048
(212) 566-7550

Monroe County Tax Sales
City Hall, Room 023B
30 Church Street
Rochester, NY 14614
(716) 428-6951

Onondaga County Tax Sales
Finance Department
15th Floor
421 Montgomery Street
Syracuse, NY 13202
(315) 425-2426

Westchester County Tax Sales
Real Property Tax Commission
110 Grove Street
White Plains, NY 10601
(914) 285-4325

NORTH CAROLINA

Mecklenburg County Tax Sales
Tax Collector
P.O. Box 31457
Charlotte, NC 28231
(704) 336-4600

Guilford County Tax Sale
County Attorney's Office
Delinquent Tax Department
301 W. Market Street
Greensboro, NC 27401
(919) 373-3852

Forsyth County Tax Sales
County Attorney's Office
704 Hall of Justice
Winston-Salem, NC 27101
(919) 727-2216

NORTH DAKOTA

Burleigh County Tax Sales
Auditor's Office
221 North 5th Street
Bismarck, ND 58501
(701) 222-6713

OHIO

Hamilton County Tax Sales
Delinquent Taxes, Real Estate
138 East Court Street

341

Room 401
Cincinnati, OH 45202
(513) 632-8570

Cuyahoga Falls
Sheriff's Department
Land Sales
1215 W. 3rd Street
Cleveland, OH 44113
(216) 443-6038

Lucas County Tax Sales
Treasurer's Office
Foreclosure Department, 6th Floor
One Government Center
Toledo, OH 43604
(419) 245-4057

OKLAHOMA

Oklahoma County Tax Sales
County Treasurer's Office
320 Robert S. Kerr
Oklahoma City, OK 73102
(405) 278-1300

Tulsa County Tax Sales
Treasurer's Office
Delinquent Tax Department
Tulsa County Admin. Building
500 South Denver
Tulsa, OK 74103
(918) 584-0471 Ext. 3340, 3350

OREGON

Lane County Tax Sales
Foreclosure Department
Property Tax Division
125 East 8th Avenue
Eugene, OR 97401
(503) 687-4174

Clackamas County Property Management
902 Abernethy
Oregon City, OR 97045
(503) 650-3335

Lehigh County Tax Sales
Tax Claims B
Delinquent Tax Office
455 Hamilton
Allentown, PA 18101
(215) 820-3119

RHODE ISLAND

Providence County Tax Sales
Tax Collector, City Hall
25 Dorrance Street
Providence, RI 02903
(401) 331-5252

SOUTH CAROLINA

Richland County Tax Sales
County Treasurer's Office
2020 Hampton Street
P.O. Box 11947
Columbia, SC 29211
(803) 748-4900

SOUTH DAKOTA

Hughes County Tax Sales
Treasurer's Office
104 E. Capitol
Pierre, SD 57501
(605) 224-9231

TENNESSEE

Davidson County Tax Sales
Chancery Court
Metro Courthouse, Room 2
Nashville, TN 37201
(615) 259-5526

TEXAS

Randall County Tax Sales
Tax Office
P.O. Box 997
Canyon, TX 79015
(806) 655-7001 Ext. 275

Travis County Tax Sales
Tax Assessor & Collector
P.O. Box 1748
Austin, TX 78767
(512) 473-9473

Harris County Tax Sales
1001 Preston Street
Houston, TX 77002
(713) 224-1919

UTAH

Salt Lake County Tax Sales
Auditor's Office
Office N-2200
2001 South State Street
Salt Lake City, UT 84111
(801) 468-3381

VERMONT

Waterbury County Tax Sales
(Ms. Sandra Brodeur)
Cost Assessment
51 South Main Street
Waterbury, VT 05676
(802) 241-3500

VIRGINIA

Richmond County Tax Sales
County Attorney's Office
2 E. Clay Street
Richmond, VA 23261
(804) 788-4408

WASHINGTON

Thurston County Tax Sales
Sheriff's Office
2000 Lakeridge Dr.
Olympia, WA 98502
(206) 786-5500

WEST VIRGINIA

Kanawha County Tax Sales
State Auditor's Office
Land Development Department
State Capitol Building
Room 212
Charleston, WV 25305
(304) 348-2262

WISCONSIN

Dane County Tax Sales
County Treasurer's Office
210 Martin Luther King Blvd.
Room 114
Madison, WI 53709
(608) 266-4151

Private Auctioneers

Many government agencies use various private auctioneers. We have compiled the following list for your use. Feel free to call them and get on their mailing lists. This list is, by no means, complete. You may need to call auctioneers from your phone book for further lists of those who do auctions for various government agencies.

This list represents private auctioneers who are not government agents. They are under a long-term or short-term contract for specific auctions held on behalf of the government agency.

ATLANTA

Jim Rouse
P.O. Box 6527
Atlanta,Georia 30315
(404) 622-4455

Arwood Auction Company
P.O. Box 250085
Atlanta, Georgia 30325
(404) 352-0110

The Dobbins Company
P.O. Box 2001 Station N.
Atlanta, Georgia 30325
(404)352-2638

Hudson and Marshall
4751 Best Road - Suite 300
Atlanta, Georgia 30337
(404) 763-0211

BOSTON

Jerome J. Manning Company Inc.
P.O.Box 10
Yarmouth Post, MA 02675
(508) 362-8171

John J. Nolan Real Estate Marketing
Services
College Park - Nantuckett
Building 720 Washington
Hanover, MA 02339
(617) 826-5452

Paul Saperstein Auctioneers
148 State Street

Boston, MA 02109
(617)-227-6553

Garrett Auctioneers
134 Newberry
Peabody, MA 01960
(508) 535-3271

Barton K. Hyte Company
15 Taft Street
Marble Head, MA 01945
(617) 720-0939

CHICAGO

Hanzel Galleries
1120 S. Michigan
Chicago, IL 60605
(312) 922-6234

Michael Natchbar
4040 N. Kedzie
Chicago, IL 60168
(312) 539-7460

Marcie Rath
38 W. 196th _ Route 20
Elgin, IL 60120
(312) 695-0388

Auction Services Inc.
5338 North Lotus Ave.
Chicago, IL 60630
(312) 631-2255

Sheldon F. Good and Company
333 West Wacker Dr. Suite 450
Chicago, IL 60606

(312) 630-0915

CINCINNATI

A-1 Auctioneers
6018 Vine St. Elmwood Place
Cincinnati, Ohio 45216
(513) 641-3467

Delbert Cox and Arthur Auctioneers
4674 Cincinnati-Brookville Rd.
Hmiliton, Ohio 45013
(513) 738-3475

Joel T. Wilson and Company
211 E. Main Street
Cincinnati, Ohio
(513) 732-6300

Semple and Associates Inc.
Box 44006
Cincinnati, Ohio
(513) 831-6113

CLEVELAND

Bankers Motor Vehicles, Inc.
4985 W. 150th Street
Cleveland, Ohio 44135
(216) 676-5920

Donn and Associates
21437 North Park Drive
Cleveland, Ohio 44126
(216) 331-5505

Hart Galleries
2311 Westheimer
Houston, Texas 77098
(713) 524-2979

Rosen and Company
319 The Arcade
Cleveland, Ohio 44114
(216) 621-1860

Grossman Inc.
3749 Grosvenor Rd.
S. Euclid, Ohio 44118
(216) 932-0777

Bambeck Auctioneers Inc.
Route 1 Box 405
Dover, Ohio 44622
(216) 343-1437

DALLAS

Keith Carey
127 Dividend Court
Arlington, Texas 76012
(817) 265-1852

Pollack, Southwest
12750 Merit Drive
Suite 830
Dallas, Texas 75251
(214) 239-9788

Rosen Systems Inc.
2520 W. Mockingbird Lane
Dallas, Texas 75235
(214) 350-2381

Miller and Miller Auctioneers Inc.
2525 Ridgemar Boulevard Suite 100
Fort Worth, Texas 76116
(817) 732-4888

Rene Bates Auctioneers Inc.
Route 4
McKinney, Texas 75070
(214) 584-9636

Jim Keepings Auctions
5103 Lawnview
Dallas, Texas 75227
(214) 388-8721

Jim Short - Nelson International
11811 Preston Rd.
Suite 100
Dallas, Texas 75230
(214) 980-7539

DENVER

Olde Cumberlin Auctioneers
1155 N. Colorado Avenue
Box 248
Brush, Colorado 80723
(303) 842-2822

Donald Freedburge & Associates
2734 S. Milwaukee St.
Denver, Colorado 80210
(303) 758-1510

McCrea & Company Auctioneers
5895 East 72nd Avenue
Commerce City, Colorado 80022
(303) 289-4437

Colorado Auction Service
P.O. Box 33
Louveires, Colorado 80131
(speak with Red Freisen)
(303) 791-7243

Larry Latham Aucioneers Inc.
320 West Olive
Fort Collins, Colorado 80521
(303) 482-2828

DETROIT

Mr. Bill Stanton
144 S. Main
Vermontville, Michigan 49096
(517) 726-0181

P.H.C. of Michigan
24001 Greater Mack Avenue, Suite C
St. Claire Shores, Michigan 48080
(313) 772-7710

Midwest Auto
14666 Telegraph
Detroit, Michigan 48239
(313) 538-2100

Farris Brothers Furniture
6665 W. Vernor
Detroit, Michigan 48209
(313) 843-5720

Robert Williams & Company
17376 W. 12 Mile Road
Southfield, Michigan 48076
(313) 559-5551

L. M. Koploy & Company
23100 Providence Dr. Suite 192
Detroit, Michigan 48075
(313) 559-0660

HOUSTON

Houston Auctions
701 N. Sheppard
Houston, Texas 77007
(713) 862-4556

Windsor Auctions
2117 Judiway
Houston, Texas 77018
(713) 680-8001

Fuller Commercial Brokers
1990 Post Oak Boulevard
Houston, Texas 77056
(713) 850-8400

Federal Auctions
713 Lehman Street
Houston, Texas 77018
(713) 688-6688

Hart Galleries
2311 Westheimer
Houston, Texas 77098
(713) 524-2979

Martin Auctioneers Company
P.O. Box 1282
Sheppard, Texas 77026
(713) 692-6837

INDIANAPOLIS

Commercial Liquidators of America
1453 East Washington
Indianapolis, Indiana 46204
(317) 632-8040

Allied Auctioneers
100 N Road
Indianapolis, Indiana
(317) 897-5268

Heimel Auction Service
59 N. Second
Beechgrove, Indiana 46107
(317) 783-9627

Herman Strakis
3333 W. Tory
Indianapolis, Indiana 46225
(317) 244-8063

Marsh Auction Gallery
1205 E. New York Street
Indianapolis, Indiana 46202
(317) 263-3030

KANSAS CITY

DeWeese Auctions (Missouri Auction School)
1600 Genesee
Kansas City, Missouri 64102
(816) 421-7117

Roger Porter

346

1036 W. Ironwood
Olathe, Kansas 66061
(913) 782-8009

Alpyne Auctioneers Company
732 G Sunnyside School Road
Blue Springs, Missouri 64015
(816) 461-0042

A-1 Auction Service
3026 S. 37th
Kansas City, Missouri
(913) 384-2775

Cable Car Auction Co.
1036 W. Ironwood
Olathe, KS. 66061
(913) 782-8009

Cates Auction & Sales Service
1301 S. Jefferson
Kearney, Missouri 64060
(816) 635-5698

LOS ANGELES

Butterfield & Butterfield
7601 Sunset Blvd.
Los Angeles, California 90046
(213) 850-7500

Van Cleves & Company
1010 Kaiser Road
Napa, California 94558
(707) 255-5850

Kohn & Megibow Company Inc.
2020 E 7th Street
Los Angeles, California 90021
(213) 624-8401

Gamson & Flans
16200 Ventura Boulevard, Suite 401
Encino, California 91436
(818) 784-3200

Kennedy Wilson
3110 Main Street, Suite 200
Santa Monica, California 90405
(213) 452-6664

MIAMI

Auction Company of Florida, Inc.
911 N.E. 199th Street, Suite 105
N. Miami Beach, Florida 33179

(305) 651-0500

Auction Compay of America
100 N. Biscayne Boulevard, 23rd Floor
Miami, Florida 33132
(305) 577-3322

Sugarman Auction Co.
18500 N.E. 5th Avenue
N. Miami Beach, Florida 33179
(305) 651-0101

Dallas Frye Auction Co.
2000 N. Dixie Hwy.
Hollywood, Florida 33020
(305) 923-0501

Harry P. Stamples Auctioneers
7875 N.W. 77th Avenue
Miami, Florida 33166
(305) 761-8744

MINNEAPOLIS

Quickie Auctions
22895 141 Avenue R.
Rogen, Minnesota 55374
(612) 428-4217

Wayne Pike Auction Company
P.O. Box 387
Princeton, Minnesota 55371
(612) 389-2700

Royal Star Liquidators & Auctioneers
7565 South Concord
Inver Grove Heights, Minnesota 55076
(612) 455-1931

Kurt Kiefer Auctioneers
P.O. Box 745
Fergus Falls, Minnesota 56537
(800) 435-2726

Anoka Fridley Auctioneers
848 E. River Road
Anoka, Minnesota 55303
(612) 427-6770

NEW YORK CITY

County Auctions
911 43rd Avenue
Long Island, New York 11101
(718) 729-0500

Jackson Hecht Associates
10 East 21st St., Suite 1608
New York City, New York 10010
(212) 505-0880

Stuart L. Medow & Associates
2935 West 5th St.
Brooklyn, New York 11224
(718) 996-2405

Greenwich Auctioneer
110 East 13th Street
New York City, New York 10003
(212) 533-5930

Bernard Magill
194 Broadway
Brooklyn, New York 11211
(718) 782-4574

PHILADELPHIA

John Hirsh Auctioneers
3330 S. 20th
Philadelphia, Pennsylvania 19145
(215) 336-8800

Freeman Fine Arts
1808 Chestnut Street
Philadelphia, Pennsylvania 19103
(215) 563-9275

Quaker City Auctioneers
2860 Memphis Street
Philadelphia, Pennsylvania 19134
(215) 426-5300

Henry Nemrod Auctioneers
137 North 3rd
Philadelphia, Pennsylvania 19106
(215) 627-6100

William F. Comly & Son Inc.
1825 East Boston
Philadelphia, Pennsylvania 19125
(215) 634-2500

PITTSBURGH

Anderson Auctioneers
A.D. No. 2 - Box 50
Georgetown, Pennsylvania 15043
(412) 734-4244

Auction Barn

20333 Route 19
Evans Ci   nsylvania 16033
(412) 77(

Hostetter Auctioneers
124 Black Hawk Road
Beaver Falls, Pennsylvania 15010
(412) 847-1880

Gerald Jackson Auction Service
522 Broad Street
Belle Vernon, Pensylvania 15012
(412) 929-2135

Johnson Auction Service
147 Flaugherty Road
Coraopolis, Pennsylvania 15108
(412) 457-1100

PORTLAND

Harvey Berlant
Beaverton, Oregon 97005
(503) 641-8989

Portland Auto Auctions
3000 North Hayden Island Drive
Portland, Oregon 97212
(503) 286-3000

American Auctioneering Service
85322 Jasper Park Road
Pleasant Hill, Oregon 97455
(503) 747-5190

Action Auctions
10025 N. E. Sandy Boulevard
Portland, Oregon 97220
(503) 256-2299
(speak with Jim Casey)

Steve Van Gordon Auctioneer
P.O. Box 106
Canby, Oregon 97013
(503) 266-1551

SACRAMENTO

Huisman Auctioneers
7923 Stockton Boulevard
Sacramento, California 95823
(916) 682-3338

Nelson Geiger Auctions
9608 Oats Drive

Sacramento, California 95827
(916) 368-0130

Roger Ernst & Associates
824 Kiernan Ave
Modesto, California 95356
(209) 527-7399

Shuffield Auctions
712 Garden Highway
Yuba City, California 95911
(916) 673-5189

Stoss Liquidators
9611-A Oats Drive
Sacramento, California 95827
(916) 368-0747

SAN DIEGO

Butterfield & Butterfield
7601 Sunset Blvd.
Los Angeles, California 90046
(213) 850-7500

Fischer Auction Company
614 Fifth Avenue, Suite A
San Diego, California 92101
(619) 233-1851

H & M Goodies Family Auction
130 East 8th Street
National City, California 92050
(619) 474-8296

Mark Gorin & Associates
18837 Brookhurst Street Suite 210
Fountain Valley, California 92708
(619) 560-1677

McCormick Auction Company
743 El. Cajon
San Diego, California 92020
(619) 447-1196

SAN FRANCISCO

A.R.S. Auctioneers
1755 10th Avenue
San Francisco, California 94122
(415) 566-6464

Ashman Company and Auctioneers &
Appraiser Inc.
21 Massola Drive

Pleasant Hill, California 94523
(415) 682-8100

Forest Faulknor & Sons
175 Sylvester Road
South San Francisco, California 94080
(415) 872-3242

Liquidators Inc.
P.O. Box 27144
Oakland, California 94602
(415) 482-2877

Rabin Brothers
660 3rd Street
San Francisco, California 94107
(916) 441-2405

Ross-Dove Company
1118 Chess Drive
Foster City, California 94404
(415) 571-7400

Van Cleves & Company
1010 Kaiser Road
Napa, California 94558
(707) 255-5850

SEATTLE

AAA Liquidating & Auction Service
17800 Des Moines Way, S.
Seattle, Washington 98148
(206) 246-7253

Auctions, Inc.
6226 196th S.W., #18
Lynnwood, Washington 98036
(206) 771-4232

Belieu Auctioneers
P.O. Box 24989
4797 1st Avenue, S.
Seattle, Washington 98134
(206) 767-6796

Harris & Harris
P.O. Box 5657
Bellview, Washington 98006
(206) 451-8922

James G. Murphy & Company
P.O. Box 82160
Kenmore, Washington 98028
(206) 486-1246

ST. LOUIS

Art Britton Auction Sales
441 Graeser Rd.
St. Louis, Missouri 63141
(314) 567-5636

Jim Bell and Son Auctioneers and
Appraisers
8290 Commercial Boulvard
Pevely, Missouri 63070
(314) 479-4075

Bob Cockrum Liquidators
3416 Brown Rd.
St. Louis, Missouri 63114
(314) 429-4112

Marks Auction Services
O'Fallon, Missouri 63129
(314) 272-2854

Robert Merry Auction Company
5501 Millburn Road
St. Louis, Missouri 63129
(314) 487-3992

Midwest Auction Service
3733 S. Service Rd.
St. Charles, Missouri 63303
(314) 946-0392

TAMPA/ST. PETERSBURG

Action Auctioneers
8955 Palm River Road
Tampa, Florida 33619
(813) 677-4677

Al Davenport Inc.
11776-1/2 58th Street, N.
Pinellas Park, Florida 34666
(813) 545-5165

Edward Bilbruk Auctioneer
1733 Indian Rocks Road
Belleair, Florida 34616
(813) 791-9541

Randall Auction Company
13605 West Hillsborough
Tampa, Florida 33615
(813) 855-9580

Tampa Machinery & Auction
11720 Highway 301
Thonotasassa, Florida 33592

(813) 986-2485

WASHINGTON, D.C./BALTIMORE

Adam A. Weschler & Son, Inc.
905 E. Street, N.W.
Washington, D.C. 20004
(202) 628-1281

Adams & Winer Auctioneers, Inc.
2720 Sisson St.
Baltimore, Maryland 21211
(301) 366-8300

Car & Truck Auction of Maryland
1370 West North Avenue
Baltimore, Maryland 21217
(301) 669-1666

Douglas K. Goldsten Auctioneers Inc.
3408 Wisconsin Avenue, N.W. - Suite 205
Washington, D.C. 20016
(202) 966-0100

R. L. Rasmus Auctioneers, Inc.
6060 Tower Court - Suite LL1
Alexandria, Virginia 22304
(202) 370-2338
(speak with Chris Rasmus)

350

State Housing Financing Agencies

Many states have housing finance for you, as mentioned in **Section Two**. Here are some of the programs and information we have uncovered about these states. Please read the information carefully to ensure you qualify before contacting them. Not all people will qualify for this type of financing.

Each state is governed by a separate agency. As a result the types of homes available, requirements for eligibility and mortgage qualifications may differ.

I've listed below some of the general qualifications that are common to all agencies which can be used as a guideline when considering these programs.

The types of homes that can be financed are new or previously occupied, single-family, town homes, and condominiums. In most cases the property must be approved by FHA or VA. Purchase prices must fall within state-established market prices.

Buyers must be first-time home owners (in many cases this means not a principal owner for three years or more). Buyers must meet income level requirements (as determined by tax returns for the past three years) and have an acceptable credit history.

They must be state residents and the homes purchased must be the principal residence of the buyer.

Mortgages that are available are usually low-interest, fixed rate, long term (25-30 years) with a minimum of 5% down payment. Processing fees and closing costs must be paid by the buyer.

It's important to remember that the funds are limited and vary by state. The funds are provided through participating lenders on a first-come, first-served basis.

ATLANTA

Georgia Residential Finance Authority
60 Executive Parkway South
Suite 250
Atlanta, GA 30329
(404) 320-4840

BOSTON

Massachusetts Housing Finance Agency
50 Milk Street, 7th Fl
Boston, MA 02109
(617) 451-3480

CHICAGO

Illinois Housing Development Authority
401 N Michigan, 9th Fl
Chicago, IL 60611
(312) 836-5362

CLEVELAND, OHIO

Ohio Housing Finance Agency
77th S. High Street
26 th floor
Columbus, OH, 43212
Within Ohio 800-458-1700
Outside Ohio 614-466-7970

DALLAS, HOUSTON

Texas Housing Agency
811 Barton Springs Rd
Suite 300
Austin, TX 78711
(512) 474-4663

DENVER

Colorado Housing Finance Authority
1981 Blake St
Denver, CO 80202
(303) 297-7376

DETROIT

Michigan State Housing Development
Authority
Plaza One Building
401 South Washington
PO Box 30044
Lansing, MI 48909
(517) 373-8370

LOS ANGELES, SACRAMENTO

Sacramento Office

California Housing Finance Agency
1121 L Street, 7th Floor
Sacramento, CA 95814
(916) 322-3991

(San Francisco and San Diego offices have
been closed)

LOS ANGELES OFFICE

5711 W. Slauson Ave.
Culver City, CA 90230
(213) 736-2355

MIAMI, TAMPA/ST. PETERSBUG

Florida Housing Finance Office Agency
2740 Centerview Dr
Suite 300
Tallahassee, FL 32399-2100
(904) 488-4197

MINNEAPOLIS/ST. PAUL

Minnesota Housing Finance Corporation
400 Sibley St.
Suite 300
St. Paul, MN 55101
(612) 296-7613

NEW YORK CITY

State of New York Mortgage Agency
(Sunnie Mae)
260 Madison Ave.
New York, NY 10016
(212) 230-4332

PENNSYLVANIA

Pennsylvania Housing Finance Agency
2101 North Front St
Harrisburg, PA 17105-8029
(717) 780-3870

CONNECTICUT

Connecticut Housing Finance Authority
40 Cold Spring Rd
Rocky Hill, CT 06067
(203) 721-9501

DELAWARE

Delaware State Housing Authority
820 N French St.
Wilmington, DE
(302) 571-3720

HAWAII

Housing Finance
7 Waterfront Plaza
Suite 300
Honolulu, HI 96813
(808) 543-2966

IDAHO

Idaho Housing Authority
760 W Myrtle
Boise, ID 83702
(208) 336-0161

ILLINOIS

Illinois Housing Development Authority
401 N Michigan Ave
Suite 900
Chicago, IL 60601
(312) 836-5200

INDIANA

Indiana Housing Finance Authority
1 North Capital Ave
Suite 515
Indianapolis, IN 46204
(317) 232-7777

IOWA

Iowa Finance Authority
200 E Grand
Suite 222
Des Moines, IA 50309
(515) 281-4058

KANSAS

Kansas Housing Finance Authority
Office of City Administrator
701 North 7th St
Topeka, KS 66603
(913) 573-5541

KENTUCKY

Kentucky Housing Corporation
1231 Louisville Rd
Frankfort, KY 40601
(502) 564-7630

LOUISIANA

Louisiana Housing Finance Agency
5615 Corporate Blvd
Suite 6A
Baton Rouge, LA 70806
(504) 925-3675

MAINE

Maine State Housing Authority
295 Water St
PO Box 2669
Augusta, ME 04338-2669
(207) 626-4600

MARYLAND

Maryland Community Housing Authority
45 Calvert St
Annapolis, MD 21401
(301) 974-3524

MISSISSIPPI

Mississippi Housing Finance Corporation
Dickson Building
510 George St
Jackson, MI 39201
(301) 974-3524

MISSOURI

Missouri Housing Development Commission
3770 Broadway
Kansas City, MO 64111
(816) 756-3790

MONTANA

Montana Board of Housing
2001 11th Ave
Helena, MT

(406) 444-3040

NEBRASKA

Nebraska Investment Finance Authority
Gold's Galleria
Suite 304
1033 O Street
Lincoln, NE 68508
(402) 477-4406

NEVADA

Nevada Housing Division
Department of Commerce
1050 East William
Suite 435
Carson City, NV 89710
(702) 885-4258

NEW HAMPSHIRE

New Hampshire Housing Finance Authority
9 Constitution Dr
Bedford, NH 03102
(603) 472-8623

NEW JERSEY

New Jersey Housing and Mortgage Finance
Authority
CN070
3625 Quakerbridge Rd
Trenton, NJ 08625
(609) 890-1300
In New Jersey:
(800) 654-6873)

NEW MEXICO

New Mexico Mortgage Finance Authority
PO Box 2047
Albuquerque, NM 87103
or
344 4th St SW
Albuquerque, NM 87102
(505) 843-6880

NORTH CAROLINA

North Carolina Housing Finance Agency
3300 Drake Circle
Suite 200
Raleigh, NC 27607
(919) 781-6115

NORTH DAKOTA

North Dakota Housing Finance Agency
1600 East Interstate Ave
Bismarck, ND 58501
or
PO Box 1535
Bismarck, ND 58502
(701) 224-3434

OKLAHOMA

Oklahoma Housing Finance Agency
1140 NW 63rd
Suite 200
Oklahoma City, OK 73116
or
PO Box 26720
Oklahoma City, OK 73126-6720
(405) 848-1144

OREGON

Oregon Housing Agency
1600 State St, Suite 100
Salem, OR 97310
(503) 378-4343

RHODE ISLAND

Rhode Island Housing and Mortgage
Finance Corporation
60 Eddie St
Providence, RI 02903
(401) 751-5566
(800) 552-1120

SOUTH CAROLINA

South Carolina Housing Authority
1710 Gervais St
Columbia, SC 29201
(803) 734-8702

SOUTH DAKOTA

South Dakota Housing Development
Authority
221 S Central
PO Box 1237
Pierre, SD 57501
(605) 773-3181

TENNESSEE

Tennessee Housing Develpment Agency
401 Church St
LNC Building, Suite 700
Nashville, TN 37219-2202
(615) 741-4968
(800) 228-8423

UTAH

Utah Housing Finance Agency
177 E 100 South
Salt Lake City, UT 84111
(801) 521-6950

VERMONT

Vermont Housing Finance Agency
1 Burlington Sq
PO Box 408
Burlington, VT 05402
(802) 864-5743

VIRGINIA

Virginia Housing Development Authority
601 S Belvedere St
Richmond, VA 23220
(804) 782-1986

WASHINGTON

Washington State Housing Financing
Commission
1111 3rd Ave, Suite 908
Seattle, WA 98101
(206) 464-7139

WISCONSIN

Wisconsin Housing & Economic
Development Authority
1 S Pinckney, Suite 500
PO Box 1728
Madison, WI 53701-1728
(608) 266-7884
(800) 362-2767

WYOMING

Wyoming Community Development
Authority
123 S Durbin
Casper, WY 82602
(307) 265-0603

ALABAMA

Alabama Housing Finance Authority
614 Adams Ave
Montgomery, AL 36130
(205) 261-4310
(800) 325-2432

ARIZONA

Arizona Department of Commerce
1700 W Washington
Phoenix, AZ 85007
(602) 542-5002

ARKANSAS

Arkansas Housing Development Agency
100 Main St
PO Box 8023
Little Rock, AR 72203
(501) 682-5900

DISTRICT OF COLUMBIA

District of Columbia Housing Finance
Agency
1401 New York Ave, NW
Suite 540
Washington, DC 20005
(202) 628-0311

355

WEST VIRGINIA

West Virginia Housing Development Fund
814 Virginia St E
Charleston, VA 25301
(304) 345-6475
(800) 654-6652

SECTION FOUR

CITY DIRECTORIES

Introducing
Rex Publishing Company's
AUCTION NEWS HOTLINE

To receive the latest auction news for the cities currently on our Auction Hotline, dial **1-813-442-1840**. When the recording directs you to do so, press "9", which is your confidential access code number, then the "star" (*) and the two-digit number assigned to the city in which you are interested.

You will be given dates, times and places of auctions to be held in or near that city in the coming weeks.

From time to time we include new cities to this list. Call periodically for addition update.

LIST OF CITIES CURRENTLY
ON NEWS HOTLINE

ATLANTA	*44	MINNEAPOLIS	*47
BOSTON	*41	NEW YORK CITY	*35
CHICAGO	*37	PHILADELPHIA	*38
CINCINNATI	*70	PITTSBURGH	*69
CLEVELAND	*63	PORTLAND	*64
DALLAS	*42	SACRAMENTO	*65
DENVER	*62	ST. LOUIS	*67
DETROIT	*50	SAN DIEGO	*66
HOUSTON	*49	SAN FRANCISCO	*39
INDIANAPOLIS	*71	SEATTLE	*48
KANSAS CITY	*68	TAMPA/ST.PETERSBURG	*46
LOS ANGELES	*36	WASHINGTON, D.C./	
MIAMI	*45	BALTIMORE	*40

INTRODUCTION

Thousands of our book buyers have requested that we isolate the available auctions in their area for immediate use, as opposed to going through the book part by part. We've made this easier for them with the city directories here in **Section Four**.

You'll find as you leaf through this section that the major cities have been covered throughout the United States. There are many extra pointers available for those who live in or near these major cities with regards to their auctions.

Please do not ignore going through **Section Three;** it contains a great deal of previously unassembled material and material which is not going to be found in these city directories. Anyone who desires to go to an auction and does so without first studying **Section Two** will also do so at his own risk. Every attempt has been made to provide the reader with up-to-date practical information about the entire auction process and all of its elements.

These city directories were originally separate booklets which we sent out to our book buyers for each person's own area. We soon discovered that there was a tremendous demand for far more cities than just the person's own. Many of our readers travel throughout the United States. The book, in its current format, provides those individuals with the opportunity to attend auctions while traveling on business or vacation. And for those who wish to make a career out of it, this is the first attempt made by anyone to provide such a complete amount of information about each city's own special auctions.

For those whose cities are not mentioned in these directories, please use the format we've laid out for you in each of those cities that were mentioned. It should not take you more than a few days in your spare time to contact the important agencies and follow those through to get the available information they do have.

Please note that if some agency has not been mentioned it will most likely have been covered in **Section Three**, which is quite extensive.

GSA - Regional Office
75 Spring Street, SW
Atlanta, GA   30303
Telephone: (404) 331-3064
(404)   4331-0972

The GSA holds 5-12 auctions a month during the "Auction Season" - March to October. Merchandise includes surplus government property, vehicles, data processing equipment, desks, typewriter and medical equipment. The bids may be open, spot or sealed - depending on the type and quantity of merchandise being auctioned. They will send you information on future dates and locations if you call and ask to be placed on the mailing list.

U.S. Marshal's Office

The Marshal uses auctioneers to handle the disposal of personal property and the few vehicles they receive for auction. All real estate goes through licensed realtors in the area. Advertisements appear in the Atlanta Journal and Constitution, under Legal Notices. Also check the official County papers and any local law journals.

FBI
77 Forsyth Street
Atlanta, GA   30303

All merchandise seized by the FBI is auctioned by the Marshal's Office.

HUD - Property
Disposition
75 Spring Street, S.W.
Room 5767
Atlanta, GA   30303
Telephone: (404) 331-4739

Available repossessed HUD properties are advertised in the Atlanta Journal and Constitution every Thursday in the Classified Section (206). To see and bid on a property contact a realtor of your choice who will submit your bid to HUD. Currently, the houses, condominiums and townhouses in the Atlanta area available through HUD, are valued between $30,000 and $90,000.

Sealed bids are opened every Thursday and the highest bid is accepted on the property.

VA
730 Peachtree Street, N.E.
Atlanta, GA   30365
Telephone: (404) 881-1776

The VA compiles a list of available properties each week and furnishes them to local licensed realtors. The realtors have keys to the properties and can show them to you. Your sealed bid must be submitted to the VA by the realtor.

U.S. Postal Service
Merchandise
730 Great Southwest
Parkway
Atlanta, GA   30336
Telephone: (404) 344-1625

Atlanta is one of five U.S. cities where undeliverable and unclaimed merchandise is auctioned. The merchandise can include any item that can be sent Parcel Post or mailed - from books, small appliances, clothing, china and jewelry to TVs and put-it-together furniture.

Everything is sold in lots: a box of books, a hamper of bedding, a box of household goods, etc. They also hold an auction of books only. The auctions are held every two months and there are bidders in attendance from New York,

Kentucky and many other states - as the merchandise is sent to Atlanta from the entire Southeastern area of the United States. The auction starts at 10:00 a.m. and the merchandise may be inspected from 8:00 a.m. to 10:00 a.m. On the day of the auction, you may register starting at 8:00 a.m. and you will be given a paddle to be used in bidding. There are minimums at which the bidding must start.

The auctions are advertised in the Atlanta Journal and Constitution but you may call the above number to be notified by mail.

U.S. Postal Service - Vehicles
3900 Crown Road
Atlanta, GA   30304
Telephone: (404) 765-7735

The Postal Service holds no auctions and surplus vehicle sales are rare. When they have vehicles available (at fixed prices) the rural mail carriers have the first opportunity to purchase.

After ten days, the public is allowed to buy, then after another ten days, the Post Office employees are given their turn at whatever vehicles remain for sale. The last sale was in November, 1988, therefore, you might check with the Post Office at the above number for further information on future sales.

IRS
Special Procedures Staff
401 W Peachtree Street
Atlanta, GA 30365
P.O. Box 875
Telephone: (404) 522-0050

The IRS holds auctions in different counties throughout the area, depending on where the properties were seized. You must attend one auction to get on the mailing list. Notices are posted in the county courthouses where the auctions are held and advertisements are published in the Atlanta Journal and Constitution.

SBA
1720 Peachtree Road, NW
6th Floor
Atlanta, GA 30309
Telephone: (404) 347-2441

The SBA uses a private auctioneer to handle its foreclosures. There are eight to nine each month and they are always held at the courthouse. The merchandise and property auctioned includes: a lot of real estate, automobiles, a few single residences, business property, large companies (up to 3/4 million dollars in appraised value), machinery, equipment, furniture, fixtures - actually anything that could be found in a store, business or office.

Advertisements are placed in the newspaper with the largest circulation in the county where the property is located. Auctioneer: Ackerman & Company - (handles auctions for SBA), 1040 Crown Point Parkway - Suite 200, Telephone: (404) 392-9999.

There are some excellent opportunities at these auctions, since they are foreclosure sales. If the outstanding balance on the loan is small, the SBA is interested only in recovering its money and it could be a real bargain for the public.

U.S. Trustees - Bankruptcy
Court
75 W. Spring Street
Room 1340
Atlanta, GA 30303
Telephone: (404) 331-4437
Recording: (404) 331-6886

Each Chapter Seven Trustee handles arrangements for the auctions of forfeited merchandise from his cases, therefore personal contact with him is necessary. To receive a list of all Chapter Seven Trustees, write a letter to the clerk - Bankruptcy Court at the above address, requesting same.

If you prefer you may go to the Clerk's Office, as all records are open to the public between 9:00 a.m. and 4:00 p.m.

Defense Reutilization &
Marketing Office
Warner Robbins
Warner 'A' Building 1602
Marchbanks Drive, R
Robbins AFB,
GA 31098-5000
Telephone: (912) 926-2164
            (912) 926-3159
            (912) 926-4541

Three auctions a month are held with merchandise from surrounding bases. Auctions usually include office furniture and equipment, refrigerators, household items, paint, auto testing equipment and hand tools. Some auctions have vehicles, some do not.

About 20 a year are sold at these auctions. The bids are open and there are no minimums. However, they reserve the right to reject a bid if it's too low. Call the above number and ask to be placed on their mailing list.

Defense Reutilization &
Marketing Office
Forest Park
Building 310-B Bravo
Forest Park, GA 30050
Telephone: (404) 363-5117

Auctions are held every other month. Merchandise includes office furniture and equipment, computer processing equipment, clothing, machinery and vehicles. They have only military vehicles at most auctions, not many automobiles - one or two at the most.

The bids are open but there are minimums. Fort Gillem is 40 minutes from Atlanta and they will notify you by mail of the next auction if you call and request it.

State Surplus Vehicles
1050 Murphy Avenue SW
Building 1A
Atlanta, GA 30310
Telephone: (404) 756-4800

These auctions are held every six to eight weeks, always on Wednesday with viewing the previous Monday and Tuesday, 8:00 a.m. to 4:00 p.m. Merchandise for auction usually includes - office equipment, kitchen equipment from state institutions; commercial stoves, baking tables, appliances and other items; automobiles, trucks, bulldozers and dumpsters.

There are approximately 100 vehicles per auction - about 50% junk and 50% good. The bidding is open and there are usually no minimum bids.

The auctioneer who handles these auctions is: Jim Rouse.

Call (404) 756-4800 and ask to be placed on the mailing list if any of the above categories are of interest to you.

366

Sheriff's Department
136 Pryor Street, SW
Room 108
Atlanta, GA   30303
Telephone: (404) 730-5100

The Sheriff holds at least seven to ten auctions a year on the steps of the County Courthouse. The Atlanta Sheriff is responsible for eight different cities, all of which auction through Atlanta.

Advertisements for the auctions appear in the Atlanta Journal and Constitution and in the Fulton County paper.

DeKalb County State Court
Marshal's Office - Room 601
556 N. McDonough Street
Decatur, GA   30030
Telephone: (404) 371-2930

They normally hold one auction a month - (third Monday or Tuesday, if Monday is a holiday) at 10:00 a.m. The merchandise is vehicles and personal property. No real estate.

Cobb County Sheriff
185 Washington Avenue
Marietta, GA   30090-9650
Telephone: (404) 499-4647

Auctions are held on the first Monday and Tuesday of each month on the steps of the County Courthouse, 30 Wadell Street, Marietta. Merchandise varies each month.

Advertisements appear in Marietta Daily Journal prior to auction with complete lists of items offered.

County Sheriff
75 Langley Drive
Lawrenceville, GA   30245
Telephone: (404) 822-8200

The Sheriff holds about four auctions a year, mainly personal property with only one or two cars available at each auction. Advertisements are published only in the Gwinnette Daily News prior to the auction and contain complete information on the sale.

Fayette County Sheriff
155 Johnson Avenue
Fayetteville, GA 30214
Telephone: (404) 461-6353

The Sheriff held eight to ten auctions last year with personal property and few vehicles being offered. He advertises only in the Fayette County News four weeks prior to each auction, listing the items to be sold. You may also call his office for information as to future auction dates.

DeKalb County Sheriff
556 N. McDonough Street
Decatur, GA 30030
Telephone: (404) 371-2397

The Sheriff holds vehicle, personal property and real estate auctions to satisfy court judgments. Last year he held approximately four auctions and while there were no particular items named, the information given was that most property sold for much less than its actual value.

Call the above number or check advertisements in the Decatur-DeKalb News Era.

Clayton County Sheriff
Courthouse Square
Jonesboro, GA 30236
Telephone: (404) 471-1122

The Sheriff holds an auction on the first Tuesday of each month at 10:00 a.m. on the courthouse steps to dispose of confiscated, abandoned or repossessed vehicles and personal property.

Advertisements appear in the News Daily prior to the auction with all information on the merchandise to be sold. There may be some good buys but the items vary from month to month and they can't say in advance what will be available. Check the advertisement to determine if any merchandise is of interest to you.

Police Department
165 Decatur Street
Atlanta, GA   30305
Telephone: (404) 658-6876

The Police Department holds auctions every three months and the merchandise consists of "anything a person could be carrying when he is arrested", TVs, radios, VCRs, stereos, tools, jewelry (assumed to be stolen items).

The bidding is open and it depends on the quality of merchandise whether there is a minimum. Advertisements are in the Atlanta Journal and Constitution.

Police Department
Property & Impound
Division
165 Decatur Street
Atlanta, GA   30305
Telephone: (404) 658-6717

There are five Atlanta Towing companies which handle the auction of boats and vehicles only. The permanent monthly schedule is as follows:
2nd Wednesday - 10:00 a.m.
 B & L Wrecking
 150 Milton Avenue
 Telephone: (404) 624-4208
  4th Wednesday - 10:00 a.m.
  Robertson & Stevens
  281 Mansford
  Telephone: (404) 624-1207
 2nd Friday - 10:00 a.m.
  Lowe Bros.
  1350 Marietta
  Telephone: (404) 792-0128
 4th Friday - 10:00 a.m.
  Bryants
  844 Regina Drive
  Telephone: (404) 799-0344
 1st Wednesday - 10:00 a.m.
 Futo
 2050 Liddell Drive NE
 Telephone: (404) 874-5926

Private Auctioneers - Atlanta

Auctioneer for State Surplus
Vehicles:
Jim Rouse
P.O. Box 6527
Atlanta, GA   30315
Telephone: (404) 622-4455

One or two auctions are held each month for the State of Georgia, SBA, GSA and U-Haul. Merchandise at these auctions usually includes bulldozers, farm and road equipment, restaurant supplies, ovens, items from the offices of dentists and chiropractors and office furniture.

From U-Haul there are miscellaneous items that people leave in storage - lawn mowers, commercial vacuum cleaners and washing machines. There are usually 120-150 vehicles at approximately eight auctions, none at the other four. The bidding is open and there are no minimum bids.

Auctioneer for City Marshal:
Arwood Auction Company
P.O. Box 250085
Atlanta, GA   30325
Telephone: (404) 352-0110

City Marshal auctions are held every four months with cars, office equipment and heavy equipment among the merchandise being offered for sale. Approximately 50 automobiles are auctioned, all in good condition. The bids are open and there are no minimums.

Arwood holds auctions in many locations in the state. Check the classified section of the Atlanta Journal and Constitution regularly for current information.

The Dobbins Company
P.O. Box 2001 Station N
Atlanta, GA   30325
Telephone: (404) 352-2638

They hold auctions for the SBA.

Hudson & Marshall
4751 Best Road - Suite 300
Atlanta, GA   30337
Telephone: (404) 763-0211

They hold auctions for Federal Reserve Bank.

GSA
10 Causeway Street
Tip O'Neil Building
9th Floor
Boston, MA 02222
Telephone: (617) 565-7326

GSA holds approximately one auction a month that offers around 60 vehicles in fair to good condition. These cars have formally been used by Government employees and have about 60,000 miles on them.

The auctions are open bidding with minimums of $2,000 to $2,800.

U.S. Marshal's Office

The Marshal holds only real estate auctions, held at the location of property to be sold and a member of the Marshal's staff conducts the auction. Advertisements on properties to be sold can be found in the Boston Globe or Boston Herald on Tuesday or Thursday under "Legal Notices". Also check official county papers and any local law journals.

FBI
JFK Boulevard
Room 900
Government Center
Boston, MA 02203
Telephone: (617) 742-5533

This agency holds no auctions. All merchandise sent to GSA.

HUD
Thomas P. O'Neal Building
10 Causeway Street
Room 375
Boston, MA   02222-1092
Telephone: (617) 565-5397
Recording: (617) 565-5398

For listings of available properties see the Sunday edition of the Boston Globe - Section A.

VA
Government Center
JFK Boulevard
Room 312
Boston, MA   02205
Telephone: (617) 565-3027

For information on available properties, call the local VA office.

U.S. Postal Service -
Vehicles
135 A Street
Boston, MA   02210-9761
Telephone: (617) 654-5771

At the present time they have no vehicles for sale. When they are available - no auctions are held. All vehicles sold at "fixed prices". When vehicles are available, they may be viewed at the above location (P.O. Garage). No advertising - call to find out if they have any vehicles.

U.S. Postal Service
Merchandise

All undeliverable mail and parcels sent to New York City for public auction.

IRS
Government Center
Scollay Square - Room E.100
(1st Floor)
Boston, MA   02203
Telephone: (617) 523-1040

For information on auctions of seized property it is necessary to go to IRS office where data is posted outside Room E-100.

SBA
10 Causeway Street
Room 265
Boston, MA   02222-1093
Telephone: (617) 565-5575

For dates, times and locations of SBA auctions, see advertisements in the Sunday edition of the Boston Globe.

U.S. Trustees - Bankruptcy Court
O'Neil Federal Building
10 Causeway Street
Boston, MA   02222
Telephone: (617) 565-6360

Any bankruptcy auctions held by U.S. Trustees will appear in the Boston Glove under "Legal Notices".

Defense Reutilization & Marketing Office
Box 69
Fort Devens, MA
01433-5690
Telephone: (508) 796-2418

One or two auctions per month are held with office furniture and equipment, stereos, military vehicles and trucks sold at open bidding. There are minimum bids. To receive fliers or catalogs on future auctions, call the above number and request that you be placed on the mailing list.

State Surplus Vehicles
1 Ashburton Place
Boston, MA   02108
Telephone: (617) 727-2920

Auctions are held every three to four weeks and consist of sedans, police cars, heavy equipment, trucks and dump trucks. They usually sell for $500 to $1,000; however, some go for as little as $1.00.

The vehicles are in poor condition and will require repairs. It is suggested that persons planning to bid bring a mechanic with them to inspect the vehicles. Advertisements appear in the Boston Globe the Saturday before the auction is to be held.

Sheriff's Department
11 Beacon Street
Room 1300
Boston, MA   02108
Telephone: (617) 227-2541

At present the Sheriff has no vehicles or merchandise available. It is usually reclaimed by the owner before an auction is held.

Barnstable County Sheriff
P.O. Box 729
Barnstable, MA   02630
Telephone: (508) 362-9578

The Barnstable County Sheriff held approximately 30 auctions last year with vehicles, real estate and personal property being offered.

The bank holding the mortgage usually buys the property back but there are bargains to be found on boats, in particular and on some personal property. As to vehicles, some are in good condition, some are not and some have liens on them so you must be cautious.

Bristol County Sheriff
P.O. Box G928
Bedford, MA   02742
Telephone: (508) 992-6631

The Bristol County Sheriff's Office primarily auctions land and real estate but many times the sales are cancelled because the owner redeems the property.

Approximately 50 auctions were held last year and they were advertised in the newspapers of the towns where the property is located. Also, according to law, notices of the auctions must be posted in the Town or City Hall.

Essex County Sheriff - Civil
2 Salem Green
Salem, MA   01970
Telephone: (508) 744-0038

The Essex County Sheriff holds about 200 auctions a year of vehicles, boats, airplanes, inventories and personal property which have been repossessed.

Literally, anything you can get a loan on and fail to repay it real estate is frequently auctioned by court order, with the bank usually buying the property back.

Norfolk County Sheriff
630 High Street
Dedham, MA   02026
Telephone: (617) 326-1787

The Sheriff of Norfolk County primarily holds real estate auctions to satisfy judgments against the owner. Many of these scheduled auctions are cancelled because the debt which created the court order is paid.

If you plan to participate in these auctions, it is recommended that you contact your attorney, do a title search and check the Registry of Deeds to determine what other liens, if any, are on the property. If you have no idea how these auctions are conducted, the best place to start is your local law library under Basic Sheriff's Sales, Chapter 235, Section 36.

Middlesex County Sheriff
P.O. Box 180
Cambridge, MA   02141
Telephone: (617) 547-1171

The Middlesex County Sheriff handles primarily equity sales, court ordered real sales and the owner has a year to redeem his property.

These types of auctions should be viewed with caution because of the redemption factor. In some instances, the buyers of the property in an auction of real estate have negotiated with the owner and purchased his "right of redemption." This should be investigated as to its legality in your particular area.

Plymouth County Sheriff
22 Pottage Street
Brockton, MA 02401
Telephone: (508) 580-2110

The Sheriff of Plymouth County posts notices of auction 48 hours prior to each sale. He also advertises each auction in the local newspaper where the property is located.

Last year he held approximately 150 auctions, some of which were single pieces of real estate. They also handle many court-ordered repossessions of personal property, due to non-payment of loans or debts.

Police Department
154 Berkeley Street
Boston, MA 02222
Hotline: (617) 247-4200

The Police Department holds auctions every two weeks with 50-100 vehicles and miscellaneous personal property, such as bicycles and stereos.

The condition of the vehicles varies because many of them are abandoned. The auction is open bidding with no minimums. For information as to time and date of the next auction call the above number.

Private Auctioneers - Boston

Jerome J. Manning &
Company, Inc.
P.O. Box 10
Yarmouth Post, MA   02675
Telephone: (508) 362-8171

They hold auctions for U.S.
Marshal and State Treasury, SBA
and U.S. Trustees.

John J. Nolan Real Estate
Marketing Services
College Park - Nantuckett
Building
720 Washington
Hanover, MA   02339
Telephone: (617) 826-5452

He does real estate only, on
Government order.

Paul Saperstein Auctioneers
148 State Street
Boston, MA   02109
Telephone: (617) 227-6553

They hold auctions for Bankruptcy
Court and SBA.

Garrett Auctioneers
134 Newbury
Peabody, MA   01960
Telephone: (508) 535-3271
        or   (617) 233-7227

They hold auctions for various
government agencies.

Barton K. Hyte Company
15 Taft Street
Marblehead, MA   01945
Telephone: (617) 720-0939

They hold auctions for City, SBA
and Bankruptcy Courts.

GSA
MS 34-5
230 S Dearborn Street
Chicago, IL 60604
Telephone: (312) 353-6061

GSA holds one auction every two to three months. They will give not give any information by telephone. If you will send a SASE to the above address, they will send information on the dates, times and locations of upcoming auctions.

U.S. Marshal's Office

The Marshal uses Hanzel Galleries to auction seized, abandoned and foreclosed merchandise and property. They hold eight to ten auctions a year, each one lasting two to three days.

Last year 1,500 pieces of property were auctioned. They advertise in the Chicago Tribune and some National Art publications.

FBI

All auctions handled by the U.S. Marshal's Auctioneer.

HUD - Property
Disposition
547 W Jackson - 7th Floor
Chicago, IL 60606
Telephone: (312) 353-5682

Available foreclosed HUD properties are listed in the Business Section of the Chicago Tribune, Sunday edition. To see and bid on a property contact a licensed real estate broker who is registered with HUD.

If you wish to determine whether a realtor is registered with HUD, call (312) 886-9771. They will not recommend a realtor but will tell you if he is registered.

VA
536 S Clark Street
Chicago, IL 60680
Telephone: (312) 663-5510

Listings of available foreclosed VA properties are published in the Friday edition of the Chicago Sun Times, Home Life Section. Every other Friday it lists what properties have been sold and on alternate Fridays what properties are available.

You must use a broker to submit your bid. The broker must be affiliated with the VA, otherwise they will not have the necessary information or forms.

U.S.Postal Service
740 S Canal Street
Chicago, IL 60607-9721
Telephone: (312) 765-4122

The Postal Service disposes of surplus cars, Jeeps and trucks three to four times a year. Cars and Jeeps are auctioned; trucks are sold at a fixed price.

Bidding is open on cars and Jeeps and there is usually a minimum bid. Advertisements for sales are published in the Chicago Sun Times and Chicago Tribune, classified section. All undeliverable and unclaimed merchandise is sent to St. Paul, Minnesota for auction.

IRS
230 Dearborn Street
Chicago, IL 60604
Telephone: (312) 435-1040

Each revenue officer sets up auctions for his seizures. The advertisements appear on Thursday and Sunday in the Chicago Tribune in the classified section.

Notices are also posted in IRS offices, with pictures and information. They do not have a mailing list.

SBA
219 S Dearborn Street
Room 437
Chicago, IL 60604
Telephone: (312) 353-4528

SBA uses Michael Natchbar to auction its foreclosed real estate and personal property. There is no set schedule. The number of auctions is determined by how many businesses insured by the SBA fail. The bidding is open and usually there are no minimum bids.

Auctions are advertised in the Chicago Tribune each Sunday in the classified section.

(See Michael Natchbar information in the Private Auctioneers section following this.)

U.S. Trustees - Bankruptcy
Court
219 S Dearborn Street
Chicago, IL 60604
Telephone: (312) 435-5693
            (Recording)

Individual Trustees arrange for bankruptcy auctions. For a Docketing Book of Sales which contains all information on upcoming auctions, go to Room 1820, 219 S Dearborn and pick it up.

Defense Reutilization &
Marketing Office
Naval Training Center
Building 3212A
Great Lakes, IL 60088-5798
Telephone: (312) 688-3655

An auction is held on the third Tuesday of each month (starting in July). Prior to July - one is held on the third Tuesday of every other month.

The merchandise to be auctioned usually includes office furniture and equipment, vehicles (surplus and abandoned), electronics, TVs and major appliances. The number of vehicles varies at each auction.

The auction starts at 9:00 a.m., with registration at 8:00 a.m. in Building 3212-C. Inspection of merchandise is scheduled on the Thursday, Friday and Monday before the auction on Tuesday. Payment must be by cash or money orders only.

State Surplus Vehicles
3550 Great Northern
Avenue
Springfield, IL 62707
Telephone: (217) 793-1813

This agency holds about six auctions a year with approximately 250 vehicles per auction and an average price of $800.00. All vehicles are auctioned in Springfield but merchandise is sometimes offered in Chicago. To be placed on the mailing list call the above number.

Sheriff's Department
Auto Pound
3146 S. Archer
Chicago, IL 60608
Telephone: (312) 890-3355

Sheriff does not hold auctions in the winter months. The number of vehicles to be sold varies but is rarely more than 50. They are usually older cars, some in good condition, others not.

The bidding is open and there may be some auctions with a minimum, depending on the vehicles to be sold. Call for the date and time of the next auction.

Cook County Sheriff's
Office - Real Estate
Division
59 W Washington
Room 701-A
Daley Civic Center
Chicago, IL 60602
Telephone: (312) 443-3341

The Sheriff holds auctions on Tuesday, Wednesday and Thursday of each week. The source of the real estate to be offered is foreclosures and properties with levies (court-ordered sales). The bids are open and the minimum is usually the judgment amount or the amount owed.

Advertisements appear in the Chicago Daily Law Bulletin available at newsstands or in Room 802 at 59 W Washington.

Cook County Sheriff's
Office - Personal Property
Division
59 W Washington
Daley Civic Center
Chicago, IL 60602
Telephone: (312) 443-3346

Personal property, either residential or business, is auctioned on Tuesday, Wednesday and Thursday of each week at the location where the property is seized. Items include household furniture, appliances, vehicles, business equipment and fixtures.

The bidding is open and the minimum bid must be "within reason", For dates, times, locations and descriptions of the merchandise, check the Chicago Daily Law Bulletin which is available at newsstands or in Room 802, 59 W Washington.

Cook County Sheriff - Civil
Division
59 W Washington
Daley Civic Center
Room 701
Chicago, IL 60602
Telephone: (312) 443-6475

The Sheriff holds auctions on foreclosed real estate when there are properties available. The sales are held at the location of the property, always on a Tuesday, Wednesday or Thursday. Officers from the Civil Division conduct the auctions. The sheriff warns the buyer to know what he is bidding on before attending an auction, as some properties have additional liens against them.

An attorney can help you determine whether there are other liens and if the title is clear.

Also, investigate the length of time the owner has to redeem his property. In some states there is a one-year "right of redemption". Sheriff's auctions of foreclosed properties are advertised in the "Daily Law Bulletin" with full details on the sales.

DuPage County Sheriff
501 County Farm Road
Wheaton, IL 60187
Telephone: (312) 682-7256

The Sheriff holds real estate foreclosure auctions and advertises in the newspapers. They also offer a "foreclosure pack" for $10.00, which explains procedures and contains descriptions of the properties being auctioned.

Some examples of real estate sold at these sales are:

Condominiums for $47,000 and $50,000, a building for $870,000; a house for $80,000. The first bid at the auction is made by the Attorney for the Plaintiff and is the amount of the judgment. After this bid the public is invited to participate in the auction. The

Sheriff also holds vehicle and personal property auctions which are held in the lobby at the above address. Check local newspapers for notices of these auctions.

Lake County Sheriff
25 S Utica
Waukegan, IL 60085
Telephone: (312) 360-6300

The Sheriff holds foreclosure auctions consisting of vehicles and personal property for banks and mortgage companies. The certified auctioneer who holds the auctions stated that some properties are sold from 20% to 50% below market value.

At foreclosure auctions, the attorney for the mortgage holder makes the first bid, then anyone can bid. Sometimes even one dollar over the initial bid can buy the property. The Sheriff advertises in the Chicago Tribune and in all of the ten counties in Illinois. If you wish to be put on the mailing list for the auctions, call the Lake County Purchasing Department, Waukegan, Illinois.

Will County Sheriff
14 W Jefferson
Joliet, IL 60431
Telephone: (815) 727-8895

The Sheriff holds foreclosure auctions on real estate; however, they have no information except the name of the owner and the address of the property. The number of auctions depends on the number of foreclosure there are.

Advertisements are published in the "Farmers' Weekly Review" and The Labor Record. Single copies cannot be purchased. They are only available through subscription. At the auction the

385

attorney for the mortgage company makes the initial bid, which is in the amount of the judgment. The public can then participate in the bidding.

Chicago Police Department
Recovery of Evidence
Division
2650 S California
Chicago, IL 60608
Telephone: (312) 744-6224

The Police Department holds auctions once every month to six weeks. The merchandise usually includes radios, jewelry, TVs, musical instruments and are from crime seizures or lost, stolen and unclaimed items.

Auctions are held at the Washburn Trade School, 31st & Kedzie. Cash only - no traveler's checks. Notices will appear in the Chicago Sun Times two weeks prior to the auction.

Private Auctioneers - Chicago

Auctioneer for U.S. Marshal's
Office
Hanzel Galleries
1120 S. Michigan
Chicago, IL 60605
Telephone: (312) 922-6234

Hanzel Galleries holds eight to ten auctions a year with merchandise from the Marshal (FBI seizures and property forfeited through bankruptcy proceedings). The bidding is open and advertisements appear in the Chicago Tribune, Auction Section.

Auctioneer for SBA
Michael Natchbar
4040 N Kedzie
Chicago, IL 60168
Telephone: (312) 539-7460

He holds one to two auctions a year for SBA with merchandise such as machinery, retail equipment, store fixtures and some real estate. The auction is open bidding and usually has no minimums. He maintains a mailing list and will send you information on request. He holds a total of 55 auctions each year.

Marcie Rath
38 W 196th - Route 20
Elgin, IL 60123
Telephone: (312) 695-0388

At least one auction each week is held with a very interesting and varied selection of merchandise being offered. Some examples are: gold coins, antiques, cars, household items, real estate, jewelry and guns.

The condition of the cars up for auction is "good" and the average price is $500.00. She also does bankruptcy auctions and bank repossessions. For current information as to dates, times and locations, call the above number and ask to be put on the mailing list.

Auction Services Inc.
5338 North Lotus Avenue
Chicago, IL 60630
Telephone: (312) 631-2255

They hold auctions for U.S. Marshal and SBA on a limited basis.

Sheldon F. Good &
Company
333 W Wacker Drive
Suite 450
Chicago, IL 60606
Telephone: (312) 630-0915

They hold auctions for various government agencies on real estate, no specific agencies.

GSA

All GSA auctions are handled out of the Chicago office. For more information call (312) 353-0302.

U.S. Marshal
Telephone: (513) 684-3594

Auctions are held to dispose of seized merchandise from other agencies and on court order and can be anything from jewelry to trucks. There is no set schedule; when enough merchandise is accumulated, a date is set for an auction.

The bidding is usually open and there may be minimum bids on vehicles if there is a lien against it. Ron's Pre-owned Cars, Blue Ash, Ohio, handles vehicle auctions for the Marshal and you may contact that company for further information. For merchandise auctions, check legal notices in the classified section of your major newspapers, as well as official county papers and local law journals.

FBI

All general merchandise is auctioned by Chicago office. Real estate is sold through local realtors in the area.

HUD
Telephone: (513) 684-2714

Available properties are advertised in Cincinnati and Dayton newspapers with descriptions and listing price.

If you are interested in a property, contact a realtor who will show it to you and submit your sealed bid to HUD. There is a ten-day period from the time a property is advertised until the sealed bids are opened. If your bid is the highest, you will be informed, usually on the same day. HUD pays the realtor's commission.

VA
Telephone: (513) 579-0505

Listings are sent to realtors in the area every three to four weeks and they can tell you what is available, show you the property and submit your sealed bid to the VA.

Contrary to popular belief, you do not have to be a veteran to buy a foreclosed home from the VA. Since the broker's fee is paid by the VA, you should take advantage of his assistance and expertise.

U.S. Postal Service
Telephone: (513) 684-5625

They do not have auctions, rather they sell surplus vehicles at fixed prices. They are in very poor condition and sell for $100. If you bought two, there is a possibility that you could combine the parts and make one of them run.

Rural carriers are given first opportunity to purchase, then the public. If any vehicles remain, they are sold for scrap.

IRS
Telephone: (513) 621-6281

In order to receive auction information, send your name and address to Bidder's List at P.O. Box 1579, Cincinnati, Ohio 45201 and request information on real estate, general merchandise, vehicles and boats.

The IRS seizes property for non-payment of income taxes and can be one of the most valuable auction avenues you can pursue. The minimum bid at these auctions is usually 20% of the market value of the items being sold.

SBA
Telephone: (513) 684-2814

The SBA office in Columbus, Ohio (614) 469-6860 handles all auction arrangements for the Cincinnati area and the frequency depends upon the number of foreclosures.

Merchandise to be sold can be store fixtures and equipment, office furniture and, in some cases, real estate and company vehicles owned by the company which defaulted on the loan. They also auction the contents of stores and other businesses which sold directly to the public. Notices will be published in major newspapers in the area and will be designated as SBA liquidation auctions.

State Surplus
Columbus, OH
Telephone: (614) 466-2850

Merchandise includes office furniture and equipment, machines, boats, vehicles and much more. Auctions are held more frequently during the summer months, especially on vehicles which are sold on an open bid basis. Call to receive fliers in advance of the sales.

Sheriff's Department
Telephone: (513) 632-8822

The Sheriff holds foreclosure sales every Thursday, with minimum bids of 2/3 the property value. Call for further information.

Police Department -
Property
Telephone: (513) 352-6371

Abandoned vehicles in poor condition are auctioned every other Saturday. Most of them would not start, even if they had the keys. Bidding is open and there is a $75 minimum bid.

DRMO
Wright-Patterson AFB
Telephone: (513) 257-4291
        (513) 257-4203
        (513) 257-7823

Auctions are held on the second Thursday of every other month with office furniture, typewriters, hardware, tools and much more. The bidding is open with no minimums. Call to be put on the mailing list.

GSA
Dayton, OH
Telephone: (513) 225-2746

There is no GSA Office in Cleveland. If interested call Regional Director - ask for Fleet Management for auction schedule.

U.S. Marshal's Office
Telephone: (2216) 522-2150

The Marshal uses Bankers Motor Vehicles, Inc. to auction all automobile. All real estate is handled by private realtors within the area.

Jewelry is sent to Houston, Texas for auction. Advertisements on upcoming auctions appear in the Cleveland Plain Dealer - Classified Section. Also check official County papers and any local Law Journals.

FBI
Telephone: (216) 522-1400

All FBI seizures handled by GSA.

HUD
Telephone: (216) 522-4057

HUD does not hold auctions. They dispose of repossessed property through real estate brokers who have the listings and keys to the houses being offered.

Some are in good condition and some are fix-ups. FHA financing is available on those designated "FHA insured" or "with repairs needed". Prices are typically $42,500 to $51,500, put into escrow. There are "uninsured cash" listings on which you cannot get FHA financing because they do not meet the agency's standards. Prices $19,000 to $22,000 are typical.

VA
Telephone: (216) 621-5050

To purchase a home repossessed by the VA, you must contact a local real estate broker and have your sealed bid submitted by him/her. brokers have the listings and access to the homes being offered.

U.S. Postal Service -
Vehicles
Telephone: (216) 443-4040

The Postal Service no longer auctions their surplus vehicles - they are sold at fixed prices. The rural letter carries and Postal employees ar offered first choice before the public has an opportunity to purchase.

The vehicles are in running condition with high mileage and include both left-hand and right-hand drive Jeeps and vans. There are also some high mileage Plymouth K-cars included. Check with the Postal Service at the above number for date of the next sale. If any vehicles remain unsold at the fixed price, sealed bids are accepted. All undeliverable merchandise auctioned by the Post Office in Philadelphia - Telephone: (215) 895-8140.

IRS
Telephone: (216) 522-2100

The IRS auctions real estate and Personal property which has been seized for non-payment of income taxes. The number of auctions depends on the number of seizures and whether the property is redeemed by the owner or whether he chooses to pay his back taxes.

The bids are open and there are no minimum bids. Call the above number to receive current information by mail.

SBA
Telephone: (216) 522-4167

The SBA uses a Private auctioneer to dispose of foreclosed real estate and equipment of failed businesses. The bidding is open and the minimum bid is usually two-thirds of the appraised value of the property or merchandise being auctioned.

For more information call Donn and Associates - (216) 331-5503 or check the Daily Legal News for advertisements on upcoming auctions.

Defense Reutilization &
Marketing Office
Telephone: (614) 238-3244

Auctions are held once a month - second Friday at 9 a.m. Merchandise usually includes office furniture and equipment, electronics, laboratory equipment, office machines, sleeping bags, military clothing and first aid kits.

They have vehicles for auction occasionally. Merchandise can be viewed on the prior Tuesday, Wednesday and Thursday from 8 a.m. to 3 p.m. and on the day of the auction from 8 a.m. to 9 a.m.

They will be glad to send you information prior to the auction. Columbus is about two hours drive from Cleveland.

Sheriff's Department
Telephone: (216) 443-6000

The Sheriff auctions real estate every Monday at 10 a.m. on the 2nd floor of the Justice Center, The bids are open with a 10% downpayment, balance due in 30 days. The minimum starting bid is two-thirds of the appraised value of the property.

Sheriff's Department
Telephone: (216) 443-6020

The sheriff holds approximately two auctions a year on property seized by levy. Check the Daily Legal News for date, time, location, and a description of the merchandise. The auctions are open bidding and there are minimums set by their appraiser.

Geauga County Sheriff
County Courthouse
P.O. Box 224
Chardon, OH 44024
Telephone: (216) 285-2222
Ext. 247

Auctions are primarily on foreclosed homes and they will mail you information in you send a SASE to the above address. Auctions are held at least one Thursday of each month with as many as three sales a day. Check advertisements in the Geauga Times.

Medina County Sheriff
Telephone: (216) 725-0028
(216) 725-9702

The sheriff holds auctions every other week, mostly real estate foreclosures, but the banks or mortgage holders usually but the property. Vehicle auctions are rare and they usually sell one car at a time. Call the above number for further information. Check auction notices in the Medina County Gazette.

Police Department
Property Room
1300 Ontario
Telephone: (216) 623-5366

The Police Department holds one auction a year at the above address. It consists of bicycles, stereos, electronics, TVs and possibly a few vehicles. The bidding is open and there is a $1.00 minimum bid. Call the above number for information on date and time of the auction.

Private Auctioneers - Cleveland

Banker's Motor Vehicles, Inc.
Telephone: (216) 676-5920

They hold four auctions a month for the Marshal with 100 to 200 automobiles and trucks being offered. These are seized, abandoned and repossessed vehicles with the condition varying, some very good - others very poor. The bids are open and there is not a minimum bid. See advertisements in the Cleveland Plain Dealer.

Donn & Associates
Telephone: (216) 331-5505

They average two to three auctions a month with real estate, business equipment, store fixtures, machinery,restaurant equipment, etc., depending on the type of business that failed.

Autos are sometimes included, also trucks and vans and they are usually in good condition. The bidding is open and the minimum bid of two-thirds of the appraised value is required. Advertisements in the Plain Dealer and Daily Legal News.

Hart Galleries
Telephone: (713) 524-2979

They handle auctions for Cleveland U.S. Marshal's Office.

Rosen & Company
Telephone: (216) 621-1860

They hold auctions for SBA.

Grossman Inc.
Telephone: (216) 932-0777

They hold auctions for SBA.

Bambeck Auctioneers Inc.
Telephone: (216) 343-1437

They hold auctions for SBA.

GSA Surplus Sales
819 Taylor, Room 6E-04
Fort Worth, TX 76102
Telephone: (817) 334-2351

No information given by telephone. A brochure will be sent on request, along with an application for a permanent place on the Mailing List. All auctions for GSA are held in Fort Worth.

GSA - Real Estate
819 Taylor, Room 11A-26
Fort Worth, TX 76102
Telephone: (817) 334-2331

This agency rarely holds auctions but they will send information if you request it. When real estate or land is auctioned, sealed bids are used to dispose of it.

U.S. Marshal's Office
1100 Commerce Street,
Room 16-F-47
Dallas, TX 75242
Telephone: (214) 767-0836

General merchandise and automobiles are not auctioned; they are awarded for official use and shared with other agencies. Seized or forfeited real estate is handled by private realtors in the area.

Advertisements appear in the Dallas Morning News or in the local newspapers where the property was seized. Also check official County papers and local Law Journals.

FBI

All seized property turned over to GSA for disposal.

HUD
P.O.Box 2905
Fort Worth, TX 76102
Telephone: (817) 885-5960

Lists of available properties appear in the Star Telegram (Fort Worth) each Friday. Contact a licensed HUD broker who has keys to the properties, the proper forms on which sealed bids must be submitted and information which could be of value to you.

Since the broker's fee is paid by HUD, it would be to your advantage to use this service.

VA
1400 N. Valley Mills Drive
Fort Worth, TX 76799
Telephone: (817) 336-1641

Lists of available properties are published in the Dallas Morning News, Tuesday edition and in the Fort Worth Star Telegram, Tuesday edition.

Contact a licensed broker who will show you the property and submit your bid to the VA. All broker's fees are paid by the VA.

U.S. Postal Service -
Vehicles
401 DFW Turnpike
Dallas, TX 75260
Telephone: (214) 760-4680

The Postal Service has a sale of surplus fleet vehicles every two to three years with half-ton and one-ton step-vans available. The general condition of the vehicles is good.

Three years ago the one- ton vans were priced at $1,800 and one-half ton's at $1,300. Call the above number for current information on available vehicles.

U.S. Postal Service
Merchandise

All undeliverable mail is sent to Atlanta for auction.

IRS
Telephone: (214) 742-2440

U.S. Marshal handles auctions of some IRS seizures and some are sold by private auctioneers.

Notices of real estate auctions are posted at the courthouse and advertisements published in the Dallas Morning News, Dallas Herald and Fort Worth Star Telegram.

SBA
1100 Commerce Street
Room 3C-36
Dallas, TX 75242
Telephone: (214) 767-0605

The SBA uses private auctioneers to dispose of foreclosed real estate and personal property of businesses insured by the SBA. Two of these auctioneers are:
Ralph Segers - (214) 343-4055
and
Keith Carey - (817) 265-1852.
See information following under "Private Auctioneers."

U.S. Trustees - U.S.
Bankruptcy Court
1100 Commerce Street
Room 14A7
Dallas, TX 75242-1496
Telephone: (214) 767-0814

The Chapter Seven Bankruptcy Trustees are responsible for auctioning off property which has been forfeited because of non-payment of debts. The proceeds from the auction are used to pay creditor, partially, for the unpaid debts of the person who declared bankruptcy.

One of the auctioneers engaged by the U.S. trustees is Pollack, Phillips and Company. A more detailed auctioneer summary will follow.

Defense Reutilization &
Marketing Office
P.O.Box 1330
Hooks, TX 75561-1330
Telephone: (214) 334-3177

Auctions are held once every three months and include such items as furniture and equipment, surplus military clothing, typewriters, tool cabinets and shop furniture.

There are surplus military vehicles available at most auctions, the condition being poor to good. They always use spot bids and a minimum bid of $20.00 is required. They will notify you of future auctions, if you call and request it.

State Surplus Vehicles

All vehicles and merchandise are auctioned in Austin.

Dallas County Sheriff
Civil Section
600 Commerce
Dallas, TX 75202
Telephone: (214) 653-6531

Auctions are held on the first Tuesday of each month and includes real estate tax sales and abandoned and confiscated vehicles.

At some sales there are no automobiles available. The bidding is open and on vehicles there is no minimum; on the real estate tax sales there is a minimum, since the taxes are unpaid and must be satisfied by the auction.

The auction is held on the first floor, 600 Commerce Street. The only source of information regarding these auctions is the bulletin board on the first floor, 600 Commerce.

Wise County Sheriff
200 Rook Ramsey Drive
Decatur, TX 76234
Telephone: (817) 627-5971

The Wise County Sheriff holds vehicle auctions with 10 to 30 cars available. He also has land auctions and bank repossessions which include vehicles, furniture, machine shop equipment and farm equipment.

There are no set dates for the auctions but they are advertised in the Fort Worth Star and the Wise County Messenger. They do maintain a mailing list and will be glad to send you information prior to the auctions. You may also call his office for information as to the dates, times and locations.

Tarrant County Sheriff
300 W. Belknap
Fort Worth, TX 76102
Telephone: (817) 334-1300

The Sheriff of Tarrant County advertises in the Commercial Recorder when he holds auctions. he does not have a mailing list but information is posted on the bulletin board in the basement of the courthouse.

Automobiles are sometimes auctioned one at a time and land may be handled in the same manner. The courts also hand down judgments on repossessed property which can include any item that a person has purchased and failed to repay the loan.

Kaufman County Sheriff
Highway 34 South
Kaufman, TX 75142
Telephone: (214) 932-4337

The Kaufman County Sheriff holds real estate auctions on the first Tuesday of each month with advertisements published on the Terrell Tribune and the Kaufman Herald.

They do not have a mailing list but the notices are posted on the bulletin board in the Courthouse. They also have vehicle auctions with seven to eight cars and also bank repossessions of tractors and farm equipment.

Collin County Sheriff
200 S. McDonald
McKinley, TX 75069
Telephone: (214) 699-1023

The Sheriff of Collin County handles Court ordered auctions of real estate for back taxes and judgments. The vehicles available are usually abandoned cars and average 15 to 20 per auction.

Six constables hold the auctions for the sheriff and they have the information on the actual merchandise but advertisements are published in the McKinley Courier Gazette with full details given.

Grayson County Sheriff
200 S. Crockett
Sherman, TX 75090
Telephone: (214) 893-4388

The Grayson County Sheriff's auctions are usually on condemned land which is being sold for non-payment of taxes. When this land is sold, delinquent taxes are all the sheriff is trying to receive.

Therefore, the potential for getting a real bargain is great. When vehicles are auctioned, they usually have only one or two cars. For further information, you may call the Denison Tax Office (214) 465-3177.

Police Department
1955 Vilbie (off Fort
Worth Avenue)
Dallas, TX 75208
Telephone: (214) 670-3350
          (214) 670-3340

The Police Department holds three different kinds of auctions at three different locations.

1. Impounded automobiles- approximately 100 held every Monday at 1955 Vilbie. Registration is at 8:30 a.m. The bidding is open and there are no minimum bids.

2. Fleet automobiles and heavy equipment - approximately 100 held about every two months at 10 a.m. This auction is held at 2761 Municipal Street, Dallas. Condition of the vehicles is "fair" with about 60,000 miles on the fleet autos. The bidding is open and there are no minimums.

3. Stolen/unclaimed goods - TVs, VCRs guns and tools - held about every two months at the corner of Chestnut and Dawson, Dallas. The bidding is open and there are no minimums.

For information on future auctions, call the above number.

Private Auctioneers - Dallas

Auctioneer for SBA:
Keith Carey
127 Dividend Court
Arlington, TX   76012
Telephone: (817) 265-1852

Mr. Cary holds auctions other than those for Government agencies throughout the Dallas area. The merchandise auctioned is varied, depending upon the government agency, company or bank involved. For information as to dates, times and locations of future auctions, call the above number. They advertise in the Dallas Morning News, Dallas Times Herald and the Fort Worth Star Telegram. Call to be put on their mailing list.

Auctioneer for U.S. Trustees
Pollack, Southwest
12750 Merit Drive
Suite 830
Dallas, TX 75251
Telephone: ((214) 239-9788

Property of individuals who have declared bankruptcy - could include real estate, automobiles, household goods and furnishings, electronics, appliances, company trucks and vans, industrial machinery and office equipment. Auctions are held at the location of the foreclosure, whether it be a business or residence.

Advertisements are published in the Dallas Morning News and the Dallas Herald and, if machinery is being auctioned, in industrial magazines. They hold auctions for other agencies and companies and maintain a Mailing List.

Rosen Systems Inc.
2520 W. Mockingbird Lane
Dallas, TX 75235
Telephone: (214) 350-2381

They hold auctions for
bankruptcies.

Miller & Miller
Auctioneers Inc.
2525 Ridgemoar Boulevard
Suite 100
Fort Worth, TX 76116
Telephone: (817) 732-4888

They hold auctions for FDIC

Rene Bates Auctioneers Inc.
Route 4
McKinney, TX 75070
Telephone: (214) 548-9636

They hold auctions for City of
Dallas and surrounding cities and
counties.

Jim Keepings Auctions
5103 Lawnview
Dallas, TX 75227
Telephone: (214) 388-8721

They hold auctions for U.S.
Marshal & Treasury Department.

Jim Short - Nelson
International
11811 Preston Rd.
Suite 100
Dallas, TX 75230
Telephone: (214) 980-7539

They hold auctions for State
surplus items.

GSA
Denver Federal Center
7 FBP-8 Bldg. 41
P.O. Box 25506
Denver, CO   80225-0506
Telephone: (303) 236-7707

The GSA has no set schedule for auctions, the frequency depends on the amount of merchandise turned over to them by other government agencies. Auctions include such items as: U.S. Government surplus vehicles, office equipment, furniture and machines, medical equipment and supplies from VA hospitals and equipment from NASA test facilities. Well maintained vehicles, no more than three years old and mileage varying between 17,000 and 100,000 miles. Never less than 50 vehicles nor more than 150. Open bids with reserve.

To be placed on GSA mailing list for prior notification of auctions, call (303) 236-7707.

U.S.Marshal's Office
P.O. Box 3599
Denver, CO   80294
Telephone: (303) 844-2801

General merchandise is handled by an auctioneer hired by the Marshal. Vehicles are auctioned by the Marshal's staff. real estate is handled by private realtors within the area. Advertisements are published in Rocky Mt. Post. Also, check the official County papers and any local Law Journals.

FBI

All FBI seized merchandise is auctioned by the GSA

HUD - Property
Disposition
Executive Tower
1405 Curtis Street
Denver, CO 80202
Telephone: (303) 844-6689
Recording: (303) 844-4061

Lists of available properties appear in Friday and Sunday editions (classified section) of Rocky Mt. News, Denver Post, Colorado Springs Gazette, Pueblo Grand Valley Sentinel and the Pueblo Chieftain. You may also call the above number for a recorded message for information.

VA
44 Union Boulevard
P.O. Box 25126
Denver, CO 80225
Telephone: (303) 980-1300

The VA has from 50 to 100 foreclosed houses each month, $5,000 to $20,000 under market value, which are located in many different areas. To bid on these properties, contact any local real estate broker for information. Your bid must be submitted through a broker or through the Board of Realtors.

U.S. Postal Service
Vehicles
915 S. Logan
Denver, CO 80209
Telephone: (303) 297-6730

The Post Office does not auction its surplus vehicles, instead they have a continuous fixed price sale on surplus Postal Service cars, trucks and jeeps (right-hand drive). At present only half-ton trucks, 1971-73 models, are for sale at prices ranging from $450 to $750. Next year jeeps and cars will be for sale.

All unclaimed and undeliverable mail and packages are sent to St. Paul, Minnesota, for public auction.

IRS
600 17th Street
Denver, CO 80202
Telephone: (303) 825-7041
Recording: (303) 844-5417

The IRS has no set schedules for auctions as they are dependent on the accumulation of seized property. Notices of forthcoming auctions are posted on the Bulletin Board in the IRS office, and in advertisements appearing in the Rocky Mt. News and Denver Post.

SBA
721 19th Street, Room 439
Denver, CO 80201-0660
Telephone: (303) 844-4291

The type of merchandise auctioned by the SBA depends on the kind of businesses being liquidated. It could be a bakery, machine shop or hardware store. There are open bids on general merchandise and minimum bids only on commercial real estate.

U.S. Trustees - Bankruptcy
Court
1845 Sherman Street
Denver, CO 80203
Telephone: (303) 844-5188

U.S. Trustees for the Bankruptcy court engage private auctioneers for disposal of real and personal property seized by the Court. Check newspapers for public notices regarding bankruptcies, finding the name of the individual declaring bankruptcy and calling the above number for that person's trustee.

Defense Reutilization &
Marketing Office
Fort Carson Building 318
Colorado Springs, CO 80913-
5044
Telephone: (719) 579-4355

They hold auctions once a month with surplus military vehicles, office furniture, and equipment and other surplus items. Bidding is by spot method with no minimums. For further information call the above number and ask that their catalogue be sent to you.

Defense Reutilization &
Marketing Office
Building 621
Rocky Mountain Arsenal
Commerce City, CO 80022-
2180
Telephone: (303) 289-0378

Auctions are held as needed and include such items as office furniture, military surplus vehicles, office equipment and typewriters. For date of next auction or further information, call the above number and ask that their catalog be mailed to you.

State Surplus Vehicles
1001 E 62nd Avenue
Denver, CO 80216
Telephone: (303) 287-7940

They will hold no auctions until 1990.

Colorado Department of
Highways - Purchasing
4201 E. Arkansas
Denver, CO 80222
Telephone: (303) 757-9236

This agency holds three to four auctions a year (in Summer) and the merchandise could include any equipment used for highway maintenance, such as graders, snowplows, dump trucks, sedans, trucks, posts and miscellaneous tools and machinery.

To receive flyers on future auctions send SASE to the above address.

Sheriff's Department
Car Pound
5160 N York Street
Denver, CO 80216
Telephone: (303) 295-4363

The Sheriff holds auctions every other Wednesday at the car pound with approximately 50 vehicles to be sold. The bidding is open and there are no minimum bids. All cars sell at every auction.

Sheriff's Department
Civil Division
City and County Building
Room 507
Denver, CO 80202
Telephone: (303) 575-5192

The Sheriff holds approximately 12-15 auctions a year on properties seized through levy. It is primarily real estate (not personal property). For additional information and specifics, call the above number. They do not maintain a mailing list.

Police Department
5160 York Street
Denver, CO 80216
Telephone: (303) 295-4361

The Police Department holds auctions every other Wednesday at the Sheriff's Car Pound, 5226 Brighton at 10 a.m. Vehicles only are auctioned, with an average of 50 to 150 per auction. The bids are open and there is no minimum bid.

Denver County Sheriff
City and County Building
Room 507
Denver, CO 80202
Telephone: (303) 575-5192

The Sheriff held over 80 auctions last year of vehicles, personal property and real estate being sold. He uses public TV and the Daily Journal to advertise the sales, and lists are posted on the bulletin board at this address.

In many cases scheduled foreclosure auctions are cancelled because the owner paid the judgment before the date of sale. Call the above number or check newspaper ads for current information on upcoming auctions.

Clear Creek County Sheriff
P.O. Box 2000
Georgetown, CO 80444
Telephone: (303) 569-3251

The Sheriff held two auctions last year but, unfortunately, no one came to the second one. There were good bargains, we were told, with one vehicle and quite a variety of personal property for sale but "no one showed up". The sheriff also holds real estate foreclosures and he advertises in the Clear Creek Courier. For information on the next auction, call the above number.

Jefferson County Sheriff
17900 W. 10th Avenue
Golden, CO 80401-2697
Telephone: (303) 277-0211

One auction is held each year with surplus vehicles, seized vehicles, boats, TVs, VCRs and other personal property for sale. Advertisements are published in the Rocky Mountain News and Denver Post. Call the number above for information on the next auction.

Private Auctioneers - Denver

Olde Cumberlin
Auctioneers
1155 N Colorado Avenue
Box 248
Brush, CO 80723
Telephone: (303) 842-2822

They handle auctions for IRS and Farmers Home Administration

Donald Freedburge &
Associates
2734 S. Milwaukee Street
Denver, CO 80210
Telephone: (303) 758-1510

They hold auctions for the State.

413

McCrea & Company
Auctioneers
5895 East 72nd Avenue
Commerce City, CO 80022
Telephone: (303) 289-4437

They hold auctions for local cities and Counties.

Colorado Auction Service
P.O. Box 33
Louveires, CO 80131
(Speak with Red Freisen)
Telephone: (303) 791-7243

They hold auctions for U.S. postal Services.

Larry Latham
Auctioneers Inc.
320 W. Olive
Fort Collins, CO 80521
Telephone: (303) 482-2828

They hold auctions for HUD, VA and FHA.

GSA
Telephone: (312) 353-6064

Because of the economy of the automobile industry in Detroit, no automobile auctions are held there. The GSA in Chicago handles these auctions. Detroit has no auctions by the GSA at present.

U.S. Marshal's Office
Telephone: (313) 226-2801

The Marshal uses his staff to auction General merchandise. items such as expensive jewelry sent to Texas for disposal. All automobiles are auctioned by Midwest Auto - (313) 538-2100; all real estate by PHC of Michigan - (313) 772-7710. The Marshal does not advertise - all advertising done by others, i.e., Midwest Auto and PHC in Detroit Free Press (no set days) and Detroit Legal News, a weekly publication. Also check the official County papers.

FBI

U.S. Marshal handles auctions of all seized properties.

HUD
Telephone: (313) 226-7144

HUD does not hold auctions. Lists of the available properties appear every two weeks in the Detroit News (Friday edition) and the Free Press (Saturday edition). Prices are in the advertisement. If you are interested in a property, Contact a licensed real estate broker to submit your bid.

VA
Telephone: (313) 226-4200

The VA holds no auctions. Sales listings come out every third Friday and only real estate brokers can receive them. To make an offer on a VA property, contact a VA-affiliated broker who can give you all necessary information. Listings include the entire State of Michigan.

U.S. Postal Service
Telephone: (313) 226-8500

The Postal Service holds no auctions but sells surplus Postal vehicles at a fixed price as they come in. To learn what is currently available, call the above number.

Undeliverable and unclaimed Postal Service merchandise is sent to St. Paul, Minnesota for auction.

IRS
Telephone: (313) 237-0800

The IRS seizes personal property and real estate for nonpayment of income taxes. Advertisements appear in the Detroit Free Press and Detroit News prior to the auction. You may also read the flyers posted at Detroit City Council, County Building and the Post Office. IRS auctions may include real estate, automobiles, other vehicles, boats, airplanes, jewelry, household goods, etc. Some excellent bargains are available.

SBA
Telephone: (313) 226-6075

There have been no SBA auctions for a number of months. They use Private auctioneers; therefore, it would be wise to check the auction advertisement in local papers for those designated "SBA Foreclosure."

U.S. Trustees
Telephone: (313) 226-7999

Bankruptcy auctions are listed in the Detroit News every Wednesday in the Classified Section. All necessary information in contained in the advertisements.

Defense Reutilization & Marketing Office
Telephone: (313) 466-4586

Auctions are held every six weeks and include Army clothing, furniture, office equipment, appliances and vehicles. There are from two to twenty autos and trucks for auction in fair condition - 50% are driveable. No major repairs are necessary.

They will notify you of upcoming auctions if you call the above number and request it.

State Surplus Vehicles
State of Michigan
Department of Management
& Budget
Office Services Division
Telephone: (517) 334-6858

These auctions are usually held twice a month and offer exceptional bargains. The automobiles auctioned are in good condition. The 1980 and up models, and all are driveable. An average of 450 automobiles and 150 trucks and vans are offered ar each auction. According to Mr. Stanton the Auctioneer, the public considers them "very good deals." Office furniture and refrigerators are also included in the items for sale.

Sheriff's Department
Telephone: (313) 494-3060

The Sheriff holds a merchandise auction on the third Thursday of each month at the Detroit Police Station, 1300 Beaubien Street. Items offered for sale are seized properties and include TVs, VCRs, stereos, clothes and sometimes jewelry. At times, a separate auction is held for jewelry only. Auction times vary - call the above number for additional information and times.

Sheriff's Department
Telephone: (313) 479-4360

This auction is held each Wednesday at one p.m. at the above address (corner of Telegraph and Sibley). They offer approximately 250 vehicles although they are enlarging the lot to accommodations more. The majority of the cars are driveable and, if not, this is announced. There are all makes and all years; some new and great. the bidding is open and there are minimum bids. This auction may also include automobiles from private individuals.

Washtenaw County Sheriff
Telephone: (313) 971-9798

The Sheriff holds one auction a year on surplus and personal property. He advertises in the Ann Arbor News prior to each auction. You may call the above number for information on upcoming auctions.

Oakland County Sheriff
Telephone: (313) 858-4950

The Sheriff holds two auctions a year, one in the spring and one in the fall. The auctioneer he uses is Robert Williams Auctioneers at (313) 559-5551. You may call their office and ask to be put on the mailing list.

Macomb County Sheriff
Telephone: (313) 469-5151

The sheriff holds one auction a year, in the fall, with personal property and vehicles available. Some surplus vehicles are included and are in good condition. Rifles, shotguns, stereos and office equipment are usually among the items available.

Police Department
1300 Beaubien Street
Telephone: (313) 596-2092

The Police department holds one auction a month at the above address at 9 a.m. Items auctioned include household goods, stereos, TVs, stoves, refrigerators, furniture and jewelry. Anything that can be found in a home is up for auction. The bidding is open and there are minimum bids.

Police Department Impound
6311 Caniff
Telephone: (313) 267-7174

Auctions are held every third Tuesday at the above address at 9 a.m. Check with the Police Department to verify dates. Fifty or less impounded vehicles are auctioned, most not driveable and in poor condition. The bidding is open and there are no minimums.

Private Auctioneers - Detroit

Mr. Bill Stanton
Telephone: (517) 726-0181

Mr. Stanton holds approximately 200 auctions a year, not primarily for the State. He auctions as many as 600 cars, trucks and buses in one day, most of which are good, average age four to five years, with approximately 60,000 miles on them. He sometimes auctions items such as antique tractors (1930's) and gas engines (1910-1920's). All of his auctions are advertised in the Auction Exchange, Box 57, Plainwell, Michigan 49080. Telephone: (616) 685-1343

420

PHC of Michigan
Telephone: (313) 772-7710

This auctioneer handles all real estate for the Marshal's Office. The properties are acquired by seizures or Court Order and the number will vary each month.

Notices of Auctions are posted in the Federal Court House, and advertised in the Detroit Free Press and the weekly Detroit Legal News.

Midwest Auto
Telephone: (313) 538-2100

Midwest Auto holds an automobile auction every Friday at 10 a.m. All types of motor vehicles are sold and the Marshal's vehicles are included. The condition of the vehicles varies from poor to excellent. The bidding is open and the owner of the vehicle has final approval of the highest offer.

Farris Brothers Furniture
Telephone: (313) 843-5720

They hold auctions for local Government cities & Counties on Estates.

Robert Williams & Company
Telephone: (313) 559-5551

They hold auctions for Oakland County & surrounding cities.

L M Koploy & Company
Telephone: (313) 559-0660

They hold auctions for U.S. Marshal's Office and trustees.

GSA

(No GSA Office in Houston. Fort Worth handles all business.)

U.S. Marshal's Office
515 Rusk, 10th Floor
Houston, TX 77002
Telephone: (713) 229-2806
Recording: (713) 229-2806

There are Jewelry sales about every two months and Estate sales every four months. Vehicles are auctioned two or three times per year, as needed. The Marshal's Office advertises in the Houston Post and Houston Chronicle and notices are posted outside the office door on the 10th Floor.

FBI

U.S. Marshal handles FBI seized vehicles and merchandise. For recorded information on upcoming auctions, locations and dates call (713) 229-2806.

HUD
2211 Norfolk
Houston, TX 77098
Telephone: (713) 653-3220

Listings of available properties each Friday in the Houston Post. You have ten days to submit a bid through a HUD broker. The bids are opened on the Tuesday ten days after the advertisement appears, and the highest bidder gets the property.

VA
2515 Murworth
Houston, TX 77025
Telephone: (713) 664-4664

Available properties are advertised on Thursday and Saturday in the Houston Post and Houston Chronicle. All information is in the advertisement - price, location and how to bid.

U.S. Postal Service
401 Franklin
Houston, TX 77201
Telephone: (713) 226-3434

Surplus Post Office Vehicles are for sale at fixed prices on an on-going daily basis. They can be viewed at a Vacant Lot - 7511 N. Shepherd Street. On occasions, when vehicles do not bring the "fixed price" - sealed bids are accepted. all unclaimed or undeliverable merchandise is sent to Atlanta, Georgia for auction.

IRS
P.O. Box 27724
Houston, TX
Telephone: (713) 965-0440

The IRS has no set schedule for auctions. Advertisements are run in the Houston Post and Houston Chronicle prior to each auction and notices are also posted in IRS Offices.

Merchandise acquired through confiscation for non-payment of taxes and can include real estate, jewelry, automobiles, trucks, vans, campers, boats, appliances and TVs. To be placed on their mailing list sent SASE to:

Special Procedures Function
P.O. Box 42837
STOP 5020H- BP
Houston, TX 77242-2837

U.S. Trustees - Bankruptcy Court
515 Rusk, 4th Floor
Houston, TX
Telephone: (713) 226-4115

Trustees do not have mailing lists. Call auctioneers in yellow pages and ask if they hold bankruptcy Auctions. Most auctioneers will put you on a mailing list.

State Surplus Vehicles
P.O. Box 13047
Capitol Station
Austin, TX
Telephone: (512) 463-3381

Auctions held in Austin every two months. The vehicles are State Trooper cars, Youth Division and other State Agencies' autos. They usually have from 80,000 to 90,000 miles on the odometer and have been well-maintained.

There are no minimum bids. Surplus merchandise such as office furniture and equipment is auctioned at the same time. To receive an application to be put on the mailing list, call or write the above Agency.

Sheriff's Department
1301 Franklin
Houston, TX
Telephone: (713) 221-6044

The Sheriff's Department does not hold auctions; eight Constables handle them. Notices are posted at the Family Law Center, 115 Congress. There is no telephone there are reading the notices is the only way to obtain information.

Harris County Sheriff
1115 Congress
Houston, TX
Telephone: (713) 221-5500

The Harris County Sheriff advertises real estate in the Houstonian and the Daily Court Review. Information on other auctions is posted on the first floor bulletin board. Real estate auctions are usually held on the first Thursday of each month. Others are scheduled as needed, with Deputies acting as auctioneers. At a recent vehicle auction a Lamborghini (model unknown) was sold for $2,000.

Liberty County Sheriff
2113 San Houston
Liberty, TX 77575
Telephone: (409) 336-8906

The Sheriff of Liberty County advertises in the Liberty Vindicator and the Cleveland Advocate. The auction information is also posted at the county courthouse. He handles real estate tax sales and court-ordered vehicle sales. You may call for further information.

Montgomery County
Sheriff
208 W. Davis
Conroe, TX 77301
Telephone: (409) 539-7989

The Montgomery County Sheriff held three auctions last year on vehicles, surplus and confiscated, personal property such as bicycles, golf carts, stereo speakers, water skis, snow skis, etc. They do not handle real estate auctions. At a recent auction 1985 and 1986 Sheriff's cars sold for $3,000 and bicycles went for $5.00 to $30.00. The sheriff advertises in the Houston Chronicle and the Conroe Courier. Grover Howell is the auctioneer used by the sheriff and you may contact him for additional information.

Fort Bend County Sheriff
500 Liberty
Richmond, TX 77469
Telephone: (713) 341-4686

The Sheriff of Fort Bend County holds one vehicle auction a year with approximately 20 - 25 cars available. The Sheriff advertises in the Herald Coaster and he will be glad to put you on the mailing list to be notified prior to the date of sale.

Chambers County Sheriff
P.O. Box 998
Anawack, TX 77514
Telephone: (409) 267-6761

The Chambers County Sheriff held one auction last year with vehicles and real estate being sold. Advertisements are published in The Progress and the Gulf Coast News or you may call the Sheriff's Office for current information.

Police Department
Vehicles
33 Artesian
Houston, TX 77002
Telephone: (713) 247-5806

The Police Department has three to five different auction locations each day. Information on locations can be obtained by calling (713) 247-5812.

Private Auctioneers - Houston

Houston Auctions
701 N. Shepherd
Houston, TX 77007
Telephone: (713) 862-4556

They hold five auctions per month, with 300 to 400 vehicles at each one. Automobiles, trucks, motorcycles and heavy equipment are included.

They hold auctions for 40 different Agencies and Companies including Banks, Finance Companies, Police Department and private individuals.

Windsor Auctions
(for SBA)
2117 Judi Way
Houston, TX 77018
Telephone: (713) 680-8001

They hold two auctions a month and the merchandise can range from automobiles to antique swords from Spain. Usually furniture, furs, jewelry, TVs stereos and typewriters are included.The automobiles are primarily early 1980 models.

426

Fuller Commercial Brokers
(for SBA)
1990 Post Oak Boulevard
Houston, TX 77056
Telephone: (713) 850-8400

They have no set schedule but hold auctions as properties are foreclosed. Brochures on available properties are available by calling the above number.

Federal Auctions
(for SBA)
713 Lehman Street
Houston, TX 77018
Telephone: (713) 688-6688

The number of auctions varies from one to four a month. They hold bankruptcy and foreclosure auctions and merchandise ranges from heavy machinery to household furniture and appliances.Call the above number to be placed on mailing list.

Hart Galleries
2311 Westheimer
Houston, TX 77098
Telephone: (713) 524-2979

They hold auctions of jewelry for U.S. Marshal in several States.

Martin Auctioneers
Company
P.O. Box 1282
Sheppard, TX
Telephone: (713) 692-6837

They hold auctions for Police vehicles.

Les Elliott
P.O. Box 1092
Del Rio, TX 78841
Telephone: (512) 774-4255

They hold vehicle auctions for the Houston U.S. Marshal's Office.

427

GSA
Telephone: (317) 226-6234

All auctions for the Indianapolis area are arranged by the Region Five SBA office in Chicago.

Advertisements are published in the Indianapolis Star or you may call (312) 353-0246 for auction information.

U.S. Marshal
Telephone: (317) 226-6566

The GSA auctions automobiles and other U.S. Marshal items along with merchandise from other agencies.

Private auctioneers are used to handle the auctions and the bidding is open with the auctioneers giving the minimum bid. Look for the GSA notices of auction in the Indianapolis Star.

FBI
Telephone: (317) 639-3301

All FBI seizures are sent to the U.S. Marshal for auction.

HUD
Telephone: (317) 226-7043

This office handles repossessed homes in the entire State of Indiana. Most are single-family homes and are usually in the $9,000 to $75,000 range. Many are "fixer-uppers" and are sold "as is".

Advertisements appear in the Indianapolis Sunday Star and on Wednesdays in the Indiana News and the Star. The properties are listed with local realtors and the advertisements contain descriptions of the properties, the addresses and the listed prices. To submit a bid, you must contact a real estate broker who has all the information about the property in which you may be interested. After the advertisement appears, there is a seven-day bidding period. If your bid is accepted, a down payment of $300 to $2,000 is required and you have 60 days to obtain financing. The broker's fee is paid by HUD.

VA
Telephone: (317) 226-7830

The Properties which have been foreclosed by the VA are advertised each Sunday in the Indianapolis Star.

You must contact a real estate broker to inspect the property and submit a bid within the 10-day period after the advertisement appears. If your bid is accepted, you have 45 to 60 days to arrange financing. A down-payment of $100.00 to $3,000, depending on the property, is required. The VA also has Trader Margin properties (those that have not sold in an acceptable length of time) and reasonable bids below the listed price will buy the property. Some of these houses, while not desirable to everyone, can be purchased at figures too low to believe.

U.S. Postal Service
Telephone: (317) 464-6081

This agency does not have auctions but holds an on-going sale of surplus Postal Service vehicles with fixed prices.

They usually have 2-1/2 ton vans and one-ton trucks. Some are left-hand and others are right-hand drive. To learn what vehicles are available, call the above number for information. All undeliverable or unclaimed merchandise is sent to St. Paul, Minnesota for auction.

IRS
Telephone: (317) 226-5477

Personal property and real estate seized for non-payment of income taxes is auctioned by the IRS They do not have a set schedule because the number of auctions depends on the property seizures by the agency.
Merchandise can include real estate, automobiles, jewelry, furs, coin collections or anything of value which can be sold to satisfy the amount of taxes due. You may call the above number to be placed on the mailing list.

SBA
Telephone: (317) 226-7272

This Agency uses private auctioneers to dispose of real estate, equipment and inventories of businesses which have failed to repay bank loans guaranteed by the SBA.
The auctions are held at the location of the foreclosed property and there are always minimum bids. In this area the banks are responsible for arranging 90% of all auctions and advertisements will be published in the Sunday Indianapolis Star (South Side Edition) under Classification 647.

Sheriff's Department
Telephone: (317) 633-5181

The Sheriff holds three to four vehicle auctions each year and the same number on seized merchandise.

The vehicle auction usually has between 20 to 30 autos available with the condition ranging from fair to good. The bidding is open and there are usually notices in the Indianapolis Star.

Police Department
Telephone: (317) 236-3474

Vehicle auctions are held every two months and include abandoned and seized automobiles, trucks and vans, in fair to good condition.

There are no minimums and the bidding is open. Merchandise auctions are held twice a year, in April and November. Merchandise includes seized, confiscated and unclaimed items such as silverware, TVs, stereos, VCRs bicycles and any household items a burglar can carry out of a home. The bidding is open, with no minimums.

State Surplus Vehicles
Telephone: (317) 232-1365

This agency holds a vehicle auction on the first Thursday of each month at 4555 Lafayette Road.

The automobiles and trucks are police cars and vehicles from County and State Agencies, in good condition with mileage between 60,000 and 100,000. The average price is $3,000; $$4,000 for 1986 and 1987 models. There are usually 50 to 75 vehicles at each auction and there are minimum bids on some vehicles. Payment in full must be made on the day of the sale. Call to be placed on their mailing list with advance notice of vehicles to be sold.

This Agency disposes of surplus office furniture and equipment by sealed bids submitted to the state office. Look for advertisements in the Sunday Indianapolis Star and the Times for more information on these sales.

DRMO
Telephone: (317) 543-6615
              (317) 543-6616

Surplus military equipment, clothing, office furniture and equipment plus many more items are auctioned every two months at the above location. Call the above number to receive fliers prior to the auction.

Private Auctioneers - Indianapolis

Heimel Auction Service
59 North Second
Beechgrove, IN 46107
Telephone: (317) 783-9627

This auctioneer handles sales for the SBA, U.S. Trustees and banks on foreclosures. His weekly auctions are held every Thursday ar 6 p.m. and are 99% consignment with jewelry, paintings and household goods offered.

On SBA and bankruptcy auctions, the real estate, household goods and vehicles are sometimes auctioned at the location of the foreclosure. Call the above number and ask to be placed on their mailing list.

432

Herman Strakis
3333 West Tory
Indianapolis, IN   46225
Telephone: (317) 244-8063

This auctioneer holds 15 or more auctions each month, including those for the SBA. There are minimum bids only on government cars and merchandise and the items will be withdrawn if the bidding is too low.

Merchandise auctioned includes real estate, commercial and residential, jewelry, household goods, TVs and stereos plus much more. Call to be placed on their mailing list.

Marsh Auction Gallery
Telephone: (317) 263-3030

This company holds sheriff's auctions, as well as Court Judgments, seizures, estate sales and consignments.

Merchandise includes furniture, linens, tools, cars, appliances, TVs paintings, china and crystal. Special auctions are held for jewelry only. There are no minimum bids as a rule and the bidding is open. Advertisements appear in the Sunday edition of the Sun Star, with a complete list of all items to be sold on the following Tuesday. The weekly auctions are held each Tuesday at 9 a.m. with inspection on Monday from 12 noon until 7 p.m.

GSA
4400 College Boulevard
Overland Park, MO 66211
Telephone: (913) 236-2523
or
1-800-392-7711
(Missouri only)

The GSA offers merchandise for auction once a month at 1500 E. Bannister, Kansas City. A variety of merchandise is available, ranging from medical and office equipment to automobiles. All vehicles auctioned are late models in good condition and low mileage.

The merchandise may be viewed the day preceding the auction and immediately before the auction begins. Merchandise and surplus GSA vehicles are auctioned through sealed bids. All newer vehicles are bid on openly. The GSA maintains a mailing list which can provide more specific information. Contact Gene Palmer at the number above to have your name placed on the list.

U.S. Marshal
811 Grand Avenue
Room 509
Kansas City, MO 64106
Telephone: (816) 426-3521

The Marshal does not have regularly scheduled auctions because the frequency depends on how much merchandise is sent to him by other agencies.

A private auctioneer, DeWeese Auctions, handles both merchandise and auto auctions for the Marshal. Real estate is disposed of through local realtors in the area.

FBI

The U.S. Marshal handles all FBI merchandise for auction.

HUD
1103 Grand
Kansas City, MO 64106
Telephone: (816) 374-6209

All foreclosed properties are advertised in the Kansas City Star on Friday. In order to bid you must contact a licensed broker who will submit your sealed bid. The broker's fee is paid by HUD.

VA
601 E. 12th Street
Room 260
Kansas City, MO 64106
Telephone: (816) 426-3782
Recording: (816) 426-2210

To receive a list of available properties, call the above number and it will be mailed to you. If there is something listed that you would be interested in seeing, contact a realtor and he will show you the property and submit your bid. (VA pays realtor's commission.)
    Missouri residents may call 1-800-392-3761 for further information. The listings are also published in the Daily Record.

U.S. Postal Service
3131 Wyandotte
Kansas City, MO 64111
Telephone: (816) 374-9231

The Post Office has an ongoing sale, with fixed prices, of surplus trucks, vans and Jeeps. To learn what is available, call the above number for information.

U.S. Postal Service
315 W Pershing Road
Room 546
Kansas City, MO 64108
Telephone: (816) 374-9231

Three or four fixed price sales are held each year to dispose of surplus merchandise such as calculators, typewriters, office furniture, carrying cases, bookcases, paper, etc. If you call the above number, they will send you this information by mail.

435

SBA
Telephone: (816) 374-6708

The SBA uses a private auctioneer to dispose of foreclosed and forfeited property of businesses which have failed to repay loans guaranteed by the Agency. (Auctioneer information follows.)

U.S. Customs

See the material on U.S. Customs in Section One, Chapter 1.

U.S. Trustees (Bankruptcy)

Each Chapter Seven Trustee is responsible for handling auctions of forfeited property of his bankruptcy cases.

By law these auctions must be published prior to the sale. The notices will specify (Bankruptcy auction) and can be found in the Legal Notices section of local newspapers.

Police Department
1125 Locust
Kansas City, MO 64106
Telephone: (816) 234-5000

The Police Department auctions vehicles on the first Tuesday of each month, 8:30 a.m., at 1st and Lydia. There are usually 300 to 400 vehicles being offered, most in poor condition as they have been towed, not seized.

Merchandise sales are held once each year, in the month of May, with TVs VCRs, bicycles and other stolen, unclaimed items available.

There are no minimum bids on vehicles but on merchandise there may be, depending on the item being auctioned.

D.R.M.O.
P.O. Box 6010
Whiteman A.F.B.,
MO 65305-6100
Telephone: (816) 687-3308

They hold auctions every three months to dispose of surplus military goods, such as office furniture, appliances, typewriters, shelving, clothing and much more. The vehicles they auction are for scrap or salvage and rarely have one that is driveable.

If you wish to receive fliers prior to the auction, call the above number and ask to be added to the mailing list.

Private Auctioneers - Kansas City

Auctioneer for U.S. Marshal
DeWese Auctions
(Missouri Auction School)
1600 Genesee
Kansas City, MO 64102
Telephone: (816) 421-7117

This company holds auctions for the U.S. Marshal, as well as for Customs, FDIC and others. To be placed on the mailing list call the above number to receive fliers.

Auctioneer for SBA
Roger Porter
P.O. Box 8
1036 W. Ironwood
Olathe, KS 66061
Telephone: (913) 782-8009

This auctioneer advertises in the Kansas City Star on Sunday, under Auctions, for the SBA and others. Merchandise can include furniture, clothing, TVs, washers and dryers; any items belonging to failed businesses, from equipment to inventories.Call the above number for more information.

GSA
4747 S. Eastern Avenue
Bell, CA 90012
Telephone: (213) 894-3210
Hotline/Recording:
(213) 894-5162

GSA holds auctions of seized or forfeited items at:
Sealed Bid Field Office
5600 Rickenbacker Road
Building 5-E
Bell, CA

There is no schedule of auctions as their frequency depends on the amount of merchandise brought to them by the U.S. Marshal, FBI and federal agencies. Call the Hotline number above for current information and write to GSA Regional Sales Office, 525 Market Street - 33rd Floor, San Francisco, California 94105 to be placed on the mailing list.

U.S. Marshal's Office
312 Spring Street, 1st Floor
Los Angeles, CA 90012
Telephone: (213) 894-2484
Hotline: (213) 894-2495

Most goods sent to GSA for auction. Private auctioneers used occasionally. Check auction section of Los Angeles Times, classified advertisements, and also official County papers and local Law Journals.

FBI
Telephone: (213) 477-6565

U.S. Marshal handles all FBI seizures.

HUD
1615 W. Olympic Boulevard
Los Angeles, CA 90015
Telephone: (213) 251-7136

Lists of available properties are published in the Sunday Los Angeles Times. You must go through a licensed broker to submit a bid.

If you see a listed property which interests you, contact a broker of your choice, see the property (broker has keys), and submit your sealed bid. HUD pays the broker's fees - no cost to the bidder.

VA
1100 Wilshire Boulevard
Los Angeles, CA 90017
Telephone: (213) 209-7175

VA foreclosed homes are listed in the Sunday Los Angeles Times, along with VA affiliated brokers to contact. The brokers have keys and can show you the homes.

Many are fixer-uppers, others are in good condition. All are sold "as is." Sealed bids on VA forms are submitted only through the brokers at no charge to the bidder. VA pays broker's fee.

U.S. Postal Service
1375 N. Western Avenue
Hollywood, CA 90027
Telephone: (213) 464-7591
         (Garage number)

The Postal Service does not auction its surplus vehicles but sells them to the public at fixed prices. The number of vehicles available varies because additional vans are continually being added to the surplus inventory.

Half-ton and one-ton delivery vans are usually the only types to be sold. Some are sold from $500 to $600 and are in poor condition. Those that go for $1,500 to $1,600 are in good condition but they may have high mileage. The vehicles may be inspected from 10 a.m. to 1.30 p.m., Monday through Friday at the above address.All undeliverable merchandise sent to San Francisco for auction.

IRS
Telephone: (714) 643-4523
Hotline: (213) 894-5777

Each revenue officer is responsible for the auction of his seizures and only he has the information as to dates, times and merchandise or property.

There could be 20 or more auctions of seized properties each month.Call the Hotline number. It gives you everything you need to know about the what, when and where of current auctions.

SBA
Federal Station
Box 1869
Los Angeles, CA 90053
Telephone: (213) 482-5535

The SBA uses private auctioneers and the advertisements are found in the Sunday Los Angeles Times, Metro Section. They have no set schedule as the frequency depends on how many businesses insured by SBA fail. Send SASE for information.

U.S. Customs

All Customs auctions of seized merchandise are handled by Northrop Worldwide Aircraft, Inc. (See Customs information in Section One, Chapter 1).

There are a number of opportunities in the Los Angeles area to pick up some real bargains at these auctions. In one recent auction, three aircraft were offered (one for salvage only), boats, gold jewelry and art, as well as less unusual items such as shoes, clothing, handbags, luggage, etc.

U.S. Trustees - Bankruptcy
Court
300 N Los Angeles Street
Room 3101
Los Angeles, CA 90012
Telephone: (213) 894-6387

The auctions are held every other month at this location for disposal of surplus County merchandise and unclaimed stolen property from the Sheriff. Merchandise can include typewriters, computers, TVs, cameras, radios, stereos - anything small enough to be carried out by a burglar. Call the above number for date of the next auction.

Los Angeles State Garage
122 S. Hill Street
Los Angeles, CA 90012
Telephone: (213) 620-4450

Approximately one auction a month is held at the above address of State vehicles, trucks, vans, pick-ups and 4-wheel drive vehicles. Usually about 60 are sold, most are running.

The bidding is open and there are no minimums. They do not have a mailing list, so it is necessary to call for the date of their next auction.

Public Administrator/
Public Guardian
Box 11526
Santa Ana, CA
(Orange County) 92711
Telephone: (714) 567-7660

This agency holds one auction every other month to dispose of

441

property of persons who died without leaving a will. He also auctions for other agencies in the State. The merchandise usually includes household furniture, TVs appliances (small), paintings, collections of many types.

There are usually two or three automobiles auctioned - some in very good condition. The bidding is open and there are no minimums. Call for information on the next auction.

Los Angeles County
Marshal
110 N. Grand, Room 525
Los Angeles, CA 90012
Telephone: (213) 974-6311

They have four auctions a month if there is sufficient merchandise. Real estate is auctioned at the above address. Automobiles and personal property at different locations.

They do not know the condition of the vehicles until they are delivered to the auction site. The make, model and year is all they can tell you prior to the auction. No mailing list is maintained - call the above number for information on both real estate and automobile auctions.

Sheriff's Department
Warehouse
6905 E. Elm
Commerce, CA 90040
Telephone: (213) 720-6952
             (Recording)

They hold approximately three auctions a year and offer only Sheriff's vehicles and heavy equipment. Sealed bids only are accepted. Advertisements for the auctions are posted on the Sheriff's bulletin board or you may request auction information by sending a postcard or letter to P.O. Box 22259, Commerce, California 90040.

Also, call the above number for recorded information.

Orange County Sheriff
1300 S. Grand
Tustin, CA 92681
Telephone: (714) 567-7660

The Sheriff and Public Administrator combined held approximately 20 auctions last year for the Police, Public Administrator and mini-storage facilities.

Some great bargains were available, for instance paintings worth thousands were sold for $25.00. Real estate foreclosures, deceased persons' estate sales (everything in some very nice homes), bicycles, jewelry, desks, TVs and car parts were some of the items available. The auctions are advertised in local newspapers and flyers are distributed throughout the area.

Ventura County Sheriff
800 S. Victoria
Ventura,.CA 93009
Telephone: (805) 654-2311

The Sheriff holds more real estate foreclosure auctions than any other kind but the frequency varies according to the number of levies and Court orders handed down.

Vehicles are usually auctioned one at a time. Advertisements are published in different newspapers depending on the location of the property.

Riverside County Sheriff
4293 Orange Street
Riverside, CA 92501
Telephone: (714) 787-2186

The Sheriff holds one personal property auction a year with jewelry, stereos, TVs - hundreds of items with many good bargains.

There are two to four vehicle auctions a year with 120 to 170 cars, trucks and heavy equipment available. The average selling price is 20% below wholesale. At a recent auction a new Porsche and a late-model Mercedes (drug related confiscations) were auctioned.

Los Angeles Police Department - General Merchandise
150 N. Los Angeles Street
Los Angeles, CA 90012
Telephone: (213) 485-3196

Three auctions a year are held - usually in April, August and December. Merchandise includes stereos, bicycles, radio's, TVs, cameras, clothing and much more. Payment is by cash only. The auction is held at 555 Ramirez Street.

The bidding is open and there are no minimums. Call the above number for information on the next auction.

Private Auctioneers - Los Angeles

Auctioneer for U.S. Marshal & other agencies:
Butterfield & Butterfield
7601 Sunset Boulevard
Telephone: (213) 850-7500

This is a very large and prestigious company which handles government auctions as well as those for estate liquidations and consignments.

The most recent government auction was for the U.S. Marshal where three confiscated Mercedes Benzs were sold. The bidding at the auction itself is open but telephone and absentee bids are accepted. Minimum bids of one third of the value of the merchandise are usually required.

Auctioneer for Narcotics
Division - Police Department
Nationwide Company
13005 Temple
City of Industry, CA 91746
Telephone: (818) 968-3110

These auctions are for "big ticket items", many confiscated and seized by the Narcotics Division. Merchandise may include city vehicles, boats, planes, tractor-trucks and trailers, construction equipment, some computers and confiscated automobiles.

One recent auction included late model Cadillacs, a 1985 Lincoln Town Car, 1984 Lincoln Mark 7, an eight-door Buick Limousine and a 1974 Rolls Royce, to name just a few. Bidding is open and there are no minimums. Auctions are held the first and third Sunday of each month.

Auctioneer for GSA
Gary Analora
5600 Rickenbacker Road
Bell, CA 90201
Telephone: (213) 894-5322

Auctions are held one to five times a month at the above address and include such items as seized personal property, government surplus vehicles, office machines and furniture, hospital and medical equipment.

The bidding is either sealed or spot, depending on the kind of merchandise being sold. At a recent auction, 70 vehicles were sold by sealed bids and 55 to 60 by spot bids.

Kohn-Megibow Company
Inc.
2020 E. 7th Street
Los Angeles, CA 90021
Telephone: (213) 624-8401

They hold auctions for IRS and SBA.

Gamson & Flans
16200 Ventura Boulevard
Suite 401
Encino, CA 91436
Telephone: (8181) 784-3200

They hold auctions for SBA.

Kennedy Wilson
3110 Main Street
Suite 200
Santa Monica, CA 90405
Telephone: (213) 452-6664

They hold auctions for SBA.

GSA
Telephone: (305) 594-5768

GSA holds one auction each month on Saturday at 6100 SW 87th - (next to Orr Water Plant). Merchandise includes vehicles, furniture, boats, jewelry and computers.

There are no minimum bids and the auction is open bidding.

There is no newspaper advertising on these auctions, but you can be on the mailing list by calling the above number. Information will be sent to you prior to each auction.

U.S. Marshal's Office

All general merchandise and vehicles are auctioned by the GSA at the Kennedy Space Center. Real estate is handled by Private Realtors within the Miami area. Advertisements appear in the Miami Herald, official County papers and local Law Journals for Kennedy Space Center auctions. Also contact GSA at (407) 867-2874.

HUD
Telephone: (305) 662-4500

Repossessed property located in Dade and Broward Counties is listed every Friday and Saturday in the Miami Herald.

You must use a Real estate broker to submit your bid. Prices range from $60,000 to $90,000 and all are fix-up, handyman specials. It is necessary to deposit 5% of your bid (up to $2,000) in escrow and you have 60 days to secure financing and close on the property.

U.S. Postal Services
Telephone: (305) 47000-0264

The postal Service sells used vehicles with "fixed prices," no bidding, approximately every two years.

In April, 1989 there was such a sale with 100 cars, half-ton trucks and Jeeps available. Condition of vehicles was poor to good. If present policy is continued, the next sale will be held in 1991.

SBA
Telephone: (305) 536-5521

SBA uses Private auctioneers. Call the auctioneers in the Miami Herald and ask when, or if, they will be holding auctions for the SBA.

U.S. Customs

All auctions for U.S. Customs are handled by Northrop Worldwide Aircraft. There are no set schedules for the auctions because they depend on the seizures made by Customs. Typical Customs auctions might include vehicles, aircraft, vessels, machinery, furniture and liquor.

The bidding is open and there are no minimum bids.

U.S. Trustees

Bankruptcy auctions are held by individual U.S. trustees who engage Private auctioneers. Notices of Auctions are published in the Miami Review, available for 25 cents at newsstands.

Defense Reutilization & Marketing Office
Telephone: (305) 257-7425

Auctions are held every three months and include such items as military vehicles, abandoned vehicles, trucks, tractors, typewriters, refrigerators, stoves, camper trailers.

The bidding is open. At times an auctioneer will withdraw an item from the sale if the bidding is too low. Call above number to be placed on mailing list.

State Surplus Vehicles
Telephone: (904) 488-4290

Auctions are held as required with approximately 150-200 vehicles for sale. Average prices: $700 to $3,700 - Cars, vans, trucks and heavy equipment are included.

Auctions are held in Tallahassee, Lake City and Marianna.

For information on future Auctions Contact:
First Coast Auctioneers
P.O. Box 7878
Jacksonville, Florida 32238
Telephone: 1-800-329-8338

Sheriff's Department
95 NW 29th Street
Miami, FL 33127
Telephone: (305) 547-7291

The Sheriff's Department has no set schedule for Auctions; they have them as often as they accumulate sufficient merchandise.

Auctions may include such items as vehicles, motorcycles, boats and dirt-bikes.

The bidding is open and there are no minimums.

For dates and locations, you may call the above number.

Metro-Dade Police Department
95 NW 29th Street
Miami, FL 33127
Telephone: (305) 547-7291

In the Dade County - Miami area, the Police Department and County Law Enforcement offices are combined to form Metro-Dade and auctions are held every three months to dispose of vehicles to satisfy Court judgments, abandoned cars and some seized or confiscated autos.

Some examples from recent sales are: 1983 BMW - $5,000; 1983 Buick - $330; 1989 Ferrari - $22,000; 1981 Jaguar - $1,300; and a 1971 BMW - $1,850. There are usually about 30 vehicles available. Advertisements are published in the Miami Herald and Miami Review two weeks prior to the auction or you may call the Metro-Dade Police Department for information.

Dade County Sheriff
73 W Flagler Street
Miami, FL 33130
Telephone: (305) 375-5100

The Dade County Sheriff's Department - Civil Division holds auctions which are advertised in the Wednesday edition of the Miami Review. Confiscated merchandise of all kinds and vehicles are offered, depending on the judgments handed down by the court.

450

Call the above agency or check the Miami Review for more information.

Broward County Sheriff
840 NW 5th Avenue
Ft. Lauderdale, FL 33311
Telephone: (305) 765-4027

At the Broward County Sheriff's Special Projects Division auction, you will find automobiles, boats and planes seized through confiscations from drug dealers. Only one auction is held each year of these typical items:

Corvettes, Roll Royces, Mercedes, BMWs, etc. Because of media coverage last year on 60 Minutes and other nationally-televised programs, 5,000 people attended the auction with only 60 of the luxury-type vehicles available. Some buyers got carried away with "auction fever" and many of the bids exceeded book value. This auction is advertised in the Fort Lauderdale News, Sun Sentinel and the Miami Herald. You may also call the above agency for date, time and location.

Palm Beach County Sheriff
P.O. Box 24681
West Palm Beach, FL
33416-4681
Telephone: (407) 355-2760

In Palm Beach County the Sheriff auctions real estate through the Civil Division of the agency. Many of the scheduled auctions are cancelled because the debtor is able to satisfy the court judgement before the date of sale.

Out of 12 scheduled for a recent month, all were cancelled. Therefore, after reading the auction notices in the Palm Beach Review, it is advisable to call the Civil Division for verification that the auction will be held.

451

Palm Beach County Sheriff
3228 Gun Club Road
West Palm Beach, FL 33406
Telephone: (407) 471-2000

The Palm Beach Sheriff also holds auctions, approximately twice a year, to dispose of vehicles, boats, yachts and other miscellaneous items which have been seized for criminal offenses (from dealing drugs to parking tickets).

There are bargains to be found here. Check the Palm Beach Post or call the Sheriff for the date of the next auction.

Police Department
2121 SW 3rd Avenue
8th Floor
Miami, FL 33129
Telephone: (305) 579-6111

The Police Department holds two automobile auctions a month, usually 25 to 30 vehicles ranging in condition from wrecks to good running vehicles. For information on dates and locations call the above number.

Police Department-Personal Property
2121 SW 3rd Avenue
8th Floor
Miami, FL 33129
Telephone: (305) 579-6455

The Police Department auctions personal property (except bicycles) three to four times a year. The bids are open and there are no minimums. Items may include jewelry, TVs, microwave ovens and general household items.

For information on the next auction call the above number.

452

Private Auctioneers - Miami

Auction Company of Florida, Inc.
911 NE 199th Street, Suite 105
N. Miami Beach, FL 33179
Telephone: (305) 651-0500

This auctioneer holds auctions for the SBA - usually three per month, with items such as antiques, jewelry and household items. Real estate is disposed of through Merrill Lynch Realty. Advertisements on auctions appear in the Miami Herald and any local newspapers where the auction is to be held.

For information on upcoming auctions and locations, call the above number. They also maintain a mailing list, if you wish to receive notices on all auctions.

Auction Company of America
100 North Biscayne Blvd.
23rd Floor
Miami, FL 33132
Telephone: (305) 577-3322

This company usually holds four real estate auctions per week, representing banks, bankruptcy trustees and the FDIC. Notices of auctions are published in the Miami Herald and in other local papers where auctions are to be held. Call the above number for current auction information.

Sugarman Auction Company
18500 NE 5th Avenue
N. Miami Beach, FL 33179
Telephone: (305) 651-0101

They hold auctions for a number of agencies. Call for information.

Dallas Frye Auction
Company
2000 North Dixie Highway
Hollywood, FL   33020
Telephone: (305) 923-0501

They hold auctions for counties
and towns.

Harry P. Stamples
Auctioneers
7875 NW 77th Avenue
Miami, FL   33166
Telephone: (305) 761-8744

They hold auctions for U.S.
Bankruptcy Court and SBA

GSA
Fort Snelling - Room G-74
St. Paul, MN   55111
Telephone: (612) 725-3625

This agency does not have a set schedule for holding auctions but they have excellent buys when they do have them. Typical autos at one of the recent auctions were 76 1985 to 1987 Ford Tempos and Capris, 1983-1987 trucks, passenger vans, etc.

The condition of the vehicles is good because they are government owned and were leased to various agencies for a period of time. This bids are open and the auctioneer may feel it necessary to have minimum bids, depending on the vehicles to be auctioned. Call the above number and ask to be notified of auctions and you will be placed on their mailing list.

U.S. Marshal's Office

The Marshal auctions merchandise for several government agencies and advertises in the St. Paul Ledger and in the Minneapolis Star and Tribune.

Advertisements also appear in the Finance and Commerce newspaper. Also check the official County papers and local Law Journals. Real estate is handled by private realtors in the area. Furs donated to charities. Vehicle auctions are handled by a member of the Marshal's staff and jewelry is auctioned In-House.

FBI

All property for auction is handled by the U.S. Marshal.

HUD

Lists of available properties appear in the Sunday editions of the Minneapolis Tribune and St. Paul Dispatch.

If you are interested in bidding on any foreclosed HUD Property, contact a licensed real estate broker who will prepare and submit your bid.

VA
Fort Snelling
Federal Building
St. Paul, MN 55111
Telephone: (612) 725-3870

The VA advertises in the St. Paul and Minneapolis newspapers when they have available properties. You may pick up the list of foreclosures at the Reception Desk in the Federal Building or from any licensed real estate broker.

It would be advisable to telephone prior to making a special trip to determine whether there are properties available.

U.S. Postal Service
Vehicles
1144 Fillmore Street, NE
Minneapolis, MN 55413-1683
Telephone: (612) 349-4990

The Postal Service does not hold auctions but has ongoing sales of used vehicles at fixed prices. Available vehicles can be inspected at the above address. Typical price for 1973 and 1974 half-ton vans is $1,000.

One-ton vans (right-hand drive) are also available. Information indicates the vans are in "fair" condition.

U.S. Postal Service
Merchandise
443 Fillmore Street
St. Paul, MN 55101-9998
Telephone: (612) 293-3084

St. Paul is one of five cities in the United States which holds public auctions on unclaimed and undeliverable mail. They are held approximately every two months (or when about 200 lots are accumulated).

Merchandise is sold by lot, for instance, a hamper of dishes, a box of jewelry, a hamper of new clothing, a hamper of record albums, etc. Merchandise will vary at each auction. They also have unopened boxes - contents unknown, which is like buying a "grab bag". There is open bidding with a $20.00 minimum on most items, $50.00 on more expensive merchandise. Cash only unless you are registered with the Post Office to pay by check. (Register at Main Post Office, Room 405, with two forms of I.D.). Auctions start at 10:30 a.m. and merchandise can be viewed from 9 a.m. - 10:30 a.m. To be placed on mailing list call (612) 293-3099.

IRS
316 N. Roberts Street
St. Paul, MN 55101
Telephone: (612) 290-3381

The IRS holds auctions of real estate and personal property seized for non-payment of income taxes. Property might include such items as jewelry, motorcycles, boats, office equipment and vehicles.

Most automobiles and other vehicles are in good condition.

The IRS uses sealed bids for real estate auctions and open bids on personal property. The IRS advertises in the newspaper with the largest circulation in the

Country where the merchandise was seized: in Ramsey County Finance and Commerce and the Minneapolis Star and Tribune. Each Revenue Officer is responsible for setting up the auction on property he has seized. They do not have a mailing list but you may call the above number and receive current information which is updated each week.

SBA
610-C Butler Square
100 N. 6th Street
Minneapolis, MN 55403
Telephone: (612) 370-2324

The SBA uses private auctioneers to dispose of foreclosed real estate and personal property. The auctions will be advertised in the St. Paul Ledger and the Minneapolis Star and Tribune.

Sheriff's Department
14 W. Kellogg Boulevard
St. Paul, MN 55102
Telephone: (612) 298-4451

The Sheriff holds about four auctions each month with confiscated merchandise being offered. Household goods of all types make up the bulk of the items to be auctioned. There is usually only one automobile in each of the auctions.

The Sheriff advertises in the St. Paul Ledger. The auction is open bidding and there are no minimum bids.

Sheriff's Department
14 W. Kellogg Boulevard
St. Paul, MN 55102
Telephone: (612) 292-6030

The Sheriff's Department holds auctions on foreclosed real estate at the above address. In a recent issue of the St. Paul Ledger there were 25 real estate auction sales and one motorcycle to be sold to satisfy a lien.

This is a paper which is used by many agencies to satisfy the requirement of publication.

Carver County Sheriff
Civil Division
600 E. 4th Street
Chaska, MN 55318
Telephone: (612) 448-2111

The Sheriff holds real estate foreclosures and vehicle auctions with Mechanic's Liens on the cars and trucks. The real estate auctions are subject to a six-month right-of-redemption for the owner to redeem the property sold at auction.

It is a "buyer beware" situation. Know what you are bidding on. Watch for auction notices in the County newspapers and check the courthouse bulletin board.

Washington County Sheriff
14900 61st N.
Stillwater, MN 55082
Telephone: (612) 439-9381

The Sheriff holds both real estate and vehicle auctions. Real estate foreclosures depend on the court-orders and vary each month. Vehicle auctions are held once a year.

Check advertisements in the Washington Gazette for the real estate auction and all major St. Paul newspapers for the vehicles.

Hennepin County Sheriff
Old Courthouse - Room 30
Minneapolis, MN 55415
Telephone: (612) 348-3744

The Sheriff auctions both real estate and vehicles each day (sometimes only one or two a day). Check the bulletin board on the 4th and 5th Street sides of the Courthouse or call the above number for additional information.

Police Department
Merchandise
350 S 5th Street, Room 33
Minneapolis, MN 55415
Telephone: (612) 348-2932

The Police Department holds an auction every two to three months of seized merchandise. Items such as bicycles, cameras, tools are some of the merchandise available. The bidding is open with no minimums.

Police Department
Vehicles
51 N. Collfax
Minneapolis, MN 55415
Telephone: (612) 348-2991
(Auctioneer - Ray Morris)

The Police Department holds one auction each month to dispose of merchandise from drug seizures. Approximately 160 cars, trucks, vans, motorcycles and boats are for sale at a public auction with open bidding and no minimums. Auction held at 10:30 a.m. on the first Thursday of each month. Sold "as is" - you are not allowed to start them. If you can't fix it, don't buy it, is the auctioneer's advice.

Private Auctioneers - Minneapolis

Quickie Auctions
22895 141 Avenue N
Rogers, MN 55374
Telephone: (612) 428-4217

They handle auctions for the Police Department.

Wayne Pike Auction
Company
P.O. Box 387
Princeton, MN 55371
Telephone: (612) 389-2700

They hold auctions for the IRS.

Royal Star Liquidators & Auctioneers
7565 South Concord
Inver Grove Heights, MN 55076
Telephone: (612) 455-1931

They hold auctions for U.S. Marshal's Office.

Kurt Kiefer Auctioneers
Fergus Falls, MN 56537
Telephone: (800) 435-2726

They hold auctions for SBA, State & Bankruptcy Court.

Anoka Fridley Auctioneers
848 Eastern Road
Anoka, MN 55303
Telephone: (612) 427-6770

They hold auctions for IRS & Bankruptcy Court.

GSA
26 Federal Plaza
Room 20-116
New York, NY 10278
Telephone: (212) 264-2035
Hotline: (212) 264-4823

The GSA holds auctions for several other government agencies at different locations, two of which are convenient to residents of New York City - 31st Street & 3rd Avenue, Brooklyn and Route 514 & Woodbridge Avenue, Edison, New Jersey. Auctions are held at the Brooklyn location on the first Friday of each month and in Edison on the second Friday of each month.

These are sealed bid auctions and the merchandise will vary from month to month. For example, at a recent auction in Brooklyn there were 50 government surplus Ford Tempos and Chevrolet Celebritys while at the Edison location there were confiscated Mercedes and several classic autos auctioned.

In addition to vehicles, auctions might include x-ray machines and other medical equipment, raw silver and gold (sold in lots), electronic equipment, TVs, VCRs, typewriters and computers. For the current information on auctions in your area, call the Hotline number above.

U.S. Marshal's Office

The Marshal holds both personal property auctions (one or two a year) and vehicle auctions (two a year). The locations of the auctions change from time to time but the dates, times and locations are advertised in the New York Times and/or New York Journal ten days before the auction is held.

FBI

This agency holds no auctions. All property is turned over to the U.S. Marshal for disposal.

HUD
26 Federal Plaza
New York, NY 10278-0068
Telephone: (212) 264-3907

Lists of available properties are published in the Daily News and News Day each Friday. The real estate market is "tight" in the New York City area; therefore, only two to three properties are advertised each each week. Fortunate buyers can acquire fixer-uppers and realize a substantial profit on their purchases.

VA - Loan Guarantee Department
252 7th Avenue
New York, NY
Telephone: (212) 620-6442

The VA does not hold auctions and there are very few foreclosed or abandoned properties in New York City. Every licensed real estate broker is furnished a list of the available properties and can give you information on their locations and prices. You should contact a broker for information on currently available properties.

US Postal Service-
Merchandise
380 W 33rd Street
New York, NY 10199-9543
Telephone: (212) 330-2931

New York City is one of five cities in the U.S. which handles all unclaimed and undeliverable mail and offers it for public auction. One auction is held each month and a great variety of merchandise is available, ranging from clothing, books, garden tools, TVs and VCRs to furs and jewelry. The bidding is open (with paddle) and there will be some minimum bids, depending on the item.

Call for date, time and location of the next auction in New York City.

U.S. Postal Service-Vehicle
Auction
29th Street
(between 9th & 10th
Avenue)
New York, NY 10199
Telephone: (212) 330-4830

The Postal Service in New York no longer sells surplus P.O. vehicles; however, the autos they offer (at fixed prices) are clean, in very good condition and reasonable. Examples of recently available vehicles are: 1982 Mercury Cougar (6 cylinder wagon), 1982 Ford Granada, Dodge K-Car, 1983 Jeep with 35,000 miles on it. This is a continuous sale. Call above number for information on vehicles currently available.

IRS
P.O. Box 60 GPO
Brooklyn, NY 11202
      or
P.O. Box 2200
Church Street Station
New York, NY 11202
Recording: (718) 780-4020

For information on current properties being auctioned, call the above number. The message is updated weekly.

SBA
26 Federal Plaza
Room 3100
New York, NY 10278
Telephone: (212) 264-0995
Auction Division

The SBA engages private auctioneers to conduct auctions on foreclosed property and merchandise. In New York there are 27 individual auctioneers for this agency and their advertisements can be found in the auction section of the Sunday New York Times.

U.S. Customs

All U.S. Customs seized merchandise is auctioned by Northrop Worldwide Aircraft Services, Inc. (Refer to Custom's Auctions Section). There are a number of auctions held in the New York City area with a wide variety of items offered. A few examples from a recent Northrop auction in New Jersey are - men's and ladies clothing, jewelry, rugs, automobiles, furniture, stone carvings, children's clothing, handbags and wallets to name just a few. Incredible bargains are available at these auctions.

U.S. Trustees-Bankruptcy Court
1 Bowling Green
Room 534
New York, NY 10004
Telephone: (212) 668-7663

Bankruptcy auctions are published in the New York Times each week, if there are any scheduled.

Surplus Personal Property
Albany, NY
Telephone: (518) 457-6335

Two to three auctions per week are held in New York City, with only cars and vans being auctioned. The bidding is open and there are no minimums. In New York City auctions are held at the Adam Clayton Powell, Jr. State Office Building, 163 West 125th Street. For current information call:
Surplus Personal Property
Telephone: (518) 457-6335

Sheriff's Department
31 Chambers Street
New York, NY 10278
Telephone: (212) 374-8223

Auctions are held by the sheriff about twelve times each month in all five Boroughs of New York City. Merchandise is primarily cars but other items are included. The autos are usually in very bad condition - you'll need to bring a mechanic with you because they cannot be started there. Sometimes you can pick up a real bargain. The bidding is open and there is a $5 to $10 minimum bid. For current information, refer to the auction section of the New York Times. The advertisements appear daily.

King's County Sheriff
Municipal Building
Brooklyn, NY 11201
Telephone: (718) 802-3545

The King's County Sheriff in Brooklyn holds real estate auctions to satisfy court-ordered judgments as they are handed down. However, some of the properties have additional liens on them and you must be very cautious when bidding on such items. Advertisements are published in the New York Times and Brooklyn Home Reporter.

466

Richmond County Sheriff
350 St. Mark's Place
Staten Island, NY 10301
Telephone: (718) 447-0041

The Richmond County Sheriff (Staten Island) advertises in the Staten Island Advance prior to each sale and they usually have one to two a year. They handle both real estate and vehicles when available and suggest you call them from time to time for information.

Westchester County Sheriff
110 Grove Street
White Plains, NY 10601
Telephone: (914) 285-3053

The Westchester County Sheriff in White Plains held six auctions last year but the frequency varies with the availability of merchandise. Call the sheriff's office for information or check for auction notices in the White Plains Reporter.

Nassau County Sheriff
240 Old Country Road
Mineola, NY 11501
Telephone: (516) 535-2113

In Nassau County, the sheriff suggests that you call his office periodically to learn of upcoming auctions. No newspaper advertisements - only notices posted on sheriff's bulletin board.

New York County Sheriff
31 Chambers Street
16th Floor
New York City, NY 10007
Telephone: (212) 374-8217

The Sheriff of New York County holds confiscated vehicle auctions, as well as merchandise and real estate when it is available. He advertises in the New York Times and notices are posted on his bulletin board. You may also call his office for further information.

467

New York County Sheriff
Bronx Division
851 Grand Concourse
Bronx, NY 10451
Telephone: (212) 293-3902

The Bronx Sheriff's Department auctions vehicles as they become available (confiscations due to unpaid parking tickets). Some are held weekly. They sell for $50.00 to $3,000 and vary in condition from poor to good.

Advertisements are published in the auction section of the New York Times or you may call the sheriff's office for location, date and time of the next auction.

Police Department
1 Police Plaza
New York, NY
Telephone: (212) 406-1369

The Police Department holds auctions every other Tuesday with 200 to 300 trucks, cars and vans being offered. The condition varies from bad to good. The bidding is open and there is a $25.00 minimum bid. The auction is held at the above address which is near Chambers and Center Street.

Private Auctioneers - New York

Country Auctions
911 43rd Avenue
Long Island City, NY 11101
Telephone: (718) 729-0500

They hold auctions for Public Administrator.

Jackson Hecht Associates
10 East 21st Street
Suite 1608
New York City, NY 10010
Telephone: (212) 505-0880

They hold auctions for the Sheriff's Department.

Stuart L. Medow &
Associates
2935 West 5th Street
Brooklyn, New York 11224
Telephone: (718) 996-2405

The hold auctions for U.S. Marshal
and New York Department of
Transportation.

Greenwich Auctioneers
110 East 13th Street
New York City, NY 10003
Telephone: (212) 533-5930

They hold auctions for U.S.
Marshal and Department of
Sanitation.

Bernard Magill
194 Broadway
Brooklyn, NY 11211
Telephone: (718) 782-4574

They hold auctions for EDA,
Bankruptcy Court and IRS

GSA
Telephone: (215) 597-1237

Auctions are held once a month and consist of vehicles only. Some are motor pool cars and have been well maintained; others are confiscated and all are sold "as is". There are usually between 500 and 600 vehicles at each auction. The bidding will be open. However, there is an upset price (not made public) that they won't go under.

U.S. Marshal's Office

The Marshal turns general merchandise and autos over to the GSA for auction. Private realtors within the area and GSA handle real estate auctions. The Marshal advertises upcoming auctions in the Philadelphia Legal News. Also, the official county papers and any local law journals should be checked.

FBI

U.S. Marshal holds all FBI auctions.

HUD
Telephone: (215) 597-2350

Lists of available properties are published twice weekly: Thursday, The Daily News and Sunday, The Inquirer. Expiration dates are contained in the advertisements. Sealed bids only are accepted and they must go through a HUD approved real estate broker.

VA
Telephone: (215) 438-5225

They do not hold auctions. Each Friday the new properties that are available are listed in local newspapers, together with previous listings that have not sold. Lists of available properties will be sent to interested parties if you call the above telephone number. Sealed bids only are accepted and a licensed realtor must submit your bid.

U.S. Post Office -
Merchandise
Telephone: (215) 895-8140

Philadelphia is one of five U.S. cities which auctions all unclaimed and undeliverable mail and packages for the U.S. Postal Service. Auctions are held every three months at the Main Post Office - 30th and Market - Room 531. Merchandise can be anything from books and furniture to jewelry. To be put on the mailing list, call (215) 895-8140. Ten days before the auction you will receive notice of the merchandise to be auctioned.

U.S. Post Office - Vehicles
Telephone: (215) 698-8100

No auctions are held. Continuous sale daily or as vehicles become available. List posted in garage at 30th and Chestnut. Jeeps usually sell from $1,200 to $1,500. Fixed prices on all vehicles.

IRS
Telephone: (215) 574-9900

No information given by telephone. To be placed on mailing list for IRS auctions and all necessary information to bid, call the above number.

SECTION FOUR - Philadelphia

SBA
475 Allendale Road - Room 201
King of Prussia, PA 19406
Telephone: (215) 962-3839

Most SBA loans are bank-serviced, in which case the banks engage private auctioneers. The U.S. Marshal handles non-bank real estate sales of commercial property. For sales of residential real estate, the SBA uses local realtors. Read the auction section of the Philadelphia Inquirer. All SBA auctions will be listed as such, along with the name of the auctioneer holding the sale.

U.S. Trustees - Bankruptcy Court
c/o Custom House
200 Chestnut - Room 607
Philadelphia, PA 19103
Telephone: (215) 597-4411

Each Chapter Seven Bankruptcy Trustee handles the auction of forfeited property by engaging private auctioneers. To receive a list of Chapter Seven Trustees send SASE to the above address requesting same.

Defense Reutilization Marketing Office
Defense Personnel Center
5500 South 20th Street
Building 26-C
Telephone: (215) 952-5914
(Sales Department)

Auctions are held at the above location on the third Thursday of each month at 9 a.m. Viewing from 9 a.m. to 4 p.m. for three days prior to the sale. All types of miscellaneous surplus goods, office furniture, electronics, tools, hardware, typewriters and computer parts will be auctioned.

From 100 to 150 Army/Navy vehicles (compressed) will be sold for salvage scrap. This number will vary from month to month. The bidding is open and there are no minimum bids.

Defense Reutilization
Marketing Office
Philadelphia Naval Base
(At foot of S. Broad Street)
Telephone: (215) 897-6586
           (215) 897-6587

There is one auction each month at this location (Building 648). Surplus vehicles, abandoned vehicles, machinery, typewriters, computer parts and TVs. Inspection of merchandise is three days prior to the sale - 7:30 a.m. to 4:00 p.m. The bidding is open and there are no minimums.

State Surplus Vehicles
Department of General
Services
Bureau of Vehicle
Management
2221 Forster Street
Harrisburg, PA 17125
Telephone: (717) 783-3132

All surplus materials are auctioned in Harrisburg, which is about a 2-1/2 hours drive from Philadelphia. There are auctions every three to four weeks with 200 to 220 vehicles at each one. Average prices: $900 to $5,000. Cars, trucks, vans and heavy equipment are included. There is no general merchandise at these auctions.

Delaware Sheriff's
Department
Telephone:
(215) 686-3534-Real Estate
(215) 686-3560
Personal Property

Sheriff's Department usually holds two auctions a month, one for real estate the other for personal property. The bids are open, however, there are minimum bids at these auctions. The auctions are advertised in the auction section of the Philadelphia Inquirer about two weeks prior to the sale.

If you send a SASE to the above address, you will be notified by mail of the upcoming auctions.

Chester County Sheriff
17 North Church Street
Westchester, PA   19380
Telephone: (215) 344-6850

The Chester County Sheriff holds real estate foreclosures and court-ordered sales one Thursday each month and there are usually one to three sales that day. The sheriff advertises in the local newspaper where the property is located. For further information you may check the bulletin board in the county courthouse.

Lancaster County Sheriff
50 North Duke Street
Lancaster, PA   17602
Telephone: (717) 299-8200

The Lancaster County Sheriff held six real estate auctions last year with 125 properties being sold. The sheriff schedules auctions every other month (January, March, May, July and September) in court room 'A' of the old courthouse. These are "buyer beware" auctions which means you should do a lien search because they don't guarantee a clean title. The sheriff advertises in the Lancaster Law Review and the Lancaster New Era, three consecutive Fridays one month before the auction.

Montgomery County Sheriff
Court House
Morristown, PA
Telephone: (215) 278-3331

The Sheriff of Montgomery County holds one real estate auction each month on foreclosed properties. The auctions are advertised in various county newspapers - Times Herald, Mainline Chronicle, Pottsdown Mercury and the Lancedale Report. For further information you may call the sheriff's office.

Burlington County Sheriff
49 Rancocas Road
Mount Holly, NJ
Telephone: (609) 265-5824

The Burlington County Sheriff handles real estate foreclosure auctions every Thursday and these sales are advertised in the Burlington Times real estate section. Vehicles are rarely auctioned and when they are available, there are no very desirable ones included. For the merchandise and personal property auctions, the listings are posted on the bulletin board. The amount of merchandise is dependent on the judgments of the court.

Camden County Sheriff
P.O. Box 769
Camden, NJ
Telephone: (609) 757-8586

The Camden, New Jersey Sheriff's Office holds foreclosure auctions every Friday at 2:00 p.m., with advertisements published in the Courier Post on Thursdays. If you find a property listed which interests you, call the sheriff for further information.

Delaware County Sheriff
Media Court House
Front and Veteran Square
Media, PA   19063
Telephone: (215) 891-4300

The Sheriff of Delaware County holds an average of two auctions a week on personal property. They do not advertise in the newspapers but suggest that you check courthouse records.

Private Auctioneers - Philadelphia

John Hirsh Auctioneers
3330 South 20th
Philadelphia, PA 19145
Telephone: (215) 336-8800

They hold auctions for bankruptcy courts and school systems.

Freeman Fine Arts
1808 Chestnut Street
Philadelphia, PA   19103
Telephone: (215) 563-9275

They hold auctions for the IRS.

Quaker City Auctioneers
2860 Memphis Street
Philadelphia, PA   19134
Telephone: (215) 426-5300

They hold auctions for bankruptcy courts.

Henry Nemrod Auctioneers
137 North 3rd
Philadelphia, PA   19106
Telephone: (215) 627-6100

They hold auctions for SBA and bankruptcy courts.

William F. Comly & Son Inc.
1825 East Boston
Philadelphia, PA   19125
Telephone: (215) 634-2500

They hold auctions for U.S. bankruptcy courts.

GSA - Motor Pool
395 Washington
Bridgeville, PA   15017
Telephone: (412) 644-2687

Two to three auctions are held each month at the above address with 80 to 100 vehicles being auctioned. These are GSA fleet vehicles, as well as confiscated and seized cars from the U.S. Marshal, IRS and occasionally one from Customs.

The GSA cars are reconditioned and detailed and have new inspection stickers. Other vehicles are sold "as is". The bidding is usually open and there are reserves which allow the vehicle to be withdrawn if the bidding is too low. At a previous auction a 1936 Jaguar Reproduction Kit car sold for $5,000. Call the above number if you would like to be on the mailing list.

GSA
Telephone: (215) 597-7253

Auctions are held approximately once each week during the summer months and vehicles are the principal type of merchandise. They are sold "as is" but you have five days prior to the sale to inspect them. During the winter months, sealed bid sales are held for medical and office equipment. At auto auctions the auctioneer will begin the bidding and for the sealed bid sales any minimums will be stated in the written description of the items offered. Call the above number and ask to be placed on the mailing list.

U.S. Marshal

The Marshal has no set schedule for auctions - the frequency depends on the amount of merchandise brought in or seized by other agencies. Typical items offered at the Marshal's auctions are jewelry, paintings, TVs, electronics, coins and sometimes fine art. All vehicles are sent to GSA for auction. Notices are published in the Legal Notice section of the Pittsburgh Press and sometimes in the Law Journal. Real estate is handled by private realtors within the area. They do not maintain a mailing list.

FBI

The U.S. Marshal handles auctions for the FBI.

HUD
Telephone: (412) 644-6519

HUD publishes lists of available foreclosed properties in the Saturday Post-Gazette and the Sunday Pittsburgh Press. If you see a property you would be interested in, contact a realtor who will show you the property and submit your sealed bid. It is necessary to send a deposit of $500 with your bid and should it be accepted, you have 60 days in which to close on the property.

VA
Telephone: (412) 281-4233

The Veterans Administration does not advertise its foreclosed properties but provides a list for you on request. If you are interested in a certain listing, call a licensed broker who handles VA property and he will submit your bid. Fee is paid by the VA.

U.S. Post Office - Vehicles
Telephone: (412) 359-7857

The Post Office does not auction its surplus vehicles but holds ongoing sales with fixed prices. They have 1973, '74 and '75 left-hand and right-hand drive Jeeps and 1974 and 1975 delivery vans, with usually about 40 vans and 25 Jeeps available. Jeeps are priced from $900 to $1,500 and the vans from $600 to $1,000. All unclaimed and undeliverable mail is sent to Philadelphia for auction.

SBA

The GSA handles all of SBA auctions in Pittsburgh.

U.S. Trustees - Bankruptcy Court

The are 16 Trustees who handle bankruptcy cases in the Pittsburgh area, but their names are not available to the public. In order to take advantage of the auctions held to dispose of forfeited property, look for Notices of Bankruptcy Auction which the law requires to be published. They can be found in the Pittsburgh Press prior to the sales.

State Surplus - Vehicles
2221 Forster
Harrisburgh, PA   17125
Telephone: (717) 783-3132

Approximately one auction held each month with 210 state vehicles and confiscated cars, trucks and vans available. Call the above number to receive fliers on future auctions.

State Surplus - Merchandise
22nd and Forster
Harrisburg, PA   17125
Telephone: (717) 787-6078

A continuous sale is held Monday through Friday from 8:00 a.m. to 3:45 p.m., with office furniture, typewriters, filing cabinets and more being offered at fixed prices.

Allegheny County Sheriff
Telephone: (412) 355-4704

The Sheriff holds real estate levy auctions the first Monday of each month at 10:00 a.m. If you bid successfully, a 10% down payment is required with the balance to be paid by the following Friday. The sheriff does not guarantee a clear title, he gives you only a deed. It is the buyer's responsibility to conduct a title search. The first mortgage must always be paid, so research into the liens against the property is most important. Advertisements on the available real estate are published the last three Mondays of the month in the Pittsburgh Post-Gazette, Pittsburgh Press and Legal Journal.

Police Department - County Garage
Telephone: (412) 355-5683

Surplus County vehicles are auctioned twice a year by this agency. They are high-mileage vehicles and are sold at open bidding auctions. Advertisements are placed in local newspapers before the sales.

480

GSA
9FBP-105
Auburn, WA 98001
Telephone: (206) 931-7856

This agency conducts approximately 30 auctions a year. Eight to ten of them are vehicles only, open bid. The balance consists of heavy equipment, airplanes and office equipment. Real estate auctions are "modified sealed bids", which means the bidder must appear on the auction location. Send SASE to above address to receive notification.

U.S. Marshal
620 SW Main Street
Room 420
Telephone: (503) 326-2209

For general merchandise, the Marshal holds auctions. The Marshal uses local realtors within the area to dispose of real estate. Advertisements in Portland Times and Salem papers on forthcoming auctions. Also, check the official County papers and any local Law Journals. You may also pick up "Marshal's Notices of Auction" at their office or send SASE to the above address.

FBI

U.S. Marshal holds all FBI auctions of seized and confiscated properties.

HUD
Recording: (503) 326-3498

HUD advertises available properties in the Portland Oregonian on Friday and Sunday. All information necessary to bid on a property is contained in the advertisement. You must use a licensed broker to submit your bid.

VA
1220 SW Third
Portland, OR 97204
Telephone: (503) 326-2484

Call the broker of your choice as he has all the information on available properties and it is necessary to have the broker submit your bid. (VA pays broker's commission). Bids must be submitted within five days after the broker receives listings.

U.S. Postal Service
Vehicles
Broadway & Hoyt (behind
Main P.O.)
Portland, OR 97208-9721
Telephone: (503) 294-2453

Post Office has an ongoing sale, with fixed prices, on surplus Jeeps (right hand drive), half-ton and one-ton Trucks. Rural mail carriers have first opportunity to purchase Jeeps, then the public may buy.

All unclaimed and undeliverable mail and packages are sent to San Francisco for public auction.

IRS
P.O. Box 4451
Portland, OR 97208
Telephone: (503) 221-3960

The IRS advertises upcoming auctions in the classified section of the Portland Oregonian.

SBA
1220 SW 3rd Avenue
P.O. Box 4451
Portland, OR 97208
Telephone: (503) 326-5207

The SBA advertises in the Portland Oregonian and the Eugene, Oregon newspaper. Properties are forfeited due to failure in repaying loans. Merchandise to be auctioned could include fixtures, equipment, office furniture and machines, real estate and other items connected with operating various types of businesses.

U.S. Trustees - Bankruptcy
1001 SW 5th Street
Room 900
Portland, OR 97204
Telephone: (503) 326-2231

U.S. Trustees for the Bankruptcy Court engages private auctioneers to dispose of real and personal property seized by the Court. The following are publications in which bankruptcies for your area are listed:
Portland Business Today/Daily Journal of Commerce
Telephone: (503) 226-1311
The Business Journal
Telephone: (503) 274-8733

Defense Reutilization & Marketing Office
Umatella Army Depot
Hermiston, OR 97838-9544
Telephone: (503) 564-8632

They have only one auction a year, the next one will be in July, 1989. They will have both military and civilian merchandise. The number of vehicles has not been finalized. For a catalog describing the merchandise to be auctioned, call (206) 967-7861 and they will put you on the mailing list.

Agency
State Surplus Vehicles
1655 Salem Industrial Drive
Salem, OR 97310
Telephone: (503) 378-4714

Approximately eight auctions held each year. They include State Police cars, other State vehicles, trucks, vans and heavy equipment. They auction approximately 100 vehicles at each auction. The bidding is open and there are no minimums. Call above number for dates.

Sheriff's Department
2505 SE 11th Avenue
Portland, OR 97202
Telephone: (503) 248-5111

The Sheriff holds two to three auctions a year to dispose of stolen, unclaimed or seized property. The auction is open bidding and includes items such as radios, TVs, typewriters, bicycles and jewelry. He uses a private auctioneer - Harvey Berlant, Beaverton, Oregon. Telephone: (503) 641-8989.

Clackamas County Sheriff
807 Main Street
Oregon City, OR 97045
Telephone: (503) 655-8218

The Sheriff holds personal property, vehicle and real estate foreclosure auctions. Last year there were over 100 sales with some good bargains available. They do not have a mailing list and all advertisements are published in the Enterprise Courier. Call the sheriff's office at the above number for further information.

Washington County
Sheriff - Civil Division
150 N 1st Avenue
Hillsboro, OR 97124
Telephone: (503) 648-8700

The Sheriff holds approximately three auctions a week primarily real estate foreclosures and a few with personal property. Advertisements are published in the Hillsboro Argus or you may call the above number for additional information.

Police Department
920 NE 21st
(City Warehouse)
Portland, OR 97232
Telephone: (503) 248-4395

The Police Department has fixed price sales on stolen and unclaimed merchandise. Items include bicycles, tools, lawnmowers, TVs, radios, stereos and small appliances. Call above number for additional information and to be placed on mailing list.

Private Auctioneers - Portland

Harvey Berlant
Beaverton, OR 97211
Telephone (503) 641-8989

He holds Sheriff's auctions for all counties in the State of Oregon. For current information in your area, call the above number.

Portland Auto Auctions
3000 North Hayden Island
Drive
Portland, OR 97212
Telephone: (503) 286-3000

Sells to dealers only on a bid basis for the City.

American Auctioneering
Service
85322 Jasper Park Road
Pleasant Hill, OR 97402
Telephone: (503) 747-5190

They handle auctions for local cities, schools and Bankruptcy Court.

Action Auctions
10025 N.E. Sandy Boulevard
Portland, OR 97220
Telephone: (503) 256-2299
(Speak with Jim Casey)

They hold auctions for VA.

Steve Van Gordon
Auctioneer
P.O. Box 106
Canby, OR 97013
Telephone: (503) 266-1551

They hold auctions for SBA.

GSA - Fleet Management Control
Federal Office Building
Suite 447
Hato Rey, P.R. 00918
Telephone: (809) 749-4344
Hotline: (212) 264-4823

Auctions are held approximately once each month with Army surplus vehicles, furniture and jewelry being offered. Advertisements are published in the San Juan Star and El Nuevo Dia. Sealed bids are used but you must be present when they are opened. To be put on the mailing list, call the above number.

U.S. Marshal
P.O. Box 3748
San Juan, P.R. 00904
Telephone: (809) 729-6780

The Marshal has auctions approximately every three months with seized merchandise, personal property and vehicles from GSA and Marshal's Fleet Pools.

There can be as many as 20 automobiles and most of them have been well-maintained and are in good condition. The spot bidding method is used at these auctions and the items sell at low prices. At a recent sale, emeralds were auctioned and there are unusual items at nearly every auction. To receive advance information on the next auction, send a letter to the above address.

FBI
Telephone: (809) 754-6000

The FBI had its last auction over a year ago. Useable vehicles are sold to other government agencies and the GSA handles confiscated merchandise such as furniture and jewelry. The Marshal disposes of any real estate that the FBI may acquire.

HUD
159 Cardon Ave., #201
San Juan, P.R. 00918-1804
Telephone: (809) 766-5203

Available homes are advertised in the San Juan Star, El Mundo and El Vocero on Fridays and auctioned on the Tuesday ten days afterwards.

Minimum bids are contained in the advertisement. Homes that are not sold at the auctions are removed from the list for a period of time and later put back on the available list. When you bid, 5% of the price is required as a deposit, with $2,000 being the maximum deposit. If you need additional information, call the above number.

VA - Property
Management Division
159 Chardon Avenue
San Juan, P. R.
Telephone: (809) 766-5141

If you would like the listings of foreclosed VA properties, call the above number and they will be mailed to you. They have been actively liquidating their inventories. Therefore, the number of properties may vary from month to month.

SBA - Liquidation
Division
Federal Building
Room 691
Carlos Chardon - Hato Rey
Puerto Rico 00918
Telephone: (809) 766-5470
         (809) 766-5523

This agency disposes of residential real estate which is sold in "as is" condition by sealed bids. The buyer must pay all back taxes and there will be no other liens on the property. The SBA conducts the title search (your protection) and prepares all of the documents.

They are not interested in equipment or inventories. The owner sells these himself. The Puerto Rico district Office also handles property in the Virgin Islands. Call the above number to have the listings sent to you.

488

U.S. Customs
Telephone: (809) 724-1935

Auctions are held to dispose of merchandise seized by Customs Agents when people cannot or refuse to pay the duty owed.

There are also some drug seizure items, such as boats, auctioned from time to time. Most auctions are held at Garcia Trucking Co., Carolina, P. R., which is about ten minutes from the airport.

Advertisements are placed in local papers up to three weeks before the auction with inspection three days to one week prior to the sale. A 20% down payment is required on all bids which are accepted. To have fliers sent to you in advance of the auctions, listing all merchandise to be sold (and any conditions, such as export restrictions), refer to the material on U.S. Customs in Section One, Chapter 1.

U.S. Postal Service

No auctions are held in Puerto Rico because of the lack of storage space. All unclaimed and undeliverable merchandise is sent to New York for auction.

Roosevelt Roads Naval Base
Roosevelt Roads, P.R.
Telephone: (809) 865-2000

Auctions are held approximately every two months with personal property being the principal merchandise being sold. They have very few vehicles being sold.

This is because they offer them first to other U.S. Government Agencies, then to the Puerto Rican Government and last to the local public. A catalog is prepared before each auction which lists all items to be offered and you may call the above number to have them sent to you. Spot bidding is the auction method used.

Ft. Buchanan Army Base
Bayamon, P.R.

The surplus vehicles from Fort Buchanan are auctioned by the GSA along with any surplus goods the Army may have. The auctions are held approximately once each month and are advertised in the San Juan Star and Nuevo Dia.

Private Auctioneers - Puerto Rico

Auto Auction
Carretera 872
R. 06 Hato Tejas
Bayamon, P.R.
Telephone: (809) 798-0123

This auctioneer is used by many banks and insurance companies in the area to dispose of their repossessed vehicles. Auctions are held each Wednesday on premises and begins at 9:30 a.m. You may inspect the automobiles on the day of the sale prior to the starting time. The bidding is open and there are no minimum bids.

Ramon Miranda
Carretara 862 Km 1.3
Bayamon, P.R.
Telephone: (809) 785-2765

Senor Miranda is not an auctioneer, per se, but he disposes of much of the merchandise held by the Court. He buys from the Court and sells directly to the public from three warehouses which he says are full.

While he has prices on his merchandise, he is open to negotiation and his prices are very inexpensive. He handles furniture, jewelry and automobiles and says

490

he can obtain anything you need - just tell him. The locations of the warehouses are:

(1) 1501 Carretera 833, Santiago Iglesias, Puerto Viejo - (809) 783-6280

(2) 23 South Carretera Estatal, Santiago Iglesias, Puerto Viejo - (809) 783-2160

Super Gangas, Inc.
Carretera 848
St. Just
Telephone: (809) 752-5760

This company buys merchandise at auctions and sells at both fixed and negotiable prices. They handle all types of machinery for light industry, such as sewing machines, etc.

Newport Sales
402 De Diego, Puerto Nuevo
San Juan, P.R.
Telephone: (809) 793-6201

This company is the largest of its type in the Caribbean and sells all materials for sewing, i.e., buttons, thread and ribbon. They do not handle fabrics. They have both wholesale and retail operations and claim to have the best prices in the area. For wholesale job lots they will negotiate prices.

Look in the newspapers for liquidation and bankruptcy sales. There are many held each month that are not handled by government agencies. In some cases the banks or lending institutions will advertise and hold the sales, in others the companies will liquidate as much as they can before bankruptcy is declared. There are excellent bargains to be had at these sales.

491

GSA
Teléfono - (809) 749-4344

Las subastas se conducen aproximadamente una vez al mes con venhículos excedentes del ejercito, muebles y joyas ofrecidas. Las noticias están publicadas en los periódicos "San Juan Star" y "Nuevo Día." Licitaciones selladas se usan y debe estar presente cuando se abran. Para ser puesto en la lista de direcciones llame al número de teléfono arriba.

U.S. Marshal
Teléfono - (809) 729-6780

El Marshal tiene las subastas aproximadamente cada tres meses con mercancía decomisada, propiedad personal y vehiculos de la flota del Marshal y GSA Ellos pueden tener hasta 20 vehículos y la mayoria están bien mantenidos y en buena condición.

La manera de oferta es en el momento y por escrito. Se acepta la oferta más alta pero la mercancía se vende muy barata. Recientemente fuero ofrecidas esmeraldas y usualmente hay mercancía rara.

FBI
Teléfono - (809) 754-6000

La última subasta del FBI tuvo lugar hace un poco mas de un año. El FBI no conduce las subastas. Vehículos usables se venden a otras agencias gubernamentales y la GSA conduce las subastas de muebles y joyas. El Marshal vende bienes raices adquiridos por el FBI.

HUD
Teléfono - (809) 766-5203

Las casas disponibles aparecen en los periódicos "San Juan Star," "El Mundo", y "El Vocero" diez dias antes de la subasta que ocurre todos los martes.

Las licitaciones mínimas se encuentran en los periódicos . Se quitan las casas que no se venden y aparecen otra vez posterioramente. Debe pagar un deposito del 5% del precio con un máximo de $2,000. Si quiere más información llame al numero arriba.

VA
Teléfono - (809) 766-5141

Si Usted quiere una lista de propiedades de la VA llame al número arriba y se lo enviarán por correo. Ellos han sido liquidando los inventaarios muy rápidamente y por lo tanto los inventiarios varían mensualmente.

SBA
Teléfono - (809) 766-5470
         (809) 766-5523

Esta agencia vende bienes raices residenciales en la condición en que se encuentran por licitaciones selladas. El comprador debe pagar todos los impuestos pero no tendrá otros cargos en la propiedad.

El SBA conduce la examinación del título (para su protección) y prepara todos los documentos. Llame al número arriba para recibir las listas de las casas. Ellos no tienen el equipo o los inventarios de los negocios. El dueño mismo los vende. La oficina en Puerto Rico tiene también las propiedades de la SBA en las Islas

Vírgenes. Llame al número arriba para recibir las listas de propiedades.

U.S. Customs (Aduana)
Teléfono - (809) 724-1935

Las subastas tienen lugar para vender mercancía embargada por la aduana cuando personas no pueden o rehusan a pagar los arbitrios debidos.

Hay también lanchas embargadas por razón de drogas que se ofrecen a veces. La mayoría de las subastas tienen lugar en los almacenes de Garcia Trucking Co. ubicada en Carolina, P.R., aproximadamente a diez minutos del Aeropuerto Internacional.

Las noticias de las subastas se encuentran en los periódicos locales aproximadamente tres semanas antes de la subasta, con la inspección tres dias a una semana antes. Se requiere un depósito del 20% para todas las ofertas aceptadas.

Si Usted quiere más información sobre las subastas y mercancía disponible, además si hay restricciones, puede referirse a la Sección de U.S. Customs (Aduana) en el Section One, Chapter 1.

Postal Service (Servicio Postal)

No hay subastas en Puerto Rico porque no hay espacio para almacenar. Toda mercancía no reclamada o que no se puede entregar se envía a Nueva York para ser subastada.

494

Roosevelt Roads Naval
Base (Base Naval)
Teléfono (809) 865-2000

Las subastas tienen lugar aproximadamente cada dos meses con propiedad personal siendo la mercancía principal vendida.

No hay vehículos en cantidad porque inicialmente se ofrecen a otras agencias Federales, luego al Gobierno de Puerto Rico y finalmente al público Puertorriqueño. Se ofrece un catálogo que contiene todos los artículos que aparecerán en la póxima subasta. Llame al número de arriba para recibir el catálogo. Las licitaciones son hechas en el momento por escrito.

Ft. Buchanan Army Base
(Base del Ejército)

El ejército usa la GSA para conducir las subastas de vehículos excedentes y artículos excedentes. Las subastas tienen lugar aproximadamente una vez al mes y las notificaciones aparecen en los periódicos "San Juan Star" y "El Nuevo Día".

Subastadores Privados - Puerto Rico

Auto Auction
Teléfono - (809) 798-0123

Esta compañía de subastas es usada por muchos bancos y compañias de Seguros en Puerto Rico para vender vehículos recuperados.

Las subastas tienen lugar en el mismo local todos los Miércoles y empiezan a las 9:30 de la mañana. Se puede hacer una inspección de los vehículos en el día de la venta antes de comenzar. Las licitaciones son abiertas y no hay licitación mínima.

Ramón Miranda
Teléfono - (809) 785-2765

El Sr. Miranda no es subastador pero él vende mucha mercancía que tiene la Corte. El compra de la Corte y vende directamente al público de tres almacenes cuales están ubicadas alrededor de San Juan. Usalamente él mantiene inventarios buenos, particularmente con muebles.

Mientras él tiene precios establecidos se puede negociar los precios. Los precios son muy baratos. El tiene muebles, joyas y automóviles y si él no lo tiene, lo conseguirá.

Los locales de los otros dos almacenes son:
1) 1501 Carretera 833, Santo Iglesias,
Puerto Viejo - (809) 783-6280.
2) 23 South Carretera Estatal, Santiago Iglesias, Puerto Viejo (809) 783-2160.

Newport Sales
Teléfono - (809) 793-6201

Esta compañía es la más grande en el Caribe para este tipo de negocio. Ellos venden botones, hilos, cintas y otros materiales de costura. No venden telas.

Ellos venden al por mayor y por menor y aseguran que ellos tienen los mejores precios. Se puede negociar precios si quiere comprar lotes por mayor.

SECTION FOUR - Puerto Rico - Español

Super Gangas, Inc.
Teléfono - (809) 752-5760

Esta compañía compra mercancía a través de subastas. Tienen precios establecidos y negociables. Ellos tienen muchos tipos de maquinaria para indústrias livianas como maquinaria de coser.

Puede leer los periódicos para liquidaciones y ventas de bancarrotas. Hay muchas ventas en el mes que las agencias gubernamentales no conducen. En algunos casos los bancos e instituciones de préstamos anuncian y conducen las ventas. En otros casos las compañías liquidan la mayor cantidad posible de los inventarios antes de declarar bancarrota. Se pueden encontrar muchas gangas cuando se vende la mercancía por este modo.

GSA
401 Broadway
Sacramento, CA 95818
Telephone:
Sacramento:
(916) 551-1605
San Francisco:
(415) 974-9800

GSA holds approximately three auctions a month and the merchandise to be sold comes as a result of seizures, confiscations and foreclosures by different Government Agencies. In addition, Government fleet vehicles are auctioned and these are generally in much better condition than the vehicles offered at many auctions. At the Sacramento auction, the spot bidding system will be used and there may be a minimum bids, depending on the merchandise being sold. GSA maintains a mailing list for those persons who would like to receive advance notice of upcoming auctions. Call the above number to be placed on the list.

U.S. Marshal's Office
650 Capitol Mall
Telephone: (916) 551-2861

Auctions held very rarely. Larger lots are handled by GSA in Sacramento. All American Auction Company handles general merchandise and automobiles. Advertisements are published in the Sacramento Bee. Also, check the official County papers and local Law Journals.

FBI
Seizures Department
Telephone: (916) 481-9110

GSA handles FBI auctions.

HUD
777 12th Street
Suite 200
Sacramento, CA 95814-1997
Telephone: (916) 551-1367

Available properties are advertised in The Sacramento Bee every Friday. Check the listings and, if you are interested in purchasing a listed property, contact a licensed realtor and he will show you the home and submit your sealed bid to HUD. The broker's fee is paid by HUD.

VA
Regional Office
211 Main Street
San Francisco, CA 94105
Telephone: (916) 929-5863

Sacramento is in the San Francisco VA Region and a list of available properties is compiled and furnished to participating brokers by the San Francisco office. The VA will also furnish the listing to any individual who calls and requests it.

The participating VA brokers have keys to show prospective buyers the properties and the proper forms on which the sealed bids must be submitted. The VA pays the broker's fee - there is no cost to the bidder.

U.S. Postal Service
Vehicles
228 Harris
San Francisco, CA 94105
Telephone: (415) 550-5212

Postal Service vehicles are auctioned three to four times a year in San Francisco. Automobiles only are auctioned - no trucks or vans. The bidding is open and there are minimum bids. Since this auction is not regularly scheduled, we suggest periodic telephone calls to determine if a date has been set and what will be available for auction. All undeliverable postal merchandise is sent to San Francisco for auction.

499

IRS

Only toll free numbers are furnished for contact with the IRS in Sacramento and it is not possible to call from out-of-state. Since IRS auctions are among those with the best bargains, we urge you to contact your local IRS office for information. Merchandise at these auctions is from seizures of real estate and personal property due to non-payment of income taxes. Items can include residential and commercial property, autos, trucks, vans, jewelry, furniture. Investigate this agency thoroughly - you may find some fantastic buys.

SBA
660 J. Street
Suite 215
San Francisco, CA 95814
Telephone: (916) 551-1426

Auctions for this agency are held because of business failures and non-payment of SBA loans, therefore, it is impossible to forecast their frequency. The Sacramento office states they average one auction a month and it could be held in a location outside of Sacramento. The auction is held at the location of the foreclosure. For this reason, a number of different auctioneers in various parts of the area are used. To determine which auctioneers handle SBA sales, the office suggests you check the Yellow Pages and call the more prominent ones..Ask if they auction for SBA.

U.S. Trustees - Bankruptcy
Court
915 L Street
San Francisco, CA 95814
Telephone: (916) 551-3300

Auctions for Chapter Seven bankruptcy cases are arranged by each U.S. Trustee for his caseload. To learn the names of the Trustees in order to contact them regarding their auctions, call the Clerk of the Bankruptcy Court. The cases of that office are a matter of public record and, as a last resort, you could go there and copy the information. It would be much simpler to contact the Trustees. For a start, one of Sacramento's Trustees is Charles Whitworth - Telephone: (916) 5312.

Defense Reutilization &
Marketing Office
DLA-YKD, Building 70
McClellan AFB
CA 95652-6448
Telephone: (916) 643-3830

This base holds auctions about once a month and the merchandise includes office furniture and equipment, typewriters, tool boxes, forklifts, military surplus vehicles. The number of vehicles at each auction can be as few as two and as many as thirty. The general condition would be classified as good. Spot bids are used and there are usually no minimums. They will send you fliers before the auction if you request this.

State Surplus Vehicles
State Garage
1421 Richards Boulevard
Sacramento, CA 95814
Telephone: (916) 445-4851

One auction a month is held with approximately 100 vehicles offered for sale. Trucks, vans and dump trucks are included and some are good high-mileage vehicles. The bidding is open and there are minimum bids, set by the auctioneer.

Sheriff's Department
6670 Elvas
Sacramento, CA 95819
Telephone: (916) 732-3841

The Sheriff holds two auctions a year with merchandise that may include stereos, cameras, TVs, clothing and other personal property. No vehicles are sold at this auction. The bidding is open and there are no minimum bids. The auctioneer for the Sheriff is Roger Ernst (separate synopsis follows). Call the above number or Mr. Ernst and look for advertisements in the Sacramento Union and Sacramento Bee.

El Dorado County Sheriff
300 Fairlane
Placerville, CA 95667
Telephone: (916) 621-5655

The sheriff usually holds one auction a year with vehicles available and the frequency of real estate foreclosures depends on the number of court orders handed down. They auction vacant lots as well as houses. Advertisements are published in the Mountain Democrat prior to the auction date.

Napa County Sheriff
1125 3rd Street
Napa, CA 94559
Telephone: (707) 253-4325

The sheriff holds one vehicle auction each year with one to three cars available. He handles real estate foreclosures auctions as the court judgments are handed down. Van Cleves Auction Company in Napa, Telephone: (707) 255-5850, handles the Sheriff's auction, as well as for many other agencies throughout California. Advertisements are published in the Napa Register prior to auction and notices are posted in the Old Post Office.

Yolo County Sheriff
P.O. Box 179
Woodland, CA 95695
Telephone: (916) 666-8880

The Yolo County Sheriff holds two vehicle auctions a year and these are advertised in the Daily Democrat prior to the date of sale. No real estate has been auctioned by the sheriff in several years.

Police Department - Fleet Sales
813 6th Street
Main Office
General Services Corporation Yard (Fleet Auction)

Police Department holds two Fleet auctions a year on unclaimed stolen property two to three times a year. The fleet sales have some terrific bargains, two year old cars that have reached the mileage limit for $150 to $500 at the last auction. They usually have about 100 cars, the Police Squad cars have had the decal removed and the buyer is furnished with the maintenance record of the vehicle. These cars are in excellent condition, according to one of the persons who set up the auctions. Call (916) 449-5316 for information on the next fleet auction and (916) 449-5237 for the merchandise auction information. They also have a mailing list.

Private Auctioneers - Sacramento

Auctioneer for Sheriff's
Department
Roger Ernst & Associates
P.O. Box 3251
Modesto, CA 95353
Telephone: (209) 527-7399

This auctioneer holds 10 to 25
auctions a year, in addition to
those for the sheriff. Merchandise
includes autos, jewelry, business
equipment, clothing, real estate,
TVs, stereos and cameras. The
number of automobiles varies
with each auction; the same is true
for the condition of the vehicles.
They range from fair to excellent.
The bids are open and minimum
bids are rare. Call the above
number to be placed on the
mailing list.

Huisman Auctioneers
7923 Stockton Boulevard
Sacramento, CA 95823
Telephone: (916) 682-3338

They handle auctions for Cal
Trans, cities & Bankruptcy Courts.

Nelson Geiger Auctions
9608 Oats Drive
Sacramento, CA 95827
Telephone: (916) 368-0130

They handle auctions for SBA &
Bankruptcy Courts.

Shuffield Auctions
712 Garden Highway
Yuba City, CA 95911
Telephone: (916) 673-5189

They handle auctions for
Bankruptcy Courts.

Stoss Liquidators
9611-A Oats Drive
Sacramento, CA 95827
Telephone: (916) 368-0747

They handle auctions for Bankruptcy Courts.

GSA

All GSA auctions for St. Louis are held in Kansas City.

U.S. Marshal
1114 Market Street,
Room 108
St. Louis, MO
Telephone: (314) 539-2212

The Marshal tries to schedule auctions the third week of each month, with advertisements in the St. Louis Post Classified Section (Legal Notices) on Friday, Saturday and Sunday prior to the sale. The auctions are always held at the market address and all necessary information will be in the advertisements. They auction jewelry and cars more than any other items but they also have boats, mink coats, microwaves and all kinds of collections. A little bit of everything can be found here. Real estate is handled by private realtors within the area.

FBI

All merchandise seized by the FBI is auctioned by the U.S. Marshal.

HUD
210 N. Tucker
St. Louis, MO 63101
Telephone: (314) 425-4783

Available properties are advertised in the Post Dispatch on Sunday and Tuesday. If you see a property listed that you may be interested in, contact a broker and submit a sealed bid through him. On FHA insured properties, $200 plus 5% of the asking price must accompany the bid. On "as is" properties, 5% of the asking price must be included.

VA
1520 Market Street
St. Louis, MO 63103
Telephone: (314) 342-1171

To learn what properties are available in the St. Louis area, call the above number and the current list will be mailed to you. If you find a property you are interested in, you may either go through licensed real estate broker or deal directly with the VA to submit your sealed bid. They do not advertise in local newspapers.

U.S. Post Office - Vehicles
1720 Market Street
St. Louis, MO 63155
Telephone: (314) 436-4324

They have no set schedule and hold auctions as the vehicles are accumulated and usually include two-ton and five-ton trucks and Jeeps. The vehicles are in fair to good condition and may be viewed at the garage prior to the auction. Notices are placed in all Post Offices or you may call to have your name placed on the Mailing List. Undeliverable and unclaimed merchandise is sent to St. Paul, Mn., for auction.

IRS
P.O. Box 1487
St. Louis, MO 63188
Telephone: (314) 342-1040

IRS maintains a mailing list and will notify you in advance of both real estate and personal property if you call the above number.

SBA
815 Olive Street
Room 242
St. Louis, MO 63101
Telephone: (314) 539-6600

The SBA uses private auctioneers to handle property of failed businesses which had insured loans. There is no set schedule as the auctions depend on the number of forfeitures. Any type of goods and merchandise associated with a business may be auctioned, i.e, hardware, sporting goods, restaurant equipment, etc. They advertise in the St. Louis Post Dispatch and local County papers.

Information on another SBA auctioneer follows in the Private Auctioneers section.

State Surplus - Vehicles
and Merchandise
P.O. Box 1310
Jefferson City, MO 65102
Telephone: (314) 751-3415

They hold at least two auctions a year, sometimes more, with cars, trucks, vans, motors, office furniture and equipment available. At some auctions Federal surplus, such as medical equipment, office supplies and equipment is included.

Sheriff - City of St. Louis
Real Estate
11 N 11th Street
Civil Courts Building
St. Louis, MO 63101
Telephone: (314) 622-4851

They usually hold auctions in August, September and October for real estate tax sales, other times as needed. The properties are advertised in the St. Louis Post Dispatch twice in the two weeks prior to the auctions. Since the addresses in the newspaper are sometimes incorrect, it is advisable to verify the address with the Collector's Office and also check to be certain there are no additional liens against the properties.

St. Louis County Sheriff
Real Estate
7900 Carondelet
Clayton, MO 63105
Telephone: (314) 889-7502

The Sheriff holds auctions of real estate with court-ordered judgments against it but has no regularly scheduled auctions because the volume depends on the court. Notices are posted in public places: court House, Fire Department, Police Department and City Garages.

Police Department
1200 Clark Street
St. Louis, MO 63103
Telephone: (314) 444-5540

This department holds one auction each year, usually in June to dispose of stolen, unclaimed merchandise. Such items such as bicycles, TVs, VCRs, clothing and cameras are offered. The bidding is open and there are no minimum bids.

D.R.M.O.
Ft. Leonard Wood
Gas Street
Building 2391
Ft. Leonard Wood, MO
29574
65473-5820
Telephone: (314) 368-7101

An auction is held every six to eight weeks to dispose of surplus military material. The merchandise may vary from time to time but you can always find office furniture and equipment, military clothing, PX property such as food service equipment, tools and hardware. Very few military vehicles are auctioned for most are sold as scrap. Bidding is open and there are no minimums. Fliers will be sent prior to the auctions, if you call the above number and request this.

Private Auctioneers - St. Louis

Auctioneer for SBA
Cockrum Auctions
2701 N. Highway 94
St. Charles, MO 63301
Telephone: (314) 723-9511

This auction company holds one auction each week with merchandise such as antiques from estates, real estate, liquidations, jewelry, furs and automobiles, late models and antiques. They also hold bankruptcy and repossession auctions with household goods, automobiles and furniture being sold.

At recent auctions a Model T Ford sold for $8,000, a Tiffany lamp went for $9,600 and a 2-1/2 carat diamond ring brought $6,000. They maintain a mailing list and you may call and request being placed on it.

GSA
880 Front Street
San Diego, CA 92188
Telephone: (619) 557-6035

The GSA holds an auction every two months with Government surplus cars, trucks, real estate, office furniture, computers and typewriters to name only a few items. They have between 50 and 60 cars which are in fair condition. The bidding is usually open, however, they do have an occasional sealed bid auction - depending on the merchandise. They maintain a mailing list and you may call and ask to be placed on it.

U.S. Marshal's Office
San Diego, CA 92311

The Marshal uses Butterfield & Butterfield in Los Angeles for general merchandise auctions. For automobiles and occasional boats, he uses Fischer Auction. Real estate is handled by private realtors within the area. Automobile auctions are advertised in the Sunday edition of the Union Tribune two weeks prior to the auction. General merchandise advertised in the San Diego Union. Also, check official County newspapers and any local Law Journals.

FBI

The U.S. Marshal handles all FBI seized merchandise.

HUD
880 Front Street, Room 553
San Diego, CA 92188-0100
Telephone: (619) 557-5596

Available HUD properties are advertised in four local newspapers: San Diego Monitor, Voice and Viewpoint, La Prenza and The Union. Real estate brokers have keys to the houses and can show them to you. Your sealed bid must be submitted through a licensed broker. HUD pays the broker's fee - no cost to the bidder.

VA
2022 Camino Del Rio, N.
San Diego, CA 92108
Telephone: (619) 297-8220

The VA advertises its available properties in the Los Angeles Times Sunday Real Estate Section and the San Diego Union on Wednesdays. Choose a VA-affiliated broker to show you any property you are interested in. The broker will then submit your sealed bid on the proper forms to the VA at no cost to you. The VA pays broker's fee.

U.S. Postal Services
Vehicles
2535 Midway Drive
San Diego, CA 92199-9721
Telephone: (619) 221-3196

The Postal Service does not hold auctions to dispose of its surplus vehicles but offers them to the public at fixed prices. They sell their vans in fair condition for $1,000 and they can be inspected at the above address during Postal Service business hours. Since these vehicles are sold quickly, it would be advisable to call and verify that there are some there to purchase. All undeliverable merchandise is sent to San Francisco for auction.

IRS
300 N Los Angeles
Los Angeles, CA   90012
        or
450 Garden State Avenue
San Francisco, CA   94101
Telephone: 1-800-422-1040

Only toll free numbers are furnished for contact with the IRS in San Diego and it is not possible to reach this office from another state. Since these auctions are among those with the best bargains, we urge you to contact your local IRS office for information. Merchandise at these auctions is from seizures of real estate and personal property due to non-payment of income taxes. Items can include residential and commercial real estate, autos, trucks, vans, jewelry, furniture, household items, appliances and furniture. Investigate this agency thoroughly - you may find some fantastic buys. Call to be placed on their mailing list.

SBA
880 Front Street
Room 4-529
San Diego, CA   92188
Telephone: (619) 557-7250
Extension 33

The SBA uses private auctioneers to dispose of property, foreclosed because of non-payment of SBA-insured loans. Property can be both real and personal, both business and residential, household furnishings and appliances, business fixtures or equipment pertaining to the foreclosure, i.e., restaurant, bakery, hardware, etc. The bids are open and there are usually no minimum bids. McCormick Auction Company, 743 El Cajon Blvd., El Cajon - Telephone: (619) 447-1196. Call them and ask to be added to their mailing list.

U.S. Trustees - Bankruptcy
Court
101 W. Broadway
Suite 440
San Diego, CA 92101
Telephone: (619) 557-5013

Call the Clerk of the Bankruptcy
Court at the above number and
ask to have a list of Chapter Seven
Trustees sent to you. Individual
Trustees are responsible for the
auction of the forfeited property
of persons who have declared
bankruptcy. Also check local
newspapers for bankruptcy
auction notices and also official
County newspapers.

Sheriff's Department
5555 Overland Avenue
Building 12
San Diego, CA 92123
Telephone: (619) 565-5200

Auctions are held every four
months or more frequently if
sufficient merchandise is
accumulated. Items auctioned
usually include office equipment,
auto parts, computers and
vehicles. At a recent auction, ten
autos in good condition were
offered. The bidding is open and
there are no minimum bids. The
auctioneer used by the Sheriff is
Mark Gorin - (619) 560-1677.
Contact him and ask to be added
to the mailing list.

Defense Reutilization &
Marketing Office
Box 337
Imperial Beach
CA 92032-0337
Telephone: (619) 437-9456

Auctions are held once each
month with items such as office
furniture, typewriters, computer
printers, vending machines and
surplus military vehicles being
sold. Both sealed and open bids
are used, depending on the
merchandise being auctioned. At a
recent auction a 1980 MG was
auctioned for $150. All it needed
was a distributor cap. Call to be
added to the Mailing List.

Orange County Sheriff
1300 S. Grand
Tustin, CA 92681
Telephone: (714) 567-7660

The Sheriff and Public Administrator combined held approximately 20 auctions last year for the Police, Public Administrator and mini-storage facilities. Some great bargains were available, for instance paintings worth thousands were sold for $25. Real estate foreclosure, deceased persons' estate sales (everything in some very nice homes), bicycles, jewelry, desks, TVs, car parts were some of the items available. The auctions are advertised in local newspapers and flyers are distributed throughout the area.

Riverside County Sheriff
4050 Main Street
Riverside, CA 92502
Telephone: (714) 787-2402

The Sheriff holds foreclosure auctions on real estate, vehicle auctions and personal property sales. The vehicle auction notices are posted in the county courthouse. He does not have regularly scheduled auctions but will mail you information if you send him an SASE.

Police Department
1401 Broadway
San Diego, CA 92101
Telephone: (619) 531-2866
          (619) 531-2000
Hotline: (619) 531-2767

Auctions are held every two to three months with such items as bicycles, VCRs, TVs, clothes, radios and stereos to name a few. (Auto's are handled at separate auctions). The bidding is open and there are no minimums. Auto auctions are held by Fischer Auction Company - (619) 233-1851. (See Synopsis which follows).

515

Public Administrator/
Public Guardian
5201-A Ruffin Road
San Diego, CA 92123
Telephone: (619) 694-3500

He holds approximately seven personal property and five auto and vehicle auctions a month. The merchandise includes household goods, furniture, paintings, china, silverware, crystal, electronics and clothing, plus more. Vehicles are sold "as is", however, some are in very good condition. The source of some of his merchandise is from the estates of individuals who die without leaving wills. After outstanding bills are paid, the balance goes to the state.

Private Auctioneers - San Diego

Auctioneer for SBA
McCormick Auction
Company
743 El Cajon
San Diego, CA 92020
Telephone: (619) 447-1196

McCormick holds one or two auctions a month for the SBA with business furniture, equipment and fixtures, real estate and vehicles. The merchandise depends on what kind of business failed. The bidding is open and there are no minimums.

Auctioneer for U.S. Marshal
Fischer Auction Company
614 Fifth Avenue, Suite A
San Diego, CA 92101
Telephone: (619) 233-1851

They hold four to five auctions a month for several Government agencies other than the U.S. Marshal, i.e. D.E.A., Border Patrol, Federal seizures, Federal Bankruptcy Court, credit companies and private individuals. Their auctions are not for vehicles only but include many items from other sources. Approximately 140 autos sold at each auction. All Government auctions are held at Family Carousel Hall, 1770 Palm Avenue, Imperial Beach, California. Call the above number and ask to be added to their mailing list. The U.S. Marshal's Auction List costs $10 a year.

Auctioneer for U.S. Marshal
Butterfield & Butterfield
7601 Sunset Boulevard
Los Angeles, CA 90046
Telephone: (213) 850-7500

This is a very large and prestigious company which handles government auctions, as well as those for liquidation of estates and consignments. The most recent government auction was for the U.S. Marshal where three confiscated Mercedes were sold. The bidding at the auction is open but telephone and absentee bids are accepted. Minimum bids of one third of the value of the merchandise are usually required.

H & M Goodies Family
Auction
130 East 8th Street
National City, CA 92050
Telephone: (619) 474-8296

They handle auctions for SBA, Farm Bureau and local school districts.

517

Mark Gorin & Associates
18837 Brookhurst Street
Suite 210
Fountain Valley, CA 92708
Telephone: (619) 560-1677

They handle auctions for the County of San Diego.

GSA
525 Market Street
Room 9FB-PS
San Francisco, CA 94104
Telephone: (415) 974-9800

GSA auctions are held in various locations throughout the Western United States and Hawaii. There are usually five to six a month and include government surplus vehicles, typewriters, hospital equipment and property seized by the U.S. Marshal and FBI. An average of 200 vehicles may be offered at any given auction and some of them are in good condition. The bidding can be either sealed or spot, depending upon the merchandise being sold.

U.S. Marshal's Office

All merchandise seized by the Marshal is auctioned by the GSA.

FBI
450 Golden Gate Ave.
San Francisco, CA 94102
Telephone: (415) 553-7400

Merchandise seized by the FBI is auctioned by the GSA. The FBI does hold two auctions a year on the agency's fleet vehicles, cars, vans and trucks, with fifteen to forty being offered for sale. The bidding may be sealed or open and there are no minimum bids. The condition of these vehicles is good, as they have been well-maintained. At the February auction, a 1984 Z28 sold for $3,500. Bargains are to be found here.

HUD
450 Golden Gate Avenue
San Francisco, CA 94102-
4848
Telephone: (415) 556-5900

Available HUD properties are listed in the San Francisco Examiner on Sunday. If you find a listing of interest to you, contact a licensed broker who will show you the property and submit your sealed bid. Properties are located in many different locations in the San Francisco area. Some are "fixer-uppers," others in good condition.

VA
211 Main Street
San Francisco, CA 94105
Telephone: (415) 495-8900

Lists of available properties are compiled every two weeks and furnished to VA affiliated brokers. These brokers have keys to the properties and can show them to you. The VA will also mail the listings to you upon request. However, your sealed bid must be submitted to the VA by a licensed VA-approved broker.

Postal Service
Merchandise
1300 Evans Avenue
San Francisco, CA 94188
Telephone: (415) 550-5400

San Francisco is one of five cities in the United States where the Postal Service auctions mail that was undeliverable or unclaimed. The bargains to be had at these auctions are fantastic.

Merchandise includes anything which can be sent by mail: brand new TVs, computer software, stereos, radio's, precious gems, crystal and merchandise from Nieman-Marcus. Auctions are held once each month except June when there is not one held. The time is 10 a.m. and you may register at 8:00 a.m. and inspect the items to be sold. Merchandise is sold in lots, i.e., a box of books, a hamper of dishes, a hamper of clothing, etc.

The auction is open bidding and there are minimum bids. Payment by cash, Postal Money Order or Cashier's Check. All sales are final - no refunds. An "Auction Catalog" is available at no charge when you attend the auction. However, if you wish to have it mailed to you, the cost is $21.00. The catalog lists all items to be sold, detailed for all months and consists of 20 pages. To order, make check payable to Postmaster, San Francisco, California and mail it to Postal Service, 1300 Evans Street, San Francisco, California 94188-5400. Attention: Joanne Davis - Superintendent of Claims and Inquiry Department.

U.S. Postal Service
1300 Evans Avenue
San Francisco, CA 94188
Telephone: (415) 550-5212

The Postal Service does not auction its surplus vehicles but sells them at fixed prices to the public as they become available. They usually have approximately 20 on hand, consisting of Jeeps, one and one-half ton trucks, vans, mid-size cars and economy-size cars. The condition of the vehicles vary but any defects are posted on the windows of each one. Advertisements regarding this ongoing sale may be found in the San Francisco Examiner, Oakland Tribune and West Contra Costa County Times. Also, call the above number for current information.

521

IRS
P.O. Box 1559
Oakland, CA 94604
Telephone: (415) 273-4382
Hotline: (415) 556-5021

The IRS auctions property which has been seized for non-payment of income taxes. There are twelve revenue officers in this office and they are assigned different cases to handle. Many times the auction will be held at the location of the seizure. Property can include real estate, residential and commercial, jewelry, furniture, vehicles (cars, vans, trucks), office equipment, any type of household goods and appliances. Some of the vehicles are in excellent condition and many are late models. At a recent sale, a 1986 Cadillac was purchased for $5,000. The bidding is open and the minimum bid is 20% of the value of the property.

We suggest that you call the above Hotline number for a description of the property and the particular revenue officer assigned to the particular sale. You may then contact the office and that officer will put you on his mailing list.

SBA
74 New Montgomery
San Francisco, CA 94105
Telephone: (415) 974-0649

The SBA uses private auctioneers for the sale of property foreclosed due to non-payment of business loans. These auctions, three to five each month, consist of residential and commercial property, office furniture and machines, restaurant equipment, art, antiques and any other assets the debtor may own. Company vehicles and some non-commercial automobiles are often included. The auctions are usually held at the location of the failed business, with open bids and no minimum.

U.S. Trustees - Bankruptcy Court
450 Golden Gate 15th Floor
San Francisco, CA 94102
Telephone: (415) 556-2250

Each Chapter Seven Trustee engages an auctioneer to handle the bankruptcy auctions of his cases. Bankruptcy Notices are published in official County papers and may appear in local legal newspapers also. Call the Bankruptcy Court Clerk for instructions as to acquiring a list of Trustees so that you may contact them personally.

Defense Reutilization &
Marketing Office
Warehouse 5
2155 Mariner Square Loop
Alameda, CA   94501-1022
Telephone: (415) 869-8309

Auctions are held on the second
Thursday of each month and
include surplus military clothing,
office furniture and equipment,
typewriters, tools, hardware,
machinery and military vehicles -
to name just a few. The number of
vehicles varies at each auction but
there are usually seven or eight in
fair to good condition. The bidding
is open and there are minimum
bids at some of the auctions.
Unusual items may be sold at
times, such as horses and sheep
which were purchased by the
military to graze a field and to be
sold afterwards.

State Surplus Vehicles
57 Ellis Street
San Francisco, CA   94109
Telephone: (415) 557-3604

All auctions are held in Los
Angeles and Sacramento.

Sheriff's Department
400 Van Ness Street
Room 333 City Hall
San Francisco, CA 94102
Telephone: (415) 554-7225

The Sheriff holds auctions every two to three months on court order. Real estate is offered and at some auctions there will be clothes, furs and jewelry. No vehicles are included in these sales. The bidding is open and there are minimum bids (to satisfy judgments). These auctions are advertised in the San Francisco Recorder prior to the date of sale. They do not maintain a mailing list; however, if you send a legal-size SASE to the above address, a flyer will be mailed to you prior to the auction with date, time, location and description of the merchandise.

Alameda County Sheriff
1225 Fallon St.
Oakland, CA
Telephone: (415) 272-6878
Recording: (415) 272-5095

No information given by telephone. Call the recording above for current auction information. Individual items to be sold, locations and minimum bids, if any, are given.

San Mateo County Sheriff
401 Marshall Street
Redwood City, CA 94063
Telephone: (415) 363-4000

The Sheriff handles real estate auctions to satisfy judgments, usually one a month but the number depends on how many the court hands down. He also holds vehicle auctions approximately every three months. Check the San Mateo News for notices of auctions.

Marin County Sheriff
Marin County Civic Center
Room 167
San Rafael, CA 94903
Telephone: (415) 499-7284

Real estate foreclosure auctions
are held on an irregular schedule,
depending on the amount of
property available.
Advertisements are published in
the Independent Journal and
notices are posted in three places:
the library, City Hall and County
Sheriff's Office.

Police Department
850 Bryant Street
San Francisco, CA 94103
Telephone: (415) 553-1377
Hotline: (415) 553-9751

The Police Department holds
auctions every two or three
months for sale of stolen and
unclaimed merchandise. Such
items as TVs, cameras, clothing
and tools may be offered. No
vehicles are included in this sale.
If you will call the above number,
you can get information on the
next auction date, as well as the
time and location.

Private Auctioneers - San Francisco

Auctioneer for GSA
A.R.S. Auctioneers
1755 10th Avenue
San Francisco, CA 94122
Telephone: (415) 566-6464

This company holds four to six
auctions a month with all types of
business equipment and fixtures,
as well as household goods being
offered. The bidding is open and
there are sometimes minimum
bids placed on an individual item
by the auctioneer. Call above
number to be placed on their
mailing list.

Auctioneer for Narcotics
Division - Police Department
Van Cleves & Company
1010 Kaiser Road
Napa, CA 94558
Telephone: (707) 255-5850

These auctions are for "big ticket items", many confiscated and seized by the Narcotics Division. Merchandise may include City vehicles, boats, planes, tractor-truck and trailers, construction equipment, some computers and confiscated automobiles. One recent auction included late model Cadillacs, a 1985 Lincoln Town Car, 1984 Lincoln Mark 7, an eight-door Buick Limousine and a 1974 Rolls Royce, to name just a few. Bidding is open and there are no minimums. Auctions are held on the second Saturday of each month.

Ashman Company &
Auctioneers &
Appraiser Inc.
21 Massola Drive
Pleasant Hill, CA 94523
Telephone: (415) 682-8100

They hold auctions for SBA.

Ross-Dove Company
1118 Chess Drive
Foster City, CA 94404
Telephone: (415) 571-7400

They hold one or two auctions a year for FDIC and Bankruptcy Court.

Forest Faulknor & Sons
175 Sylvester Road
South San Francisco,
CA 94080
Telephone: (415) 872-3242

They hold auctions for U.S. Customs.

SECTION FOUR - San Francisco

Liquidators Inc.
P.O. Box 27144
Oakland, CA 94602
Telephone: (415) 482-2877

They hold auctions for IRS, State, Bankruptcy Courts and cities.

Rabin Brothers
660 3rd Street
San Francisco, CA 94107
Telephone: (916) 441-2405

They hold auctions for U.S. Bankruptcy Courts.

528

GSA
15th and C Streets SW
Auburn, WA 98001-6599
Telephone: (206) 931-7566

This agency holds both vehicle and personal property auctions five or six times a year at the GSA warehouse, a half mile south of the intersection of 15th and C Streets. The vehicles are from various Government agencies and are approximately three years old with mileage limits reached. Most are in good condition. The bidding is open and the minimum bid is 90% of the loan value. They also have personal property auctions of seized, confiscated and surplus properties with the sealed bid system being used. Call the above number to be placed on the mailing list for upcoming auctions.

U.S. Marshal's Office
U.S. Courthouse
Room 300
1010 5th Avenue
Seattle, WA 98104

This agency uses a private auctioneer for vehicle auctions - James Murphy Auction Company, Kenmore, Washington, Telephone: (206) 486-1246. To dispose of real estate, private realtors within the area are given the listings. Advertisements appear in the Daily Journal of Commerce. You should also check the official County paper and any local Law Journals.

FBI

All seized and confiscated property auctioned by U.S. Marshal's Office.

HUD
1321 2nd Avenue
Seattle, WA 98101
Telephone: (206) 442-1700

HUD foreclosed properties are advertised in the Sunday Times, Real Estate Section. If you are interested in any of the listings, contact a licensed real estate broker and he can show you the property and submit your bid. HUD pays the broker's fee. Seattle's area is large, extending north to Bellingham, south to Vancouver and east to Spokane. They list from 80 to 120 properties each week.

VA
915 2nd Avenue
Seattle, WA 98101
Telephone: (206) 624-7200

VA foreclosures are not advertised in the newspapers in Seattle. Once each month a list of available properties is compiled and furnished to licensed, VA-affiliated real estate brokers. It is also available to any individual who calls or goes by the office to pick it up. Your bid on a property must be submitted by a broker (VA pays the fee), on the forms supplied by the VA. At present the market is very active and there are a number of homes available.

U.S. Postal Service
301 Union Street
Seattle, WA 98101
Telephone: (206) 442-6340

Post Office surplus vehicles are offered to the public at fixed prices, not auctioned and may be purchased when available. Half-ton cargo vans and jeeps are the only types available. Recently they had only two vans for sale at $895.00 each. To learn what vehicles they have, call the above number and you will be given information as to availability, price and location to inspect. All undeliverable mail is sent to San Francisco for auction.

IRS
915 2nd Avenue
Seattle, WA 98101
Telephone: (206) 442-1046
Hotline: (206) 442-0703

Each revenue officer is responsible for setting up auctions on the property he has seized. Only the officer involved in the seizure has information on the auction. The IRS Office above does not keep lists. Call the Hotline number; it will provide you with the information you need. The auctions are held because of failure to pay income taxes and can include real estate, all household goods (furniture, appliances, paintings, etc.), vehicles and possibly business equipment. Be sure to look into this one.

SBA
915 2nd Avenue
Room 1792
Seattle, WA 98174-1088
Telephone (206) 442-1420

The SBA forecloses on businesses who have failed to repay loans. Property can be both real and personal - real estate, both business and residential, household furnishings and appliances, business fixtures or equipment pertaining to the foreclosure, i.e. restaurant, bakery, hardware, etc.
The SBA uses private auctioneers to dispose of their foreclosed property, the two principals are: James G. Murphy Company and Auctions, Inc. Information on these autioneers follows. Advertisements on auctions will be published in the Seattle Times.

U.S. Trustees - Bankruptcy Court
810 Park Place Building
Seattle, WA 98101
Telephone: (206) 442-2000

U.S. Trustees are responsible for Chapter Seven bankruptcy auctions. To obtain a list of the Trustees in order to contact them for information, send a letter requesting the list to Clerk, Bankruptcy Court, at the above address.

Defense Reutilization &
Marketing Office - (Lewis)
P.O. Box 92056
Tillicum,
WA   98492-0056
Telephone: (206) 967-4890

They hold two auctions each month with all types of government surplus merchandise available. Typical would be office furniture and equipment, clothing, tools, hardware, appliances, small boats, military and abandoned vehicles. The auction is held in Building 96-71, Logistic Center, Tillicum. This is about one hour's drive from Seattle, Exit #123 off I-5. They maintain a mailing list and will send fliers prior to each auction with merchandise listed, if you call and request they be mailed to you.

State Surplus Vehicles
Building 5 - Door 49
2805 C Street, SW
Auburn, WA   98001
Telephone: (206) 931-3931

These auctions dispose of surplus vehicles for many state agencies and are held five to six times a year, with 150-170 being sold. They include cars, trucks, vans and motorcycles. The condition of the vehicles ranges from fair to good. The bidding is open and there are usually no minimum bids. Call for information on future auction dates.

Sheriff's Department
516 3rd Avenue
Seattle, WA 98104
Telephone: (206) 296-4078

The Sheriff holds three to four auctions each year for disposal of unclaimed stolen personal property and abandoned vehicles. Merchandise usually includes radios, TVs, bicycles, stereos, cameras, etc. The condition of the vehicles is usually bad; the merchandise is generally good or it would not have been stolen. The bidding is open and there are minimum bids - usually low ones. Call Officer George Minich at the above number for current information.

Island County Sheriff
P.O.Box 5000
Coupeville,
WA 98239-5000
Telephone: (206) 679-7310

The sheriff holds 24 to 30 real estate foreclosures each year,' as well as bank repossessions on improved and unimproved goods. No vehicle auctions are held by the sheriff. You are cautioned to investigate liens and conduct a title search before bidding. Advertisements are published in the Real Estate Times and in the County newspapers where the property is listed. Personal property auctions are posted on the bulletin board.

Pierce County Sheriff
930 Tacoma Avenue
Tacoma, WA 98402
Telephone: (206) 591-7522

Mather Auctioneers holds all auctions for the Sheriff at an average of one every two months. Bicycles, stereos, cameras, TVs, cars and motorcycles are some of the merchandise frequently found at these sales. Six to ten cars and trucks are usually sold, in fair to good condition. For information on future auctions, call (206) 847-9161.

Police Department
Merchandise
610 3rd Avenue
Seattle, WA 98104
Telephone: (206) 386-1234

The Police Department holds merchandise auctions once or twice a year on stolen property which was recovered or known to be stolen and unclaimed. Items include household goods, TVs, stereos, radios, VCRs, cameras and clothing. Literally, anything a burglar might steal. The bids are open and there are no minimums. Call for information on future auctions.

Police Department
610 3rd Avenue
Seattle, WA 98104
Telephone: (206) 386-1234

Auctions are held approximately once each month on seized vehicles - cars, trucks and vans. The condition of these vehicles is usually not good, therefore, there are no minimum bids and bidding is open. Call above number for current dates and information.

Private Auctioneers - Seattle

Auctioneer for SBA and
Bankruptcy Trustees
Auctions, Inc.
6226 196th S.W. #1 B
Lynwood, WA 98036
Telephone: (206) 771-4232

They will give no information by
telephone but you can be put on
their mailing list if you call them.

Auctioneer for U.S. Marshal
and SBA
James G. Murphy &
Company
P.O. Box 82160
Kenmore, WA 98028
Telephone: (206) 486-1246

Call to be placed on their mailing
list.

Belieu Auctioneers
P.O. Box 24989
4797 1st Avenue, S
Seattle, WA 98134
Telephone: (206) 767-6796

They hold auctions for City,
County and Port of Seattle.

Harris & Harris
P.O. Box 5657
Bellvue, WA 98006
Telephone: (206) 451-8922

They hold three to four auctions a
year for SBA and Bankruptcy
Court.

AAA Liquidating & Auction Service
17800 Des Moines Way S
Seattle, WA 98148
Telephone: (206) 246-7253

They hold auctions for School districts, Bankruptcy Courts and U.S. Customs.

GSA
Telephone: (407) 867-2874
Hotline: (407) 867-7637

There is no GSA office in Tampa. All auctions are held at Kennedy Space Center. They hold one auction each month with about 100 vehicles to be sold. Other items are added each month - such as jewelry, but the auction is primarily vehicles. Call to get on the mailing list.

U.S. Marshal's Office

All merchandise and vehicles are auctioned by the GSA at Kennedy Space Center. Call (407) 867-2874 or (407) 867-7637 for dates and information.

FBI
St. Petersburg & Tampa

Seized merchandise is turned over to the U.S. Marshal for disposal. All U.S. Marshal items are auctioned by the GSA at the Kennedy Space Center. For information and dates or to be placed on mailing list at Kennedy Space Center call the above numbers.

HUD
Telephone: (813) 228-2551

Available properties are advertised in the classified section of the St. Petersburg Times, Orlando Sentinel and Tampa Tribune.

Approximately 150 houses are listed each week and can be purchased by sealed bids through a licensed real estate broker.

VA - (Regional Office)
Telephone: 1-800-282-8821

Every two weeks a new list of available properties is sent to 6,000 brokers. Interested parties must contact the brokers to determine if they handle VA foreclosures. Bids must be submitted through them.

U.S. Postal Service - Vehicles
Telephone: (813) 323-6516

All Postal Service vehicles are sold at fixed prices, not auctioned. Prices range from $1,200 to $2,000. When vehicles are available for public sale, advertisements are placed in local newspapers and notices posted in all local Post Offices. All unclaimed and undeliverable mail and packages are sent to Atlanta, Georgia for auction.

IRS
Telephone: 1-800-424-1040

To be placed on mailing list for this area call the above number. No auction information given on telephone.

SBA
Telephone: (813) 228-2594

SBA uses private auctioneers to dispose of forfeited merchandise. In order to get information, call individual auctioneers and ask to be placed on their mailing lists. Also, check auction section of the St. Petersburg Times and Tampa Tribune for current auction information.

U.S. Customs

The Customs Office holds no auctions. Northrop Worldwide Aircraft handles all seized Custom's merchandise and the sales are held in various locations in the United States.

U.S. Trustees - Bankruptcy Court
Telephone: (813) 225-7064

Individual Trustees engage private auctioneers to dispose of forfeited merchandise. To obtain a list of Trustees call the above number.

State Surplus Vehicles
813-B Lake Boulevard
Tallahassee, FL   32304
Telephone: (904) 488-4452

Tallahassee holds one large auction on state-owned vehicles, usually in the fall. The vehicles are in good condition and sold by sealed bid.

State Surplus Vehicles
Bureau of Motor Vehicles & Watercraft
Larson Building- Room B-69
Tallahassee, FL   32399-0950
Telephone: (904) 488-4290

Auctions usually held as required with 150-200 vehicles for sale. Average prices: $700 to $3,700. Cars, trucks, vans and heavy equipment are included. Locations in Florida where auctions are held: Tallahassee, Lake City and Marianna. For information on future auctions call First Coast Auctioneers, Jacksonville - Telephone 1-800-329-8338.

Police Department - Tampa
Telephone: (813) 893-7555

No set schedule for auctions - held when sufficient property is accumulated. Advertisements appear in the auction section of the Tampa Tribune and the St. Petersburg Times prior to the sale.

Tampa Police Department
Telephone: (813) 225-5880

Auctions held every three weeks at the Police Impound Lot, 410 South 34th Street. The merchandise consists of unclaimed stolen property and abandoned vehicles. The bidding is open and there are no minimum bids. Call the above number for future auction dates.

Defense Reutilization &
Marketing Office
McDill AFB
Telephone: (813) 830-2871

Auctions held every three to four months and consist of office equipment and furniture, typewriters, TVs and some vehicles. The bidding is open and there are usually no minimum bids. Call the above number and ask to be placed on their mailing list.

Pinellas County Sheriff's
Department
250 West Ulmerton Road
Largo, FL 34648
Telephone: (813) 587-6200

The Sheriff's Department does not hold auctions. They sell only one item at a time and handle only merchandise which has a levy against it. The Pinellas County Review will contain information on upcoming sales.

Hillsborough County Sheriff's
Department
2008 8th Avenue
Ybor City, FL
Telephone: (813) 247-8140

Sheriff holds auctions every two to three months at the above location. Items to be auctioned include bicycles and small items such as radios, TVs and appliances. No vehicles are sold. The bidding is open and minimum bids are on very expensive items only.

541

Hillsborough County Sheriff
P.O. Box 3371
Tampa, FL
Telephone: (813) 247-8000

The Hillsborough County Sheriff advertises personal property to be auctioned by court order in the Tampa Tribune. He also auctions any seized or confiscated merchandise at these sales There are bargains to be found here, especially on the seized property. On real estate foreclosures there is no set schedule, since these are held only by court order. For the real estate auctions, read the notices in the Free Press, Tampa Record, La Gazetta and the Penny Saver.

Pinellas County Sheriff
P.O. Drawer 2500
Largo, FL   34649
Telephone: (813) 587-6200

The Pinellas County Sheriff, Largo office, auctions personal property on which the courts have issued levies or judgments. The frequency depends on the number of court orders received by the Sheriff. Advertisements appear in the Pinellas Review.

Manatee County Sheriff
515 11th West
Bradenton, FL   34205
Telephone: (813) 747-3011

The Sheriff of Manatee County in Bradenton holds very infrequent auctions on seized and stolen property such as TVs, stereos, radios and cameras, to name a few typical items. Watch for advertisements in the Bradenton Herald.

Sarasota County Sheriff
2071 Ringling
Sarasota, FL   34230
Telephone: (813) 951-5800

There is very little auction activity in Sarasota County. The Sheriff holds sales, not auctions, on real estate and the number of sales depends on how many judgments are received from the courts.

542

Pasco County Sheriff
8700 Citizens Drive
New Port Richey, FL 34654
Telephone: (813) 847-5878

In Pasco County the Sheriff holds about four auctions a year on vehicles and these are advertised in the West Pasco Press and the Pasco News. This auction is held at the office on Citizens Drive.

Pasco County Sheriff
7530 Little Road
New Port Richey, FL 34654
Telephone: (813) 847-5878

The main Sheriff's office turns over all seized and confiscated property to the county which combines them with surplus county vehicles, office furniture and equipment for an auction held each year in July or August. This is advertised in the Pasco Edition of the St. Petersburg times prior to the sale. You can call the county for date, time and location. There will also be a large sign outside the Courthouse.

Pasco County Sheriff- Civil Division
7530 Little Road
New Port Richey, FL 34654
Telephone: (813) 847-2411

The Civil Division of the Pasco County Sheriff's office handled 50 real estate auctions last year with many properties selling 20% to 50% less than market value. These are usually foreclosures and the notices are published only in the West Pasco Press. There are good buys to be found at these auctions.

Pope County Sheriff
455 North Broadway
Bartow, FL
Telephone: (813) 533-0344

The Pope County Sheriff holds a personal property sale twice a year with bicycles and miscellaneous merchandise (seized, confiscated and stolen) being offered. Advertisements will appear in the Lakeland Ledger prior to the auction or you may call the sheriff's office in Bartow for details.

The Lakeland office handles vehicle auctions at the Sheriff's Garage with First Coast Auction and Realty of Jacksonville being the auctioneers. Local radio announcements and advertisements in Lakeland newspapers are used by the auctioneers to publicize the auction.

Private Auctioneers - Tampa/St. Petersburg

Tampa Machinery & Auction
11720 Highway 301
Thonotasassa, FL 33592
(6 miles N. of State Fair Grounds)
Telephone: (813) 986-2485

One auction held each month for the Sheriff's Department. Merchandise consists of government vehicles, abandoned and seized automobiles also some sold for salvage. Open bidding.

Edward Bilbruk Auctioneer
1733 Indian Rocks Road
Belleair, FL 34616
Telephone: (813) 791-9541

They hold auctions for SBA.

Randall Auction Company
13605 West Hillsborough
Tampa, FL 33615
Telephone: (813) 855-9580

They hold auctions for SBA

Al Davenport Inc.
11776-1/2 58th Street N
Pinellas Park, FL 34666
Telephone: (813) 545-5165

They hold auctions for counties and local cities.

Action Auctioneers
8955 Palm River Road
Tampa, FL 33619
Telephone: (813) 677-4677

They handle one or two a year for State of Florida.
Attention: Mr. Bob Elting

GSA - (Surplus Sales Center)
Telephone: (703) 557-7785
Hotline: (202) 557-7796

This agency holds three different types of auctions each month:
1) Office furniture and equipment every Monday & Wednesday from 8:30 a.m. to 11:00 a.m.
2) Warehouse clearances
3) Vehicle auctions

The warehouse clearance offers a wide range of merchandise including computer equipment, office machines, laboratory equipment and electrical items.

The vehicle auction offers 100-150 cars, trucks and vans at each sale - 1984-86 models in good condition. The bidding is open and there are minimum bids on vehicles.

U.S. Marshal's Office

The Marshal's Office disposes of seized and forfeited merchandise for a number of government agencies. The amount of merchandise varies, therefore, there are no set schedules for auction dates. The items offered could include autos, jewelry, boats and yachts. Two private auctioneers are used by the Marshal to conduct the auctions, one in Baltimore and one in Washington, D.C.
Information on these auctioneers follows

FBI
Washington, D.C.

The FBI holds no auctions. All seized or confiscated property is disposed of by the U.S. Marshal.

HUD
451 7th Street, NW
Room 3158
Washington, DC 20410
Telephone: (202) 453-4592

The list of available properties is published every Friday in the Washington Times with more than 20 offered. Most are single family homes and small apartment buildings in "good condition". The asking price is listed in the newspaper advertisement. Contact a licensed real estate broker to submit you bid.

VA
941 N Capitol Street NE
Room 9112
Washington, DC 20421
Telephone: (202) 275-1325
(202) 275-1326

Available properties are advertised in the Washington Post on the third Wednesday of each month. Licensed real estate brokers have keys to the properties, the forms on which bids must be submitted, and information which would be helpful to you. Since the VA pays the brokers' fees it is to your advantage to deal with them.

U.S. Postal Service
980 V Street, NE
Washington, DC 20018-9601
Telephone: (202) 832-0212

They presently have one-ton step vans at a fixed price of $650-$700, and one ton cargo vans for $600. You may view them at the above address Monday to Friday from 8 a.m. to 4 p.m.

IRS - Special Procedures
P.O. Box 1076
Baltimore, MD   21203
Telephone: (301) 962-1838

To be placed on the mailing list for auctions in your area, call (301) 962-5102. Merchandise was seized for non-payment of income taxes and could include real estate, vehicles, jewelry, paintings, coin collections and other personal property.

SBA
P.O. Box 19993
Washington, DC 20036
Telephone: (202) 634-1500

SBA uses private auctioneers. See information following.

U.S. Customs

No Customs auctions are held by Northrop in Washington, D.C.

U.S. Trustees - Bankruptcy Court
Washington, DC   20544
Telephone: (202) 633-6231

Bankruptcies are listed in the Washington Post when there are auctions. Some months there are no bankruptcies, some months there may be two.

Defense Reutilization & Marketing Board
Fort Belvoir, VA   22060-0566
Telephone: (703) 664-6553

Auctions are held every third Tuesday with others randomly scheduled throughout the month. The merchandise varies at each auction as to the number of vehicles. There is always office furniture and equipment, miscellaneous tools and hardware. To receive information on auctions call the above number and ask to be added to their mailing list.

State Surplus Vehicles
2000 Adams Place, NE
Washington, DC   20018
Telephone: (202) 576-7850

Auctions held on the third Thursday of each month at 10:30 a.m. at the above address. Merchandise includes all property except real estate - could be office furniture and equipment, heavy machinery and there are usually 70-100 vehicles a month. The bidding is open and there are minimum bids. For further information call the above number.

Fairfax County Sheriff
4110 Chainbridge Road
Fairfax, VA   22030
Telephone: (703) 246-3227

Ten days before each auction a notice is posted on the bulletin board outside the courthouse. There are no regularly scheduled auctions because it depends on the number of court-ordered sales and the amount of merchandise accumulated. Call the above number for information on upcoming auctions.

Montgomery County Sheriff
50 Courthouse Square
Rockville, MD   20850
Telephone: (301) 217-7000

The Sheriff holds two auctions a year and uses Tom Kay as his auctioneer. For information on upcoming auctions you may call and be put on the mailing list.

PG County Police Department
Vehicle Audit Unit
4920 Ritchie Marlboro Road
Upper Marlboro, MD   20772
Telephone: (301) 952-1873

The sheriff holds approximately 13 auctions a year and he advertises in the PG Post, prior to each auction. After you have attended one auction, they will put you on the mailing list and notify you in advance.

Police Department
2235 Shannon Place, SE
Washington, DC   20018
Telephone: (202) 767-7586

Auctions held on the first Tuesday every month on Blue Plains Drive, SW (the Police Training Academy). Merchandise usually includes 25-30 vehicles in very good condition, clothing, jewelry, refrigerators, tools, TVs, VCRs, bicycles and coins.

Private Auctioneers - Washington/Baltimore

Auctioneer for SBA & U.S. Marshal
Adam A. Weschler & Son, Inc.
905 E Street, NW
Washington, DC   20004
Telephone: (202) 628-1281

Two types of auctions are held by this auctioneer. Each Tuesday consignment auctions are held. These are inexpensive items which might include household furniture, dishes, glassware, lawnmowers and lawn furniture. Then there are the catalog sales which are usually held two or three times a month. This auction consists of antiques, carpets, paintings, crystal, fine china, jewelry, etc.

Catalogs are printed for each of these sales and may be picked up at the above address for $15.00 or mailed to you at a cost of $17.00. When merchandise from the U.S. Marshal or SBA is auctioned, it is done along with the consigned items - not separately.

Adams & Winer Auctioneers Inc.
2720 Sisson Street
Baltimore, MD   21211
Telephone: (301) 366-8300

They hold auctions for U.S. Marshal's Office.

REX PUBLISHING COMPANY

Dear Colleague:

As the author of the book you have just received from REX PUBLISHING COMPANY, I wanted to drop you a little note and help you get started on your adventure.

The whole subject of Government Auctions is quite an adventure. I first heard about these auctions from various friends. One of them, who was not at all wealthy, purchased a beautiful late-model car each year, sometimes every six months. When I asked him how he could afford to spend so much money on cars, and where was he getting all this money, he just laughed at me and said: "Heck, I'm getting these cars for about $1500-2500 each. I drive them around for a few months and then sell them for a profit." I didn't know at the time that he had been going to Government Auctions. I thought he was part of some secret club or association. No one told me that anyone could go to these auctions.

Another friend, who was also not wealthy, told me a story how he had just purchased 10 single-family homes with his credit cards for a total of $15,000. I thought he was just exaggerating until he explained that he had found them by using a little-known secret--that same secret is found in the book you have just received. Each of the homes immediately began generating a positive cash flow, which means that he profits above and beyond his expense in purchasing and maintaining these homes! I don't know if he's a millionaire but he sure is on his way to becoming one.

One colleague is a millionaire. Being curious I asked him just how he got to become one. He told me that he'd been going to government auctions for years. He would buy merchandise inexpensively at military base auctions and resell them for handsome profits. This past July one nationally-syndicated columnist conducted an in-depth investigation into government auctions and called them a "virtual giveaway". All the information you need to find out about military base auctions and how to participate in those is found right in the book you are about to read.

You'll discover, as I have, that going to government auctions is not only an educational experience but a richly rewarding one as well. I've talked with auctioneers, government officials and numerous auction-goers to provide you with all the necessary information you need to get started. We spent several thousands of man-hours compiling this book for your easy use. It cost quite a small fortune gathering all of this information for you so that your job will be easier.

When you finish reading the book and go to an auction, please remind yourself to drop me a note and let me know about your experiences. Nothing brings an author more satisfaction than knowing his readers have been successful using his advice. And if you run into any difficulties and need a hand, please call **REX PUBLISHING COMPANY**'s Customer Service Department and ask for help. The Customer Service Department is there to help you with something you don't understand and to consult with you--at no cost to you--so that your experience at auctions will be successful. Give them a call between 10 a.m. and 4 p.m. Eastern Time at (813) 446-1602.

Please keep in mind that each of the government agencies mentioned in the book is there to help you get to an auction. Occasionally some government agents aren't very helpful. In fact, I was just reading in the newspaper how government bureaucrats don't rate very well with regard to providing service. If you do run into trouble with any, please let us know so that we can help you.

One last note, for a limited time, we are providing a free auction update service to help you find out about some of the government auctions going on in your area. It's a short-cut, but it will help you get there fast. The phone number and the confidential access codes are mentioned in the book. Call anytime of the day or any day of the week. It's an electronic voice-mail service with a menu so it's always available for you. We update this every week on Monday mornings, so call anytime after noon on Monday for a fresh update.

Good luck on your auction adventure!

Best wishes,

George Chelekis

Mailing Address:
107 Garden Ave.
Clearwater, FL   34616

Telephone (813) 446-1602

CONFIRMATION OF INFORMATION GIVEN TO THE CUSTOMER

(Customer's name) DAVID M. Barnum

contacted me at REX PUBLISHING COMPANY'S 800 telephone number on
(date) 1 / 9 /90 at 8:30 am/pm as a result of REX PUBLISHING COMPANY'S
commercial announcement on/in (radio, television/print). At this time a charge was made on
his/her credit card (type of credit card) MC in the amount of $109.95
for the purchase of:

THE ACTION GUIDE TO GOVERNMENT AUCTIONS AND REAL ESTATE

I vouch that during our phone conversation each of the following was done, as witnessed by my
initials for each item and my signature below.

KMF 1. I informed the customer of the correct price of the product he/she requested to
purchase as written above.

KMF 2. I informed the customer of the approximate delivery date.

KMF 3. I informed the customer that THE ACTION GUIDE TO GOVERNMENT AUCTIONS and
enclosed materials would help the customer to get on the government's available mailing lists. I
also explained that the customer's participation and following the exact instructions in the book
were both required in order to be placed on those mailing lists.

KMF 4. I informed the customer as to the approximate number of auctions available in their
area.

KMF 5. I informed the customer that he/she must adhere to the rules of the agencies in
order to continue receiving the auction notices on a continuing basis.

KMF 6. I attest that this order was taken only upon the approval of the customer and only
after confirmation by a verifier.

KMF 7. I informed the customer of our standard refund policy in detail, including the $25
reprocessing fee, as it appears on the enclosed customer's warranty.

KMF 8. I informed the customer that the charge would appear on his/her credit card in the
name of Rex Publishing Company, Inc.

Kristi Flora 9654   1-9-90
Operator Name & Number   Date

Ken Roe 9039   1-9
Verifier Name & Number   Date

FOR YOUR CONVENIENCE WE HAVE CUSTOMER SERVICE STAFF TO ANSWER YOUR QUESTIONS AND
ASSIST YOU WITH THE BOOK TO HELP YOU SUCCEED WITH THE ACTION GUIDE TO GOVERNMENT
AUCTIONS AND REAL ESTATE. PLEASE CALL AT (813)446-1602 BETWEEN THE HOURS OF
9AM-5PM EASTERN TIME.

If you are a homeowner
WE HAVE GOOD NEWS FOR YOU!

HOW WOULD YOU LIKE TO GET $10,000, $20,000, $40,000, OR MORE BACK OUT OF YOUR MORTGAGE? THE MORTGAGE REDUCER is the homeowner's guide to the little used banking secrets that will put thousands of your hard-earned dollars back in your pocket.

WOULDN'T YOU LIKE TO KNOW HOW TO TAKE CONTROL OF YOUR MORTGAGE? Learn how to build your equity two, three, even four times faster. THE MORTGAGE REDUCER will show you how to own your home years sooner. You will find out why you are spending thousands of dollars needlessly on your home...and how to get started on putting all that money into your pocket.

HERE'S WHAT YOU WILL LEARN:
•How to put thousands in your pocket.
•Build your equity two, three, even four times faster.
•Knock years off the life of your loan.
•How to control your financial security.
•How to use the forms that are needed by the bank or mortgage lender
AND MUCH, MUCH MORE...

> **THE MORTGAGE REDUCER IS THE MOST POWERFUL AND UNIQUE PRODUCT OF ITS KIND AVAILABLE TO THE HOMEOWNER TODAY! NOW YOU CAN CONTROL YOUR MORTGAGE INSTEAD OF YOUR MORTGAGE CONTROLLING YOU!**

This is what you will receive with **THE MORTGAGE REDUCER:**

•76 PAGE MANUAL
•30 MINUTE VHS VIDEOCASSETTE
•20 MINUTE AUDIOCASSETTE
•FREE NINE-PAGE COMPUTER ANALYSIS OF
YOUR MORTGAGE

ORDER NOW! SAVE 30%! 1-800-822-2470

WARRANTY CERTIFICATE

ACTION GUIDE TO GOVERNMENT AUCTIONS AND REAL ESTATE

1. No refund will be given unless submitted with the following items:

   a) Proof that you have been put on the government's mailing list. This can be a flier notifying you of an upcoming auction or a sealed bid catalog--not just an application form to be put on the government's mailing list. You must show you were actually put on the mailing list.

   b) Proof that you placed a bid at an auction. This can be a bidder's card or a returned sealed bid form. You must actually send us the bidder's card.

2. All returned books must be received in undamaged and resalable condition and returned by either UPS, Certified mail or Federal Express.
   Any stains, notes or other examples of damage immediately invalidates a refund.

3. Books must be received by us no later than 60 days from shipment date.

4. A $25 repackaging and reprocessing fee will be charged on all refunds (this includes the shipping fee).

R.L. Rasmus Auctioneers Inc.
6060 Tower Court-Suite LL1
Alexandria, VA   22304
Telephone Hotline: (703)
370-5760

They handle auctions for U.S. Bankruptcy Courts, military bases and airport authority. Auction fliers available for $35.00 per year.

Douglas K. Goldsten
Auctioneers Inc.
3408 Wisconsin Avenue, NW
Suite 205
Washington, D.C.   20016
Telephone: (202) 966-0100

They hold auctions for FHIC.

Car & Truck Auction of
Maryland
1370 West North Avenue
Baltimore, MD   21217
Telephone: (301) 669-1666

They hold auctions for all agencies in the area.

GLOSSARY

This glossary consists of the legal and specialized terms found in this book. It has been set up in the back of this book for easy access. Credit has been given previously to the sources of these definitions. They have been taken from a variety of dictionaries in order to provide you with accepted and working definitions of those words. I hope that you will frequently refer to this glossary as you study and re-study the book. Terms are listed alphabetically for your easy use.

ABANDONED: Deserted. To abandon is to leave to forsake completely and finally, to discontinue, give up, withdraw from. As in "abandon a sinking ship."

ABSOLUTE: Free from any restriction, limitation or exception.

ABSOLUTE AUCTION: Strictly to the highest bidder, regardless of price.

ADJUDICATION: The determination of a controversy and a pronouncement of a judgment based on evidence presented; implies a final judgment of the court. To adjudicate is for a court to make a decision on something.

AGENCY: An organization that provides some service.

AGENT: A person or thing that acts or has the power to act. A person authorized by another to act on his behalf.

ASKING PRICE: The list price that an owner would like to receive. For example: Abel advertises a property for sale at a price of $100,000. The advertised price is Abel's asking price.

ATTORNEY: This is one of a class of persons admitted by the state's highest court or by a federal court to practice law in that jurisdiction.

AUCTIO SUB HASTA: To increase under the spear. This dates back to Roman times when auctions were held under the spear.

AUCTION: A public sale to the highest bidder; the sale of real property or goods by public outcry and competitive bidding.

AUCTION BLOCK: The place from where goods are sold or the table or podium which the auctioneer uses to strike his hammer. In Roman times this was an actual block of stone.

AUCTIONEER: A person who conducts sales by auction.

AUCTION WITHOUT RESERVE: The Uniform Commercial Code retains the common law rule for sales "without reserve" in that once the auctioneer calls for a bid, the article for sale cannot be withdrawn unless there is no bid within a reasonable time.

BANKRUPT: The state or condition of one who is unable to pay his debts as they are, or become, due. The term includes a person against whom an involuntary petition has been filed, or who has filed a voluntary petition.

BANKRUPTCY: A legal process under federal law intended to not only ensure fairness and equality among creditors but also to help the debtor by enabling him to start anew with property he is allowed to retain as exempt from his liabilities, unhampered by pressure and discouragement of pre-existing debts.

BANKRUPTCY CODE: A federal law for the benefit and relief of creditors and their debtors in cases in which the latter are unable or unwilling to pay their debts.

BANKRUPTCY COURT: The forum in which most bankruptcy proceedings are conducted.

BANKRUPTCY DISCHARGE: The Order of Bankruptcy Court which discharges the bankruptcy from all dischargeable obligations and debts.

BANKRUPTCY TRUSTEE: The person who takes legal title to the property of the debtor and holds it "in trust" for equitable distribution among the creditors. In most districts, the trustee is appointed by the bankruptcy judge or selected by the creditors and approved by the judge. In a limited number of "pilot districts," a United States Trustee, appointed by the Attorney General, serves as or supervises the trustee.

BID: The amount someone offers to pay for something.

BIDDING: The activity of making offers for something at an auction.

BIDDING PADDLE: A hand-held instrument, shaped like a ping-pong or table tennis paddle, with a number that is used to identify the bidder.

CERTIFICATE OF TITLE: A statement of opinion on the status of title to a parcel of real property based on an examination of specified public records.

CHAPTER ELEVEN: (Bankruptcy) Petitions for relief under Chapter 11 permit the debtor to undertake a reorganization to pay his debts.

CHAPTER SEVEN: (Bankruptcy) Most assets of the debtor are liquidated as quickly as possible to pay off his creditors to the extent possible and to free the debtor to start anew. The debtor receives a discharge from most debts incurred prior to the time he filed for relief.

CLAIM: The assertion of right to money or property.

CREDITOR: One to whom money is owed by the debtor; or to whom an obligation exists. A creditor is one who voluntarily trusts or gives credit to another for money or other property. In its more general and extensive sense, it is one who has the right by law to demand and recover of another a sum of money on any account whatever.

CONFIRMATION: For a sale to be complete, the seller must accept the bid.

CONVENTIONAL LOAN: A loan that is not insured or guaranteed by a government or private source.

COURT: The branch of government which is responsible for the resolution of disputes arising under the laws of government. A court system is usually divided into various parts which specialize in hearing different types of cases.

COURT HEARINGS: Proceedings of relative formality (though generally less formal than a trial), generally public, with definite issues of fact or law to be tried, in which witnesses are heard and parties proceeded against have the right to be heard, and is much the same as a trial and may terminate in final order.

CUSTODY: Not ownership. A keeping, guarding, care, watch, inspection, preservation, or security of a thing.

DEBT: Money, goods or services owing from one person to another. An absolute promise to pay a certain sum on a certain date, or any obligation of one person to pay or compensate another.

DEBTOR: One who has the obligation of paying a debt; one who owes a debt; one who owes another anything, or is under any obligation arising from express agreement, implication of law, or from the principles of natural justice, to render and pay a sum of money.

DEFAULT: A failure of the mortgagor to pay mortgage installments when due.

DEFENDANT: One who is sued and called upon to make satisfaction for a wrong complained of by another.

DEFICIENCY JUDGMENT: Imposition of personal liability on a mortgagor for unpaid balance of mortgage debt after foreclosure has failed to yield the full amount of due debt.

DEPOSIT: Money paid in good faith to assure performance of a contract. Deposits are commonly used with sales contracts and leases. If the person who put up the deposit fails to perform, the deposit is forfeited, unless conditions of the contract allow for a refund.

DOWN PAYMENT: The amount one pays for property in addition to the debt incurred.

EARNEST MONEY: A deposit made by a purchaser of real estate to evidence good faith. It is customary for the buyer to give the seller earnest money at the time a sales contract is signed. The earnest money is generally credited to the down payment at closing.

ENCUMBRANCE: A lien, such as mortgage, tax or judgment lien, an easement, a restriction on use of the land, or an outstanding dower right that may diminish the VALUE OF THE PROPERTY.

EQUITABLE: According to natural right or natural justice, marked by due consideration for what is fair, unbiased, or impartial.

EXECUTION: The process of carrying into effect a court's judgment, decree or order. It is the end of the law. It gives the successful party the fruits of his judgment.

FAIR MARKET VALUE: The price that goods or property would bring in a market of willing buyers and willing sellers in the ordinary course of trade.

FORCED SALE: A sale which the vendor must take immediately, without the opportunity to find a buyer who will pay a price representing a sum approaching the reasonable worth of the property sold.

FORECLOSURE: The cutting off or termination of a right to property; specifically, an equitable action to compel payment of a mortgage or other debt secured by a lien. As to real property, it is precipitated by non-payment of the debt, and leads to selling of the property to which the mortgage or lien is attached in order to satisfy that debt.

FORFEITURE: The permanent loss of property for failure to comply with the law.

GOVERNMENT: That form of fundamental rules and principles by which a nation or state is governed, or by which individual members of a body politic are to regulate their social actions.

GOVERNMENT AGENCY: A subordinate creature of federal, state or local government created to carry out a government function or to implement a statute or statutes.

GOVERNMENT AGENTS: Those performing service and duty of a public character for benefit of all citizens of the community.

INVOLUNTARY PROCEEDINGS: An equitable proceeding for the purpose of impounding all the debtor's non-exempt property to distribute it equally among creditors, and to release the debtor from liability.

INSOLVENCY: A financial condition in which one is unable to meet his obligations as they mature in the ordinary course of business or in which one's liabilities exceed his assets in any given time.

JUDGMENT: The determination of a court of competent jurisdiction upon matters submitted to it; a final determination of the rights of the parties to a lawsuit.

JUDICIAL: Pertaining to courts of law or to judges; or to the administration of justice; giving or seeking judgment , as in dispute or contest.

JUDICIAL SALE: Sale conducted under a judgment, order, or supervision of a court as in a sale under a petition for partition of real estate or an execution. A "judicial sale" is one which must be based upon an order or decree of a court directing the sale.

JURISDICTION: The power to hear and determine a case. In addition to the power to adjudicate, a valid exercise of jurisdiction requires fair notice and an opportunity for the affected parties to be heard. Without jurisdiction, a court's judgment is void.

LAW: The legislative pronouncement of the rules which should guide one's actions in society.

LAW OF THE LAND: Due process of law. By the law of the land is most clearly intended the general law which hears before it condemns, which proceeds upon inquiry, and renders judgment only after trial. The meaning is that every citizen shall hold his life, liberties, and property and immunities under protection of general rules which govern society.

LEGAL: Conforming to the law; according to the law; required or permitted by law; not forbidden or discountenanced by law; good effectual in law. Created by law. Lawful.

LEVY: To raise or collect; to seize; to asses, as to levy a tax. When one levies, or places a levy upon some property, it is seized and may be sold to satisfy a judgment.

LIABILITIES: Signifies monies owed. A liability is an obligation to do something; an obligation to pay money.

LIEN: A charge, hold claim or encumbrance upon the property of another as security for some debt or charge; not a title to property but rather a charge upon it; the term connotes the right which the law gives to have a debt satisfied out of the property, by the sale of the property if necessary.

LIEN SALE: Comes after a judgment lien on a judgment debtor's property in favor of a judgment creditor. When a judgment has been entered in a civil case, and the party liable for the judgment fails to pay it, the judgment creditor may file a lien against the property of the party liable, to give notice that the property is subject to sale in satisfaction of judgment. The judgment creditor may enforce the lien by having the sheriff seize the property and sell it at a sheriff's sale.

LIS PENDENS: A pending suit. A notice of lis pendens may be required in some jurisdictions to be placed in the public records to warn persons (such as prospective purchasers or others having an interest in the property under suit) that the title to the property is in litigation and that they will be bound by the possibly adverse judgment.

LIQUIDATE: To settle; to determine the amount due, and to whom due, and, having done so, to extinguish the indebtedness.

LOT: A distinct portion or parcel of anything, such as merchandise. The manner in which articles, items, equipment or real estate is sold at an auction.

MAILING LIST: A compilation of possible customers prepared as for use in direct mail solicitation. Through the use of these specially prepared lists, the direct mail advertiser is able to pinpoint almost exactly the TARGET MARKET for the advertised product.

MARSHAL: An officer of the peace, appointed by authority of city or borough, who holds himself in readiness to answer such calls as fall within the general duties of a constable or sheriff. An office in each federal district which performs the same duties as the sheriffs do for the states. Federal marshals also execute writs and orders issued by the Federal Courts.

MINIMUM BID: The least or smallest offer which will be accepted by the government agency or auctioneer at a public sale, spot bid, or sealed bid auction. To bid successfully and have your offer accepted you must bid higher than the minimum bid in most cases.

MORTGAGE: A written instrument that creates a lien upon real estate as security for the payment of a specified debt. The borrower gives the mortgage, which pledges the property as collateral. The lender gives the loan.

MORTGAGEE: One who holds a lien on property or title to property as security for a debt, usually the bank or mortgage company.

MOTGAGOR: One who pledges property as security for a loan, usually the homeowner.

NEGOTIATED SALE: The way merchandise or property is sold by discussion, with a small number of buyers or a single buyer, a price and arranging the sale in that manner, avoiding a public auction. A series of offers and counter-offers until both parties are satisfied with the price.

OPEN-BIDDING AUCTIONS: Public auctions or public sales where bids are accepted from the auction-goers in person and are done vocally or in some similar manner.

OPENING BID: The first offer made by an auction-goer to the auctioneer.

ORAL AUCTION: A voice auction where bids can be made to the auctioneer buy stating the bid, raising one's hand or paddle or numbered card, or in some other obvious and accepted manner until a winning bid is made, the bid accepted, and the merchandise sold.

PERSONAL PROPERTY: Things movable, as distinguished from real property or things attached to the realty. In a broad and general sense, everything that is the subject of ownership, not coming under denomination of real estate. Generally, all property other than real estate.

PETITION: A formal written application to a court requesting judicial action on a certain matter.

PLAINTIFF: A person who brings an action; the party who complains or sues in a civil action and is so named on the record. A person who seeks remedial relief for an injury to rights.

POSSESSIONS: Those things which a person has, holds or maintains in his own power or command.

POSSESSORY LIEN: A lien is possessory where the creditor has the right to hold possession of the specific property until satisfaction of the debt or performance of an obligation.

PROCEEDINGS: The succession of events constituting the process by which judicial action is invoked and utilized. The form in which actions are to be brought and defended, the manner of intervening in suits and of conducting them, the mode of deciding them, opposing them, and of executing judgments.

PROPERTY: Ownership. The exclusive and unrestricted right to a thing. The right to dispose of a thing in every legal way, to possess it, to use it, and to exclude every one else from interfering with it.

PUBLIC AUCTION: A sale upon notice to the public and in which members of the public may bid.

PUBLIC SALE: The legal phrase most commonly used to describe a public auction and which distinguishes it from a private auction house's auction.

QUIT CLAIM DEED: A conveyance by which the grantor transfers whatever interest he or she has in the real estate without warranties or obligations.

REAL ESTATE: Land and everything more or less attached to it. Ownership below to the center of the earth and above to the heavens.

REAL PROPERTY: Land, including the surface, whatever is attached to the surface such as minerals and the area above the surface.

REPOSSESSION: Seizure or foreclosure. The method by which a secured creditor satisfies a debtor's obligation after the debtor has defaulted.

RETAILER: A merchant whose primary activity is to sell directly to the consumers.

RETAIL PRICE: The price at which goods are identified for sale or are sold.

SALE: A contract or agreement by which property is transferred from the seller (vendor) to the buyer (vendee) for a fixed price on money, paid or agreed to be paid by the buyer.

SATISFACTION: A discharge and subsequent release of obligation by the payment thereof. Discharging an obligation by paying a party what is due him (as on a mortgage, lien or contract).

SEALED BID: Each party interested submits a bid in a sealed envelope, and all such bids are opened at the same time and the most favorable, highest bid wins.

SEIZURE: The act of forcibly dispossessing an owner of property under actual or apparent authority of law. Also, the taking of the priority into the custody of the court for the satisfaction of a judgment.

SHERIFF: The chief executive and administrative officer of a county, being chosen by popular election.

SHERIFF'S SALE: A sale of property by the sheriff under authority of a court's judgment and writ of execution in order to satisfy an unpaid judgment, mortgage lien or other debt of the owner.

SPOT BID: An auction where attendees write in their bid on a form and submit to the auctioneer. It is done, generally, in person at the auction and in writing and is signed by the bidder.

SURPLUS: That which remains above what is used or needed. An amount, quantity, greater than needed.

STRAIGHT BANKRUPTCY: In this form of bankruptcy most assets of the debtor are liquidated as quickly as possible to pay off his creditors to the extent possible and to free the debtor to start anew.

STATUTE: An act of legislature, adopted pursuant to its constitutional authority, by prescribing means and in certain forms such that it becomes the law governing conduct within its scope.

SUBJECT TO SELLER'S APPROVAL: The seller must accept the bid for the sale to be finalized.

TAX: A rate or sum of money assessed on a person or property for the support of the government, and commonly levied upon assets or real property, or income derived from wages, or upon the sale or purchase of goods.

TAX SALE: A sale of land for the non-payment of taxes.

TITLE: Ownership. Having title to something means having the right to possess the thing.

TITLE INSURANCE: A policy insuring the owner or the mortgagee against loss by reason of defects in the title to a parcel of real estate, other than encumbrances, defects, and matters specifically excluded by the policy.

TRUSTEE: One who holds legal title to property "in trust" for the benefit of another person, and who is required to carry out specific duties with regard to the property, or who has been given power affecting the disposition of the property for another's benefit.

UNCLAIMED: That which has been forgotten or abandoned.

UPSET PRICE: The price at which any subject, as lands or goods, is exposed to sale by auction, below which it is not to be sold.

VOLUNTARY PROCEEDINGS: Proceedings whereby any debtor entitled to the benefits of the Bankruptcy Act may file a petition to be adjudged a voluntary bankrupt.

WAREHOUSEMAN'S LIEN: Right of warehouseman to retain possession of goods until storage charges have been paid.

WARRANTY: A written statement arising out of a sale to the consumer of a consumer good, pursuant to which the manufacturer, distributor, or retailer undertakes to preserve or maintain the utility or performance of the consumer good or provide compensation if there is a failure in utility or performance.

WARRANTY DEED: A deed in which the grantor fully warrants good clear title to the premises. Used in most real estate deed transfers, a warranty deed offers the greatest possible protection of any deed.

WHOLESALE: To sell goods in gross to retailers, who then sell the merchandise to customers.

WHOLESALER: An individual who buys and sells goods to retailers and other users but does not sell in significant amounts to the consumer.

WRIT: An order issued from a court requiring the performance of a specified act, or giving authority to have it done.

WRITE OF EXECUTION: A writ to put in force the judgment or decree of a court.